# Opening Paths to a Moral Economy

# THE SOUL

*of*

# CAPITALISM

# WILLIAM GREIDER

SIMON & SCHUSTER

New York   London   Toronto   Sydney   Singapore

SIMON & SCHUSTER
Rockefeller Center
1230 Avenue of the Americas
New York, NY 10020

SIMON & SCHUSTER and colophon are
registered trademarks of Simon & Schuster, Inc.
For information about special discounts for bulk purchases,
please contact Simon & Schuster Special Sales at
1-800-456-6798 or business@simonandschuster.com

*Book design by Ellen R. Sasahara*

Manufactured in the United States of America

1 3 5 7 9 10 8 6 4 2

Library of Congress Cataloging-in-Publication Data
Greider, William
The soul of capitalism / William Greider.
p.   cm.
Includes bibliographical references and index.
1. Capitalism—United States. 2. Capitalism—Moral and ethical aspects—
United States. 3. Capitalism—Social aspects—United States. I. Title.
HB501.G6472 2003
330.12'2'0973—dc21          2003053007
ISBN 0-684-86219-0

*To the memory of Peter L. Milius*

A wise and rigorous reporter, generous teacher and friend,
who lived in the spirit of Wendell Berry's dictum:
"Be joyful though you have considered all the facts."

# Contents

1. This New Moment    *1*

2. The Soul of Capitalism    *23*

3. Work Rules    *49*

4. Imperious Capital    *94*

5. Consuming the Future    *153*

6. Command and Control    *205*

7. Public Works    *263*

8. Thinking Forward    *325*

*Acknowledgments*    *338*

*Notes*    *341*

*Index*    *351*

# THE SOUL

*of*

# CAPITALISM

# 1

# This New Moment

FIRST, we pause to acknowledge the ancestors. The discontents of present day American life are real enough but can seem quite trivial and self-indulgent when laid alongside the American past. Modern pressures lack the hard and often tragic bite of what earlier Americans commonly endured. Three or four generations ago most Americans lived in dwellings that lacked indoor plumbing, not to mention electricity and central heating. Most families were tenants, not owners. Life was simpler, certainly, but also much shorter. Half of the children born in 1900 were dead by the age 40 (in our time, 95 percent of the new babies will live to 40 and half will be still alive at 79). People, it is said, were more God-fearing in olden days, and probably so, since their lives were ruled by stark, random insecurities that dwarf our own: bad weather that could destroy livelihoods or abrupt waves of economic disorder; unspeakably harsh working conditions and inadequate incomes; the blind cruelties of uncontrollable diseases. Parents regularly experienced the sudden death of small children, an event that no doubt encouraged faith in an afterlife, the promise of a heavenly reward.

What would they make of us, surrounded as we are by luxurious goods and plentiful variety, the profusion of entertainments and electronic machines that allow our minds to leap freely across time and space? The departed ancestors naturally would be astonished by the reckless speed of modern life and the hedonism. They might be alarmed by our size (Americans are taller now) and amused by the preoccupation with fitness (many of our leisure activities would look to them like unnecessary work). They surely would be puzzled by contemporary obsessions with inner pain and personal ghosts, by the various "syndromes" that describe new maladies, and by the new drugs invented to treat them. Their descendants are fabulously wealthy by comparison—bizarrely wealthy—and the ancestors might insist that even our poor people are rich in everyday comforts and exotic possessions. How can a child be truly poor who owns $125 sneakers and a GameBoy?

Before there were designer labels the distinctions of class status were recognized easily by all because they were delineated bluntly in terms of the most basic amenities. In 1918, only a third of laboring families had a bathroom in their dwellings (though often not hot water), while three-fourths of the salaried class enjoyed this new convenience of indoor plumbing. The peculiar social habits and artifacts of luxury Thorstein Veblen identified in the early twentieth century as tribal markings of the "leisure class" have since become generalized throughout the population (though the leisure class still manages to distinguish itself with a higher order of conspicuous consumption). Our humble forebears might recognize a brave, new cosmopolitanism in our everyday tastes (Episcopalians who eat Mexican food, truck drivers who vacation on Caribbean cruises), but they would perhaps also see us adrift in a sea of empty follies.[1]

One feels awe for the past, yet also estranged. It was so different. The extraordinary changes in American lives—especially life spans that are now twenty-five or thirty years longer—are the universal bounty delivered by industrial capitalism during the last century and before. The deep transformation in living conditions and expectations was wrought by the wealth-creating processes of investment and production—the rewards of mass consumption. It is mistaken, however, to think that the architects of plenty came only from business and banking. Scientists and doctors developed the great life-saving cures, often with no profit to themselves beyond the satisfaction of aiding humanity. It was government, not private enterprise, that built the sewers and water systems that eradicated common illnesses and thus extended longevity; government also built the roads and schools and financed technological development. Life-enhancing changes also were wrought by social reformers, from working-class labor organizers to the martyred advocates of racial equality to upper-class humanitarians—all morally angered by obvious injustices, pointless brutalities. And we also should mention the brave politicians who took up these social causes before they were in fashion, who coaxed business enterprise to behave more responsibly, and who, finally compelled them to do so with new laws.

All the while, the plain people struggled. Their stories usually get left out of the history texts, since they are too diffuse to describe easily, too small and pedestrian as experiences of hope, defeat, triumph. Rachel Bella Calof was one among the millions, a young woman who left a miserable orphan's life in Russia in the 1890s to take up an even more harrowing existence as an American farm wife homesteading with her new husband, Abraham, on the trackless prairie of North Dakota. They lived in a 12-by-14-foot shack that each winter was crowded with relatives, livestock, and babies (Rachel had one after another, it seemed), all struggling to get through the desperate, cold months without starving. *Rachel Calof's Story* is an unsentimental narrative she wrote late in her life, the original in Yiddish. It is one of those honest, richly descriptive texts that modern children might read to understand where American life actually came from (if Rachel Calof had not been a homesteader, she might have been a writer):[2]

The wheat grew well and, at last, was ready for cutting. . . . Our spirits soared. A better life awaited just ahead. Dear reader, it was not to be. . . . Shortly after the noon meal a dark cloud suddenly boiled up in the northwest sky. We both knew what such a formation could mean and we watched in fear and trembling as the sky became darker and assumed an ominous hue. Then suddenly the hailstorm, the scourge of the prairie farmer, was upon us. It was of such intensity that in a few minutes all for which we had suffered and labored so long was destroyed. The wheat crop was hammered into the ground. The storm water washed away the grain which had already been cut. . . . Our two horses were killed running frantically into the wire which surrounded their pasture. The windows of the shack were smashed. Destruction was everywhere. We all, children and parents, huddled under the table for protection, but the shack became so filled with water we feared we would be carried away.

A century later, North Dakota still has hailstorms—but also crop insurance and well-built houses. Farmers need not submit family and self to the naked terror of nature. Life's dangers are managed in our time through the science of risk assessment. Yet, strangely enough, Rachel Calof discovered a sense of triumph in the terrible storm that destroyed everything: "I suppose this was as good a time and reason as any to give up the long unequal struggle. But we had become resilient and tempered by hardships and, surprisingly, our first emotions were joy and thankfulness that we had been spared. We knew now that we could win out."

These hard stories are numerous in the American past—incredible stories usually passed along within families—and they can be read as a rebuke to the present. We seem so soft. Most immigrant families did stick with it, and eventually most did "win out," as Rachel Calof put it, and achieved the secure, prosperous life that was the original purpose of their sacrifices. So we may choose to believe that the ancestors would be happy for us. They might be pleased to see that their struggles were not repeated by later generations but have been rewarded fulsomely. Are we happy for ourselves? The stories reveal the heart and fiber of becoming American. We are left to ponder whether we inherited their strengths along with the legacy of plenty.

When I consider the profusion of goods and recreational delights of our time, I think of my own grandfather, a Scotch-Irish farmer named Franklin S. McClure whose well-ordered life now seems eccentric in its simplicity. Never rich, never poor, but moderately prosperous in their own terms, the McClures had farmed in the hill country of western Pennsylvania since the 1790s, an area established by Revolutionary land grants, and the name had come to be well regarded in the vicinity. His lifetime was overtaken by the first waves of industrialization during the first half of the twentieth century— overwhelmed by modern life. But he stood his ground, resisted what seemed frivolous to him, defended what seemed most valuable. I can still see an occasional puzzlement in his face as he contemplated the newness of things.

Grandpa kept a small dairy herd and pasteurized his own milk, selling some to the coal miners' families living along the hollow. On two hundred acres, half woodlands, he grew feed for the livestock and food for the family, maybe sold some grain when market prices were good. He never attended college but read law books as the township's justice of the peace, and enjoyed a well-developed cultural life, music and classical literature, the Bible. He was self-sufficient unto his time and place, his sense of independence anchored in the fact that he owned his own land, managed and operated his own means of production. In 1900, when steel and coal were already booming along the Monongahela River valley, this young farmer (my mother was a newborn) reported to a U.S. census taker that he was "unemployed." So did the other neighboring farmers in Forward Township. They meant, I assume, that they worked for themselves, not for coal mines or steel mills or any other employer.

As a child, when I spent summers on that farm, it was a living window on an already vanished past. For whatever reasons, never fully explained to us, my grandfather and grandmother declined to participate in the modernizing luxuries of their own era. Other farmers around him became mechanized, bought the first tractors and trucks, later the large threshing machines and combines. Grandpa continued to farm with his horses. He plowed and spread manure and harvested with horse-drawn implements, milked the cows by hand. When he grew too old to farm, he turned the horses out into the woods every day and leased the fields to neighbors with their machines and chemical fertilizers.

The center-hall farmhouse had no electricity, no telephone or plumbing (an indoor toilet and tub were installed once but never functioned properly). Twice a week, we went into town to purchase a new block of ice for the white-enamel icebox in the kitchen. The parlors and bedrooms, with lofty Victorian ceilings, were softly illuminated by the glow of gaslights, each mantle lit by hand everyday at dusk, the natural gas supplied by a well on the farm. The outhouse was a long, dark walk from the kitchen porch, past the washhouse and chicken coop, by the far end of a double-sided corncrib.

Grandfather did decide once to install electricity at the farmhouse. But, when Grandmother saw the first poles marching up the lane, she objected. The wires ruined her view from the kitchen window, the gentle vista across fields and woods rising to a distant ridge dotted with white farmhouses, unpainted barns. She was strong-willed, too. He took down the poles. They lived on with gaslights and the icebox. Empty bleach bottles accumulated under the corncrib where she stored them. It seemed a waste to throw them away, though Grandmother had no use for them. The new age of packaged goods was creeping into their lives, with quite different values about what was useful, what was wasteful.

I admire the stubbornness of their resistance—their willingness to stare down intrusions—but this is not a romantic lament for the lost simple life. The truth is, after a week or two on the farm, my brother and I would turn quarrelsome, tired of toting pails of water from the spring, sharing in hot field work, listening over and over to the same old phonograph records on the windup Victrola. We were bored silly by the simple life. We longed to return home to suburban civilization.

In their own terms, however, this well-ordered life on the farm was not at all simple for my grandparents. Like most farmers, even today, my grandparents were, by necessity, workers with numerous skills. They knew animal husbandry (hogs, chickens, horses, cows) and horticulture (vegetables and fruit orchard, maple sugaring and crop rotation). They did carpentry, bookkeeping, occasional school teaching, mending, and sewing. Grandma used to bake daily when she was younger (bread and fresh pies for breakfast). Grandpa was a machinist who fixed axles and other gear in his small blacksmith shop (though he never got the plumbing right).

Though I never heard this said, my hunch is that what my grandparents resisted was the encroaching loss of self-reliance, the steadily vanishing complexity of their own self-contained lives, the capacity to do many things well and provide well enough for themselves. Put in those terms, it seems a huge and frightening loss. They were unwilling to accept the trade-offs.

Their situation illustrates, first, how far the concept of economic necessity has traveled in two or three generations, and how greatly we have been liberated from hard daily labor by the fruits of industrial production. Yet, oddly enough, their sense of encroachment also parallels the modern experience. The new technologies of this era are much more complex, far too esoteric for common understanding, much less to repair at home, but the disorienting effects may be similar. When my grandfather rejected the obvious comforts produced by the previous industrial revolution, he must have recognized, perhaps with a hint of terror, that his very own personal qualities were being commodified by the new inventions—his tasks and skills converted into products that are bought and sold, machines and manufactured goods that would be many times more efficient (cheaper) and more effective (uniformly reliable and productive) than the labor of a single, skillful farmer could possibly match.

The same alienating exchange is occurring in our own time, and not just for those workers displaced by new technologies. Life's daily chores—cooking dinner, rearing children, even walking the dog—are commodified as services we hire others to do for us or as goods we purchase instead of making ourselves. Of course, it requires more cash income to acquire these liberating conveniences, and often the "time-saving" devices become needs, not luxuries, and some of the saved time will be devoted to more work, not leisure. Since we are by now several generations removed from any illusions of self-reliance, people may experience this dread of personal loss less starkly, as a small kernel of inner doubt and helplessness. One recognizes a deepening dependence on the mysterious new machines and on the complicated organizations of modern economic life, which are operated by distant systems of decision making, themselves opaque and mechanical. One paradox of the information age is that, while we are able to find out instantly so many more things than the ancestors could ever know, the anchor of self-knowledge—who we are and where we fit in, what we count for in this new scheme—seems to be weaker.

In historical perspective, however, the technological changes of the present era, even the astonishing advances in telecommunications, do not involve life transformations as profound as what those earlier generations experienced—they were confronted by cars, airplanes, telephones, electric lights, indoor plumbing. Nor do the social and economic upheavals seem as severe for most of us (though they are still brutal for some). We can resist the machines (and many choose to do so), but we cannot blame them. Anyway, the machines are not going to go away because they do deliver, reliably, what many want in their lives, what people soon find they need. My digression into the distant past is intended to stimulate a little doubt and suspicion about our modern pretensions. Despite the progress of machines and money incomes, the fundamental terms of human existence do not change over time or even across centuries (see Ecclesiastes on this point). But we have perhaps forgotten some important elements of life that the ancestors readily understood.

IF THE NEW TECHNOLOGIES do not explain what is distinctive about the modern American condition, then we have to look elsewhere for an explanation of what agitates the social discontents and tensions. The answer is a breathtaking new fact of history, so simple and obvious one hesitates to announce it as news. The United States has solved the economic problem.

America, that is, has solved the ancient economic problem known to all previous millennia of human toil. We have escaped the elemental struggle that has stalked human societies since the origins: hunger, scarcity, the burdens of producing enough for human survival and a general standard of well-being that is not restricted to the powerful few, the king and high priests. The United States is not alone in this happy condition but still the rare case in the world. The constant threat of scarcity is what sowed the desperation, but also inspired the invention and enterprise. For the fortunate minority who live in the most advanced nations, the fundamental economic threat is now, quite literally, extinguished. Indeed, basic human needs are now eclipsed—even overwhelmed, like my grandparents—by the overflowing abundance and variety produced by the modern economic system.

The problem is solved. Yet the United States pushes on strenuously, like a long-distance runner who has won the race yet keeps running beyond the finish line, not looking back and not quite sure who or what drives him on. A similar observation arguably could have been made about the United States thirty or forty years ago, but it would not have been taken seriously by a population that had lived through the sufferings of the Great Depression or the deaths and sacrifices required by the mobilization for World War II. The point of overwhelming abundance is now plainly in our face and beyond argument, yet seldom discussed as the new central premise of the economic condition. The incompleteness at the core of American life, I believe, is also about this new fact of history. Our situation is unique—learning how to live amid endless plenty and, ironically, how to live well in spite of it. Our ancestors never had to face such a struggle. We cannot escape it.

In 1893, Samuel Gompers, the first president of the American Federation of Labor, was asked: What does labor want? "More," he answered. Of course, more. At the time, it sounded vaguely belligerent and greedy. Gompers's business adversaries used the one-word answer to demonize labor unions as a monstrous threat to civil order. But what organized labor sought—more—was merely the general ambition of all Americans and a deeply held objective of the nation. It still is. From the beginning, one could say "more" was the organizing principle for American life—the goal of immigrant sacrifices, the motivation for ferocious contests in economic life. It drove the expansion westward (pushing aside indigenous peoples who did not live by acquisitive precepts). It spawned great inventions; it justified the hard work and bountiful production. "More" is the bluntest expression of how we have defined the "pursuit of happiness." Only during the last several generations have dissenting voices begun to articulate a different question: more of what?

The question is answered easily and imaginatively. More of the old and more of the new. More cars and urban pickup trucks; more off-road vehicles for adventure. More and larger houses and, for some of us, two houses, or even three. More electronic connections, worldwide, handheld, and 24/7, as tech hipsters say. More wealth, more food, more travel, more wilderness, more money and more work, more sports channels, more movies, more miracle drugs, more ailments to be cured, more incinerators and landfills, more bottled water, more fat, more sugar, more lakes, more security guards, more

toys. The chase of modern life can be exhilirating and gorgeously satisfying, also exhausting and terribly wasteful. One recalls the mordant
bumper sticker that used to be seen on suburban pickup trucks:
"Whoever Finishes with the Most Toys Wins."

All Americans across the differences of class and status—all but the
very poor—achieved self-sufficiency in basic needs (food, shelter,
clothing, and so forth) nearly a half century ago. Clair Brown, an
economist at the University of California–Berkeley, meticulously
tracked consumption patterns across the last century in *American
Standards of Living* and found the spending for the basics declined
steadily as a share of incomes from the 1950s onward, replaced by
goods and services that are increasingly recreational or described as
"variety" or "status." Scholars have engaged in a dense sociological
controversy over exactly what drives the material desires—who is
keeping up with whom in modern America? The designer labels, for
instance, suggest that people of modest means strive to participate in
the tribal markings of the leisure class, even if the identity of refined
taste is determined at a superficial level. On the other hand, the consumption of cultural goods seems often to work in reverse, with the
affluent mimicking lower-class tastes. Think of those white suburban
teenagers, alone in their rooms, listening to rap music and identifying
with insistent lyrics derived from violent urban life. The questions of
class mimicry can be intriguing but go past the larger point. At nearly
every station and status level, most Americans share, one way or the
other, in the common experience of plentiful consumption, notwithstanding the differences in content and volume. Brown evoked the
reality with these details:

> In 1988, typical working families with incomes between
> $30,000 and $50,000 (in 1998 dollars) owned their homes, had
> air-conditioning, owned at least one car, spent a quarter of their
> food budget away from home, and went on 1.5 vacations annu-
> ally that cost $655 each. . . . They spent $1,140 yearly on a vari-

ety of household furnishings such as sofas, refrigerators and decorative items, and another $1,635 on household operations,
including telephone service, gardening, and cleaning supplies.... From a world viewpoint or a historical viewpoint, these
families were not living a meager life style; yet in modern-day
America thoughtful commentators find it lacking.[3]

What could possibly be lacking? Time, most obviously. Americans
on average work longer hours than their counterparts in other leading
industrial economies, as much as three hundred or four hundred more
hours per year. The pressures on time, combined with the need for rising incomes to maintain these patterns of consumption, undermine
personal lives and family, but also deny any stable sense of fulfillment,
given the erosion of job security, family savings, and pension rights. Indeed, for a broad swath of Americans, who are not themselves poor, it
sounds wildly wrong—and offensive—to talk about the extraordinary
comfort levels of modern life. For them, the economic problem remains a month-to-month struggle of keeping up with the rent or
mortgage payment. The statistics suggest a general affluence that is un-
deniable, yet they know and feel precariousness in their condition.

Federal Reserve Chairman Alan Greenspan expressed his own
puzzlement when he discovered that levels of anxiety and insecurity
seem to be rising inversely to the supposedly healthy conditions of
the economy. "As recently as 1981, in the depths of recession, International Survey Research found 12 percent of workers fearful of losing their jobs," Greenspan told the American Council on Education
in early 1999. "In today's tightest labor market in two generations, the
same organization found 37 percent concerned about job loss." How
could this be so? Plausible explanations are not exactly a secret. They
start with the rigorous new style of management that adjusts to transient fevers from financial markets by discarding long-experienced
and well-paid employees. This helps the stock price while it sows
doubts and fears in the society.

For a time, the rising price bubble in stock markets was thought to be an antidote to these rising insecurities, the way in which even small investors could accumulate sufficient assets to make their lives secure for the distant future. A TV commercial for Scudder Investments adroitly captured the ironic tensions embedded in contemporary prosperity: "What if you want to stop working for a living? What if you want to start living for a living?" The new passion for stock-market investments became an alluring kind of substitute for many people—a defense against the pressures on family, an escape from the immediate worries. It was not to be. When the bubble burst, American households swiftly lost $3 or $4 trillion in putative wealth. The mutual funds where they had parked their savings fell back to the same levels of four or five years earlier, before share prices had begun their great—but temporary—inflation.

The illusions were deeply felt, however. A popular financial guru for middle-class investors, Suze Orman, instructed her followers: "Money is a living entity and it responds to energy exactly the way you do. It is drawn to those who welcome it, those who respect it." Her insight sounds plain wacky now that stock prices have collapsed, despite the sincere devotion of share owners. In my grandfather's time, describing money as a "living entity" would have been regarded as blasphemy. His financial balance sheet was trivial compared to modern standards of personal wealth. Yet somehow he was able to feel more secure and more independent, despite his relative poverty. This is not a trivial anomaly, but the new paradox created by America's extraordinary abundance.[4]

One could go on at length cataloging similar symptoms of distress and social disorder—the dysfunctional qualities of "more"—but many other books have already filled that purpose. Most Americans, I am convinced, have at least a vague sense that something is wrong in the contours of their supposed prosperity. In my experience, I do not find these complaints restricted to the poor or struggling working-class, though their struggles are obviously more stark and often desperate. In affluent living rooms one hears the same conversations about stress and disappointment, the same exasperation and futility, often laced with an edgy bitterness toward those who are supposed to be in charge. Despite the class differences, I have heard people from nearly every income level express an oddly similar sense of confinement, as if their lives were trapped by the "good times" rather than liberated. Short of renouncing modern life and going off to live in the woods, they do not see any sure way to break free of what binds them. Think of the paradox as enormous and without precedent in history: a fabulously wealthy nation in which plentiful abundance may also impoverish our lives.

Brown's study suggests a set of resigned choices people have made during the last generation, especially the working families whose hourly wages have been steadily depressed in purchasing power since the early 1970s. "Feeling powerless to influence public problems that significantly undermined their own standard of living, people have turned inward to focus on their private consumption," she wrote. "Disillusioned with society's ability to tackle social problems, much less solve them, people have withdrawn to their private lives and sought solace in consumption of variety and status. For many people, the demands in their private lives of going to work and taking care of family deplete their time and energy. Yet social pressure to maintain consumption norms prevents them from expanding leisure time or focusing on social problems."

Even the cycles of rising prosperity can begin to feel tyrannical. As each new generation of products (and subsequent upgrades) appears, the context surrounding one's circumstances is altered and there's no easy escape. A family may decide to keep its food in an icebox, but where do they buy the block of ice? One does not actually *need* a television for entertainment, but without one you are utterly lost in office conversations. Some people do opt for the simple life and clear away the gadgets and unnecessary complexities (a virtuous choice surely, though not one I would choose). Achieving the simple life requires stern character and a kind of solitary withdrawal, like my grandparents' resistance. The willpower will be easier to sustain if the children do not watch TV (and are not allowed to visit friends who do).

Character and values can guide people toward wiser choices, but neither individuals nor the society can easily escape the present system because the principles of "more" are everywhere. "More" is embedded in the behavior of every business enterprise and the principles of marketing, in the self-interested decisions of every investor and consumer. The pursuit of "more" guides politics and government policy and describes the core objective of formal economics. Faith in "more" as a blunt instrument for achieving the greater good for the greatest number is what legitimizes the confinements and social distress, from families to communities. It does require real character to step back and question what others regard as natural law.

The regime of "more," individual grievances aside, also leads to an unfulfilled society, as some people are beginning to recognize. This was actually the point Samuel Gompers was trying to make back in 1893, though his remarks were maliciously caricatured. What the labor leader said in full was: "Labor wants more schoolhouses and less jails; more books and less arsenals; more learning and less vice; more constant work and less crime; more leisure and less greed; more justice and less revenge; in fact, more of the opportunities to cultivate our better natures." Gompers's list of "demands" seems uncannily relevant to our present dilemma. It suggests a *social* definition of "more"—a general prosperity that does not confuse and destroy life itself.[5]

The British economist John Maynard Keynes, who was wise about the human condition as well as money matters, predicted this dilemma of plenty more than seventy years ago in an essay entitled, "The Economic Possibilities for Our Grandchildren." Capitalism, Keynes observed, was generating surplus wealth for investment at such a rapid pace that, combined with scientific discovery and sound engineering, the process of wealth creation should eventually eradicate the ancient afflictions of human want and material suffering. This, he thought, could occur for the advanced countries within one hundred years, notwithstanding occasional setbacks from war or depression. At the point of triumph, Keynes declared, people would at last be free—truly free of the old fears and struggles—but would then face the larger, more permanent questions of mortal existence. What does it mean to be truly human?

"For the first time since his creation," Keynes wrote, "man will be faced with his real, his permanent problem—how to use his freedom from pressing economic cares, how to occupy his leisure, which science and compound interest have won for him, to live wisely and agreeably and well." The prospect of such liberation can be deeply frightening since, without the well understood burdens of economic struggle to define our lives, what are we to do? We will face "the panic of having to create our own lives," as Raoul Vaneigem explained in *The Movement of the Free Spirit*. Our social challenge—discovering how to live "wisely and agreeably and well" with our abundance—is more elusive than whatever the ancestors endured, also less harsh and threatening, but it is fundamentally a pioneering frontier beyond anything they faced. Like earlier pioneers, it will require a kind of forward-looking courage—stubborn faith in a future that does not yet exist.[6]

America clearly has arrived at the threshold Keynes described. There is plenty to go around, more than enough for everyone by any reasonable measure. Yet the accomplishment does not prompt great celebration because, as everyone knows, the overflowing abundance is obvious in the economic data but not in the society. One-sixth of the population, the government reports, still lacks the means to provide even the minimum essentials of food and shelter for themselves. By official measure, one-fifth of America's children live in this old-fashioned condition of poverty.

Yet the burdens of inequality are spread more broadly than that and are more central to the discontents amid the abundance. Amartya Sen, a Nobel Prize–winning economist, has described a more supple social definition of poverty that is more relevant to our condition. Poverty, he suggests, is when people lack the means to appear in public without shame. By that standard, many more Americans are impoverished than the government has calculated, and Sen's definition perhaps captures the real inner dynamic driving mass consumption beyond acquiring the basic necessities. It is not simply a matter of keeping up with the Joneses or mimicking refined tastes. The consumption is required to keep up with American life itself. To avoid experiencing public shame in this society a family needs far more than food and shelter and, whatever personal desires one feels, the marketing mechanisms of commerce continuously reelaborate the social definition of what "more" means.

Looking backward, one can say that the mass consumption society constructed during the twentieth century was an egalitarian triumph in the sense that nearly all were enabled to participate, albeit at vastly different levels of luxury. But the future of mass consumption is now, paradoxically, threatened by the growing inequalities of wealth and incomes. As Clair Brown reported, a large portion of Americans, mainly in the laborer and wage-earner classes, is now faltering, diverging in their consumption patterns from the better-off classes. This fissuring of the middle-class—first noted with alarm in the 1980s—is driven basically by the diverging fortunes of American families in personal wealth and the widening gulfs in incomes. People, to put it crudely, don't have enough money to keep up. Nevertheless, they are trying—struggling heroically, one might say—to remain good consumers and thus avoid the public shame.

From the 1950s to the early 1970s, Brown explained, virtually all classes enjoyed a robust expansion in their discretionary spending on "variety" and "status" consumption. Even the poor gained a much improved standard of living, thanks to more generous public subsidies. However, during the last three decades, as hourly wages stagnated in real terms, working families were squeezed in their ability to maintain an expanding participation in the mass consumption. They more or less succeeded, though at a steadily slowing pace. How did they accomplish this? First, they worked harder and longer, mainly with women, wives and mothers, entering the full-time workforce and other family members taking on part-time jobs. Second, they borrowed against their savings, with credit cards and lines of bank credit that steadily drew down the accumulated equity they owned in their homes. This process explains the mountainous debt levels households built up amid the booming nineties. After storing up savings through home ownership during the sixties and seventies, the average homeowner drew down home equity dramatically during the last two decades, from 70 percent to 51 percent of mortgage value.

The problem with both of these strategies—working longer hours, spending the family savings—is that neither can be repeated during the next twenty years. Sooner or later, people will run out of the time to take on another job or additional overtime shifts. Sooner or later, they will run out of savings. An economic crunch seems unavoidable unless the distribution of incomes is altered significantly. When this reckoning occurs in sufficient numbers, the normal assumptions of our mass-consumption economy should be severely challenged, as broad ranks of working people are compelled to change their values as consumers—to get by with less and endure the social shame. Professor Brown is not sanguine about how this rancorous transition will unfold. "Continued wage stagnation will eventually translate into stagnation of living standards," she predicts. "In the absence of a major transformation of social values, our class conflicts over income and what it buys can be expected to intensify."[7]

In those circumstances, Americans might at last be compelled to reconsider the underlying economic assumptions of "more." The internal logic of economic theory is derived, after all, from the historic expectation of permanent scarcity—scarcity confronted by infinite potential for human needs and wants. Thus, capitalism ingeniously strives to produce more output from less input—the efficiency that demands (according to its own definitions) the most effective allocation of resources and capital. The assumption that scarcity is with us always claims the highest priority in public affairs and efficiency regularly trumps social aspirations. An impossible burden of proof confronts intangible social goals that are not marketable commodities and thus have no priced value. What is the rate of return? How much might this social improvement damage the production of "more"? Both liberals and conservatives accept these efficiency premises; their policy arguments in macroeconomics are generally over the best way to achieve the "more."

The standard assumptions of efficiency, however, are regularly mocked by real life outcomes. The faith in efficiency was shaken most recently by the horrendous disintegration of stock prices that destroyed somewhere between $6 and $8 trillion in capital, including especially the retirement savings of working families. The financial system's managers shrugged this off as an unfortunate occurrence and lamely explained that these things are to be expected in the tides of free-market capitalism. But where does one find "efficiency" in this process, the stern disciplinarian who designs lean production systems and squeezes costs down to the penny?

The system, remember, arduously accumulates its surplus and savings by imposing painful sacrifices and brutal dislocations on innocent participants such as workers or communities. Then it artificially inflates the supposed value of those savings as invested in the assets of financial markets. Then it abruptly collapses those assets, leaving millions of families with devastating losses and a much bleaker future. The savvier big players are able to accumulate still larger fortunes while the ignorant herds experience the bracing tonic of free-market insecurity. Where, for that matter, is the "social efficiency" in such a system? One thing is obvious: Because ordinary people lost still more of their financial cushion, the reckoning that Professor Brown foresees for mass consumption likely has been hastened by these events.

More of what? The question does not much interest formal economics. Abundance and its social consequences are regarded as a matter of consumer taste—let people decide for themselves what makes them happy. If you don't want it, don't buy it. This sounds vaguely democratic until one remembers that in the economic realm the power to decide things is distributed in dollars, not as individual rights, so many lose their voice by consequence of their meager assets. Some citizens, furthermore, have examined the accounting principles behind the economists' efficiency and found huge fallacies in the justifications. The destruction of nature by enterprise, they discover for instance, is regarded as cost-free by the economic model, an archaic premise of capitalism that lives on despite contemporary understandings of ecological crisis. Thus, what looks like "growth" in orthodox accounting terms may actually be "decline" when the broader social considerations such as environmental destruction are included in the bookkeeping. In any case, goods-producing activities that generate increased economic output do not necessarily generate what the society wants and needs.

The house of economics is due for major renovations, if not a complete tear down, because the economic order has lost one of its main emotional suppositions: the motivating fear of scarcity and deprivation. The dread of scarcity lives on, however, in public consciousness, in law and politics and civic ambitions. As people come to terms with this new condition (and there is scattered evidence that some young people are asking themselves, More of what?), many fruitful questions about the future are opened for discussion. What now justifies the harsh personal sacrifices imposed on people's lives in the name of sustaining the abundance? Why does the capitalist process continue to defend or ignore its many forms of social injury—especially the ecological destruction—when the pursuit of accumulation is no longer a matter of human survival but more often an elaboration of surplus? If there is plenty to go around (as there clearly is), why does the economic order still require a permanent subcategory of the impoverished and dependent—Marx's famous "reserve army" of the unemployed? For that matter, why must society accept a capitalism that persists in generating greater inequalities, generation after generation, as the required terms for sustaining general abundance? If ever greater concentrations of wealth and power are the inescapable result of our economic system, then what future is there for ever achieving genuine democracy in place of an elite plutocracy? These matters and other systemic disorders usually are blamed on people, on human error or weakness, on the failure of schooling or the political system or society itself. The only remedy, we are assured, is achieving still "more."

Many Americans no longer believe this. Skeptics are found especially among those who see the ongoing ecological destruction as the most critical contradiction overshadowing our prosperity. There are others who protest that the quality of private lives is degraded needlessly by the terms and conditions of work, even as society's commonly shared assets, from parks to communication airwaves, are reduced by enterprise to private commodities. Still others object that the growing maldistribution of power reflected in private wealth steadily degrades public confidence in democracy, capturing the representative self-government as a private asset. These perspectives and some others are active in politics certainly, but also largely frustrated. It is not so easy to think through plausible, equitable solutions because the various discontents generated by "more" are tangled up together and the supposed reforms often interact at cross-purposes. After all, the engine that reliably produces "more" and distributes its goods so broadly is the same engine that devours nature at a pace that logically cannot continue. It is the same economic machinery that cannot be slowed down without severely injuring masses of ordinary working people. And yet, even in its most robust phases, it generates an ever greater maldistribution of assets and incomes and, not coincidentally, imposes on most citizens the sense of loss of self-sufficiency and independent control over one's own destiny.

This historical moment allows us—in fact, impels us—to look directly at the engine itself, that is, at the nature of American capitalism. The purpose of this book is to examine more deeply how and why our brilliant economic system collides with so many of society's broader aspirations and regularly frustrates them. The subject is daunting, of course. Yet we are able to ask these questions now, and probably for the first time in American history, without the shadow of desperation and scarce necessity hanging over the answers. The terms of inquiry, however, must be very different from the standard politics of the past, as I will explain in the next chapter. Our objective is to identify the functional routines and relationships within the system itself that might be altered—in fact, must be altered—in order to achieve the more fulfilling society that ought to be possible now, given our great wealth.

The idea of reinventing American capitalism sounds far-fetched, I know, and especially improbable considering the market-centered orthodoxy that reigns in conventional thinking. I can report, nevertheless, that many Americans are already at work on the idea in various scattered ways (though usually not with such sweeping declarations of intent). They are experimenting in localized settings—tinkering with the ways in which the system operates—and are convinced that alternatives are possible, not utopian schemes but self-interested and practical changes that can serve broader purposes. This approach seems quite remote from the current preoccupations of big politics and big business, but this is where the society's deepest reforms usually have originated in the American past. The future may begin among ordinary people, far distant from established power, who are brave enough to see themselves as pioneers.

# 2

# The Soul of Capitalism

THE big, fundamental questions have all been answered, or so we are told. Continuing disputes among economists or business and political leaders typically involve the subsidiary issues of how best to manage things for maximum output and efficiency. The economic system is marvelously well-developed, sophisticated, and intimidatingly complex, and one does not doubt it is the great engine of our abundance. In these circumstances, society itself seems becalmed; at least, people are not mobilized by any great causes challenging the existing order. Most citizens, either because they are contented with things or resigned to fate, have essentially withdrawn from the arena of political action, perhaps sensing that politics has nothing larger in mind for them or no intention of addressing their personal discontents. America, meanwhile, describes itself to the world in unblushing superlatives: the richest, freest, most powerful and capable nation on earth. Indeed, this is what we tell ourselves.

Notwithstanding the settled stillness, this book proceeds from an opposite premise: that a more contentious time is approaching, when big questions about American economic life are back on the table again for serious reconsideration. Not overnight perhaps, or with any dramatic announcements, but the deeper rhythms of the national story are pushing us toward a renewal of doubt and questioning, a skeptical reexamination of long-accepted arrangements in American capitalism that govern life and work and enterprise. This agitating inquiry will occur not for ideological reasons but because the practical necessities of everyday life and the country's unfulfilled aspirations gradually persuade more and more citizens that something in our system is seriously out of whack and ought to be changed (even if they cannot identify exactly what is wrong or how it might be corrected).

Someday hence, if my premise is right, Americans will be talking again about the fundamentals, asking themselves if it is possible to alter the system in various ways and how they might proceed. We will be arguing anew, for instance, over the terms and conditions of work, and about the ways in which investment and production are organized. We may ask ourselves why the decision making in important institutions of business and finance is so closely held among a relative few when their decisions have such great impact on our lives at work and at home. We may explore more rigorously how our savings are deployed as investment capital and whether the results are pleasing or alarming. Indeed, why does the economic system seem so indifferent, even hostile, to the intangibles in life that have the deepest meaning for people and society? We might even ask ourselves: What *is* the meaning of wealth now that America is so awesomely wealthy?

Our subject is the nature of American capitalism and how it organizes life for us and for society at large, why it generates great injury and destructive consequences right alongside the material abundance. This book is not intended as another bleak catalog of those consequences—the social dislocations and gross wastefulness, the confinements on personal liberties and enduring injustices, the inequalities and the ecological destruction. I expect most readers are familiar, one way or another, with the deleterious impact of capitalism on lives or community, but they may also feel largely powerless to do much about it. Furthermore, I suspect many Americans, including among the affluent, experience a vague sense of personal shame because they regularly encounter conflicts between their own values and human aspirations and the imperatives of the economic system—conflicts they are unable to resolve. They either do not earn enough to "live well" in material terms. Or they earn more and more, yet still find themselves unable to "live well" in human terms. Unable to find fulfillment in their material circumstances, some reluctantly accept the incompleteness as a sign of personal failure. The hunger is unnamed—and embarrassing to acknowledge—but seems part of the price one is obliged to pay, part of what the system expects or demands.

These peculiar consequences of modern prosperity are examined in order to get to the larger question: Why does it have to be this way? Are Americans inevitably consigned to a series of dispiriting trade-offs between their lives and values and social obligations, on one hand, and the demands of gorgeous, beckoning abundance? Or might people, instead, actually change the nature of American capitalism? This book offers a very hopeful story of the possible, one that tells how our society can alter the operating values of capitalism instead of the other way around, and thus can establish basic human needs and aspirations as the dominant force in our economic life. That promise suggests people are not as powerless as they imagine and, in fact, they are not. As I will explain, Americans have the potential, collectively, to acquire decisive influence over large questions of business and finance that are now decided remotely by a limited number of powerful institutions. If that sounds excessively optimistic given the present dominance of business values, remember that profound systemic changes are not made quickly or easily. But the supporting evidence will show that many efforts toward transformation have already begun.

My premise—that American capitalism is ripe for reinvention—is not based on fanciful supposition. The most compelling reason for expecting deep reform is the new circumstance described in Chapter 1—the paradox of secure abundance accompanied by the stressed social reality. We are on new ground as a country, yet neither the operating assumptions nor the governing institutions have been adjusted to conform. The absence of profound adjustments promises to raise the threshold of collateral pain until sooner or later, for better or worse, the system's operating assumptions are changed or society becomes resigned to the new, starker version of inequality that is emerging.

A second reason is that, until rather recently, the very idea of transforming the terms of American capitalism was regarded as a taboo subject. During the Cold War decades, questioning the functional realities of the U.S. system sounded vaguely subversive, as if maybe you were working for the other side. Then the Cold War ended and an ideological contest with communism that had stretched across 150 years was abruptly, definitively resolved. Capitalism won. State-owned economies disintegrated. This event swept away stale ideological baggage on both sides and opened new political space—the first opportunity in half a century to ask bigger questions about capitalism itself, how it works or fails to work on behalf of the general society. This new space remains largely unfilled as yet, but I seek at a minimum to show people that it's now okay to think and talk critically about capitalism's own shortcomings. At this point in history, it may even be the patriotic thing to do.

There are good reasons why capitalism has prevailed across five or six centuries while alternative economic systems faltered and eventually failed. To understand the American system's blind spots and how they might be overcome, one must also appreciate its enduring strengths. It produces more from less more reliably than other systems did. Its processes are also always forward-looking and constantly adapting to new circumstances—thus, always progressive, according to its own objectives. These qualities are not self-evident to social critics who focus on the system's stubborn destructiveness, but the operating techniques of capitalism involve a kind of continuous flexibility, evolving to meet new conditions and threats. On the margins, inventive dissenters are always trying to do things differently, more profitably, and when those firms succeed, others will rush to emulate them. This fluid ability to adapt probably explains as well as anything why the communist systems could not keep up with the capitalist reality.

This flexibility also helps explain why the system is more vulnerable to change than it appears. Some of the positive reforms I will describe actually are underway within the system itself—crucial experiments that already are succeeding in visible ways, though still ignored or belittled in conventional practice. Furthermore, as we examine the internal routines that produce so much collateral damage, it will become clear that many of the institutional arrangements and operating principles in the American system are utterly outmoded. Most were devised a century ago more or less for circumstances that no longer exist, either in the economy or society, yet they continue in place. If these arrangements were perhaps once justifiable, they exist now only as convenient fictions—disguising the power relationships that serve certain narrow interests but effectively deprive the general population of any voice or influence, even over their own money. Knowledge is power. This deformity cannot survive if enough people come to understand its meaning. The process of self-education is underway.

Above all, I have considerable confidence that the new subject is reforming capitalism itself because I have seen so many Americans already engaged in the challenge, one way or another. You will meet some of them in these pages. They are a scattered and eclectic lot, mostly operating beneath the media's attention and not yet taken seriously by the citadels of business and financial power. Many are even unaware of parallel efforts by kindred spirits elsewhere. It would be premature to describe them as a "movement" to reinvent capitalism since none yet exists. At this point, their activities are no more than interesting fragments—big ideas, small isolated triumphs, the seeds perhaps of something larger.

These are the people I think of as the pioneers, the risk takers in our time trying to open up new territory within our highly elaborated economic system. Some are practical-minded men and women in business—engineers, accountants, managers—who see themselves as problem-solvers, not ideologues. Others are visionary thinkers and activists with sweeping concepts of industrial transformation in mind. Some are innovative labor leaders or aggrieved farmers or even financiers of a rebellious spirit. Some are teachers and some are students. What they have in common is a shared sensibility (and some level of active anger) about how important social imperatives and cherished aspects of the human experience are being ground up by the economic system, which is largely oblivious to the destruction. Prosperity, they insist, does not require that it has to be this way and, indeed, people cannot long endure this version of prosperity.

Many of them speak only of concrete projects—not grand pronouncements about altering capitalism—and have engaged themselves in a long and undramatic process of practical experiments and purposeful tinkering to discover what works, what doesn't. Many are occasionally derided as dreamers or crackpots, yet they see themselves, much as the pioneers did, as down-to-earth pragmatists trying to fashion something new and replenishing out of this era's conflicted prosperity. It does sound audacious—setting out to change the value system of capitalism on behalf of society.

The contemporary culture ignores this tedious, slow-moving route to progress. But American history confirms that the most important social and economic transformations have always originated in this humble fashion. The reform objectives were sustained at first by ordinary people with nerve and conviction, long before the leaders embraced their ideas. Starting small and localized, motivated by both practical self-interest and idealism, trying and failing, then trying again. Above all, this approach requires patience—a radical kind of patience, one might say—but that too is very much in the American tradition.

———

THE FEDERAL GOVERNMENT cannot do this for people. That is hard for many to digest, but anyone who takes seriously the possibility of reforming capitalism in fundamental ways has to start by abandoning some inherited political reflexes. The government has the power to articulate society's larger aspirations, but it is not equipped to execute this deeper kind of economic transformation or, at this point, even lead the way. If the political community were so inclined (and obviously it's not), legislative leaders would not know where to begin, what new arrangements to command by law or to encourage with subsidy. If an activist president set out with good intentions to rewire the engine of capitalism—to alter its operating values or reorganize the terms for employment and investment or tamper with other important features—the initiative would very likely be chewed to pieces by the politics. Given the standard legislative habits of modern government, not to mention its close attachments to the powerful interests defending the status quo, the results would be marginal adjustments at best and might even make things worse.

Government's handicaps are more substantial than the conservative mood. Washington, as we explore later on, has itself become a principal barrier to reformulating the economic system, and it regularly acts as unwitting collaborator in much of the social damage. In any case, the political system is not yet ready for big questions. Transforming ideas are always difficult to advance in American politics and it is virtually impossible if they are not driven by the energies of robust popular demand (the abolitionists agitated for fifty years before the Civil War resolved the slavery question). Reformers must first develop the outlines of an alternative social reality, existing examples of successful reforms that are made visible to ordinary Americans and look like plausible remedies for their own circumstances. It takes time to achieve that political condition—time for trial and error and discovery—which many of the pioneers well understand. Government eventually can be mobilized to assist pioneering ventures and promising new ideas (and to stop subsidizing capitalism's destructive practices), but the arena of electoral politics is not the place to discover which ideas, which ventures and arrangements, are the most viable solutions. People on the ground have to do that for themselves.

This observation is intended to disturb the settled habits of thought, especially among left-liberal progressives, and discourage the notion that they can count on government to descend like a deus ex machina and miraculously resolve these deeper conflicts between society and the economic realm. As a clarifying thought experiment, imagine that government doesn't exist or that on the big questions it mainly serves the other side. That assumption should focus minds and energies on the true subject: the system of enterprise and how it really functions and malfunctions in our lives, not who will win the next election. Turning to electoral politics to correct what's wrong or unfair is the deeply established reflex inherited from the twentieth century and even small-government conservatives share it. Notwithstanding their desires to shrink government's role, the right regularly employs the governing powers to serve its business clients or to impose conservative causes on the society. Their "school voucher" campaign, for example, seeks to compel U.S. taxpayers to provide financing for private religious schools—not exactly a project of small government.

I am not suggesting that politics and political struggle will end; of course not. Nor do I do argue that government should cease to use its powers of regulation (though the regulatory system is now badly deformed). I do suggest that given the decayed condition of representative democracy the political system must itself undergo a profound reformation before government will be trusted again as the reliable voice speaking for society's nobler aspirations. Since I am increasingly skeptical that regular politics will reform itself, I suspect the best route to restoring our democracy might begin elsewhere, confronting the undemocratic qualities embedded in the economic system which are, in fact, a principal source of democracy's decline.

The great accomplishment of twentieth-century reform politics was to establish government as the counterforce to capitalism, the rival power center that confronted business and finance on behalf of society, that could brake the encroaching domination of private economic power, curb the excesses and abuses, or clean up the social wreckage that business left in its wake. And government succeeded brilliantly in many enduring ways. It created financial systems for economic security and laid down public rules governing the behavior of private enterprise, from child labor and tainted meat to monopoly power. It also served as a principal benefactor to private enterprise, providing public resources (public property and the taxpayers' money) to advance the fortunes of businesses in the name of the common good. These measures and others were integral to creating the broad prosperity that now exists.

Yet there is another discomforting reality to face: Government in the long run did not succeed in resolving the deeper collisions between society and capitalism. These conflicts wax and wane from one decade to the next, but no one could argue at this point that the enduring aspirations of people and society are fulfilled when so many of these public goals are in retreat and more insecure. Government instead has become the battleground for ongoing political conflicts over what exactly society is allowed to want or what it can afford, within the terms of business accounting. This contest has always inevitably involved the heavy hand of private interests deploying their influential resources to seek correct judgments from the public officials, but in our time the democratic contest has been unhinged by money. I do not say this to belittle the great political accomplishments of the past or to second guess the many significant improvements government interventions have achieved. What I do assert is that "strong government" is an insufficient response to the underlying problem of capitalism. The imperatives of accumulation have rolled over competing social values and proliferate distress and dislocations right alongside the growing abundance, while many of the government's past achievements have been deformed or eviscerated.

31

The welfare state survives in an increasingly porous condition and is frequently redirected to ameliorate the very real stresses of middle-class life rather than the desperate struggles of the weak and destitute. The regulatory state has become a deeply flawed governing mess. Many of the enforcement agencies are securely captured by the industries they regulate, others are blocked from effective action by industry's endless litigation and political counterattacks. Stronger laws are tortuously difficult to enact and invariably studded with purposeful loopholes designed to delay effective enforcement for years, even decades. Thirty years after the Clean Air Act of 1970, the Environmental Protection Agency is still not permitted to impose emissions standards on hundreds of older power plants that were "grandfathered" in as exempt under the original law. These plants now generate the bulk of America's electricity—and the bulk of its air pollution. The Federal Communications Commission was created as "public trustee" to protect the public's great common asset, the broadcasting airwaves, but it has evolved into a friendly auction house for the largest media conglomerates, assisting the further concentration of this valuable and limited resource. Labor laws enacted in the 1930s to protect workers' right to organize unions and bargain collectively for themselves are now a tool of management, routinely and systematically violated by corporations without legal consequences.

I could go on and on with such examples. This is not an argument against regulation. Citizens (myself included) will continue to push for stronger rules and real enforcement. But it ought to be obvious by now that these protective laws are highly vulnerable to political mood swings, not to mention the swarms of lobbyists and lawyers and old-fashioned forms of corruption. Despite the grace notes provided by modern public relations, business is still business.

The modern resurgence of conservative ideology did not create these governing disorders but effectively exploited them, arguing on principle that the only way out of the rampant political favoritism is to withdraw government from its many obligations as protector and intervener (a policy choice better known as deregulation). Yet, aside from ending welfare guarantees for the poor, conservatives did not have the nerve (or the congressional votes) to achieve much outright repeal of laws that most citizens want and support. So conservatives often did the next best thing: They hollowed out the laws through business-friendly jurists or by appointing hostile enforcement officers or by squeezing agency budgets to ensure the weakness of regulators.

Thus, the constancy of law is subject to the variables of the next election. The commitment of government to certain goals shifts from year to year (most obviously in the enforcement of environmental protection) and many companies are thus encouraged to delay compliance, knowing that the next cop on the beat may be friendlier. Worse than that, many corporations have taken the looser supervision from government as an opportunity to revert to antisocial and inequitable practices that ostensibly were abandoned or even prohibited long ago. The sweatshops came back. Government was looking the other way.

The larger point, as these examples illustrate, is that the collision between society and capitalism has endured over many years, despite the laws and shifting political sensibilities, because it is essentially a clash of two different value systems. Government has not succeeded in reconciling the clash because, though it issues many rules of dos and don'ts for enterprise to follow, it not does attempt to alter the underlying values that shape capitalism's behavior. To be enduring, that change has to occur inside capitalism, like altering the gene system of a plant or animal.

The U.S. version of capitalism, we should remember, is substantially different from other, quite successful systems that were developed elsewhere by major rivals such as Germany and Japan. Socialists in western Europe, while they did not succeed in replacing capitalism with state ownership, created a much gentler version than America's. Private enterprises were compelled to accept elaborate social obligations and restraints, while governments enacted broad, universal support systems for families, workers, and society at large. Japan, likewise, created its own distinctive web of social-economic understandings that hold firms and investors responsible for what happens to people and for protecting many of society's noneconomic priorities. *The Wall Street Journal* once grumpily disparaged Japan as "the only communist nation that works."

Each nation's political response to capitalism has evolved from its own cultural ethos and historical experiences, its own ethical and religious foundations. The solutions that work in one society are nearly irrelevant to what may succeed in another. So American capitalism is not going to be refashioned by copying the collective social obligations invented in Germany or Japan or Sweden. The United States, more likely, will solve these conflicts in its own distinctive terms or not solve them at all.

In *Development as Freedom,* Nobel economist Amartya Sen of Cambridge University wrote a gently argued critique of the contemporary economic orthodoxy and asserted that the further evolution of capitalist systems is necessary and perhaps inevitable. "To see capitalism as a system of pure profit maximization based on individual ownership of capital is to leave out much that has made the system so successful in raising output and in generating income," Sen wrote. The intangible elements of human freedom—dignity, equity, democratic expression, and self-realization—usually are seen as the end goal of a successful economy, but Sen explained that these softer values are actually the necessary means for achieving economic success. Capitalism will thus have to change further, Sen declared, in order to cope with the great and growing problems of inequality and the ecological crisis, to learn how to husband the "public goods" that everyone owns collectively. "The solution to these problems," he wrote, "will almost certainly call for institutions that take us beyond the capitalist market economy." Professor Sen stands with the optimists.[1]

What Americans should by now be able to see is that neither the laissez-faire marketplace nor strong government has given them a satisfying or permanent resolution. The problem is not the marketplace and it is not government. The problem originates in the contest of clashing values between society and capitalism and, since this human society cannot surrender its deepest values, it must try to alter capitalism's. As we look deeper for the soul of capitalism, we find that, in the terms of ordinary human existence, American capitalism doesn't appear to have one.

IN THE ECONOMIC SPHERE, efficiency trumps community. Maximizing returns comes before family or personal loyalty. What seems priceless in one realm may be wasted freely or even destroyed by the other. Human experience is sacred to society, a marketable commodity in capitalism. We hear the echo of these clashing values in everyday conversation when people speak—either reverently or ominously—about "the bottom line." For some, it provides self-evident justification for the stern measures required by business. A company closes the plant and dismisses long loyal personnel for balance sheet reasons that have nothing to do with their performance or productiveness. A conscientious manager shrugs and does his job, carries out the decision, and finds rationales so he can live with himself. If the company doesn't do well, then everybody loses. I have no choice; it's my job. For others, "the bottom line" resonates with callous indifference and even greed. The phrase evokes the imperious aloofness of companies that do not seem to know or care about the human consequences of their actions, that disavow any responsibility for the wreckage their profitability leaves behind in society or nature.

We can take our text from the words of a Protestant theologian, the Reverend Emil Brunner, who declared his contempt for capitalism more than seventy years ago: "This system is contrary to the spirit of service." He meant Christian service. "It is debased and irresponsible; indeed we may go further and say it is irresponsibility developed into a system."

It seems odd to recall now that in the early decades of the twentieth century Christian ministers like Brunner were leading voices in the critique of American capitalism. Their moral outrage was stoked by the vast and visible suffering associated with unregulated capitalism: children working in factories and coal mines while the new plutocrats built fabulous mansions and founded great art museums from their private collections. The reform theologians came to be known as the Social Gospel movement and reached an apogee of influence during the extreme suffering of the Great Depression. Many of these religious thinkers (Reinhold Niebuhr was the best known) thought of themselves as socialists and were convinced that capitalism would someday be replaced by a more humane economic order, though they were vague about how this new system was supposed to function. The Reverend Brunner, a minister of the Swiss Reformed denomination, was more conservative than others. He protested the injustices and inhumanities of capitalism, but did not expect salvation to be found in earthly possessions or any economic system that produced them.[2]

The past teems with such forgotten voices asking fundamental questions about the nature of economic life that are surprisingly relevant to our time. This book, I stipulate, contains very few ideas that are genuinely new, but it revives some valuable ideas and insights from the distant past, ideas that were passed over at the time or pushed aside by competing approaches. Some of the ideas seemed too visionary; some were rejected as insufficiently radical. Possibly, the people and economic circumstances simply were not ready to see them through. In this new moment, when the long ideological conflict with communism has finally ended and general abundance is now secure, some of those old ideas may get a second chance.

". . . irresponsibility developed into a system." A generation or so later Milton Friedman emerged as the leading apostle for the revival of laissez-faire capitalism, and he put a quite different spin on the

Reverend Brunner's observation. Irresponsibility, Friedman explained, is what makes capitalism succeed. "So the question is," Friedman once said, "do corporate executives, providing they stay within the law, have responsibilities . . . other than to make as much money for their stockholders as possible? And my answer is, no, they do not." His interpretation reigns today, as anyone who reads the business pages understands. Indeed, Friedman turns the logic upside down and argues that Brunner's "irresponsibility" is actually the moral obligation for companies and their managers. Think of these two men as the polar opposites. Which side are you on?

American capitalism is, of course, no longer so raw and savage as in the early twentieth century, nor as frankly hostile to society's demands. Very few firms in commerce can now afford to be seen as blatant rogue or robber baron, not without damaging the brand name and inviting popular retaliations. Still, the last twenty years have revealed how little the underlying imperatives have changed, despite the mantle of public laws commanding socially responsible behavior. As the era of deregulation reduced legal restraints on firms, as new technologies and globalization quickened the competition, one major corporation after another was persuaded to back away from its long-standing commitments to employees and communities, even to national identity. The corporation's unwritten "social contract" was torn up. Some firms who hesitated suffered the disfavor of financial markets. Others charged ahead enthusiastically and boosted returns enormously, often by pushing their costs onto others—their workers and communities, the environment and, more discreetly, their own customers. The most aggressive companies became the most esteemed.

A crucial counterpoint exists, however. Not all companies chose the low road to solve the cost-price problems of intense competition. Many large and small firms resisted and prospered nonetheless. Whether this choice reflected the personal values of managers and owners or simply smarter business strategies, their success does hint that there is much more space for successful alternatives, even in the global context, than the stern sermonizers of the free-market culture are willing to acknowledge.

Americans at large, not only managers, live with the recurring moral dissonance between the two realms. And usually it's not so easy to choose sides. We want and need enterprise to succeed, yet also recoil at the adverse consequences visited upon people or the community or our own lives. This conflict of purposes lies just beneath the surfaces of modern American life and is difficult to visualize because, obviously, people and institutions are intimately enmeshed in both society and capitalism. We take direction and values from both—our social relationships and our place in the economic sphere. We enjoy the benefits of participating in both. We occasionally encounter different forms of disapproval or discipline from both. Yet these two interwoven realms are not the same. Each has its own distinctive goals and values, different concepts of right and wrong, different understandings of what matters most in life.

When critics complain that corporate behavior is "unethical" or "socially irresponsible," they make the problem seem easier than it is. A systems analyst might say, more accurately, that we function within two different ethical systems, each one with its own distinctive logic and moral code, each pursuing self-interested goals and operating premises, each one contesting for primacy in our thoughts and actions. The bottom line does not count humanity in its bookkeeping because to do so would violate its own ethical principles. When society resists the bottom line's imperatives, it does so to preserve the integrity of its own moral values.

Most Americans, I suspect, have come to accept this tension as an inescapable condition of living in a prosperous nation. Depending on their situation, they may feel cheerful or sullen about it, oblivious or dimly guilt-ridden. But the emotions do not dissolve the dilemma for them. What could be more dispiriting for the "pursuit of happiness" than a regimen of doing what is necessary and expected (closing the plant, firing innocent employees), and then feeling something is wrong about it?

This dilemma, I suggest, is one aspect of why so many modern Americans feel trapped and powerless, even many of those who enjoy great abundance themselves. It is about more than bad feelings. Under the present terms of capitalism, people have been rendered concretely powerless to resolve these matters of competing value systems for themselves and are intimidated by the scale of the conflict. To reach the kind of human fulfillment that Keynes envisioned—learning to live wisely and well with the permanent abundance—requires a search for reconciliation in which people must first discover how to overcome their sense of powerlessness.

THE LOGIC OF CAPITALISM is ingeniously supple and complete, self-sustaining and forward-looking. Except for one large incapacity: As a matter of principle, it cannot take society's interests into account. The company's balance sheet has no way to recognize costs that are not its own, no reason or method to calculate the future liabilities it causes but that someone else will have to pay. The incentives, in fact, run hard in the opposite direction. The firm will be rewarded with greater returns and higher stock prices if it manages to "externalize" its true operating costs. It does this by by pushing the negative consequences off on someone else: the neighbors who live downstream from a factory's industrial pollution or its own workers, who lose job security and pension rights, or the community left with an empty factory, shattered lives, a ruined environment.

Corporate accountants will also correctly reject any liability for intangible costs to society, the ruptures to family life or the loss of stability and equable relationships, the broader social injuries that will require expensive remedial action by society in the distant future but do not represent costs for the company's present-day production. With the invention of public relations early in the last century, capitalism did recognize that good business practice requires companies to acknowledge society's broad sensibilities, and their advertising regularly pays emotional homage to public values. But the accounting principles are clear: A firm need not accept responsibility for collateral damage to society. Unless criminal acts are involved, there is virtually no accountability for that kind of corporate behavior, not to the communities where the company operates nor to the larger society nor even to the company's putative owners who are shareholders. This freedom from responsibility is, not surprisingly, described by business-friendly economists as one of the American system's great virtues. It reduces the company's operating costs enormously. It provides valuable flexibility to management in determining the surest path to increased efficiency and profit.

One can admire the functional beauty of capitalism's internal logic without forgiving the damage done to innocent bystanders. The available resources, whether human labor or mined ore or livestock on the hoof, are first priced as commodities for sale or as the cost inputs for production. These valuations are necessarily rigorous and unsentimental, excluding social feeling or other irrelevancies, because the cost-price decisions at every stage will determine how to achieve the highest level of efficiency, that is, the greatest value in output from the least possible cost in inputs. More from less. Achieving that disciplined efficiency, in turn, promises to maximize returns—the greatest possible wealth creation, expressed in profit and expanding incomes, from the least possible investment.

Maximizing returns is not primarily a function of greed (though there are plenty of greedheads in business who act as though it is). Maximizing profit from investment is morally justified by capitalism because it increases the surpluses of new wealth that will be fed back into the same process—the capital that feeds new lending or investing and thus enables further expansion of the system of production and, if things go right, will generate still more output, more new wealth.

This constant recycling of capital is the brilliant core that makes the capitalist process so dynamic and creative, an engine that continuously borrows old money earned from past enterprise to launch new enterprise into the future. The surplus of wealth does not sit idle in miserly piles. It finances a continual regeneration. Thus, capitalism adapts more readily to the unknown future because, in a sense, it is continuously reinventing the future.

And all of these forward-looking initiatives and price valuations are steadily vetted and disciplined by the suspenseful, trial-and-error process known as market competition. Get the price wrong on the product, you lose and the other guy wins. Devise a new method for cost-saving production, you gain market share from competitors who lose it. Bet the company on a new product line that nobody wants to buy, shareholders dump the company's stock. The many forms of competitive testing follow endlessly complex and often brutal variations. But, in the moral logic of capitalism, the combat is what leads to the greater good, first for the particular winners, but ultimately for society at large, which will acquire a larger base of material wealth to finance its future. The fierceness of the competition is what requires the stern business practices, again morally justified by an assumption that using people, commodities, and capital with greater effectiveness is required to produce more from less. The maldistribution of who shares in those surplus returns is generally brushed aside, regarded as an external social problem that cannot be corrected without fouling up the brilliant engine. Besides, everyone is living better, aren't they?

Society's values seem frail and insubstantial by comparison—unbusinesslike. The valuations made by people in their lives are necessarily less concrete, since they are mostly based on consensual understandings, not on hard calculations with mathematical precision. But society's softer principles are no less logical or powerful than capitalism's. The moral obligations felt by people in their lives constitute a distilled sum of the collective human experience: what we learned as small children; the lessons taught by family and church; the national culture's ethical expectations for how we are supposed to treat one another. Though unwritten, these social understandings are, arguably, more deeply felt and self-interested than any economic principles, because they define everyone's mutual rewards and responsibilities toward life itself—toward family and neighbors, toward the whole of society, and even beyond one's life. These commitments, as an everyday fact, are the source of happiness that is more central to our lives than material accumulation. And these obligations are more demanding than the rules of commerce. They form the basis for living well, with or without lots of money.

As we know intuitively, people accept much deeper responsibilities in life than what economics defines as self-interest or can be easily explained by daily practicalities. These social verities constitute the universal obligations everyone assumes (or should) as the terms for their human existence, commitments that transcend any class distinctions and, indeed, do not vary greatly across cultures, despite the great contrasts between rich and poor. Without wandering into theology or genetic determinism, we can list some of the most obvious binding commitments that people accept and that society at large wants and needs. People assume responsibility:

for realizing one's own mortal potential, the hard work and joy of uncovering what is within us and learning how to use our lives fully, productively;

for adhering to the society's common code of right and wrong in personal behavior and relations with others;

for the nurture of children and family; the enthralling and somewhat mysterious task of sustaining the human cycle beyond one's own mortality;

for husbanding the collective inheritance from the past, a society's accumulated wealth of knowledge, beauty, and wisdom, the

common richness that is always far greater than personal fortunes or great buildings;

to the future as well as the past, the obligation to build beyond
our own needs and leave something valuable behind for those
yet unborn;

for the natural world that sustains all life, the great green earth
that infinitely delights and intrigues us, as it also supports us and
other living things;

for the sacred (though sacred meaning is defined in conflicting
ways), to honor humanity's transcendental expectations, to
respect eternal mysteries forever beyond the understanding of
mere mortals.

This list is only a rough approximation. Readers may wish to add
other elements I have overlooked. But the list is important to our
story because, one way or another, these intangibles constitute society's motivating subtext for defending itself against encroachments.
The moral content of life is expressed in these elements, the
inescapable commitments and the joys in living. None of us (unless
we are on the path to sainthood) has utopian expectations that we
will fulfill all of these obligations entirely, not without frequent error
or failings. Yet we cannot walk away from them either, not without
shrinking the dimensions of mortal existence. The social order, one
could say, teaches stern obligation to these intangible verities and
promises the most rewarding satisfaction in life to those who heed the
lessons and defend them.

Is it fair to say that market capitalism teaches roughly the opposite?
Enterprise and investors are rewarded concretely for refusing responsibility toward these same values. In raw simplicity, capitalism is
merely oblivious to them. But, in practice, it is also often actively
destructive. There is no way for the bookkeeping to value these intan-

gibles and, thus, no way to incorporate them in the factors of production. Everyone knows life is intrinsically cherished by society and the individual but, when industry makes its cost-benefit estimates, the value of lost life is calculated on the lost output of dead workers plus hospital and funeral bills. That sounds heartless, of course, but how could it be otherwise? This is what the Social Gospelers meant when they said capitalism lacks a soul.

On the whole, the Americans I describe who are engaged in purposeful experiments are trying to defend these values—community and self—against the relentless engine of capitalism. While they would not describe themselves in such grandiose terms, this set of common values is what unifies the scattered efforts of many thousands, their unexpressed commonality of purpose. Whether in large or small terms, they are attempting to act on behalf of society's core values as those values come into collision with the imperatives of capitalism. They are not hostile to material accumulation, but they are arguing for a deeper understanding of wealth and a moral economy in which society's values come first. Life's intangible obligations, they would concede, are awesome burdens, but they are also the priceless assets of human existence that cannot be bought or sold.

The conflicting valuation of assets defines the collision of the two realms. And it explains why society cannot yield. It cannot allow capitalism's values to prevail without forfeiting its own meaning. Capitulation may in the short term produce greater material wealth, but eventually is sure to destroy society itself, turning it into a place stripped of human sympathy and relations. This is not a new insight either. Since the rise of industrial capitalism two centuries ago, social philosophers and even some economists have observed the deep, destructive collision and warned of the dangerous implications. The Viennese economist Karl Polanyi described in *The Great Transformation,* published in 1944, how the struggle for domination between free-running capitalism and society's values led to the cataclysmic breakdown known as the Great Depression and gave rise to the violent, irrational politics of fascism. Polanyi wrote:

> To allow the market mechanism to be sole director of the fate of human beings and their natural environment, indeed, even of their purchasing power, would result in the demolition of society. For the alleged commodity "labor power" cannot be shoved about, used indiscriminately, or even left unused, without affecting also the human individual who happens to be the bearer of this peculiar commodity. In disposing of a man's labor power the system would, incidentally, dispose of the physical, psychological, and moral entity of "man" attached to that tag. Robbed of the protective cover of cultural institutions, human beings would perish from the effects of social exposure. . . . Nature would be reduced to its elements, neighborhoods and landscapes defiled, rivers polluted.[3]

Polanyi's recitation of the endangered elements resonates familiarly because it invokes many of the same injuries and grievances that society experiences today. Though the plateau of prosperity is many times higher and far more inclusive, Americans encounter the same pressures tugging at the public's precious assets, from defiled landscapes and rivers to workers robbed of self. In the absence of scarcity, people may at last find themselves free to reconsider the dilemma and seek a new balance in their obligations to the two realms, to reject social injuries once considered inescapable, to refuse sacrifices that add material increase at the expense of life itself. How these trade-offs might be approached and eventually realigned is our subject.

Irresponsibility is the heart of the American problem, as the Reverend Brunner declared long ago, but successful American capitalism has refashioned the terms of irresponsibility to be far more inclusive. It no longer suffices to limit the indictment to the powerful few, those who control the largest corporations or own the greatest accumulations of wealth. The irresponsibility is generalized now, thanks to the mechanisms and relationships institutionalized by modern business and banking and often codified in law. Irresponsibility is passed around to all.

Corporate managers are purposely shielded from accountability to their putative owners, the stockholders, who themselves are protected from personal liability for what their company does to others.

The everyday investors, large and small, are passively insulated from the social consequences of their desires, yet also denied the chance to assert their values in the enterprises they presumably own.

Consumers are supposedly carefree in their choices but also typically impotent in accepting any responsibility for the products they buy.

Workers, for the most part, are confined to a subordinate position that gives them little or no role in the firm where they work, nor any right to share the surplus wealth their work creates. Workers are thus free to be utterly irresponsible regarding the future of their firm, and voiceless on the content of their work.

The labor-management relationship defined by Federal law expresses the spirit of the American system. By law, it invites confrontation and regulates the disputes and assumes a recurring contest between irresponsible demands from both sides. The American version of capitalism requires edgy distrust among people supposedly working together. Read the fine print in the contract. Hire the best lawyers. If things go bad, sue your partner.

The other side of irresponsibility is powerlessness. These insulated and disconnected roles and relationships evolved from genuine economic objectives (and many continue to provide economic benefit in the narrow sense), but they also effectively shrink individual expression and authority. The mechanisms are a main reason why most participants—employees and investors, also managers and consumers—find they have very little influence in the system or even control over their own behavior (but also not much accountability to others). This distancing of the personal—the separation of self from the consequences of one's actions—is convenient to the system's smooth functioning, of course, and lends flexibility. It also provides a screen of moral opacity that participants can hide behind.

The essential challenge of reinventing capitalism requires us to restitch the relationships and alter mechanisms so that people may reclaim their individuality. This does not displace self-interest, but broadens its meaning beyond the narrowness of economics. It can empower individuals to assert themselves and their values, but it also depends upon fashioning new webs of mutual obligation and accountability. In a word, I am pursuing questions about ownership—the essence of capitalism—but I intend to explore the meaning of that word in a broader context. Can Americans be said to own their own lives? Do they own their work, their voice and self-expression? Does the ownership of financial assets have any meaning beyond the port-folio's monthly balance statement? Does it involve any influence or responsibility? Can sovereign citizens claim responsibility for the governing decisions made in their name? Who owns the common assets that are ostensibly shared by all? These and other questions are not theoretical abstractions. I examine them in the everyday facts of practical reality in order to identify obstacles and suggest some ways around them.

The vision shared by the many Americans who are experimenting—and the central premise of this book—is not a utopian society here on earth but the conviction that the arrangements within capitalism can be changed, little by little, to make more space for life, through innovations that eventually become common practice. Since government is unavailable to promote sweeping change, it may be just as well that people have started on the margins, where the goals are smaller, the barriers less formidable. They can move to confront the centers of power only after the ideas have passed the reality test and won broader followings.

In subsequent chapters, my inquiry digs into the complexities by exploring the main components of the capitalist process: work and the terms of employment; the commanding influence of finance capital; the pathological patterns of consumption and production; the corporation's supple influence on life and society; government's reactionary stewardship of economic life; and finally, some optimistic speculations on the future of reconciliation.

My optimism, the conviction that American capitalism can be made to conform more faithfully to society's broad values, requires one more proposition: that ordinary people are capable of doing this without much help from the very powerful. People of every station are more ready and able than is generally supposed to exercise greater responsibility for their own lives and for the social destiny, more willing than it appears to confront the confinements and discontents. Not everyone is, of course. Many Americans are doubtless content with passivity, uninterested in taking on larger burdens, and others are simply too intimidated by life's daily demands. But others have the personal confidence to try and to help hesitant friends see the prospects. If they succeed they will open a path that can lead to more fulfilling lives, more material security perhaps, and also more liberating space for self and family. In time, we may discover that trying to construct a moral economy from capitalism is also a crucial step toward restoring faith and meaning to democracy, the society in which citizens are responsible for governing themselves.

# 3

# Work Rules

Y ES, the country is fabulously rich in material terms, but are Americans really free? The question itself sounds like civic heresy. It offends national pride and the promise of liberty expressed in our founding documents, but also runs counter to the twentieth-century history of political accomplishments that greatly expanded individual rights to cover once excluded groups. Yet the disturbing contradictions are visible everyday when people go to work. The loss of freedom goes largely unnoticed because it is so routinely part of their lives.

In pursuit of "earning a living" most Americans go to work for someone else and thereby accept the employer's right to command their behavior in intimate detail. At the factory gate or the front office, people implicitly forfeit claims to self-direction and are typically barred from participating in the important decisions that govern their daily efforts. Most employees lose any voice in how the rewards of the enterprise are distributed, the surplus wealth their own work helped to create. Basic rights the founders said were inalienable—free speech and freedom of assembly, among others—are effectively suspended, consigned to the control of others. In some ways, the employee also surrenders essential elements of self.

This stark imbalance of power is embedded in the standard terms of employment and properly described as a master-servant relationship, as economist David Ellerman puts it. Stripped of social coloring and modern legal restraints, the arrangement for work in contemporary America resembles the same terms that functioned during feudalism. But this is more than an echo from distant times. The employment system is the defining structure for maintaining a still dominant hierarchy among citizens, those with stunted rights and those with expansive power over others. Centuries ago, the feudal lord owned the land and all who worked or lived on his land were subject to his rule. In the present, these terms are typically assumed, less bluntly and brutally, by the firm that operates the factory, shop or office. Individual freedom, equitable relationships, and self-empowered lives are severely compromised still.

The description sounds too harsh, of course, because people in workplaces develop their own informal accommodations that soften the everyday interactions among them. The actual circumstances of work vary dramatically across different companies and sectors, from free-spirited and highly collaborative firms to the harsh systems of clockwork supervision that oppressively monitor every move and moment in a worker's day. For most Americans, nevertheless, the underlying reality is this: The terms of their rights, the quality of their work life, the tangible and intangible rewards are determined at the discretion of the employer. For better and for worse. Under feudalism, there were kind and caring lords and there were abusive lords. Either way, no one doubted his power to command the serfs.

Anyone may test this proposition for themselves. Ask yourself if it sounds right, ask others. Is work in America organized around a master-servant relationship? In my occasional random samplings, I have yet to encounter anyone who thinks the premise is wrong. Some pause to ponder the matter. Others respond instantly, Of course. Isn't that obvious? I have put the question to managers and owners as well as rank-and-file employees; neither group wishes to argue the basic point. A recognition of these underlying terms seems jarring only because the relationship is so deeply internalized in nearly everyone's life expectations, just the way things are and probably immutable (unless one aspires to become the boss). Thus, despite great leaps forward in technological invention and productive efficiency, despite the rising abundance and various civil protections, the economic realm of work continues to function in distinctly premodern terms—master and servant—an arrangement that sets limits on human liberty as surely as the laws and the Constitution.

I start from this fundamental proposition because it is a bedrock source for so many of the largest discontents and disorders that continue to accompany the capitalist process in America, despite the presence of general prosperity. It is from this malformed power relationship that workers encounter often cruel confinements on their larger lives, the inequities and inequalities that warp and divide. The authorities typically attribute these consequences to "market forces," an abstraction that sounds neutral and objective. But the outcomes also emanate, more concretely, from a top-heavy structure of command and control in which those down below have little or no capacity to appeal or resist.

This feudal remnant helps to explain a lot about American life. It is an important subtext, though not the only one, for the persistent and growing inequalities of income and wealth, a lopsided and self-interested distribution of rewards by those in charge that redundantly favors those who already have great accumulations. It produces many stunting effects on people's life experiences that show up as stressful demands and insecurities imposed upon workers, often ensnaring well-paid professionals as well. A lack of voice and influence obviously injures people in the lower tiers most severely, but also spreads general damage—beyond the money—for many others who experience the deteriorating content of their own work. The inherent qualities and challenges in one's work—the source of much personal satisfaction and self-meaning—often are reengineered for greater efficiency, thereby degrading and sometimes destroying the coherence and integrity of what people do. The inner narrative of one's life often is embedded in one's work, in the satisfying routines and sense of fulfillment, in the sheer pleasure of doing things well. For many Americans, that story has been obliterated in the present age.

Social consequences flow from these conditions in many different directions: the longer working hours that tear up family life and weaken community; a broadening sense of sullen resignation that may feed social resentments and acquisitive envy; the continuing conflicts pitting workers against coworkers or against larger interests of the community. The most serious consequence, however, is political, not personal. It is the deleterious influence upon democracy itself.

Elaine Bernard of Harvard's trade union program explained the connection: "As power is presently distributed, workplaces are factories of authoritarianism polluting our democracy. Citizens cannot spend eight hours a day obeying orders and being shut out of important decisions affecting them, and then be expected to engage in a robust, critical dialogue about the structure of our society. Indeed, in the latter part of this [past] century, instead of the workplace becoming more democratic, the hierarchical corporate workplace model [came] to dominate the rest of society."[1]

Where did citizens learn the resignation and cynicism that leads them to withdraw as active citizens? They learned it at the office; they learned it on the shop floor. This real-life education in who has power and who doesn't creates a formidable barrier to ever establishing an authentic democracy in which Americans are genuinely represented and engaged. The socialization of powerlessness is probably far more damaging to politics than the special-interest campaign money or the emptiness of television advertising. Indeed, both of those malign influences feed off the disillusionment.

Statistics do not capture the texture of these confinements very well. And sweeping generalizations are always misleading or wrong, given the vast diversity in Americans' work experiences. To make the point concretely, let me flash through some snapshots from American workplaces.

In Baltimore, Maryland, a service technician named Joseph Bryant is fired after twenty-four years with Bell Atlantic (now Verizon) because he refuses to work overtime on weekdays. Bryant couldn't stay late on the job. As a single parent, he had to pick up his kids from school by 6:00 P.M. His supervisors are unyielding. Bell Atlantic "rationalized" its workforce, reduced employment by 15 percent, and instructed the others to pick up the slack by working longer hours. Overtime pay is actually cheaper (more efficient) for a firm than hiring additional workers who collect full benefits. Bryant's union, the Communications Workers of America, wins his job back—one small victory for family life.[2]

Middle-level managers, though presumably more powerful, frequently resent their unionized subordinates who seem to enjoy better job security and protections, according to Professor Russell L. Ackoff of the Wharton School of Business. When managements attempt to encourage greater teamwork—the celebrated Quality of Work Life movement—reforms are often sabotaged by midlevel personnel who were ignored in the discussions. "Their quality of work life is often worse than that of production workers," Ackoff explains. While genuine progress has been achieved by many companies, Ackoff cautions: "The QWL movement has not died, but it is in a coma."[3]

In Georgetown, Kentucky, a young "team leader" at Toyota's plant denounces inhumane conditions at the factory, regularly rated the most efficient auto assembly plant in North America. "What I think we have here is a high-priced sweatshop," Tracy Giles tells me. "Four team members in my area were out of work for shoulder surgery. If you're a temp worker and you're injured, which happens a lot, you are sent home and there's another person waiting in line to get the job." At one point, a new time-motion study raised the output goals and speeded up assembly at his workstation where the workers lift forty-pound modules sixty-five times an hour. "We couldn't keep up, and my team members were practically passing out," he says. "I can't stand it; it makes me sick to my stomach. For me, as team leader, it's more of a moral dilemma than anything else."

In the little town of Martinsville, Virginia, one man announces that he has held forty-six jobs in the last three years. He has the pay stubs to prove it. He is a temp worker and the town of 14,000 has nine temporary employment agencies that hire out labor for a few days, a few weeks or months, to do low-wage assembly and packaging jobs. The transaction is more like a short-term rental, only it involves human labor instead of equipment, because the agency collects an overhead fee for each hour of work, ranging from 35 to 45 percent of the wage. Employers are willing to pay a higher cost for temp laborers because they are disposable. "We call it pimping people out," says Suzie Qusenberry, "because that's really what it is. 'I'm going to pimp you out for $8 an hour and all you're going to get is $5.35.' They take the money and you do the work. Isn't that just like pimping?"

If one jumps from a depressed backwater in Virginia to the leading edge of American industry, the fabulous, wealth-creating center known as Silicon Valley, there is a similar snapshot in high-tech production. Temp jobs are the valley's sixth-largest job sector. Major names like Hewlett Packard, Sun, and Apple "outsource" work to smaller component suppliers where the average wages are 30 percent lower. Until the high-tech bust halted expansion, the "virtual employer" was the area's second-fastest-growing source of employment. At one time, Microsoft in Seattle had a third of its employees on temp status, long-term employees who call themselves "permatemps" and wear orange badges instead of the regulars' corporate blue. Nearly 30 percent of American workers are now employed in so-called "nonstandard" jobs: temp workers, part-timers, contract employees, on-call and day laborers, or the self-employed. A minor portion have skill specialties and high-end wages. Most experience the opposite.[4]

Efficiency obliterates identity, the sense of self-meaning in work, and not just for temp jobs or assembly lines. In Puget Sound, Boeing's 20,000 engineers and technicians staged a successful forty-day strike, but the central issue was not money. "Why the heck did we strike? At the highest level, it really was about respect, respect for what engineers do," says Charles Bofferding, executive director of the Seattle Professional Engineer Employees Association. A new, computerized design system was gumming up production. The white-collar engineers weren't consulted, though they possess intimate, problem-solving knowledge of how to build jet aircraft. "They did it the old-school way, brought in a big plan and said this is how it's going to be," Bofferding recalls. "We tried to insert ourselves and, well, we failed." The engineers, hurt personally and professionally, turn uncharacteristically belligerent. "We're not fighting to hurt Boeing, we're fighting to save it," the union leader explains. "It's all short-term thinking, everybody's focused on what the stock price is doing. You're not respected any more. The employees get squeezed. The reason we have design-built teams, integrative product teams, is because we know there are varying perspectives in the company and, unless you honor them all, you're going to come up with a suboptimized product. People matter. Our professionalism matters as well."

Doctors, pro athletes, airline pilots, graduate students—these and other esteemed professionals seek protection from rigid work structures or exploitative terms of employment. It is one of the perverse twists of modern prosperity that many who have very high incomes and the supposed leverage of highly specialized talents employ the collective power of unionization at a time when the older industrial unions are declining in size, some perilously. An AFL-CIO survey focused on the attitudes of young workers, union and nonunion, but uncovered a startling point about their elders: Most young people have hopeful expectations, as they should, but most employees over thirty-five years old have concluded that "working hard isn't enough any more because employers are not loyal." The longer one is employed, the more one knows about the masters. Social trust is among the casualties of work.[5]

These snapshots suggest, among other things, that the brilliant technologies of modern life, while potentially empowering and democratizing, may be employed just as readily to deepen the confinements. Automation displaces workers, of course, but that is the idea: Labor-saving devices raise human productivity. For many firms, however, the new machines allowed them to disembowel the content of work, dumbing down the tasks and challenges by reducing workers to robotic functions. The electronic devices, likewise, enable managers to adopt oppressive systems of intimate control. A survey of business organizations by the American Management Association found that 78 percent use surveillance mechanisms to monitor their employees' communications and performance. "It's got to add stress when everyone knows their production is being monitored," one employer said. "I don't apologize for that."[6]

The contemporary workplace is where energetic capitalism collides, most visibly, with the softer values of human existence. At a large Boston bakery, sociologist Richard Sennett found a grim contrast between the 1970s, when he first observed workers there, and the modernized bakery twenty years later. "In this high-tech, flexible workplace, where everything is user friendly, the workers felt personally demeaned by the way they work. . . . Operationally, everything is so clear; emotionally so illegible," Sennett wrote. He found the workers confused and sullen, indifferent to their work and colleagues, also with much lower wages. Punching computer icons is easier work, but it robs them of the logic and consequences in their actions. They no longer know how to bake bread; many never even see it. The automated ovens also produce lots of waste, daily mounds of misbaked, blackened loaves. Sennett found only one worker in the bakery resisting these "improvements," a Jamaican-born foreman who seemed perpetually angry, frustrated by the wastefulness and also by his fellow workers. "He told me he believed many of these problems could be sorted out if the workers owned the bakery," Sennett reported.[7]

To recapitulate, the snapshots convey that the confinements on human dignity, equity, and self-worth are not restricted to the lower tiers of employment. The deteriorated quality and discontents are far more inclusive now. Their impact stretches upward on the ladder of occupational status and incomes, even to much admired and supposedly privileged stations. The reengineering of work has left many white-collar workers feeling bereft of security and satisfaction. The purposeful efficiencies of downsizing and restructuring are blind to the human identity of a chemical engineer as much as to that of a machinist or casual laborer.

The essential economic transaction modern management has performed, especially in larger companies where the leaders are more distant from the followers, is to shift the burdens of risk and cost from the firm to the employees, economic risks in many forms, but also the personal costs that cannot be counted up. "We did a lot of violence to the expectations of the American workforce," an executive vice president of General Electric acknowledged upon retirement.[8]

Still, it is important to acknowledge the countervailing reality: Many Americans, myself included, are lucky enough to have found jobs we love, work so fulfilling and important to our identity we can't seem to get enough of it (family and friends sometimes see this devotion to work as an addictive disorder). In a perfect world, everyone would find satisfying work—regardless of skills or income—useful tasks that are rewarding in everyday, routine ways and draw out the best of what is within us. But envisioning an economic system where such satisfaction becomes broadly possible for all collides with our deep cultural prejudices. A condescending bias prevails in American life, especially strong among the well-educated elites but also internalized by many working people, that presumes those who do "brain work" are somehow more meritorious than those who work with their hands.

"Our culture says, if your hands are involved, you can't have a brain," Ronald Blackwell, an AFL–CIO official and former clothing-union leader, observed. "The seamstress and the machinist and nearly every kind of job involves brain as well as hands, but the intellectual content of working with your hands is ignored."

Anyone who has closely observed a carpenter at work—or a seamstress, a machinist, or a truck driver, for that matter—will recognize Blackwell's point. Doing any job well requires abstract reasoning and a continuous process of thinking through choices, just as most intellectual work involves patterns of familiar repetitions and reflexive responses. A skillful brain surgeon might, for instance, be a less creative thinker than a skillful carpenter. A capable trash collector who performs his job effectively may experience greater satisfaction at work than an overwrought bond trader. If we had to decide which occupations the society cannot do without, some of us might choose trash collectors and carpenters over bond traders and brain surgeons.

The point is, the cultural stereotypes attached to work are arbitrary and create their own destructive social divisions. They are generally wrong—inferences made at a distance about people whom we do not know, based upon their status in the occupational hierarchies. Industrial capitalism organizes jobs and work in a broad-based, layered pyramid with a commanding pinnacle, just as feudalism did, though with more productive logic, the division of labor. The pecking order of work is a convenient artifact of capitalism, not the natural order of human existence.

These observations may simply deepen the despair for some readers. If white-collar professionals are as voiceless as blue-collar workers in influencing the conditions of their work, it seems even harder to imagine that anything can change. The first step toward remedy and action, however, is the recognition that there exists a broader, unacknowledged unity among very different working people in the nature of their shared powerlessness. To see this is not easy. It means backing off the familiar conceits and biases about one's status and abilities compared to others. It means accepting the possibility that people have a common self-interest deeper than class or income. It suggests fellow employees need to start talking with one another, despite the vast differences in their jobs and status.

The fundamental solution can be bluntly summarized: People must figure out how to "own" their own work. That is, individually and jointly, they own the place where they work. They accept responsibility, collectively, for the well-being of the firm. They authorize the managers who direct things, but all participate in the rule making and other important policy decisions. They share the returns from the enterprise and agree upon the terms for sharing. None of these structural changes exempts anyone from the harrowing competition of capitalism or the demand for effective practices and productivity. Nor would this protect anyone from the normal human folly and error—the risks of loss and failure.

But does anyone doubt that, if employees acquired such self-governing powers, the terms of work would be reformed drastically in American business? Or that, if they owned the enterprise together, the rewards and risks would be reallocated in more equitable ways?

What follows is an exploration of this idea of self-ownership—the promise and the difficulties. The concept seems utterly remote to the standard terms of enterprise (and it is), but it is not utopian. Millions of Americans already work in such circumstances, or at least possess important aspects of shared control and responsibility. They are mutual owners of the firm and have a voice in running it. They work in employee-owned companies and cooperatives and partnerships or hybrid variations of all three. Some are highly paid professionals, some are assembly-line workers, some are clerks or janitors. They make it work—together—or they fail. The vision is most difficult to achieve, but many do succeed in practical reality. Running a successful business is difficult, and self-ownership is more so, because people must also alter their own attitudes and aspirations and develop new, more trusting relations among themselves. Profound change is always difficult, yet it is always required to reach the next important stage in human fulfillment.

---

The master-servant legacy embedded in modern enterprise poses a fundamental question: How can genuine individual freedom ever flourish except for a privileged few—or democracy ever be reconciled with capitalism—so long as the economic system functions along opposite principles, depriving people of rights and responsibilities, even denying their uniqueness as human beings? David Ellerman, an economist with the rare ability to apply moral philosophy to the underlying structure of economic life, has answered the question with an uncompromising argument. This power relationship is inherently illegitimate as a matter of natural law, Ellerman reasons, and is based upon "a legalized fraud." The "fraud" is the economic pretense that people can be treated as things, as commodities or machines, as lifeless property that lacks the qualities inseparable from the human self, the person's active deliberation and choices, the personal accountability for one's actions.

The fact that human beings have accepted this arrangement over the centuries—or were compelled to accept it—does not alter the unnaturalness. The fact that some people prefer mindless subservience to responsibility and self-realization does not confer legitimacy on their masters. Ellerman, formerly a staff economist at the World Bank, has devoted years to constructing a multilayered brief for "economic democracy," melding philosophy, law, and economics to illuminate long-existing fallacies. This discussion does not do justice to the rich complexity of his case but follows his lead in sorting out the fundamental terms. The ideological underpinnings are important to understand because they make clear why the structure of capitalism confines human existence illegitimately and how this might be transformed.*

---

*David Ellerman's principal text is *Property & Contract in Economics: The Case for Economic Democracy,* Blackwell, 1992. Still largely unheralded, his work is beginning to draw respectful consideration among philosophers, though not yet from many economists.

The subservient nature of the work relationship has been papered over by myth and comforting metaphors, inherited "wisdom" generally accepted by society and firmly codified in its laws. But Ellerman poses an awkward question: What exactly makes the modern system so different from serfdom? The American republic, remember, originated in a Constitution that explicitly recognized the right to own people as private property. The institution of slavery, as a productive capital asset protected by law, was not abolished until the thirteenth amendment, less than 150 years ago. Social traces of the iniquity linger still.

Formal economics has an answer for Ellerman's question, though not one that satisfies his objection. "Workers may not be bought and sold, only rented and hired," Alfred Marshall, a preeminent economist in his time, wrote in 1920. Paul Samuelson, author of a standard textbook for present-day Economics 101, sticks to the same distinction. "Since slavery was abolished, human earning power is forbidden by law to be capitalized [bought and sold as property]," he wrote. "A man is not even free to sell himself; he must rent himself at a wage." The "rented" worker is certainly much better off than the "owned" worker, no question. Yet, as their language suggests, the distinction between slavery and freedom is narrower than supposed, and aspects of property still heavily influence the transaction. Human labor is treated as an input of production no different from the other inputs—machines, raw materials, buildings, capital itself—and these inputs are interchanged routinely in organizing the elements of production. Employees are now described as "human resources," the oddly dehumanizing usage adopted by modern corporations.

The trouble is, people are not things. They are autonomous human actors, not mere "resources." They cannot be reduced to physical inputs, even if they assent, because they are conscious, responsible agents of self, endowed with inalienable rights and inescapably liable for their behavior, legally and otherwise. Ellerman put the point in a way anyone can grasp: "Guns and burglary tools, no matter how efficacious and 'productive' they may be in the commission of a crime, will never be hauled into court and charged with the crime." Human beings, on the other hand, will be held accountable for their behavior in myriad ways because their actions carry a presumption of individual will and decision. "A hired killer is still a murderer even though he sold his labor," Ellerman observed. Thus, people cannot be "rented" anymore than they can be "sold" without presuming to detach them from the core of what makes them human. This point of collision with capitalism is what makes life and liberty seem incomplete to many Americans.

The violation of natural rights, Ellerman explained, is needed to sustain the fictitious relationship within a company that allows it to exclude the employees from any claim to the new wealth their labor creates—the product and profit of the enterprise. "The capitalist, like the slave owner, has used a legalized fraud, which pretends the worker is an instrument, to arrive at the position of being the 'owner of both instruments of production' [labor and capital] so he can then make a legally defensible claim on the positive product," Ellerman wrote. Workers collect "rent" on their time and exertions but, in most situations, the terms of employment do not allow them to share in the company profits—the surplus wealth their contributions have produced. This contractual reality helps explain the great redundancy of concentrated wealth that persists in American society, why the rich get richer. As the firm's insiders and investors, they own the entire output, both finished product and profit. The "rented" employees whose lives and knowledge are intimately engaged in the firm's functionings are entitled to none (unless the insiders decide to share).

The employment system is thus a main engine generating American inequality, and perhaps the most powerful one. Its functional structure effectively guarantees that the gross inequalities of income and wealth will endure in our society, largely unaltered and replicated for each new generation, despite any ameliorative actions by the government. The system is designed to produce this outcome. The steep ladder of personal incomes, from top to bottom, is reflected by the enormous and growing wage disparities in which the CEO earns more than five hundred times more than the company's average workers. But it is the harvesting of the profits exclusively by insiders and distant owners, instead of by the working employees, that has the greatest impact. This arrangement is not logically inevitable in capitalism—workers might own their own work and harvest the surpluses for themselves—but this is the format that blanketed American life a century ago as Americans moved from farm to factory, from self-employed work to the contract terms of wages and hours.

The contract for employment, its explicit and implied terms, determines these outcomes, but its central impact is obscured and mystified by the aura of property rights, a convenient veil inherited from the feudal order that lends a sense of customary correctness to the domination of labor by the owners of capital. The man who owns the factory, it is generally assumed, commands the workforce and collects the profits as a function of his rights as the property owner. This is an historical myth, in Ellerman's analysis, one that must be demolished if people are to see the situation clearly and recognize the opportunity for changing their condition.

"Marx bought the myth," Ellerman explained. That is, Karl Marx started from the same premise of property's mythological power over others. Whoever owns "the means of production" will rule under capitalism, he asserted (and gave the system its name). Thus, his theoretical solution involved abolishing private property and establishing state ownership of the productive assets. In theory, this would make everyone a "virtual" owner, though in fact they were in charge of neither their work nor their lives, as history has amply demonstrated. The idea that workers "rented" by a government-owned enterprise would be better off somehow—empowered—compared to workers "rented" by private capital was a central fallacy of communism. It failed the test of reality—spectacularly.

The fallacy is easier to recognize in modern capitalism than it was in Marx's time. Many large and successful companies today actually do not own great assets themselves. Their control derives from the insiders' role in organizing the contractual relationships among all of the various elements that contribute to production: the employees; the suppliers; the providers of capital; and the firm's controlling insiders, who may or may not own the factory or contribute much of their own capital to the enterprise. A firm's organizers, if they choose, may "hire" the land and buildings, "lease" the machines, "borrow" the capital or "sell" shares in their ownership, just as they "rent" the workforce. Property ownership, if things are organized shrewdly, is superfluous to their claim on the final product and profits.

The real basis for the insiders' power and their legal claim to the profits is their acceptance of responsibility for the firm, their contractual commitments to pay the costs of production and to absorb the negative consequences of losses and liabilities as well as the positive results. Employees, in a sense, are awarded an opposite status: irresponsibility in the fortunes of the company and, thus, no share in its success unless the management decides to grant one. In exchange for this privileged irresponsibility, workers are rendered powerless. They accept the master-servant status, are subject to the command of others, and have no voice in the company's management or any claim to its returns.

Stated in those stark terms, it does not sound like such a good deal. But understanding the basic contractual relationship prompts a liberating thought: Contracts can be changed. If the power is derived from the employment contract and not from inherited notions of property rights, then the active participants in a company might renegotiate their roles and responsibilities or even create a new firm that reflects a different balance of power. Ellerman describes the opportunity: "Instead of capital hiring labor, labor hires capital."

Labor hires capital? The role reversal seems beyond the plausible until one remembers that this transaction is approximately what does occur in many existing enterprises. The workers, in fact, borrow the capital to own and operate the firm themselves, then pay back their loans from the returns of the enterprise, an arrangement known as the employee-owned company. The ESOP transaction (for employee stock ownership plan) resembles a leveraged buyout in which company insiders borrow capital to take over a controlling position in company stock, then pay back creditors with the company's profits. Or workers form partnerships, like a law firm, collectively assuming responsibility and thus sharing in the governance and the returns. Or they create a cooperative enterprise that, roughly speaking, blends some elements of partnership and employee ownership.

The same essential reversal is present in all three cases: the workers are the "insiders" who organize the firm's contractual relationships; they accept shared responsibility for the firm and allocate the profits among themselves, not with absentee stockholders. The result, in Ellerman's words, is "people jointly working for themselves in democratic firms." Quite literally, they own their own work.

At the start of this new century, around 10 million Americans are worker-owners in some 11,000 employee-owned companies, with total assets of more than $400 billion. Thousands of cooperative enterprises also operate around the country, ranging from some 300 worker cooperatives in manufacturing and services to cooperative day-care centers and small banks to the mammoth agricultural marketing cooperatives owned collectively by the farmers who produce the foodstuffs. The professional partnerships—lawyers, doctors, architects, and others—incorporate similar principles, as do many small firms of the self-employed. These are the meaningful exceptions, however. Most Americans have no ownership of enterprise whatever. For those who do own stock shares, the "owners" are typically confined to a weak and attenuated status.[9]

Self-ownership was the road not taken in American history. The cultural memory still enshrines independent yeomanry—the small farmer toiling in his own fields—but the modern organization of work largely obliterated those values.

It seems odd but necessary to point out that Americans did not always live like this. Just as my grandfather McClure proudly reported himself "unemployed" to the census taker in 1900, workers during the nineteenth century regarded wage employment as alien and inferior to their independent lives. They typically called it "wage slavery" because, as sociologist Charles Perrow has explained, "slavery was the closest thing to factory bureaucracy that people could conceive of; it was the closest precedent in history. Another precedent was also invoked—the military—and people referred to the 'industrial army' in attempting to describe the new situation." For a time, machinists and other craftsmen maintained independent worker-owned shops that sold their output to larger manufacturing firms, but these were gradually pushed aside. Just as the cultural meaning of "unemployed" changed, "free labor" was replaced in the language by "labor supply."[10]

During the explosive rise of industrial capitalism in the second half of the nineteenth century, some organizations of workers, like the Knights of Labor and the American Federation of Labor's early formation, did fight for a larger vision based on worker and community ownership of enterprises, described as the alternative to "wage slavery." But those efforts were overwhelmed by the force and effectiveness of the emerging national corporations, both their scale and deft management of divisions of labor in industrial processes. Advocates of worker ownership lacked the means and resources to carry it out, or their vision seemed insufficiently militant for the ferocious fight underway with capitalists of that era. Led by guilds of skilled craftsmen, unions did fight for control of the workplace (and still do in some sectors), but the contest between labor and capital gradually devolved to the narrower conflicts over wages and job benefits. Labor's victories on these issues were an essential element in creating the broad middle-class prosperity of modern times.

Organized labor, which built the model for collective action in the first half of the twentieth century and mobilized workers to secure political rights for collective bargaining, has since withered greatly in size and power. Its ranks are reduced to 13.5 percent of the workforce overall and to only 9 percent in the private economy. Federal labor law is now archaic and confines workers rather than liberates them. It is used routinely by employers as a blunt instrument to thwart efforts to organize a collective voice, that is, a union. If union members tried to open conversations with middle managers about their shared discontents with the employer such talk would violate the National Labor Relations Act, which imposes legalistic and unnatural divisions upon the broad ranks of employees (in any case, the middle managers likely would be fired for consorting privately with union members). The companies' preferred antiunion weapon is fear—fear of being fired—and the NLRA provides very weak penalties that companies ignore with little consequence (20,000 U.S. workers are fired illegally for union organizing every year, according to Human Rights Watch). Management lawyers game the technicalities for years. When the fines are finally imposed, the fired workers are long gone, the organizing campaign has already been broken. Yet labor lacks the political power to reform the laws.[11]

Labor's weakened position is reflected in the deteriorated terms and conditions of work for union and nonunion members alike. It suggests another discomforting acknowledgment: The mobilization of organized labor, at least as we have known it, has not proved an adequate response to the confining powers of American capitalism. Unions still do win important victories in many arenas, and renewed organizing energies in some unions may yet produce a turnaround in labor's strength. But, to prevail at this point in history, the ethos and spirit of collective action requires, ironically, a much more ambitious vision, one that might reignite sympathies and energies among Americans at large.

That agenda would start from a more fundamental perspective: attacking the compromised civil rights of working people and articulating a critique of the deteriorated conditions of work that speaks also for employees in the many occupations not covered by union protections. The case for self-ownership is a much better fit with present circumstances than it was for struggling workers a century ago. Employee ownership and self-management provide a plausible route toward eventually achieving greater wage equity, reforming the quality of work, and fostering accumulation of financial wealth among the many instead of the few. Eliminating the artificial dividing line between master and servant would open a vast new horizon of possibilities for individual fulfillment. The obvious problem with this approach is that it requires commitment to the long term—and enormous patience—at a time when most unions are embattled on many defensive fronts at once. Some unions are dispirited bureaucracies without hope or ambition and alienated from their rank-and-file members. Some union leaders assume, condescendingly, that their members are not interested in ownership and that the issue would merely undermine class consciousness, confusing the old labor refrain: Which side are you on?

The redeeming fact, however, is that some forward-looking labor leaders, often driven by necessity, have swung around impressively on the subject of ownership during the last few decades. Led by former president Lynn R. Williams, the United Steelworkers of America, one of the most embattled "old industry" unions, became the pioneer twenty years ago in engineering employee takeovers of troubled companies, retaining viable plants that larger corporations were discarding and saving thousands of jobs as well as valuable productive assets. Unions now actively engaged in employee ownership and worker takeovers range from machinists to papermakers, from autos to clothing and textiles. The largest employee-owned company is the troubled United Airlines that along with other major airlines filed for bankruptcy in 2002. The machinists' and pilots' unions are together the majority shareholders with seats on the board, but United got into deep financial trouble for approximately the same reasons as its competitors. The unions ostensibly have controlling power, but they have not yet figured out how to assert their power effectively or to reform United's corporate strategy and management behavior.

On the fringes of organized labor some rank-and-file activists are searching for a larger vision. "Imagine that in place of our half-century-old labor law . . . we had a labor law based on the constitutional rights of free speech, assembly and labor freedom," the Labor Party, an allied political group, declared. The new labor law, the party suggested, would be based on legal principles found in the thirteenth amendment abolishing involuntary servitude.[12]

In any case, the idea of self-ownership no longer belongs to labor alone, and unions are not present in the overwhelming majority of employee-owned firms. Given the many obstacles that burden unions, this transformation is often led by managers and owners. The idea does not belong to either left or right. Indeed, in an earlier era, some enlightened leaders of capitalism shared the progressive vision that corporations might someday be owned entirely by their employees. Owen D. Young was CEO of General Electric in the 1920s when he described the dream: "Perhaps someday we may be able to organize the human beings in a particular undertaking so that they truly will be the employer buying capital as a commodity in the market at the lowest possible price. It will be necessary for them to provide an adequate guarantee fund in order to buy the capital at all. If that is realized, the human beings will be entitled to all the profits over the cost of capital. I hope that day may come when the great business organizations will truly belong to the men who are giving their lives and their efforts to them, I care not in what capacity."[13] Labor hires capital. Workers reap the new wealth. General Electric was a very different company in those days.

THE TEMPORARY EMPLOYMENT AGENCY called Solidarity provides a dramatic illustration of what can happen to ordinary people when they assume the role of owners (so dramatic, in fact, some readers may find it hard to believe). The temp agency operates in Baltimore, Maryland, and is organized as a cooperative. It belongs to the same temp workers it sends out everyday to fill various short-term jobs. They work at the city convention center arranging chairs and setting tables for huge banquets or do light manufacturing jobs or rehab old buildings or fill temps slots at small businesses, hotels, and construction sites. These men come from the "inner city" and the loose pool of workers once known as "casual labor"—the very bottom of the American job ladder. The vast majority of them are recovering narcotics addicts and/or have criminal records and time in prison.

Their firm is thriving and expanding. They earn wages a dollar or two an hour higher than rates paid by competing temp agencies plus they have health insurance coverage. When a new client seeks to hire their labor, Solidarity workers go out to check the employer first and inspect the terms and conditions of work. At year's end the regulars will receive a bonus check from the firm's profits, typically several thousand dollars each. None of these men expect to get rich (some saw a lot more cash when they were dealing drugs), but the idea of owning something themselves is a powerful experience.

"Naturally, when it's your company, your productivity is bound to go up—it belongs to you," said Curtis Brown, a forty-seven-year-old worker who had scuffled in low-wage jobs since he was seventeen. "It's not us against them; it's all us. You're all fighting against the same thing. I've seen guys, I know myself, glad to go to work, happy to go to work. Everybody's working to get the job right."

Oddly enough, their personal troubles turned out to be an asset for the firm. Workers know each other from the streets, but mainly from attending the same Narcotics Anonymous meetings. "How I would I describe it? It's almost like a spiritual thing among the guys," Brown explains. "A lot of us knew each other. When a new guy comes in, we usually recognize him. We seen him in the rooms." "In the rooms" is their phrase for identifying a fellow Narcotics Anonymous member who attends meetings, someone who's been through the same fire and is working on the struggle for personal redemption.

Within the cooperative, this powerful subculture has been a source of trust and teamwork, but also for self-discipline. Nobody cons others who are also "in the rooms."

Avis Ransom, an idealistic MBA graduate who left her business consulting career to manage Solidarity, found the firm has competitive advantage in its shared ethos of "self-policing in the workplace—one employee going to another and telling him, 'You're goofing off; start working.' When we started out, our members would come to work and get in prayer circles outside the convention center. Workers from the other [temp] agencies would join them, sometimes even managers. We began to see how easy it was to take workers and jobs from our competitors." Solidarity regularly trains workers and pays the seasoned ones to serve as teachers. It increases the level of training as the firm gains better jobs—do simple math, swing a hammer, read a shop-floor plan. Workers meet every two weeks to air out complaints and share ideas. Not all of them survive the self-criticism. They are not ready to meet the cooperative's standards.

"The greatest problems," Ransom explains, "are workers don't show up on time. They don't show up in the numbers ordered. The client orders ten; eight show up. Or they don't show up work ready. They're sleepy or high or badly dressed or unclean. We called a meeting of workers, maybe twenty or so, and explained these problems. They said, We can fix that. If we have to start work at two, tell us to report at one. If they need twenty people, send twenty-five and, if they don't need the extra workers, send them home with two hours' pay. Now we call it show-up pay. They said, We don't want our clients to see us as not work ready, so you screen us at the work site. Pick out the ones who aren't ready and send them home. We started doing that for every job and it got to the point where we were regularly sending extra people and they would get hired because people from the other agencies didn't show up. We've got an excellent reputation with our clients."

Solidarity made a profit its second year—$50,000—and Ransom

called the members together to announce the good news. "The workers made it clear to me: This was *their* money; they had already earned it," she said. "But they wanted to keep the money in the company to develop more alliances with businesses and get a stronger foothold in the industry. For folks who are making eight dollars an hour, that's a phenomenal decision." Profits rose fourfold in the third year and workers collected profit shares based on how many hours they had worked.

It should be obvious that, in these humble circumstances, the workers could not have launched this alone. They had an experienced and influential sponsor in BUILD, a community organization that for twenty-five years has mobilized Baltimore's citizens and neighborhoods, drawn together from black and white churches across the city, to push their own civic agenda of housing, education, and other concerns. BUILD launched the nation's first "living wage" campaign and won a city ordinance boosting incomes for low-wage employees of public contractors and suppliers, an idea that has since spread across the country. Affiliated with the Industrial Areas Foundation's nationwide network of sixty-three grassroots organizations, BUILD adheres to the IAF's "iron rule": "Never do anything for people that they can do for themselves—never." In this case, the organizers patiently canvassed the city's powerless temp workers and helped some of them take the leap to a self-owned firm. BUILD provided a $35,000 line of credit and used its political clout to persuade some public agencies and private employers to become the first clients.

Solidarity, though still fragile like any small start-up, is expanding laterally into new fields of employment and moving workers upward in skills and income. An environmental consultant trained the workers to do the work on a major contract refitting public buildings for energy efficiency: caulking, weather stripping, and other tasks. In exchange, the workers "carried" the contractor for a few weeks during his own early cash-flow problems by temporarily deferring half their pay. Rehab work on church-sponsored halfway houses (a place these men had passed through themselves) is being done by Solidarity members as both workers and contractors.

This is small stuff, to be sure, but it illustrates how, with self-ownership, the work itself can become a leveraging asset. One by one they were hapless temp workers tumbling in and out of jobs. Collectively they possess a little bargaining power to open more doors for the cooperative and to ratchet up the content and value of their own work. This sort of transaction requires business savvy, but also a strong foundation of trust. Solidarity draws inspiration and a model from Mondragon, a much-celebrated network of more than one hundred cooperatives in the Basque region of northern Spain, where workers share ownership and returns in scores of affiliated enterprises, from small manufacturing companies to a major supermarket chain. Mondragon has no stockholders, but relies upon its own self-financing bank and a strong fabric of mutual support among its many small parts. Collectively, Mondragon resembles a powerful business corporation with more than 20,000 employees.[14]

Solidarity's lead organizers, Arnold Graf and Jonathon Lange, have a larger, less tangible vision: changing the culture of work in Baltimore, starting from the bottom up and eventually affecting others far up the line. They have been scouting for a building convenient to main bus lines that BUILD could turn into a "workers center," a service center and social hall for low-wage workers and their families, equipped with recreational materials and a library, computers and a chapel, music and art, a barbershop and banking services. BUILD may not have the resources to start its own bank like Mondragon, but they are talking to local bankers about forming a self-interested alliance— a worker-friendly bank.

"There's such a terrific breakdown in community places, nowhere for people to come together and call it their own," Graf says. "What excites me is trying to change the culture of what people expect from the economy, what they consider the nature of work. Do I have a right to a living wage and a job where I have something to say about decisions? Or is it just the boss? These are concrete ways of rebuilding community through different aspects of work. We had originally thought about community in terms of the neighborhoods, but we are beginning to see a different kind of vision—the community that is based in work." Solidarity's organizing activities resemble what aggressive labor unions in garment making and other sectors did for low-wage and immigrant members three generations ago. "Somebody accused us of trying to reinvent the wheel," Lange said, "but we take pride in that."

Actually, the example of Solidarity makes the cooperative process seem easier than it is. These working men, after all, may have needed some outside help, but they did not need to create a culture of trust and self-criticism. They already had absorbed that "in the rooms." Mondragon, likewise, is a brilliant model of successful cooperatives but draws power from the unique separateness of the Basque people, an embattled minority struggling to preserve its cultural integrity while also achieving prosperity. In the American experience, immigrant groups similarly rely upon ethnic solidarity—pooling their meager resources and sacrifices—to build something real for themselves. Muslims and Koreans today, Irish, Italian, and Jews in yesteryear.

Given the splintered condition of America's social relations, this is very hard work in most circumstances—constructing a social texture that binds people together in mutual trust and endeavors—and it is especially difficult within large, complicated business organizations. Teamwork is an elusive quality and cannot be faked (nor bought and sold). Modern Americans are remarkably capable people, skillful and inventive in many ways, but they are not so good at talking to one another across their vast differences of social class and economic status. Shared ownership may make it easier to have such conversations and encourage trust but, paradoxically, shared ownership is unlikely to succeed unless the trust becomes real.

"OWNING YOUR OWN WORK" is not as exotic as it may sound. College professors and lawyers essentially enjoy jobs in that circumstance, protected from arbitrary dismissal, secure in their rights of self-expression, empowered to influence their institution's operating values and policies, and for lawyers, guaranteed a share of the profits. No one familiar with law firms or college faculties would idealize those alternatives to the regular employment system, but they do illustrate that systems of self-governing workers exist and that, plausibly, similar democratic protections can be devised for those who lack formal professional credentials.

As it happens, both the tenured professors and the lawyers who are partners in law firms enjoy great personal benefit from their own versions of exploitation: pyramidal organizational structures that take gross advantage of their younger, less experienced colleagues. In universities, the teaching assistants (anxious to become tenured professors themselves someday) are underpaid and do the mule work for the full professors: heavy teaching loads and tedious research projects so the professors will have more free time to do the big thinking. On many campuses, the TAs are rebelling against these terms and organizing their own unions to fight back. In law firms, the junior associates (likewise ambitious to become partners someday) are typically subjected to horrendous work loads and other routine indignities on behalf of the firm's full partners.

Professor James Coleman of Duke University Law School, formerly a partner in a premier Washington law firm, Wilmer, Cutler & Pickering, explains the basic economics of law firms: "Leveraging the associates—that's where you make the money. The more associates a firm has in relation to partners, the more the partners make. When you're an associate, they work you and get as much out of you as possible. Associates always want more partners in the firm so they will have a better chance of making partner themselves. Like college tenure, it's usually up or out after seven to ten years."

The tradition of tenured faculty is intended to protect the lone, dissenting scholar against the tyranny of the majority or from outside political pressures, thus opening the space for independent thought. In practice, the tenure system produces much less free thinking than the theory supposes and instead may create a tyranny of the elders: established professors are the gatekeepers to tenure and can impose their mode of thinking on junior scholars as the price of advancement. "In reality, the young scholars, as they seek to win tenure, are forced to approach certain problems in a certain way and that leads them to the same conclusions," Coleman says. "You don't get as much independence of thought as the tenure system seems to promise." It would make an interesting experiment, for instance, if economics professors agreed to forfeit their protected status and submit to the invigorating competition of free labor markets (as they regularly recommend to other workers). Would market forces generate more free thinking in the academy than the professors' protected guild status? You can be sure we will not find out.

Notwithstanding its negative qualities, the law firm is a practical model of how a cooperative work system functions when organized according to shared ownership. "Once you become partner, you have tenure," Jim Coleman explains. "You can't be fired except for extraordinary causes. The partnership at base depends upon the will of the majority. All partners are considered equal but, of course, they're not, because some partners will have more control over the economics of the firm. As partner you're an owner, entitled to a share of the proceeds and also responsible for its liabilities. The profits are shared, but losses are spread over the partners too." Some more innovative firms give job tenure to lawyers but without an ownership share; some large Los Angeles firms share profits with junior associates who have not made partner.

The core of the partnership, however, is shared governance of the firm. "A majority can vote down anything—in theory and in fact—though it doesn't often happen," Coleman explains. Typically, the management committee proposes the rules, compensation schedule, and which associates will make partner, followed by lots of arguments among all the partners, most often about their compensation. Each new partner is required to invest capital up front ($100,000 or more in the big firms) with the money typically deducted from future pay or borrowed from the bank (labor hires capital). When partners resign, they take their accumulated capital with them, their share of the firm's present value.

The democratic governance becomes most intense when partners are arguing over the values of the firm. "That's usually a huge fight," Coleman says. "Do we want to take in someone who's really a good lawyer and can attract clients but who is the biggest SOB in town? Do we want to bring in a hot new securities lawyer and his associates when we really don't know a lot about them and the culture of their practice? Do we want to continue to emphasize pro bono cases by partners and associates over their billable hours and the bottom line?"

The Washington law firm where Coleman was a partner, for instance, decided it would not take any tobacco companies as clients because so many partners objected. Wilmer, Cutler also honored the "significant minority" rule. "The rule says a significant minority can defeat actions by the majority of the partners if those actions would create serious conflicts in the firm," Coleman explains. When Wilmer, Cutler decided to represent a South African airline during the boycott against that country's apartheid, Coleman and a colleague, John Payton, both active in civil rights issues, invoked the rule and asked for a firm meeting to voice their objections. No meeting was required. The South African client was turned away.

Partnerships became the standard organization format for lawyers, not for economic efficiency, but to protect the lawyer's professional responsibilities (many states and the American Bar Association's ethics code prescribe partnerships for lawyers representing multiple clients). "The rules of the profession require lawyers to be responsible for their conduct and, therefore, they have to be organized in a way that allows them to be collectively responsible for their conduct," Coleman says.

"That's the meaning of partnership—bound together, collectively responsible."

Ordinary workers of nonprofessional status are, by contrast, unprotected in their actions, shorn of ethical responsibility for their work, voiceless in company policy. They can be fired for doing what's right—making a moral choice—and they frequently are. Some workers do have a legal right, at least after the fact, to challenge a company's internal behavior, if they are covered by a strong union contract or are protected by antidiscrimination laws. Coleman, who has both argued and mediated discrimination lawsuits against large corporations, noted the paradox: "Antidiscrimination laws give protected groups [e.g., women, racial minorities, the elderly] the basis to characterize some kinds of behavior as discriminatory and thus to challenge some work practices that employees are normally unable to challenge," he explains. "But a white male employee subjected to the same kind of conduct has no recourse, no way to challenge the employer. So they resent the people who are protected and they can't see any way out of the contradiction. We ought to find a way so that white employees can also challenge this kind of conduct, force the companies to deal with this kind of complaint, whether or not racial or gender discrimination is involved."

In the present era, as major law firms have become much more obsessed with expansion and millionaire incomes at the top, the cultural understandings of partnership have weakened considerably. Indeed, very successful lawyers and law firms are experiencing some of the same distress and alienation that afflicts other, less remunerative occupations, especially among disillusioned younger lawyers.

"The problem we are dealing with now in the legal profession is unhappiness," Coleman observes. "And it's very, very serious, especially among associates. It's not about pay. In fact, some people think it is the consequence of the very high salaries. The associates feel like they are fungible—all the firm wants to know about you is that you made the minimum billable hours, that you have no other meaning to the firm or attachment. So you have a lot of very unhappy associates, some of whom leave the firm for other careers and some who stay and become unhappy partners."

In any setting, people will flourish or fail depending in part on their own behavior, regardless of the terms of employment. There are no magic routes to self-fulfillment. A cooperative partnership, nevertheless, does provide the space and democratic mechanisms that allow individuals to take more responsibility for their own work and for the quality of their performance—and the firm's. Can we imagine people who do other kinds of work, even in very large companies, applying the same principles to jobs that lack the prestige and protections of professional status?

Ethical codes, after all, express a universal of human existence: the shared expectation of moral responsibility in one's behavior, a clear understanding of right and wrong, whether or not the rules are written anywhere. Coleman believes (and so do I) that formal ethical codes can be liberating for the individual. "They define your obligations to each other and to the public; they can protect the individual's rights and allow them to resist unethical behavior," he says. Most workers in most situations are instead confined by a different value system, one they cannot easily resist.


THORSTEIN VEBLEN, whose corrosive critiques of American capitalism in the early twentieth century remain relevant and wickedly entertaining today, had one tender spot in his thinking. Veblen believed in engineers. The engineer, he wrote, is not captive to the money compulsion and other malignant illusions associated with capitalism. Engineers gain their satisfaction and status mainly from figuring out how to make things work better. Veblen's romantic notion was that someday engineers and the other dedicated technicians in business would rise up and take control from the absentee owners. Then they would redesign the production system so that it works better for humanity. I share Veblen's soft spot for engineers and similar types. My father, Harold W. Greider, was a research chemist and chemical engineer in a midsize manufacturing company, a prolific inventor and practical-minded optimist of twentieth-century industry who believed problems could be solved if people applied their minds rigorously (at the end of his long life, his mind was working on the ecological crisis).

I was reminded of Veblen's vision when I talked with Joseph Cabral, the CEO of Chatsworth Products Inc., a small and very successful California manufacturer owned 100 percent by its employees. Joe Cabral was schooled in accounting—"I'm one of the bean counter guys," he says—but became an executive whose business sensibilities harmonize with Veblen's. Cabral's manner is can-do practicality and rigor with the facts, yet he also nurtures a big-think understanding of how the system should be reformed. Experience tells him that making capitalist enterprise more equitable and human scale—more like "family"—actually makes it more productive and enduring.

"We have a wonderful capitalistic society that makes the United States really inventive, but as with anything, you find some flaws in it," he told me. "The way our society has rolled out, the wealth that's created through that vehicle called capitalism ends up in too few hands. The entrepreneur who's fortunate enough to be there at the start ends up really receiving a disproportionate amount of the wealth. And all the working folks who enabled that success to take place share in little of that wealth. So we end up in a society with a wealth structure where the top one percent owns 90 percent or something like that. It's so disproportionate that, in my heart, I'd say that kind of ownership structure is not sustainable. At some point, capitalism is going to burst because we haven't done right for the folks who have actually created that wealth."

Cabral discovered the alternative of self-ownership in 1990. The Chatsworth operation in the San Fernando Valley, where he was comptroller in division management, was discarded by the conglomerate that had acquired it only a few years before. The plants would be closed down, since the only interested buyers simply wanted to purchase the machinery and other hard assets for pennies on the dollar. Chatsworth was small and low-tech—it fabricates the metal frames for stacking computers in data-storage centers—while the Harris Corporation wished to be known as high-tech. The faddish practice of "rationalizing" product lines and balance sheets (better known to workers as downsizing) is popular with large corporations because it typically boosts the stock price and provides tax write-offs. It also destroys a vast, unmeasurable volume of viable production, not to mention jobs and careers. The destruction is what often motivates the preventive takeovers by employees. They know what is being lost.

"We valued ourselves higher than any outsiders would value us," Cabral said. "I must tell you, we had all the confidence this would work." After Harris stripped away some elements it wanted to retain, only one hundred or so employees remained but, led by eight top managers, they organized an employee stock ownership plan (ESOP). The ESOP's trust arrangement enables workers to borrow the money to buy all or a portion of their firm, then pay off the debt from the company's future earnings. The ESOP device was invented nearly half a century ago by Louis Kelso, a San Francisco investment banker who elaborated his own seminal critique of capitalism's maldistribution between capital and labor. His idea did not really take off until the 1970s, when Senator Russell Long of Louisiana, chairman of the Senate Finance Committee, pushed through a series of tax breaks to sweeten the deal for owners and bankers. Long was a conservative Democrat with a deep understanding of how the American system really works. His father was Huey Long, the inflammatory 1930s populist whose "Share the Wealth" crusade deeply frightened the American establishment during the Great Depression. Russell Long used to say: "Remember, it was my father who was the revolutionary—I'm a reformer."

"When I read about ESOPs in *CFO* magazine, I thought, yeah, this really makes sense," Joe Cabral says. "Everybody is sharing in the wealth that they're creating. There's a fundamental philosophy of, We're all in this together. We're not just doing this for some outside shareholder, we're doing it because *we* are the shareholders. In most companies you want to do well in order to have a job or career advancement, but you're basically in it for the paycheck. In CPI we created this wonderful foundation of ownership and people were totally aligned with the success of the company."

The bonding of interests between Chatworth's managers and assembly-line workers was tested up front. Under the two-year purchase option Harris agreed to reduce the $2.5 million sale price if Chatsworth employees could cut operating costs and boost profits in the meantime (in effect, sharing the income gains with the workers). "We did some amazing things, making old equipment work for us and learning to operate with a lot less inventory," Cabral says. "It was kind of a neat period in that way, seeing how creative people can be when they're put in a situation, how they work their way through it." The employees managed in one year to knock $1 million off the purchase price. They raised some money from personal savings, borrowed the rest, and bought total control.

Through the nineties, Chatsworth Products flourished spectacularly, riding the Internet boom because its equipment supplied the celebrated Silicon Valley firms building the huge data-storage centers. CPI's employment grew more than sixfold. All six hundred became owners (a majority of the workforce is composed of minorities, Hispanic and Asian). Their privately held stock rose in value from $4 a share to $121. When the Internet bubble burst at the end of the decade, CPI hung on for a year and a half, treading water and furiously cutting costs, before it too was compelled to shrink its workforce. "We lost 150 owners," Cabral says. "It was traumatic, painful, but nobody was surprised or shocked. They knew how hard we tried to avoid this, that we pulled out all the stops. They created the wealth and, when they leave the company, their wealth goes with them. That's what it's all about."

People who started with Chatsworth in 1991 (and most who came in afterward) departed with six-figure checks or considerably more. Some of those who invested personal savings ten years before have accrued balances of more than a million dollars. "These folks could never have accumulated that kind of wealth in any other way," Cabral says. "Nobody ever got rich on a paycheck."

Chatsworth's success is not typical, of course, since most employee-owned companies have less glamorous stories and less spectacular wealth accumulations Nor is Joe Cabral a typical ESOP manager. Many of them are flinty, old-fashioned bottom-line guys, bemused or even irritated by his lofty talk about the just distribution of wealth. Cabral represents a hybrid type not widely recognized in the American business culture but that would have fascinated Veblen. "Humanist-populist-capitalists," ESOP consultant Christopher Mackin of Owner-ship Associates has dubbed them. His oxymoron mixes hard-nosed and idealistic, savvy accounting and human-scale vision.

Among the ones I've met, the social values seem fused with their practical business instincts, so comfortably integrated it is difficult to know which came first. Did they engineer the sale of a family-owned company to faithful, long-term employees because it seemed the "right thing" to do? Or to save the enterprise from failure and corpo-rate predators? Or was the ESOP simply a "smart money" move to harvest the tax breaks? The deal, they would say, "made sense" for lots of reasons. Perhaps these "humanists" are an unintended by-product of American abundance, business people who know how to make lots of money but look around and ask: Is that all there is to life? In any case, their presence is strong enough among ESOP managers that Joe Cabral was elected board chair of the ESOP Association and speaks for thousands of them.

Louis Kelso's vision for achieving broadened, even universal own-ership of the nation's capital assets is sometimes compared to the homesteading movement in the nineteenth century, when the federal government gave away millions of western acres to the families who settled the land if they made it productive. In the modern industrial economy stock shares are roughly equivalent to land as the principal income-producing asset. The ESOP process is not "free," however. The new owners must "work off" the loan by producing profitably. The transaction may also dilute share value for other stockholders, though they will be well rewarded if the new worker-owners make the firm successful and more profitable. A better comparison may be with the New Deal credit reforms in the 1930s that enabled ordinary families to buy their own homes through liberalized mortgage terms. Two generations of broadening home ownership brought stability and a long-term time horizon to people's lives. Ownership anchors the "American dream" of middle-class prosperity that now feels threatened for so many families.

In the best of circumstances, an economy functioning with broadly shared ownership of enterprises would not eliminate the stark inequalities that already exist. But, over several generations, spreading wealth laterally through the society would generate profound social consequences, including greater family security, time, and satisfaction, as well as more deeply rooted connections with others. In time, the dominating political influence of concentrated wealth, both corporate and individual, on democracy would be greatly diluted, if not entirely extinguished. In time, if families accumulate substantial nest eggs, Kelso envisioned the financial assets generating a second stream of income that would make people less dependent on the "wage slavery" that early labor leaders decried and still exists for many Americans.

Essentially, there are three main arguments on behalf of a system of self-ownership that would replace employment as we know it. The first is David Ellerman's argument that the natural rights of people are inescapably violated by the enduring master-servant relationship, illegitimately separating them from self, from the personal accountability one never escapes in human existence. As a result, lives are stunted, confined, commanded, and dominated. People need democratic governance in the system of production in order to realize their full capacities as human beings.

The second argument, grounded in the economic theories of Louis Kelso, holds that universal ownership—and thus broad distribution of capitalism's returns—is not only more just, but is necessary to prevent an eventual economic and political crisis for the present system. As technology increasingly displaces labor in production processes, Kelso argued, the depressing pressures on wage incomes intensify while the wealthy minority accumulates a still greater imbalance of power. The economic danger, he suggested, is an eventual failure of available demand when workers lack the incomes to purchase what the economic system can produce (much like the reckoning for mass consumption that Professor Clair Brown described in Chapter 1). When these conditions develop, Kelso warned, the government will face unbearable pressures to enlarge the welfare state and to intervene more profoundly in the free-running economy. As a libertarian conservative he dreaded that outcome, yet he saw it as inevitable unless workers accumulate the income-producing assets— that is, shares of ownership—that can complement their wage incomes.

The third argument, which draws on both of the others, simply observes that businesses perform better when the employees share a stake in the ownership. That is, the companies are more efficient because workers contribute more readily to the processes and signal managers when something is amiss. The emerging academic research on employee-owned companies supports this claim. ESOP companies, compared with similar firms where employees have no ownership, generate greater annual sales and faster employment growth. They are also more likely to survive profitably, pay higher wages, and provide benefits like diversified pensions.

Chris Mackin, whose Ownership Associates counsels both labor and management on employee ownership initiatives, summarized the research results from Joseph Blasi and Douglas Kruse of Rutgers University, as well as other scholars: "The combination of a substantial employee ownership stake and an effective program to communicate it and thereby realize the previously untapped imagination and enthusiasm of employees leads to competitive advantages of between 8–11 percent over the conventionally structured competition."[15]

WHY, one might ask, should this surprise anyone? As Curtis Brown, the Baltimore temp worker, says: "Naturally, when it's your company, your productivity is bound to go up—it's your company." Logically, people treated with respect and with a real stake in the outcomes work harder—and smarter—than people treated like mindless cogs, mere commodities. As many major corporations have realized, encouraging honest collaboration in the workplace can unlock valuable insider knowledge known only to those who do the work. They understand where the wasteful inefficiency is buried because they see it every day. Professor Ackoff of the Wharton school studied the dramatic turnaround at an ALCOA mill and interviewed two workers who recommended important money-saving changes. How long had they known about these ideas? "Fifteen years." Why did they wait so long to propose them? "Those sons of bitches never asked us before."

The seldom discussed reality in American business is that employees, both white collar and blue collar, know a lot of things about the company that the managers do not know. Why would workers not share this with the boss? Paul Adler, professor of management at the University of Southern California's business school, uncovered the answer by talking with them. Workers, he found, are predisposed to share their intimate knowledge of the firm with managers but are often discouraged by "fairly clear signals that management is going to use this knowledge to hurt them." Professor Adler found the expectation well-founded; their pretense of ignorance is self-interested silence. The much-celebrated systems of participatory management have great limitations, sociologist Perrow reported. "One may treat slaves humanely," he wrote, "and even ask their opinions on matters with which they are more familiar than the master. But to transform their basic dependence and this presumption of their incompetence with regard to their own interests, there must be an institutional order or public process where the opportunity and capacity for legitimate self-assertion is guaranteed."

Yet, the risk I see in making claims that ESOPs perform better as businesses, even assuming the claims are correct, is that this argument may buy into the narrow logic of "more" and fallacious definitions of what constitutes greater "efficiency" for the society. If worker owners put themselves in the same harness as conventional management— pursuing the single-minded goal of maximizing short-term profit— they will have forfeited the open-ended search for reforms in pursuit of life's broader goals. In orthodox business, after all, maximizing returns is at war with those other values—family and personal fulfill- ment, the community, the environment—and reflexively pushes them aside. The great possibility opened up by self-ownership and demo- cratic governance is that people have the chance to experiment for themselves and make different choices about their priorities, not to sacrifice the firm's well-being but to reengineer the trade-offs. People in this situation will make surprising choices—like the temp workers in Solidarity who reinvested their profits rather than take the cash— and their social inventions may turn things in directions none of us could have predicted or imagined. Meanwhile, it is still true: The company has to survive and flourish according to the conventional measures.

In any case, the relationship between ownership and performance isn't altogether settled. Some academic studies report a crucial caveat: ESOP companies are likely to become more productive only when they also introduce systems for participatory decision making. In many employee-owned companies, this doesn't happen. The workers remain passive and without real influence in the firm (no better off than ordinary shareholders) or the mechanisms for voting rights and systematic collaboration don't exist or the managers are hostile to the whole idea. These changes are difficult to achieve, as I said, because people must change too.

Lynn Williams, the retired steelworkers president who pioneered the labor movement's first employee buyouts, recalls: "The greatest challenge was finding managers who both knew their business and had the sensitivity to work with employee owners, to appreciate where such owners are coming from, to truly participate with them in an open, constructive and creative way. About three years ago there was a strike at one of the Steelworker's ESOPs, largely, if not entirely, in my opinion, the result of insensitive and inadequate corporate leadership. We assisted in finding a new president and CEO and the situation is entirely turned around."

Another important barrier to achieving democratic participation is scale—small is obviously easier than large—though ESOP advocates believe that internal reorganizations can overcome problems of size even in major industrial corporations. "Most business managers think I'm crazy," Joe Cabral says. "I've been told, 'Joe, you can't do these operating units as small as you envision them.' Our philosophy is, we don't want any unit beyond a certain size—our magic number is around 150 people—because you need an environment of family. Everyone working together knows each other, they care about each other, and they're willing to help each other out. When you get above a certain size you end up with walls, and workers become just faces rather than people or, god forbid, numbers."

The crucial question, not yet fully answered, is whether employee ownership can succeed at a major corporation in changing the management culture and sharing power with the usual insiders. The experiment at United Airlines has not failed entirely—not yet—but it certainly has not succeeded in those terms. When UAL was distressed in 1994 the machinists' and pilots' unions bought majority control by trading away nearly $5 billion in "sweat equity"—wage and pension concessions—that gave them three seats on the board and virtual veto power over major policy decisions. But neither the unions nor the company really attempted to engage rank-and-file workers in the managerial decision making or in exploring what an employee-driven business strategy might look like. Instead, United stuck with the same path followed by the other major airlines and all went through the same crippling, often self-inflicted crises, climaxed for UAL (and some others) by bankruptcy. The unions engaged in head-banging conflicts with management, and three or four CEOs came and went, while the two unions pursued their own diverging priorities instead of searching together for original solutions to the industry's structural dilemmas.

In any situation, worker-owners have to reconcile the ancient combat between owner and employee—when they become both—and they have succeeded in many substantial companies. The conflicting self-interests were described by Captain Rick Dubinsky, the pilots' union president who was an early champion of the labor takeover: "We may be 'shareholders by night' keenly interested in the profitability, but we are 'employees by day' who must be concerned about the size of our paychecks and security of our jobs." As his remark suggests, the UAL worker-owners never found the way to harmonize these two interests. Indeed, they hardly had a chance.

Amid the airline industry's roller-coaster perils neither United management nor the unions undertook sustained rank-and-file education, patient discussions of what the new culture required of them or what the grassroots members thought a new business strategy should look like (now it may be too late). Only that kind of bottom-up exploration, Chris Mackin explains, could overcome conflicting obligations and create an agenda for genuine change. By inherited tradition, many labor leaders are indifferent or hostile to ownership on the grounds that it would confuse their bargaining positions and possibly undermine the fighting fervor of their members at contract time. So they stick with the "us against them" approach, which implies a limited vision of their own members' potential as human actors. Unions, meanwhile, continue to decline as an economic factor.

The question of scale—the overbearing size and impersonal distance of major corporations—is, of course, at the heart of many of the conflicts between capitalism and society (we return to this issue in subsequent chapters). Big fish swallow little ones, then frequently spit them out. Smaller companies strive for bigness seeking many kinds of advantage, including not getting swallowed and driven out of business by behemoth competitors. Small businesses in general have a very high mortality rate.

Employee-owned firms and cooperatives (and perhaps partnerships patterned after law firms) have the potential to escape from dilemmas of big versus small—in theory at least—by forming specialized alliances among themselves, overcoming the weaknesses of their size through the purposeful sharing of skills and resources, even of sales and purchases, with other small fish. To date, this approach is more often a matter of earnest conversations than actuality. But the idea of forming networks of like-minded firms that can share the costs and opportunities common to small business resonates with social promise. Some see it as a pragmatic American version of what the Basque people created in Mondragon.

John Logue, a professor at Kent State University and director of the state-funded Ohio Employee Ownership Center, is one of those patient pioneers with big ideas. Ohio now has nearly 500 employee-owned companies with more than 375,000 owners, many of them coached and encouraged into existence by Logue's center. Some failed utterly; some failed to develop the internal reality of worker self-governance. But most are flourishing and each year generate $25 to $37 million in new wealth that belongs to workers, not absentee owners. Logue is well familiar with all the difficulties, yet he also understands that "employee ownership alone is not enough." To make enduring change for workers and their communities, smaller companies have to build strengthening networks among themselves. Some

Ohio firms have made a modest start in their Employee-Owned Network that sponsors jointly financed training programs for workers and managers, teaching business skills, leadership style, and method, the mechanics of shared governance.[16]

Logue's long-term dream is creating "Mondragon in Ohio," a cooperative network of firms that can pool business functions such as finance or accounting through mutually held firms, or share the cost burdens of sophisticated services such as marketing and environmental engineering—the luxuries small businesses typically cannot afford. When people asked him why Ohio can't develop something like the Mondragon cooperatives, Logue used to say, "Because we just don't have enough Basques." The answer was too flip, he decided, after touring Mondragon and studying its structure. Yes, ethnic solidarity and Catholic social teaching are vital elements in Mondragon's success, but the cooperatives survive and prosper because of their integrated economic structure, the pooling of resources and skills among the cooperatives, especially the central financing institution that insures them access to stable, long-term credit. The chaotic go-it-alone spirit of American enterprise does not much encourage such cooperation. Neither does American law.

Yet the idea of cooperation opens up the social imagination of ordinary people. The condescending assumption that working people are too narrow-minded to harbor such vision or that they don't much care about larger matters like the environment misunderstands the situation. The problem for working people is that they lack the power to change much of anything—and they know it—so naturally they tend to focus closest to home, where they might have some influence. Workers as owners will not sacrifice their self-interest any more freely than any other group in economic life. But would they make wiser choices for society, based on a broader understanding of self-interest, than the current regime of business managers? On the whole, I think they would. We can't say for sure, but it would be interesting to find out.

At an annual meeting of the Ohio Employee Ownership Association I listened to John Logue lead a workshop discussion on what people might want if they could create "an employee-owned industrial park," one filled entirely with worker-owned companies. The people in the workshop were rank-and-file workers, managers, and a few professionals, some unionized, some not, from very different lines of business. Logue simply threw out the question: "What features would we envision for such an industrial park?" Their conversation swiftly produced two dozen ideas. Joint waste disposal. Sharing the employment of high-salaried people with specialized skills. Common legal and payroll services. Common shipping and purchasing. Cogeneration of power. The closed-loop recycling of industrial wastes for ecological sustainability.

Their suggestions gravitated to personal and social concerns. The industrial park should have a shared day-care center, a common park and playground, and an exercise room. It might need a community center to engage the social concerns from surrounding neighborhoods. It could provide the employees' own children with real-life educational experiences, regular exposure to the workplace, job internships, and hands-on vocational counseling. It might work out a labor pool agreement that helps people and firms cope with layoffs, recruiting, and job hunting. These and other suggestions sounded plausible—all of them—and generated a lively enthusiasm, though no one seemed to have illusions about how soon they might accomplish any of them. Building cooperative enterprise is hard to do; it takes time and patience, trial and error. They already knew that.

The work reality central to people's lives is also powerfully conditioned by the other foundation elements of capitalism. We turn next to examine capital and the awesome influence of financial markets over American life. When the advocates and activists of worker ownership talk about the obstacles, capital usually comes up first in the discussion. They lament the scarce working capital available to pioneering firms and the lack of long-term commitments from banks or investors, the stringent credit terms, and wrong-headed valuations.

When I asked Joe Cabral why employee ownership doesn't spread more rapidly, he paused and replied: "That's the sixty-four-million-dollar question. I happen to think it's greed. The people who have the power want to retain the power. And the capital is very concentrated in the investment banking community in Wall Street; my own 40l(k) dollars are placed in Wall Street. Big changes have to take place, but trying to turn that steamship around to a different way of doing things, that's really difficult. It means a sea change in the way our society works."

# 4

# Imperious Capital

I F capitalism were someday found to have a soul, it would probably be located in the mystic qualities of capital itself. The substance begins simply enough as personal savings and business profits, then flows like oxygen through labyrinthine channels into the heart and muscle of economic life. Once set in motion, the surplus wealth (Marx provocatively called it "stored labor") becomes one of capitalism's three classic factors of production, alongside human labor and nature (the land and resources consumed to make things). Capital puts up the money to build the factory, buys the machines, and pays the company's bills until its goods are produced and sold, thus yielding the new returns that pay back the lenders and investors with an expected increase. It is not simple, but that is the essence.

As financial markets and the banking system deploy this wealth to firms that will use it, the capital is transformed into myriad shapes and meanings, mostly represented by pieces of paper (stocks, bonds, investment agreements, and many hybridized variations) that express legal claims on the borrowed money or the productive assets it helps create or perhaps as the privilege of sharing in the profit. In the maw of finance, the very nature of the capital becomes abstracted and etherealized, mystified by dense mathematical calculation and accounting definitions, invested with unknowable intangible qualities like corporate "goodwill." Capital may even be transformed through the artistry of Wall Street's "financial engineering" into securities that exist simultaneously as "debt" and "equity." To the tax collectors the financial instruments are described as "debt" and tax deductions are claimed on the interest payments. For shareholders, they are called "equity" that increases the company's capitalization.

By this point, one can no longer concretely see the capital or know for certain where it is, but the valuations function well enough for the system so long as financial agents and investors share consensual faith in the reality of the accounting. The trust is somewhat mysterious itself, since many valuations regularly turn out to be wrong. They often are based on false hopes or transient illusions, misunderstandings corrected daily and sometimes violently by the financial markets buying and selling the pieces of paper. Even worse, some valuations turn out to be purposeful fictions and wind up as fraud claims and bitter lawsuits.

The faith endures generally, not only because of the material successes, but because the complicated processes of finance capital actually are grounded in a very human impulse: trying to see the future and alter it. This quality is capitalism's redeeming glory and also the core source of its overbearing social power. Despite the recurring failures and frauds, despite the gross inequities and greedy excesses, the financial mechanisms allow ordinary mortals to reach into the future and influence outcomes beyond the present certainties. At least they may try. And they have enough history to know that their acts of inspiration—or shrewd hunches and acquisitive maneuverings—do not all end in illusion. This noble spirit—defying the bounds of time and destiny—is an ancient human trait, of course. Think of Columbus sailing forth to discover new worlds. Think of Icarus and Daedalus flying toward the sun on wax wings.

In modern finance, both the courage and folly are largely obscured by pretensions of scientific exactitude. The mathematical forecasts of promised returns give confidence to the insiders (and may reassure their nervous investors) but are quite unreliable in the long run. The history of capitalism is littered with repudiated theories and failed formulas, the bones of sincere but bankrupt capitalists. In the recent past we have witnessed many episodes of such spectacular failure and debunked certitudes. The "science" of investing is bound to be defeated by reality, sooner or later, because finance capitalism is inescapably a human system—imbued with the endless variability of human behavior, operated by mere mortals prone to sin and error who sometimes display their stupidity in herdlike stampedes. Despite the "information age" of proliferating numbers and equations, human beings simply are not able to see the future, not really, not without divine assistance. Given this immutable condition, one appreciates the bravery involved in trying.

These human qualities, virtuous and otherwise, provide a context for demystifying the full epic force of finance capital's imperious influence over society at large. These are not Promethean titans and Nobel-class wizards magically creating new wealth. They are self-interested and fallible people like the rest of us, purposefully pursuing what their own value system holds to be right and true: the goal of maximizing returns, then doing it again and again. Given the vast wealth of the country, the financial system forms a rather narrow funnel through which tens of trillions of dollars are continuously poured. Yes, the transactions are dizzyingly diverse and complex, involving thousands of large and small financial firms, but the work itself actually is done by a fairly small number of people. In Wall Street (an emblem of the system now dispersed nationwide) fewer than one million Americans manage the money. And only a relative handful of those people make the big decisions. Collectively, they are very, very powerful. Nobody elected them, but their exalted position in American life is reflected in their incomes.

My central complaint is with the narrowness of their value system rather than the financial mechanisms (though I will examine some grand illusions and contradictions in how the financial plumbing works). With a few important exceptions, the agents of capital operate with dedicated blindness to capital's collateral consequences, an indifference to the future of society even as they search for the future's returns. The capital system does not authorize financial agents to think about such things and may well penalize them if they do. Yet, because capital reaches out to change the future, heroically or egotistically, it continuously alters the landscape in which all of us dwell, for good and for ill. Finance capital creates or destroys what society cherishes, rewards and punishes the behavior of innocent bystanders, commands or blocks the ways in which society can think about its own nonfinancial aspirations.

Indeed, in our own time, it is the financial system that shapes and polices the "social contract" in America, far more effectively than the government, which has largely retreated from that role. Capital oversees the affairs of cities and states as well as business and imposes its own singular concept of correct thinking. Finance accomplishes this by promoting and underwriting innovative business strategies and practices or by consolidating capital assets into huge new business organizations that may roll over competitors, but will also sweep across the existing social landscape. These decisions can create fabulous returns and new wealth if they work out, but may injure society whether they work out or not. The terms and conditions of employment, the ongoing ecological destruction, settled understandings of community, and the outlines of how the future will function, these considerations and others are all subjected to the commanding gaze of finance, which alters them, sometimes profoundly, without much thought to society's competing views.

This examination into the nature of finance capital confronts three big subjects. First, the fundamental illegitimacy of the financial system, and especially the stock market, as it presently is structured and functions. Second, the manner and method by which financial power reshapes our lives and the social landscape oblivious to complaints or alternative aspirations of powerless citizens. Finally, how active pioneers are intruding on this reality, literally creating a parallel system and inventing investing techniques that give them effective influence over finance and a path toward decisively altering the values of American capital. This chapter moves back and forth among these three dimensions because they are inseparable. To grasp why financial power is vulnerable to change, one must first understand how and why the system deceives and manipulates through convenient fictions, but also how it subverts basic principles of genuine capital investing. Knowing how finance capital really works, one can begin to see the openings for leveraging profound change. If people can overcome their ignorance, they will see they are not powerless, only ignorant.

Americans recently have been educated by events on the deceit and manipulation by Wall Street firms, so that is probably the easiest point to grasp. But we are not talking about the recurring matter of accounting fraud or conflicts of interest among stock analysts. These disloyalties and purposeful deceptions are embedded in the design of any Wall Street house, from Citigroup to Morgan Stanley, that describes itself as an "all-service financial firm." Its customers include major corporations *and* the investors who buy stocks in those companies. The brokerage cannot tell the truth to one customer—the ignorant shareholders—without risking injury to its other, far more important clients—the corporations. This is an important scandal but still not the heart of the matter. The structure of the financial system and its closely held power combine to disserve the ordinary public in far more systemic ways: manipulating the herd toward the short-term illusions while shortchanging the long-term interests of both the economic system and the society.

For these reasons, finance and banking represent the crowning pinnacle of conflict in the collision between society and capitalism, the place where society's values are most visibly and powerfully eclipsed. For those who seek to advance society's nonfinancial aspirations, finance capital should be understood as the most significant battleground. If they cannot win a foothold here, they are unlikely to win lasting victories anywhere else. That sounds bleak, I know, given the formidable scale and seeming permanence of Wall Street's concentrated power. But this chapter offers surprising evidence that Wall Street's operating values are far more vulnerable to outside influence—and profound change—than either the titans or their critics yet understand. In fact, on the margins, some promising changes are already underway.

A transformation of Wall Street's core values is not only possible, but eventually likely to occur, I predict. Though this will take many years (maybe decades) to achieve, it would represent a generational accomplishment more enduring and meaningful than any of the current preoccupations of politics, since the very foundations of public life would be altered. My optimism may seem incautious, but it starts from an appreciation for how dynamic capitalism evolves continuously from its own restless energies. Within the monolith of finance some adventurous players are always experimenting with new methods and theories, trying to take profit from what the larger herd doesn't yet see or understand. When renegades succeed, the system typically steals their ideas and tries to emulate their approach.

Right now, I see evidence of this process unfolding around social perspectives, small and fragmented efforts to be sure, but demonstrating that much of what the money guys believe about social imperatives is simply wrong. A few scattered innovators—hardheaded capitalists within the system—are defying conventional wisdom, most profitably, by aggressively investing in and managing corporations that accept social commitments the market players assume are losers. Their success, as it becomes more widely understood, is sure to upset the club and especially its customers.

A more fundamental reason for optimism is the simple fact that Wall Street finance operates mainly with other people's money, people whose own values and preferences are now effectively excluded in the investing process, people whose own money often is put to uses that do injury to them and to the qualities in life they most value. Obviously, this is an anomalous condition and beginning to encounter questions and challenges as more Americans learn how to make the connection between their own savings and what Wall Street does with them. Some people, in fact, are beginning to take responsibility for the consequences of their own wealth, or at least are trying to figure out how to do so. Some are withdrawing from the regular system and parking their money elsewhere (a bit like guerrillas forming up in the mountains). Others are creating new, freestanding financial institutions that will be loyal to their social purposes.

Many more are confronting the larger storehouses of wealth, where their savings mingle with money from millions of others, and arguing that Wall Street's narrow, mechanistic way of thinking is harmful not only to the social future, but to their well-being as citizens *and* as investors. These are mostly isolated skirmishes at present, but they reveal the front lines slowly forming around the commanding heights of finance. The citadel does not yet take any of this very seriously. When it eventually does, agents of finance can be expected to resist the implications fiercely, since their own closely held power will be threatened.

The social complaint is not new to finance capital, of course, nor is the general sense of powerlessness. In the Victorian age Marx depicted the ascendant industrial capitalism as a roiling revolution, continuously disturbing and destroying society's settled verities and relationships: "All that is solid melts into air, all that is sacred is profaned." Nearly a century later, the great conservative thinker Joseph A. Schumpeter made similar complaints, lamenting finance capital's ability to obliterate personal loyalties to time and place: "The capitalist process, by substituting a mere parcel of shares for the walls of and the machines in a factory, takes the life out of the idea of property. . . . Dematerialized, defunctionalized, and absentee ownership does not . . . call forth moral allegiance as the vital form of property did."

What he meant was that owning one's own home or farm or small business elicits deep commitments of personal responsibility—an owner's concern for the property's condition and its neighboring context. This felt responsibility dissipates—"melts into air"—when the property consists only of pieces of financial paper representing an "ownership" share in a distant corporation.[1]

Schumpeter's insight identified a dehumanizing quality within the capitalist process that is a primary source of the irresponsibility in the modern system: ownership distanced and depersonalized from its real-world meanings, insulated from the real-world consequences. The millions of shareholders have no genuine "moral allegiance" to the companies they theoretically "own" nor much real knowledge of how those companies operate. They have no influence, because the insiders—corporate executives and financiers—understand they can safely ignore the transient shareholders who, except for the returns, are indifferent to their "property." In the great drama of shaping the future, the supposed "owners" are treated like useful but powerless spear-carriers. The "moral allegiance" has, of course, deteriorated still further in the modern era, as the ownership of shares has dispersed laterally throughout American society, as modern technologies allow people to buy and sell stocks with even less thought about what it is they "own." These millions of new "absentee owners" represent—potentially—a collective force that can help alter the operating standards within capitalism, though it is safe to say most do not recognize that possibility or have ever thought about it.

First, we need to explain a counterintuitive reality: Americans, collectively, possess far more financial power than they probably realize; they just don't know where or or how to apply it. This is not the revolution of 1848, when Marx observed the propertyless proletarians struggling against bourgeois exploitation. It is not even the 1940s, when Schumpeter first published *Capitalism, Socialism and Democracy*. At that time, the majority of American families still did not own their homes, much less equity shares in corporations. Since then, the great expansion of financial wealth and its modest dispersal among the working middle-class have created a predicate for forging new relationships within capitalism, especially if small holders develop ways of acting collectively. The same quick information technologies used to distance people from their wealth also could help them become more intimate owners.

Meanwhile, individual wealth remains highly concentrated in America. Despite what you may have read in the newspapers, the stock market did not become "democratized" during the recently departed bull market. America's wealthiest families, the top 1 percent, hold 47 percent of all forms of the financial wealth owned by households (as opposed to institutions) and 49 percent of the family-owned stocks and mutual-fund shares. Their share of the household wealth grew even more lopsided during the last two decades. The top 10 percent effectively owns 85 percent of family-held stocks plus an overwhelming share of the private equity investments in business.

Nevertheless, the broader middle-class did make headway as investors. The number of families who own stocks directly or indirectly through their personal retirement accounts has doubled since 1983, from 24 to 48 percent. They still represent less than half of the whole society, and the average value of stock holdings remains quite small for middle-income families (less than $5,000 on average for three-fourths of those who own shares). The median wealth of American households, as economist Edward N. Wolff of New York University has explained, actually declined a bit during the 1990s, both because middle-income families were spending more than they earned, and borrowing heavily to do so, but also because their stored wealth was mainly invested in housing or low-return savings accounts, not the high-flying stock market.[2]

Inequality of wealth is gross and growing, but the financial position of ordinary Americans looks a lot more substantial when it is expressed in dollars. Leaving aside their stock holdings or equity in their homes, U.S. households own in aggregate nearly $4.5 trillion in financial assets, most of it safely parked in savings accounts at banks, credit unions, or savings and loan associations. This form of wealth holding also is maldistributed among the income classes, but it is not nearly as skewed as in stocks and bonds. Most ordinary Americans are cautious investors of their nest eggs, typically accepting a lower rate of return from a savings account in exchange for greater safety, including federal deposit insurance. In any case, as financial economist Jane D'Arista, research director of the Financial Markets Center, observes: "We are not a nation of widows and orphans. We have quite a lot of money, and people control some of it. They might ask why they don't control more of it."

By far their greatest store of savings is not subject to their control—the $6 trillion held in their behalf by pension funds—though Americans at large are the "beneficial owners" of this wealth. These accumulated trillions ($10 trillion before the stock market meltdown) represent the deferred wages of working Americans, what the company promised in its terms of employment or the union negotiated by contract in lieu of bigger wage increases. The money put aside for them (and exempted from income taxes) carries heavy fiduciary responsibilities, a pension fund's legal obligation to husband the assets, to invest safely and soundly and only in the beneficiaries' interest, to make certain the growing store of wealth can pay for the future retirement benefits. This is a national savings program of awesome dimensions and, as astute observers like Peter Drucker, Jeremy Rifkin, and Randy Barber pointed out a generation ago, it has the potential capacity to reshape the nature of American capitalism.

Pension funds are now the universal owner in the stock market, the largest sector of available capital. Along with the other financial institutions that have fiduciary obligations to their beneficiaries—mutual funds, insurance companies, trusts, and a few others—they literally "own" the American economy. Altogether, these institutional investors hold half of all the corporate shares publicly traded in the United States (and 21 percent of all varieties of financial assets). At a given point, the fiduciary institutions owned 48 percent of General Electric, 41 percent of Exxon, 49 percent of Coca-Cola, 60 percent of Philip Morris, and 52 percent of Merck (as well as 64 percent of Enron just before the company disintegrated). Collectively, they hold roughly 60 percent of shares in the nation's one thousand largest corporations (some of which also vanished when the stock market bubble collapsed).*

Despite their dominant position, pension funds are passive owners. A private investor can gain control of a company by acquiring a minority of its shares, even as little as 10 percent, but the pension funds are so huge and self-conscious of their size that they typically invest in a neutral fashion across the entire market spectrum. They do not buy on the good news or sell on the bad, but continuously adjust the share weightings in their portfolios to stay roughly indexed with the broader stock market. This is regarded as safety first, since any large moves by the major funds might disrupt the entire stock market and injure their other shareholdings (though the funds still lose hugely whenever the market itself swoons). Whether or not this practice of passive diversification is sound, as portfolio theory holds, it definitely delivers a massive volume of available capital to the financial markets—with no strings attached, often no questions asked. The fiduciaries, with a few important exceptions, are thus inertly aligned with the values of finance capital. Not surprisingly, the money managers like it like that and so do the corporate CEOs.

The "beneficial owners" are not consulted. The strict laws governing fiduciary obligations treat them, more or less, like helpless "widows and orphans" whose money must be managed for them by wise and trustworthy agents. Most of their pension wealth, about $3 trillion, is actually in the hands of private corporations, their employers, many of whom routinely manipulate the pension accounting to

---

*These statistics on holdings should be read only as representative, since they change regularly as markets rise and fall and investment portfolios are shifted.

enhance the company's own bottom line. Employees, as a matter of common fairness, ought to have their own representatives sharing a supervisory role in the corporate pension funds (including the fast-growing domain of 401[k] plans), but this won't happen until federal pension law is changed, an unlikely reform given the political system's fealty to business and finance.

The broader ranks of citizens, however, do have a substantial opening to influence the investing values—and to hold managements accountable—through the mammoth public-employee pension funds at state and local levels (which as of 2003 hold nearly $2.6 trillion). A much smaller but more promising advocate for workers are the 1,200 union-managed pension funds ($400 billion), since they are supervised jointly by labor and management trustees. The largest public-employee funds have enormous leverage of their own. Before the collapse of stock prices, CalPERS (the California Public Employees' Retirement System) owned $171 billion in assets. TIAA-CREF (Teachers Insurance and Annuity Association–College Retirement Equities Fund) held $273 billion. New York State's employee pension fund had around $124 billion. Florida's had $106 billion. In many instances the trustees include elected public officials like the state treasurer or comptroller and, in some cases, trustees elected by the employees. These overseers are naturally more likely to listen seriously to the public's expressions of social concerns, and sometimes even respond. Public employee and labor pension funds are therefore a leading edge in the broad struggle to change the customary thinking. Active citizens and unions are pushing them to take a more assertive role.

As it happens, without quite acknowledging it, American capitalism has entered into a fundamental new stage, a different constellation of wealth ownership that promises to intensify the conflicts over whose values are being served. At some point during the decade of the 1990s, a historic threshold was crossed, though not widely noted.

The fiduciary institutions have surpassed individuals as the leading stockholder. Back in 1965, American households, mainly the wealthy and very affluent families, owned 84 percent of the stock market. Yet, by 1999, households held only 42 percent of the market, despite the doubling of shareholding families. Individual wealth was displaced by the fiduciary funds, and so even the very wealthy now stand in the larger shadow cast by these institutions. They resemble an eight-hundred-pound gorilla that declines to throw its weight around, owners who would just as soon their potential power remains unnoticed. This anomalous condition—concentrated yet passive power—is likely to become less stable, as more citizens figure out the meaning and the consequences for their own lives.[3]

In *The Rise of Fiduciary Capitalism,* business economists James P. Hawley and Andrew T. Williams of Saint Mary's College of California describe this new reality as the third stage of American capitalism. The first stage, of "personal" capitalism, unfolded more than one hundred years ago, when titans like Carnegie, Ford, and Rockefeller owned and operated the emerging industrial giants intimately. That era of personal owners was eclipsed by "managerial" capitalism early in the twentieth century, as control passed to the professionalized management systems. The newly powerful managers still had to answer to finance, but they consigned the broad ranks of shareholders to the weak position they still occupy. Under "fiduciary" capitalism, ownership has reconcentrated again, only now it resides in the faceless and ostensibly neutral bureaucracies known as institutional investors. But who owns these bureaucrats? And whose interests do they really serve? The gorilla treads lightly because its position is fraught with explosive questions.

The financial system is astride a paradox that unsettles conventional thinking on all sides. During the last generation the rich got richer and still more influential (as critics, myself included, regularly pointed out). Yet, at the same time, the countervailing trend of wealth accumulating in the fiduciary institutions steadily shifted the center of gravity in an opposite direction—toward collectivized wealth. This shift potentially—only potentially—gives ordinary citizens a source of leverage they have never before possessed in the history of American capitalism or democracy. This leverage does not arise from the familiar contours of class conflict, but from the unique qualities of pension funds. They are, by nature, collective organizations required to act in behalf of the many millions, not for narrow commercial interests. As wealth holders they must necessarily take the long-term view of economic life (the law at least tells them to do so). In fact, as fiduciaries, they are supposed to act *only* in the long-term interests of their future retirees.

So the pivotal arguments for this new era will be about how those "long-term interests" are defined and defended. Labor and environmental advocates, for example, have argued with increasing force and sophistication that it is wrong for pension funds to invest in a corporation deliberately abusing its own workers, destroying their jobs for short-term gain or wrecking their communities with pollution or engaging in other antisocial practices. A fund's indifference to such social consequences, they argue, violates the spirit of the fiduciary obligation, if not also the law. These reform advocates have made only limited headway so far with shareholder proxy fights and other tactics, but they are persuading some pension trustees to drop the most offensive companies from their portfolios (tobacco companies are the easiest target since they admit liability for vast injuries to public health).

Most pension funds, however, stick to the narrow traditional definition: fiduciary obligation is about maximizing returns, not anything else. Ignoring other consequences, the fiduciary managers are as "irresponsible" as corporate managers. But the premises of this debate are changing dramatically. New intellectual insights developed by leading shareholder activists are arguing for fundamental change and with a logic that is profound and powerful. Their case resembles a stick of dynamite with a slow-burning fuse.

Pension funds, it is argued, must become active investors who pressure and punish companies for their deleterious practices, not as a gesture of social conscience, but because the corporate antisocial behavior damages a pension fund's own wealth. These funds, because they are "universal owners" and hold large, enduring stakes across the entire economy, will pay the negative costs, one way or another, for the "externalities" generated by individual companies—the firms that dump the toxics in the river or consistently injure their workers or in other ways push their operating costs off on society. The individual company improves its profits by "externalizing" these costs, and so these actions are accepted practice in American management. But the costs *will* be paid by someone and thus injure the growth and efficiency of the broader economy in which the pension funds are invested. Other companies, government, workers, and taxpayers generally, all will sooner or later have to pay for the company's evasion of its true operating costs, whether it is cleaning up a landscape ruined by toxic pollution or the health care bills for injured workers or the ameliorative aid to an injured community. The pension fund's broad portfolio gives it a direct stake in the lost economic output caused by the company's irresponsibility.

In the same sense, pension funds lose real value when corporations extract short-term profit by refusing to undertake positive actions that will enhance the overall economy—cutting their research and development budgets or creating training programs to improve employees' productivity. The corporate executives save money and argue that such positive programs are a waste of their investment capital, since the well-trained workers might go elsewhere or the new processes and products from R&D spending might in the end be exploited by other firms. Yet, in every instance, the pension fund benefits from these expenditures regardless, since all enhance growth in the overall economy the pension fund owns. General Electric is a celebrated example, since that company commits all of these antisocial practices and many others to support its rising profit. GE is well loved by shareholders, admired for its quarterly earnings gains. But who pays the tab for GE's brilliant style of management? The economy and society at large. More specifically, the pension funds and their beneficial owners.

This new concept—understanding pension funds as the "universal owner" of America's major business corporations—provides an economic rationale, unsentimental and self-interested, for why the funds should enforce social objectives; that is, they should punish corporations for irresponsible behavior by moving their capital elsewhere. The discipline would be exercised through the stock market. The wealthy enforcers simply would be fulfilling their fiduciary duties to their beneficial owners. The insight of the "universal owner" originated with Robert A. G. Monks and Nell Minow, two long-standing leaders in shareholder activism in their book, *Watching the Watchers.* Their thinking is developed further and more explicitly by Hawley and Williams in *Fiduciary Capitalism.*

Monks, by the way, is a wealthy Republican businessman from Maine who served in the Reagan administration as assistant secretary of labor for pension rights. He and Minow have together developed a sophisticated and purposeful response to the disjunctions of power within modern capitalism and are attacking the status quo on many fronts. "If pension trustees have this great power, it has to be accountable to someone else," Monks explains. "We have to find a way to make trustees respond to the long-term interests of their beneficiaries—people who are now the innocent fish exploited by everyone else."[4]

Executives in corporate boardrooms are not quaking; neither are Wall Street money managers and pension fund trustees (most are doubtless unfamiliar with how the idea of "universal owners" will someday alter their operating values and behavior). But this reconception of the role of social imperatives in finance capital starts the society down a promising road toward overcoming its deeper conflicts with capitalism. The work of fleshing out the practical implications (and substantiating the core logic with concrete examples) has begun on different fronts. Some of the largest public funds, like CalPERS, are at least listening respectfully.

The straightforward message for pension trustees—with a hint of retaliation if they don't get it—is that trustees must back off their passivity and the formulaic diversification of holdings that distances them from real-world consequences. They must learn how to become active investors, picking companies or rejecting them on more than abstract portfolio theory. They invest to maximize returns, of course, but this objective has to rely on far greater knowledge of how individual companies are helping or hurting the long-term returns for society and for their own future pensioners. Indeed, if the trustees fail to do so, they may be violating their fiduciary obligations

Our view of the financial system thus far has been from the mountaintop, so to speak. Now I descend into the messier landscape of everyday realities, where I examine more closely conventional fictions surrounding the stock market and the actual ways in which finance capital shapes our social reality.

JOHN MAYNARD KEYNES, the great economic theorist, was also an exceptionally astute investor. During the Depression years and World War II, he managed a stock fund that averaged annual returns of 13 percent, while the British stock market was averaging zero returns. Yet Keynes despised the stock market's preeminent role in finance capital. He called it "a casino" where people mainly gamble on the short-term moves in stock prices, utterly ignorant of what genuine investing requires for developing the future. He had no sympathy for the restless crowds, especially restless Americans, since most were merely "speculators," not true investors. His strongest contempt was for the financial professionals who advised them. The pros, he explained, track and manipulate the "market psychology" to generate recurring flights of enthusiasm or fear, churning the action from which their own profits are derived.[5] Keynes wrote:

It might have been supposed that competition between expert professionals, possessing judgment and knowledge beyond that of the average private investor, would correct the vagaries of the ignorant individual left to himself. It happens, however, that the energies and skill of the professional investor are mainly occupied otherwise. For most of these people are, in fact, largely concerned, not with making superior long-term forecasts of the probable yield of an investment over its whole life, but with foreseeing changes in the conventional basis of valuation a short time ahead of the general public. . . . The actual, private object of the most skilled investment today is 'to beat the gun,' as the Americans so well express it, to outwit the crowd and to pass the bad or depreciating half-crown to the other fellow.

Seeing the future is hard work. Genuine investing involves patiently, even tediously, gathering real knowledge of real-life companies and their economic context, then investing in a few firms with the most promising prospects while accepting that future events and risks are largely unknowable. "The social object of skilled investment should be to defeat the dark forces of time and ignorance which envelop our future," Keynes explained. It is far easier, he acknowledged, to profit instead by tracking market moods three months or a year ahead of the crowd, nudging average opinion in one direction or another. "We have reached the third degree," he complained, "where we devote our intelligences to anticipating what average opinion expects the average opinion to be."

The unreality of stock market behavior is not harmless play, he said. It wastes enormous amounts of a nation's capital. It destabilizes long-term valuations for the serious investors focused on creating new wealth in the future. It exaggerates immediate gains at the expense of the long-term prosperity. "Speculators may do no harm as bubbles on a steady stream of enterprise," Keynes wrote. "But the position is serious when enterprise becomes the bubble on a whirlpool of speculation. When the capital development of a country becomes a by-product of the activities of a casino, the job is likely to be ill-done."

Keynes's wisdom is before us again. A few years back, when the giddy boom and stock market bubble were lifting all spirits, most Americans would not have been able to grasp his meaning and doubtless would have dismissed him as an anachronistic crank. But his analysis has been reconfirmed vividly by the reckless inflation of stock market prices in the late nineties and its punishing aftermath for hapless investors and the economy as a whole. For households, $3 or $4 trillion of illusory "wealth" melted into air. Price gains from the bubble were completely extinguished for average mutual-fund investors by the autumn of 2001, when the average equity fund had subsided to a five-year rate of return actually below the historical pattern. By the summer of 2002, the price bubble had disappeared completely; all of the major stock indexes were back to the very same levels they had reached five years before. Diversified investors went up the hill and down again and came away five years later with zero returns.

The biggest losers, naturally, were the fiduciary institutions holding money for ordinary working Americans—the pensions, mutual funds, and others described above. Collectively, these trustworthy agents owned 64 percent of Enron just before it went bust and lost as much as $50 billion on one rotten company. Despite rigorous management and its squads of professional advisers, CalPERS lost nearly 30 percent of its stored wealth—shrinking from a peak of $190 billion to $135 billion in assets—and CalPERS did better than most. The fact that Keynes's critique, written seventy-five years ago, accurately describes the modern debacle demonstrates that the fundamental fallacies in the Wall Street system are deeply rooted in its structure (and indicates that these flaws were not corrected by finance-regulation reforms enacted by the New Deal in the 1930s).

The crowd was outwitted once again, but on a grand scale. In the present system, the true victims are those ordinary working Americans, the broad middle-class, whose accumulated savings are one way or another put in play—the people Robert Monks called "innocent fish." They would doubtless be enraged if they fully understood what had happened. Perhaps more of them do now because the dramatic unwinding epitomized by the collapse of Enron has revealed systemic deception and betrayed loyalties in Wall Street: in plain English, lying, cheating, and stealing. Corporate earnings turned out to be accounting concoctions and some of the best old names of finance, like J. P. Morgan and Citigroup, were implicated. While the brokerages continued to tout "buy" orders in failing companies, the insiders sold out early, harvesting billions in personal fortunes by passing the "bad half-crown" to the next fool. Most of these fraudulent practices were not entirely new, only brazenly exaggerated in scale. Financial fraud costs investors and creditors $400 billion a year, according to one industry estimate that, based on the recent scandals, appears to understate the true losses.[7]

In the financial world, such larceny is decriminalized. Culprits typically settle in cash, paying fines or negotiated awards to injured investors, without admitting guilt, but promising not to do it again. Just as the "moral allegiance" of property owners is dissipated when they own financial paper, so has personal culpability dematerialized for the agents who sell the paper. All in all, the market collapse and subsequent revelations add up to a spectacle of irresponsibility centered in finance capitalism but also involving an epic failure of government regulation. The very reform laws enacted during the 1930s to prohibit the abuses Keynes witnessed in his time were either gutted by political fixers or repealed entirely in the name of modernization. Not surprisingly, the same crimes and outrages flourish anew. An embarrassed Congress has enacted modest measures to restore order and trust, but it seems improbable that elected politicians will find the nerve to impose effective regulatory discipline on the very people who finance their campaigns.

Fraud and venality aside, Keynes was making a larger—and more radical—point about the stock market. It is, by its nature, an ineffective and unreliable vehicle for distributing capital to the enterprises that need it, and Keynes regarded it as an institution of dubious legitimacy in the larger scheme of finance capital. Despite industry clichés, the stock market draws staggering sums of wealth into the short-term plays and away from the slower, more plodding processes of genuine investing for the long run. The sometimes violent price fluctuations undercut the sober estimates of long-term investors and may derail new enterprises decisively by making existing ones seem temporarily cheaper. And the stock market inevitably encourages the exploitative relationship between professionals and the ignorant crowd of investors they advise (including even major pension funds). While the brokerage literature piously instructs investors to buy and hold for the long-term, the brokers devote enormous energy to provoking the opposite behavior. These contradictory objectives and conflicted interests led Keynes to conclude that Wall Street "cannot be claimed as one of the outstanding triumphs of laissez-faire capitalism."

The contradictions originate, ironically, in the stock market's supposed virtues for investors: liquidity and diversity. Liquidity is a fancy way of saying investors can always get out quickly if things go bad. In our high-tech world one can dump a corporate stock faster than one can cash a personal check. Diversifying one's holdings in the broad market, often by buying shares in a mutual fund, is meant to spread the exposure, insulating one against the bad surprises that can occur in individual firms—but not helping much when the entire market tanks. Both of these strengths are meant to reduce risk for investors but, logically, they pull in opposite directions. Owning diversified stocks and holding them forever is like buying a claim ticket on future growth and profit in the American economy with an expectation of collecting the moderate long-term rate of return (around 5 to 7 percent) confirmed by historical experience.

But this passive posture of diverse holdings works reliably only if the investor never uses the easy exit that liquidity provides—getting out for safety or jumping to other stocks that are soaring. Because human fallibilities come into play, including greed and fear, all but the most devoutly conservative investors will occasionally ignore one commandment or the other. The stock market thrives on the crowd's inconstancy. Since 1970, stock turnover has risen from 15 percent a year to more than 50 percent. Even institutional investors, despite their supposedly long-term perspective, experience portfolio turnover of 40 percent annually.[8]

Whatever returns may be realized, liquidity and diversity are also the root sources of the weak position assigned to ordinary stockholders. Why should these "owners" have any influence in running the firm if they are free to dump their shares the next day? Why should any CEO listen seriously to the shareholders' values when they have protectively dispersed their modest holdings across a broad swath of firms rather than select the few good companies they actually understand and care about? Risk avoidance has its costs too. Above all, it obliterates the ability of ordinary Americans to assert their broader social values in the operation of companies they ostensibly own. Keynes himself invested in a small number of firms (chosen very carefully) and scorned the idea of liquidity. Nothing in the maxims of orthodox finance, he declared, "is more anti-social than the fetish of liquidity." While investors use it to abandon investments, Keynes noted, "there is no such thing as liquidity of investment for the community as a whole."

As this line of reasoning suggests, investors with broader social objectives need to rethink the nature of their own risk-taking, that is, to find a more informed balance between avoiding risks and accepting responsibility. People have the power to do this, simply by withdrawing some or all of their financial savings from Keynes's casino and placing it with other financial venues that invest more faithfully according to their long-term values. Depending on the wisdom of their choices, they do not necessarily lose money by redeploying their wealth and may well see greater returns, partly by avoiding the occasional implosions. To make such choices generally available to Americans, pioneers are now creating new investment firms and venture capital funds and community banks—freestanding intermediaries not beholden to Wall Street's dominant value system. The development of these community alternatives is in its infancy but spreading rapidly, usually in response to local capital needs that the major money managers ignore. Think of this as a parallel financial system, rising slowly and gaining practical experience, still small and scattered but attracting more and more investors who see the connection between finance and their own circumstances. In short, the road to imposing a more responsible value system on Wall Street begins with the "innocent fish" taking responsibility for themselves.

As it happens, millions of Americans are already attempting to do this, at least in the tentative first steps known as "socially responsible investing." Leading social funds like Domini, Calvert, Trillium, and others invest according to explicit commitments *not* to hold stocks in the corporations associated with various antisocial products or practices: nuclear weapons and gun manufacture, for instance, or tobacco or unsafe factories or notorious environmental records. Social investment funds screen out the "bad guys" from the portfolio, and it is easy enough to ridicule, as Wall Street cynics regularly do. The screening looks like a feel-good way to stand aloof from sinfulness but without visible impact on the corporate sinners, since they can raise sufficient capital regardless. Ever adaptable capitalism, however, recognizes this as a new market niche, and Wall Street houses have opened dozens of such socially responsible investment funds to serve high-minded customers, even if the money managers don't much believe in the exercise.

Despite the obvious weaknesses, the concept is spreading dynamically, like the bow wave of a deep shift in American social consciousness. According to an industrywide survey by the Social Investment Forum, holdings in the various forms of socially responsible investing surpassed $2 trillion in 2001, up from $40 billion in the forum's first survey back in 1984. That's an astonishing figure, and one has to treat it with considerable skepticism since it includes huge pension funds that, for instance, may have stopped buying tobacco stocks but are otherwise thoroughly conventional investors. Nevertheless, the trend line is real and impressive. It represents people starting to reclaim purposeful control of their own money. One may envision a day when the growing galaxy of SRI funds learns how to act in concert and becomes a force for focusing concrete social pressure on finance capital and corporate managements.[9]

The other explosive fact about social investing is that it produces smart returns for the investors; indeed it appears to produce better returns than investing passively across the broad market. The Domini 400 Social Index, pioneered by Amy Domini in 1991, gained an average annual return of 20.83 percent during the 1990s, compared to 18.70 percent for the Standard & Poor's 500. Calvert's SRI fund reported an 11.6 percent return in the market's very bad year of 2000, when the S&P 500 was in negative territory, off 20 percent or so. Even Dow Jones has gotten aboard the train with the new "global sustainability" index it launched in 1999, tracking the top 10 percent of the best environmentally conscientious companies worldwide. Dow's "sustainability" group is outperforming Dow's broader global index by two or three percentage points. Financial experts are still arguing over what these differences mean but, when hundreds of billions are in play, an investing edge of 1 or 2 percent adds up to serious money.[10]

These results also contradict the familiar folklore of American capitalism. Investors are routinely warned that they will sacrifice returns if they try to include social sentiments—collateral issues like protecting nature—in their investment choices. This shared conviction of the hard-nosed money managers turns out to be wrong. The corporate world, likewise, always argues that environmental protection adds deadweight costs to a company's bottom line and, therefore, must be imposed only sparingly, if at all, by government. Is it possible that the opposite is true? That environmentally conscious enterprises turn out to be more profitable (and, by implication, more efficient) than the casual polluters? Social investing has opened up some profound questions the conventional wisdom cannot answer. And once derided ideas are starting to have real bite in financial circles.

A financial advisory firm called Innovest, based in Toronto and New York, has taken the logic of social investing a giant step further by applying "EcoValue" investment-risk ratings to thousands of corporations here and abroad. This creates a way for investors to apply a "positive screen" on which corporate stocks to buy, not just which bad guys to avoid. First, Innovest identified several hundred indicators of company performance on ecological and social concerns, tangible markers such as the company's liabilities for past pollution, its present risks in hazardous waste disposal, the energy efficiency of its production systems, and management's active policies on corporate governance, employee training, environmental auditing, and many other areas. From this baseline, the firm assigns risk ratings to companies from AAA to C, much like the Moody's or Standard & Poor's ratings for creditworthiness. Innovest's C rating is "a company where there are significant doubts about management's ability to handle its environmental/social risks and liabilities and where these are likely to create a serious loss." These intimate examinations identify vast differences in behavior between companies that might look more or less alike in the narrow accounting terms used by finance.

It turns out that companies with higher "EcoValue" ratings perform stronger as stocks, with returns that are 1.5 to 2.4 points higher for a diversified portfolio of several hundred "good guys" matched against a comparable portfolio of "bad guys." Even in high-risk sectors such as petroleum and chemicals, the "performance premium" Innovest found between the top half of the sector and the bottom half is striking: a 15.9 percent difference in U.S. chemicals; 17.2 percent in oil; 12.4 percent in electric utilities. Innovest, in other words, is upending the familiar maxim of passively investing across-the-board. Its rigorous company-by-company analysis demonstrates that, if a firm or pension fund (or single investor) concentrates on the high-end companies with the best environmental-social performance and simply stops investing in the low end, the returns improve substantially. This evidence has the potential to shift capital flows on a large scale—and eventually impose capital-risk penalties on the poor performers—once finance capital absorbs the distinctions. Morgan Stanley tested the Innovest model and confirmed the advantage. Leading pension funds are exploring the implications for their investment strategies.[11]

"Our ultimate purpose is reengineering the DNA of Wall Street," says Matthew J. Kiernan, Innovest's executive managing director. "The fairly simple-minded strategy is that, if you want to change corporate behavior, you have to start with their financial oxygen supply, producing solid information from social-environmental areas that have been completely opaque to financial markets. While the Wall Street crowd looks at people like us as woolly-minded, I would argue that the apparent sophistication of their analysis is pretty spurious, since most of it comes from accounting-based numbers that are completely unreliable. Depending on who's doing the accounting, a company either made $300 million last year or lost $300 million. If financial markets can see that these environmental and social issues matter to them financially, if they have good information they can rely on, then the markets are pretty good at punishing and rewarding. So we are really increasing the transparency levels of corporations with the objective of using the financial markets as an engine of reform and positive change rather than destruction."

Peter M. Camejo, founder of Progressive Assets Management in San Francisco, is also a trustee of the $3 billion public employees pension fund in Contra Costa County, California—the first U.S. pension fund to employ Innovest's "positive screen" (the Netherlands's ABP pension fund with $175 billion was the first in the world). Camejo thinks the Innovest model, once proven in wider application, may inspire others to examine company performance on questions like working conditions, employee satisfaction, and community relations because what the Innovest methodology may actually be measuring is the management's soundness. "The theory goes that what you're really discovering with this Innovest screen is something fundamental about the company," Camejo said. "With a company that has a very high rating on the environment, they're doing everything right, what you are really seeing is that the management team has got its head on straight: they avoid litigation; they avoid these problems; they know how to handle themselves; they're thinking ahead. With a company that's very bad, that cuts corners and gets in trouble all the time, you may be discovering that they've got internal management problems they don't admit to, that maybe they don't even recognize."

That commonsense logic may be more reliable than Wall Street's formulas and this new analytical approach to investing represents another big step toward rewiring the internals of capitalism with permanent social obligations. Even so, conscientious investors who use the standard would still be far distant from the central decision making of finance capital, the arena that shapes corporate strategy and thus the social circumstances. "The argument that social investing outperforms has incredible leverage because it puts Wall Street in total contradiction with itself," Camejo said. "Unfortunately, the driving force is still financial performance, and I think we need to get beyond that to achieve actual change." To influence corporate behavior before the fact—instead of punishing companies after the damage is done—one must dig deeper into how the financial system actually influences the social reality "going forward," as financial players like to say.

SUPPOSE, as a harmless thought experiment, that the stock market did not exist. Or, more realistically, suppose that the stock market's size became substantially smaller as people discovered other, more promising and trustworthy ways to invest their savings. American enterprise would not wither and die for lack of oxygen. The dynamic and forward-looking investing process that is the core of American capitalism would not seize up. Elements of finance capital would be severely disrupted (with lots of brokers looking for new work), but the main stem of Wall Street would adapt and continue to function, as it does now, as the principal provider of capital to enterprise. Despite the hearty corporate rhetoric about serving "shareholder value," the stock market plays only a minor role in delivering capital to companies. Indeed, the stock market is largely an after-the-fact institution itself, since virtually all of its trading involves secondhand shares derived from long ago business transactions and passed along from owner to owner over many years, sometimes for generations.

Mature corporations raise their capital elsewhere, mainly by retaining most of their annual profits for internal reinvestment rather than distributing the surplus earnings to shareholders as dividends. Companies raise their day-to-day working capital by selling commercial paper—corporate "certificates of deposit"—in the short-term money markets. They assemble the major packages of capital by borrowing through corporate bond issues or huge syndicated bank loans or by arranging private infusions of equity capital from major players. All of these transactions, one way or another, pass through the scrutiny and approval of the largest investment houses and banks or hundreds of smaller specialized firms. This is where the real power to shape the future is located, not in the stock market. The investment bankers design the packages of debt securities and sell them to investors, embrace the corporate visions or reject them, oversee the company's performance, and occasionally demand vigilant application of the brutal operating practices intended to sweeten the returns.

The major exception, obviously, is the entrepreneurial start-up company, which is developing a new product but not yet able to raise investment capital from its own profits (since it may not have any).

During the late 1990s we saw spectacular examples of profitless "new economy" firms raising billions by "going public," e.g., issuing their very first stock shares in "initial public offerings" (some survived the market bust, some disappeared). Even those new companies, however, were initially launched, not in the stock market, but with private capital provided by venture capital firms or wealthy individuals. Virtually all of them had to go to Wall Street bankers (or their West Coast cousins) to sell their first publicly traded shares. Indeed, the IPO became cash-out time for many insiders, the moment when they became personally wealthy by passing along "ownership" to the eager but unwitting crowds.

If the stock market is not the essential source of capital, then why do most corporate CEOs worry so intensely over their company's share price? Among the many reasons, not least is the fact that the top executives' own compensation packages, including stock options, are closely linked to their stock market performance. More fundamentally, modern finance employs the stock price in its fiendishly complex capital deals as an easy-to-read meter on corporate performance—and as a triggering mechanism for dispensing rewards or penalties. If the stock price rises smartly, it may liberalize credit terms for the company or allow its major lenders to convert their bonds into stock. When the stock price falls persistently, it will disturb—and might cut off—the company's access to capital from the money market, bond borrowing, and nonmarket sources. In the modern era, as financial value has become increasingly abstracted from a company's real assets or everyday production, Wall Street has devised rarefied mathematical formulas to determine and predict corporate "value" for investors. Despite continual errors of volatility, the stock price is a key anchoring fact for these calculations. Thus, as Keynes observed in simpler times, the short-term variations in stock prices can perversely disrupt long-term plans for genuine investment; only Keynes might despair at the far greater complications today.

A more substantial reason why CEOs are preoccupied with their share price is that it gives them the potential power to "print money." That's real power. They can do so by cranking out additional stock certificates and using them in the buying or selling of existing corporate assets—not just factories and office buildings, but entire operating divisions or subsidiaries, and often the entire company. This trade in existing capital assets is a leading function of modern Wall Street, and stock shares are the principal coin of the realm, not hard cash. If the share price soars, the CEO can begin looking around for things to buy, perhaps including nettlesome competitors. When the stock is down, the company looks like a cheap buy and the CEO starts watching over his shoulder for predators. Or the CEO may decide instead to "pretty up" his company for potential buyers by shedding unsexy elements, like the small workaday plants that are profitable but don't appeal to the modern business imagination (if the sale price is good, the CEO may be out of a job but wins too by cashing his stock options). When takeover deals are done, large sums of capital typically are borrowed to aid in the financing, but the essential transaction involves an exchange of one company's stock to buy the shares of the target company—enough shares to gain control.

Since the first great wave of conglomerates in the 1960s (substantially unwound by divestitures a decade later), Wall Street has operated "an institutionalized market for corporate control," as Harvard historian Alfred D. Chandler, Jr., wrote in *Scope and Scale,* his epic chronicle of twentieth-century industrial capitalism. Chandler described this marketplace as a new phenomenon in American capitalism: "the buying and selling of corporations as an established business, and a most lucrative one at that." The rationale for the tumultuous contests of mergers, acquisitions, and hostile takeovers is the search for "shareholder value": unlocking potential returns by dumping underperforming assets or acquiring new ones; by merging enterprises from unrelated lines of business or redividing them into smaller pieces; by reorganizing the assets and strategies of companies—even entire sectors—to operate more effectively, efficiently, profitably.[12]

Sometimes it works out brilliantly, but Chandler was skeptical of the overall impact. He feared that the deal making, while spectacularly profitable for participants, often "reduced and even destroyed the capabilities essential to compete profitably in national and international markets. . . . The rapidity with which a number of capital-intensive industries in the United States have lost market share at home and abroad . . . suggests long-term investment may have been sacrificed for short-term gain." The process itself—the continuous pressures to rearrange capital assets and the sheer size of conglomerated holding companies—has also distanced top executives from the internal realities of their own companies, Chandler observed. They no longer have the time for personal relations with the heads of operating divisions (never mind rank-and-file employees) nor much genuine knowledge of the products and production processes. As business decisions increasingly morphed into abstract financial decisions, guys from the finance office replaced engineers on the executive ladder. Indeed, the modern CEOs often come straight from Wall Street.

Anyone who spends a little time around major corporations will hear similar complaints from the people who work there—not just from the assembly-line workers, but from engineers, sales people, clerks and chemists and middle managers. They sense, correctly in many cases, that the folks in charge don't really understand how things work inside the company, or much care. Their insecurity and resentment—their sense of disenfranchisement—are intangible by-products of modern finance. The "market for capital control" has introduced a blind force into their lives capable of destabilizing their workplace with harsh new terms or abruptly altering their careers, while sometimes also wrecking the company. Some companies, of course, do need to be reorganized. And some companies deserve to fail. What angers people, however, is when they see their company mindlessly deformed for other reasons—the distant calculations of finance.

The single-minded model of "shareholder value" helps explain why contemporary CEOs enjoy such bloated incomes—531 times larger than the average worker's, compared to 14 times in 1940, as the grassroots group, United for a Fair Economy, calculated. The executive pay contract, including generous stock options provided by the management's own printing press, aligns the CEO's personal self-interest with the financial model rather than the company's long-term fate. If CEOs typically survive for only three years or less, why think long term?

The financial model helps explain why some major corporations are imposing mandatory twelve-hour work days in their factories, trying to squeeze a little more "value" from the workforce. The model justifies the repeated downsizings that Wall Street analysts encourage and applaud. The model also justifies the abandonment of viable, productive plants deemed incompatible with the company's "core strategy," a strategy devised in consultation with its investment bankers. If companies fail to take such stern measures, finance capital rebukes them in various ways and the share price falls. There are some stouthearted executives who ride out the scorn and keep their eye on the company's long-term future. Many of them succeed, many are sacked.

In broad terms, this is how Wall Street shapes the "social contract"—without much public discussion outside the private ranks of major investors. Collateral social consequences are regarded as not relevant to these capital transactions, though the architects cannot claim to be innocent of what they are doing to other people. The essential logic of "shareholder value" involves extracting something of value from the other contributing participants in an enterprise—the employees and supplier firms, the community, and sometimes the customers. In various ways, their claims to the company's earnings and its future well-being are reduced and transferred as new "value" for the shareholders, but especially for the corporate and financial insiders.

Perhaps the cruelest aspect of these transactions is that they are largely financed by the same fiduciary institutions, including pension funds, that hold the savings of ordinary Americans. In the recurring waves of mergers and restructurings, the newly powerful institutional investors were enlisted as the most important source of capital (joined by foreign investors wishing to buy into the American corporate club). The pension funds share in the gorgeous short-term returns, oblivious to the consequences for society or even for their own beneficial owners. Portfolio managers at pension funds know even less about the internal realities of a company than the Wall Street managers, and they see no need to learn more since they are fulfilling their narrow fiduciary obligation to maximize returns. Indeed, some major pension funds, in the name of improving "corporate governance," became aggressive advocates for this new order, directly pressuring corporate boards of directors to tighten still further and extract more "value" for the nameless shareholders.

Financial agents, with rare exceptions, will profit regardless of the outcomes, collecting huge fees and commissions for packaging the deals, even if shareholders never see their promised new "value." Actually, investment bankers are careful never to make explicit promises, lest they be sued later by the investors for fraud. "Bond agreements are worded in such a way as to protect all concerned," investment banker Christopher Whalen explains. "They never talk about the future, never include projected returns. When you go out to sell an IPO, the research assistant comes along and will do verbal guidance for the investors, but they never put it in writing. That would constitute a 'forward-looking statement' [as defined by securities law] and, if you don't hit it, you'll get sued." Corporate announcements of new financial offerings are always accompanied by a boilerplate disclaimer: "Actual results could differ materially from those projected or suggested in any forward-looking statements." The brave process of seeing the future is thus legally hedged and made deliberately opaque—an ironic legacy of the securities laws enacted to protect the innocent public.

Financial power does not just break up companies, but also communities. When Boeing's top management announced in 2001 that it was moving its corporate headquarters from Seattle, it literally was withdrawing from an eighty-year-old family relationship with the people and communities of Puget Sound. Most of Boeing's employees live and work there, but only a small core of top executives moved to Chicago. Many of those left behind understood this was a likely prelude to nasty upheaval in their lives. Getting distance from Seattle would make it easier for the executives to close down hometown production and move more jobs overseas to low-wage China or to spin off internal functions to cheaper subcontractors—to reorder and "rationalize" the former family. The Boeing executives, at a minimum, wished to convince Wall Street that they are not prisoners of sentiment, the mushy values like loyalty or community. The brief corporate press release announcing the move mentioned "shareholder value" seven times.

Financial power often also reshapes the behavior of an entire industrial sector and all of the affected cities and citizens. A dramatic example is the reorganization and corporate concentration in the airline industry. Starting in the 1980s the leading airlines were encouraged by Wall Street investment bankers to create a new, more efficient system of flight operations based upon a handful of hub cities, each one as home base to a different airline. Building the new infrastructure for this scheme would consume many billions from investors— and from the hub cities building mammoth new airports—but Wall Street believed in the vision and made sure the financing was available, since the promised cost savings were expected to deliver enormous new "shareholder value." Not coincidentally, only a handful of the largest airlines were capable of undertaking this vast rearrangement and it promised to give them commanding market position— three, at most four, dominant companies that would own air travel, impervious to challenge.

It has not worked out that way. The hub system may or may not have led to operating efficiencies, but all of the largest airlines became debt-burdened and unprofitable, their stock prices depressed. Meanwhile, a small upstart like Southwest Airlines—offering lean, low-priced, and terrific service to travelers and with a strong culture of employee engagement—made more money in a single year than all of the big boys combined. By late 2002, when all the major airlines were in deep financial crisis, American Airlines announced that it was backing off costly features of the hub system, and the other big boys were expected to follow. Travelers can judge for themselves whether the hub system has improved their traveling experience, but my point is not whether the original idea was sound. The point is that this great upheaval in American living patterns was generated by a very small universe of decision makers with the power to change things on a vast scale for their own interests without consulting customers or employees or even the passive shareholders.

Financial power also reorders the daily content of our lives, less directly perhaps, but as intimately as the quality of the daily newspapers we read. The tradition of family-owned newspapers, long one of the most profitable business sectors, was perhaps inevitably going to be eclipsed as the new electronic media coopted big chunks of audience and advertising revenue. But the fateful moment occurred for many newspapers when the publishing family decided to "go public" and sell stock shares. This gave the publishers access to capital and enabled them to buy many other newspapers and become chains (or sell out to one at very handsome prices). But it also ineluctably made them hostage to Wall Street accounting and Wall Street's values.

Gannett was the most aggressive leader in acquiring scores of local and regional newspapers with distinctive character and swiftly reducing them to knockoffs of Gannett's bland, low-budget model. The Knight-Ridder chain, which once included some of the best newspapers in the country, responded to "shareholder value" by steadily squeezing the newsroom budgets. A series of its most admired editors, from San Jose to Philadelphia, valiantly resisted, then resigned rather than preside over the hollowing out. The business managers always described these retrenchments as a matter of survival—adjustments to market realities. But Michael Janeway, author of *Republic of Denial,* provided a translation of what they said: "Wall Street was a more important constituency than those for whom the news was reported and edited."[13]

As this example suggests, the narrow funnel of finance capital also plays a central role in the homogenization of American culture. It built the ubiquitous fast-food chains and arranged the financing for consolidation of the handful of media conglomerates now astride films, television, books, magazines, and (coming soon) the Internet. It invests in the formulaic action movies and the multiplex theaters with six small screens and in the splendidly appointed chain bookstores that are driving out small independents. This dimension of capital's imperious influence is probably the one most visible to ordinary Americans. I mention it not to open arguments over taste or to second-guess the business plans, but to illustrate a simpler point: The concentration of power in the financial system lends itself naturally to the concentration of everything else. Large and powerful investment organizations, believing in the virtue of their own capital allocations, may reflexively seek to replicate the same qualities of uniformity and overwhelming scale in others, whether the project is industrialized hog factories or monopoly drugstore chains. I doubt the money managers sit around and talk about this, but the question of scale—the overwhelming bigness of things—inevitably drives the behavior of finance itself (I return to this important subject of scale in the next chapter).

Let's face it, it's a lot easier—and cheaper—to do one big financing deal for one major corporation than to do thousands of little deals for small, unfamous companies (also immensely more profitable for the deal makers). As a consequence, the broader ranks of smaller American enterprises—probably most of them—exist in a state of recurring oxygen deprivation, unable to raise enough capital to grow or to improve themselves or even to survive securely. This seems a puzzle at first, considering the awesome sums of capital cycling through the system, but owners and managers of small or medium-size companies will attest that their firms generally do not have access to the large pools of capital. They are either too small and unpromising or unwilling to conform to the Wall Street accounting and its idea of correct business practices. For credit, they must go to local commercial banks where the lending is typically short term and risk averse. This deformity in capital allocation has a reverse social impact of vast but unknowable dimensions, pushing smaller enterprises either to seek bigness or perish or to pursue that happy moment of extinction when the owners get rich by being swallowed by a larger enterprise.

One of the most pernicious fictions promoted by the Wall Street propaganda—embraced unblinkingly by most politicians—depicts the stock market as the miraculous engine of job creation. The reality is nearly the opposite. It is not the 10,000 or so publicly traded companies that produce America's job growth, but the hundreds of thousands of smaller, less celebrated companies that are privately owned and not even listed on any stock exchange. Frank Borges of Landmark Partners, which invests direct-equity capital in the private companies, said that during the most recent five-year-period these privately held firms generated virtually all of the net new jobs in the country with growth of roughly 20 percent, while the Fortune 500 companies were shrinking their employment by 4 percent. If more American capital flowed into the smaller enterprises and less to the larger ones, the economy would not suffer but benefit.

If one could somehow take the $400 billion lost every year in Wall Street fraud and magically deliver the wasted capital to promising small businesses across the nation, the effects would be transformative, not only for local employment and business prosperity, but probably also in the quality of people's lives. John Logue, who directs the Ohio network of employee-owned companies, explains the dilemma for smaller companies:

"The financial industry is really Wall Street–focused, pulling savings out of what might have gone into local businesses through the local financial institutions that are now also endangered themselves by all the big bank mergers. We now have almost as many mutual funds in this country as we have publicly traded stocks but, when you get right down to it, I'll bet seventy percent of those mutual funds are invested in the same stocks, the same big companies. What our companies need is long-term capital. They are forced to borrow short, five to seven years at the longest, instead of ten-year loans, or ideally fifteen years. We should have local mutual funds, funds that are specific to a city or state. I would like to put at least some of my retirement savings in an Ohio mutual fund that would undergird the Ohio economy, that invests in turnarounds and family-owned businesses that anchor the capital closer to home. Right now, I can't do that."

Joe Cabral, the CEO at Chatsworth Products Inc, describes the financial system's narrow vision from his own business experience: "It's value by perception rather than value by reality. I can buy my house with thirty years of credit. I can't do that if I go to a bank for a business loan. The bank wants collateral, even security, for a three-year loan. We need somebody who would be willing to put a stake in the company and take what I would consider a reasonable percentage of the ownership, and we could know that they are in for the long haul, doing it because they want to experience the value creation these employees will deliver. I don't know if there are any people like that."

One sure way to influence the reigning value system in finance (and thus in business) is to create an active competition with the status quo that succeeds on its own terms, a multiplicity of alternative financial venues that produce their returns by channeling capital into the diverse smaller companies ignored by the big system but also, crucially, to the pioneering firms attempting innovative products and practices—innovations the big system may actively oppose. "This is tough to do, very tough," says Logue, who is among the people trying to create localized investment funds. "What happens is that Wall

Street sucks in the kind of people interested in running funds, so we almost have to educate a whole generation of fund managers with different values."

The idea is spreading, nevertheless, as more communities decide to do capital investing for themselves. At present, some thirty chartered community development banks are up and running around the country, directing local deposits into the kind of local enterprises that regular bankers won't touch. Plus, 180 credit unions with similar commitments. Plus, nearly 60 local venture capital funds and more than 100 community-development loan funds. Collectively, these localized financiers hold only $7.6 billion, peanuts alongside the big system, and even trivial compared to the challenges they are undertaking. Most of the firms are quite new, small and still learning, but then most of them did not exist ten or fifteen years ago. The community banks or capital funds will succeed and grow only if their track records establish their soundness, if their lending and investing make real differences in the communities. Still, they have put their hands on the process that shapes their future. They now have something to say in the matter, closer to home, and can change things without waiting on approval from local government.[14]

The great, underappreciated paradox of American finance is that despite the gargantuan scale of many players and projects, the power to shape the outcomes still depends upon intimacy, even in the largest deals. That is, the closer one is involved in the financial transaction and the enterprise, including the willingness to hold an investment stake, the greater influence one will have in deciding the terms of the project, in defining its operating values and priorities. Any investment banker who is not witless understands this intuitively. The major investors, likewise, prefer the intimacy of a controlling position because then they can set the terms. In other words, the style and purpose of investing decisions—the inherent values—are not a function of immutable economic laws or disinterested experts. Neither is the expected rate of return, which is bound to be much larger for the insiders since they are, by definition, assuming a greater share of the risk. For better or worse, the values in finance capital are determined by those who do the deals and assume the risks.

Ordinary citizens—whom the system teaches to be distant and passive—cannot easily do this themselves, obviously, unless they have found faithful intermediaries to deal in their behalf. But the opportunities for forging a different value system through intimate and unorthodox investing are much greater than generally supposed. The evidence for heresy is plainly visible within modern capitalism itself. Many of the most successful—and influential—investors violate the ruling mythologies of the status quo, not just now and then, but with deliberate and profitable consistency. They draw themselves quite close to the companies in which they are investing and ignore the standard financial calculations. They take a controlling interest and supervise the company with a clear understanding of its strengths and weaknesses. They also expect—and get—far greater returns on capital than anything available to the transient crowds.

Warren Buffett is the most admired example; also, the richest. He became a billionaire because of his brains and nerve, but mainly because over four decades his investment strategy brushed aside Wall Street dogma and followed distinctly old-fashioned premises. Buffett's methodology is not secret and has been described by him and in numerous books. It is a modern variant of personal capitalism. Before investing, he wants to know the company managers, not only their plans and strategies, but what kind of people they are. He studies the product and its qualities closely and gathers insight into likely future demand. He asks lots of hard questions about earnings and capital allocation, but ignores market theory, macroeconomics, and the arcane formulas for predicting share prices. Robert G. Hagstrom, author of *The Essential Buffett,* wrote: "[H]e looks for companies he understands, businesses that have favorable long-term prospects, are operated by honest and competent people, and, importantly, are available at attractive prices. It has always been Buffett's preference to own a company directly, for it permits him to influence the most critical issue in a business: capital allocation."

Does this begin to sound familiar? Buffett is a kindred spirit to John Maynard Keynes. It's a long way from folksy Omaha, Nebraska, to an intellectual aesthete in Cambridge, England, but, as Hagstrom observed, the investing principles are quite similar, smart and patient. Buffett's record—a 24 percent rate of return compounded annually over thirty-five years—looks a lot better, but not if one remembers the adverse times in which Keynes invested. Like Keynes, Buffett buys a limited portfolio and holds onto it, a few famous names like Coca-Cola, but mainly uncelebrated firms like GEICO, See's Candy Shops, Nebraska Furniture Mart, and Scott & Fetzer. "Buffett believes the only investors who need wide diversification are those who do not understand what they are doing," Hagstrom wrote. In other words, Buffett takes responsibility and stays close to his capital.

Might we perhaps clone Warren Buffett? I am not offering a brief for Warren Buffett's personal social values (though they look pretty good compared to Wall Street's), but suggesting that only the creation of new financial institutions is likely to free the present structure of finance capital from its profitable attachment to short-term gain. Actually, Senator Russell Long, when he chaired the Senate Finance Committee, had a similar notion. Long recognized the hopelessly ignorant position of American families becoming new stock market investors, and he talked about creating a dozen or so government-chartered mutual funds to be run by fund managers committed to following the Buffett principles. This would be good for the small investors, Long told his aides, but also good for the astute allocation of patient capital. Nothing came of his idea, but it neatly illustrates the dilemma for small holders and for the country.[15]

The same mechanics employed by Buffett to exercise intimate control for the long term are, of course, also used for short-term windfalls by the slash-and-burn buccaneers, the raiders who take control and fire the management, strip the company of assets, or brutalize the workforce, then exit quickly with extraordinary returns on their capital, typically 35 percent and often much higher. They too must become intimately familiar with the company and its capital assets, but with the gaze of a rip-and-run scavenger. The point is, the techniques themselves are morally neutral. The operating values and the outcomes depend entirely on who's in charge.

During the last decade this playing field of private direct-equity investing has become a fast expanding domain in finance, presumably because it is so profitable for those willing to focus closely on the internal realities of American companies. Some are bandits and short-term opportunists, but the more general premise now is that the direct investors will make concrete improvements by taking control, injecting new capital, and reorganizing so that the corporate property has much greater value when its controlling shares are sold back into the public stock market in four or five years. These firms generally are not in it to foster social change.

Kohlberg Kravis Robert is probably the best known, but the Carlyle Group claims to be the world's largest now, managing $14 billion raised from investors around the world (including the bin Laden family of Saudi Arabia, whose stake was terminated right after the 9/11 terrorist attack on New York City). Carlyle uses its extraordinary political connections both to raise investor funds and to insure its oil and defense deals succeed (leaders include former secretary of state and treasury James A. Baker and former defense secretary Frank Carlucci; ex-president George Bush, Sr., is a senior advisor and former British prime minister John Major chairs the European office). Carlyle has completed 213 corporate and real estate deals since it was founded in 1987 and reports a gross internal rate of return of 30 percent, higher than average for buyout firms. CalPERS has invested $3.5 billion to buy 5 percent of Carlyle's management company. Major banks also do direct-equity investing through their merchant-banking operations. Before they merged as J. P. Morgan Chase, Chase Manhattan had board directors representing it in 560 companies and

J. P. Morgan reported 1,450 direct-equity transactions since 1984 with an internal rate of return exceeding 40 percent.[16]

Major wealth holders and financial institutions can afford to play in this realm, but could ordinary citizens prudently take such risks? Only if they have real pros doing the deals on their behalf. Only if their money passes through a trustworthy financial intermediary that can spread the risks across different projects (preconditions that do not exist—not yet—for unwealthy individuals). But the prospect of using direct investment to produce social change as well as returns is not as remote as it may sound. As the financiers understand, risk always accompanies the act of assuming greater responsibility, but so does the prospect for greater returns. The investor gives up liquidity— the quick, easy exit—and commits for the long haul because this enables the investor to engineer real and fundamental changes. The same principle applies to altering the social values.

To demystify the direct-equity process, one should understand that the essential source of the spectacular returns is not risk alone, but doing the deals with lots of leverage—borrowed money—just as American families do when they buy a home. Think of it this way: A family typically puts up its own capital as a down payment on the house, usually only 20 percent of the actual purchase price. It borrows the remaining 80 percent from a bank and, if the family lapses on the mortgage payments, the bank owns the house. The family, in other words, bears the risk, while the mortgage lender is protected by the collateral. But, if the family exercises "moral allegiance" over the years and keeps the house in good condition, the family—not the bank—will reap all of the home's appreciated value when it is eventually sold. A $60,000 home, purchased with $12,000 down, is sold some years later for, say, $100,000 as neighborhood housing prices have risen steadily. The family, not the bank, gets the $40,000 in added value—more than three times its initial capital.

The same essential transaction is employed when takeover firms acquire control of a company, using their stake as leverage to borrow too. If the company fails, the bank lenders own the factory and the investors lose their capital, just as foreclosed homeowners lose everything. Could these same mechanisms be used for deals that might be called "social takeovers"? That is, investors take control of a company because they intend to reform its productive performance in the usual ways—and also to alter its social behavior? The answer is clearly yes. Such pioneering deals already exist in the real world. A few investment firms, not many, have figured out that one way to improve a company's troubled bottom line is by regarding the workforce as partners, instead of as hostile opposition, and sometimes by even bringing the employees into the deal. This is new ground in American capitalism, still largely unexplored but with enormous potential for the reconciliation of ancient conflicts. The alternative, in social terms, is passivity and distant alienation, less risk perhaps, but also a familiar sense of powerlessness.

ORGANIZED LABOR is widely disparaged as a weak and anachronistic force in American life but, in one important matter, the labor movement is the vanguard. Union leaders, the forward-looking ones at least, have a vision for transforming the nature of American capitalism and are actively pursuing important elements, not through the usual political channels, but in the capital markets. Like other reform approaches I have described, labor's efforts face formidable barriers and repeated frustrations. Nevertheless, some unions are making practical advances toward their larger goal: repositioning the capital that effectively belongs to working Americans to serve the true self-interests of those workers and, therefore, society's long-term interests too. Labor may be greatly weakened from its heyday, but one thing it possesses are capital assets—the power of the $400 billion in union-managed pension funds and the trillions in public-employee pension funds where labor unions can exercise real influence over the patterns of investment.

"It's very much a capitalist project; it's not socialist or revolutionary," says Ronald Blackwell, head of the AFL-CIO's corporate affairs department, which includes its Center on Working Capital and the Office of Investment. "It's a project to improve capitalism through direct intervention."

Blackwell, an economist formerly with the clothing and textile workers union, described the purpose in terms that Warren Buffett would recognize or progressive business-school professors might use themselves. "The core responsibility of a company, from a social point of view, is to create wealth, not to push it around by redistributive policies that benefit one group at the expense of another," Blackwell says. "That is why society allows these organizations to exist, why corporations are given limited liability and legal personality and other privileges not given to other forms of business. Because we decided this form of organization fosters the creation of wealth that we, as a society, need."

Institutional investors, especially the pension funds, "are well designed to provide this important social value that we need—patient capital for long-term wealth creation," he says. "Instead, they are driving things down the low road, following the same destructive practices the capital markets favor. Our vision is to change that. Since it's our money, we would like to realign the private purpose of business, which is making money, with its broader social purpose, which is wealth creation, and to convince pension funds to recognize that real security for retirees requires wealth creation, not short-term gains."

But what exactly is "wealth creation"? Blackwell's meaning goes far beyond financial accumulation and encompasses the larger necessities in life. "I am not talking about money," he said. "I am talking about wealth in the old classical sense—the ability of things to supply human needs. As Keynes said, the economy does nothing more than to secure the material basis for civilization. Nature is an aspect of wealth, in that sense. As environmentalists explain, we are simply not paying the full costs [of consumption] in terms of the true wealth human beings need to live, because we need air and water and also our aesthetic needs. Achieving this social purpose is not the individual businessman's responsibility—he's there to make a buck. I've worked with some of the best in business, and they face very tough choices in the real world. It is society's responsibility to structure things so these social purposes are served." Defining "wealth" in this deeper sense is a fundamental question—central to reforming economic life—and I return to it later.

Blackwell's intellectual framework resonates with the opening premise offered in this book, that society has to find ways to reorder the capitalist system rather than allow capitalism to reorder vital aspects of society, randomly and recklessly. Blackwell believes, as I do, that this is possible to achieve, though he perhaps has fewer illusions about the obstacles since he butts up against them nearly every day.

The first and most formidable obstacle is the ignorance that accompanies passivity, a general ignorance, even in very high places, of the alternative ways of thinking about how capitalism might work. The Center for Working Capital is, above all, an educational campaign aimed at pension-fund trustees, accompanied by the AFL's Office of Investment, that stings the corporate status quo regularly with its focused campaigns. The collapse of Enron and accompanying scandals became a great teaching opportunity, and the AFL organized the facts for reform, pushing politicians to think bigger about corporate governance, the disloyalty of money managers to their customers, the blindness of pension funds to what exactly they are investing in. Labor (ironically, given its reputation) reintroduced the language of prudential and trustworthy financial performance.

Most of its efforts are outside politics, however. It helps organize the shareholder proxy fights and lawsuits stirred up by shareholder activists from churches and issue groups, but the AFL also gets up close and personal with the money managers. The question is asked of them: You are collecting handsome fees for investing labor's money, but are you "worker friendly"? State Street Global Advisers in Boston manages a lot of union pension money but, meanwhile, the firm made itself a leading advocate for privatizing Social Security. After CalPERs and some other major funds indicated they were reviewing this apparent contradiction, State Street announced it was withdrawing from President Bush's Social Security coalition.

The AFL's Office of Investment won a pivotal victory for all mutual-fund investors in early 2003 when it persuaded the SEC to require that mutual funds must disclose how they vote the proxies in corporate-governance shareholder fights. Fidelity and Vanguard, the two largest mutual funds, led the industry in opposing the measure and for good reason. These investment firms regularly vote against the interests of their own rank-and-file investors in order to curry favor with corporate managements. Why? Because the corporations hire them to manage corporate-run pension funds and 401(k) plans. If Fidelity and Vanguard vote against the corporate boards, they will lose lucrative contracts. If their votes against the investors are revealed, they will lose lots of them. Disclosure thus opens up a new front for leveraging corporate behavior and enforcing the fiduciary obligations in finance. When mutual funds continue to vote against their own customers, the AFL and other shareholder activists will target them as a bad place to park your money.

When Goldman Sachs organized a $13 billion bond package for Petro China, the AFL persuaded pension funds worth more than $1 trillion to boycott the sale, based on the oil giant's notorious record with worker repression and rogue regimes. The bond issue shrank to one fourth its original goal, and similar deals were shelved. This is real influence in Wall Street, and other investment houses began consulting Blackwell's shop on how they might avoid opposition. CalPERS and the New York State public employees fund subsequently adopted investment guidelines for emerging markets that require companies to honor the established international principles on worker rights.

Morgan Stanley, the "all-service" financial house, provided one of the most blatant examples of how Wall Street firms betray their clients from organized labor. Three Morgan Stanley analysts issued an advisory on investment strategy in November 2002 urging investors: "Look for the union label . . . and run the other way." Companies with unionized workforces, the firm warned, have rising pension liabilities and health care costs that may hurt their stock prices. "At the risk of encouraging the ghost of Joe Hill to come back and haunt us, we suspect investors should avoid heavily unionized industries today more than usual," the report recommended.

Labor officials were not amused by the droll tone. Scores of union pension funds hire Morgan Stanley for investment advice and park huge sums in the firm's various investment funds. As the labor clients raised protests, Morgan Stanley scurried away from the meaning, drafting a pro-union declaration for the AFL's approval. Nevertheless, Morgan Stanley had issued antisocial advice to corporate executives: if you want a better stock price, avoid pensions and health care benefits for your employees, avoid unions, avoid decent relations with your workers.

The primary target for education and informed pressure, however, are the pension fund trustees, starting with the Taft-Hartley pension funds that are directly supervised by labor and management representatives. The $400 billion invested by these labor-managed funds is the best available leverage for engineering change but, until quite recently, most labor trustees have been as passive and conventional as their corporate counterparts. "The culture of the financial industry is intimidating," Blackwell explains. "The trustees are spirited off to conferences in Hawaii or wherever there's a golf course and the fear of God is put into them on their fiduciary responsibility. On top of that, these trustees are workers, they don't have the time to become experts, or the technical and legal support to question the investing decisions. So we are providing that."

The AFL now publishes its own data for pension trustees, much like the advisory materials from Wall Street firms, only it asks different questions. The "Investment Product Review" examines the Wall Street funds that claim to be "worker friendly" and tells pension trustees which ones are authentic. Its "Key Vote Survey" rates the money managers on how they vote their fund's shareholder proxies on key corporate-governance issues. "If the money managers end up with a low rating, the money doesn't go there," Blackwell says. On scores of issues, from CEO compensation to reforming boards of directors, the center is slowly, patiently, teaching the labor trustees how to become active investors. Eventually, he envisions, labor trustees will be putting some of their investment capital into the localized capital funds that are springing up—guided by the rank-and-file union members on the ground who know the community's problems and what makes sense, what doesn't.

"The capital that belongs to working people should serve their purposes and values; right now it doesn't," Blackwell says. "If this can be accomplished, I envision the labor movement will step forward as an able critic of business as usual. Labor, which has frequently been seen as a narrow special interest, would become an advocate for real development and the whole community—and labor will have real money in its pocket to back up its advocacy."

Blackwell is thus describing a reconception of the labor movement that many labor leaders do not yet grasp, much less endorse. Working men and women would engage large public concerns on three fronts: as employees with real knowledge of the firm; as shareholders with patient capital to invest; as citizens focused foremost on their strongest attachments, family and community. "You can't do this alone," Blackwell says. "You have to have allies, and the allies you get are not going to be built around worker solidarity but around community solidarity."

If all this seems *too* visionary to be plausible, the startling fact is that some of these ideas are already at work in practical and tough-minded situations. "Working capital" is investing directly in some struggling corporations both to turn them around and to alter their social behavior. Aggressive pioneers in the labor movement have connected with a few kindred spirits in finance capital, investment bankers who understand the destructive side of how the present system functions and recognize that there are profitable opportunities for real "wealth creation" if the employees, union and nonunion alike, are brought into the deal. The first successful model for labor's direct investing was fashioned by its most conservative sector: the building trades who overcame years of traditional legal obstacles and won the right to invest their pension money directly in housing and development projects that create jobs for union members.

Together, the capitalists and the workers, not many but a few, are now doing "labor friendly" corporate takeovers—the direct-equity investment deals that used to be the exclusive domain of the wealthy and powerful. Only a handful of such deals exist at present but, as the engineers of these novel ventures demonstrate success, they are attracting more capital from labor pension funds *and* from traditional institutional investors. The returns are very strong, typical of direct-equity investing. It is the operating values that are different. And the "deal flow," as investment bankers call the essential task of spotting new investing opportunities, often originates with local union leaders, people intimately familiar with both the failures and the unrealized potential in business enterprises.

Leo Gerard, now president of the United Steelworkers of America, became an early apostle for mobilizing labor's capital, as he watched small manufacturers in the industrial Midwest decimated either by financial maneuvers or their inability to raise capital. Gerard, who is Canadian, helped engineer Canada's largest worker takeover of a company, Algoma Steel, and many smaller rescues in the United States. He created the Heartland Labor Capital Network that promotes the goal of replicating Canada's successful labor-sponsored investment funds (Quebec's Solidarity Fund, by attracting small investors with tax incentives, has become the largest source of venture capital in the province). "American politics, as regressive as it is at the national level, makes it extremely difficult to do this here," Gerard says. Congress did create new tax subsidies for local venture-capital funds, but the tax breaks go only to large investors, banks, and businesses.

Gerard envisions a growing galaxy of like-minded investment firms that do "control investing" for corporate rehabilitations, with union pension funds putting up some of the capital. In return, the takeover insiders would have to agree at a minimum to honor employees and their rights: to remain neutral on union organizing and guarantee speedy recognition of new locals through card-checking registration by a majority of workers rather than laborious fights over NLRB elections. More substantially, workers should be given a role in decision-making processes and, sometimes, an owner-ship stake with seats on the board. Writing such collateral conditions into direct-investment deals—special terms demanded by major investors—is standard practice. In the language of finance, these are commonly known as "covenants," a biblical term that nicely expresses the social function of shared commitments.

Only a handful of specialized investment firms committed to a "worker-friendly" mode exist now, but more are in development. They do different kinds of deals and work at different levels, from small firms under $250 million to some industrial producers of $2 billion or larger. "If you can create these alternative forms, then you can show that capitalism doesn't have to do the brutal stuff it does," Gerard says. "Then you have a meaningful, articulate voice that can show a different way of doing things—call it social capitalism as opposed to Darwinian capitalism."

Oddly enough, David Stockman, the tenaciously bright young conservative who served as Ronald Reagan's controversial budget director in the 1980s, is leading one of the "labor friendly" firms—the $1.4 billion Heartland Industrial Partners (evidently, he borrowed the name from Gerard). Stockman's venture may startle those who remember his combative style in Washington politics, but he impressed labor people with some of the deals he did for the Blackstone Group of Wall Street. Stockman managed large and successful industrial turnarounds by working with the employees and unions, instead of rolling over them. Since he launched his own firm in 1999, his "buy and build" strategies have focused entirely on restoring midsized manufacturing companies to good health and profitability: auto parts, home furnishings, aerospace components, and other sectors. In all, Heartland manages around $10 billion in industrial companies, probably the largest fund of its kind. The Canadian Pension Plan and Michigan's state employees fund, as well as the steelworkers', are investors, alongside major private players like J. P. Morgan Chase and AIG, the insurance giant. Heartland's literature talks about industrial renewal and shareholder value, not about workers' rights.

"David is buying controlling ownership of these companies, and he's actually turning them around, and he's not doing it by beating the shit out of the workers," Gerard says. "David came to me very early on with his idea, and we decided to support it. David made his presentation to the trustees of the pension fund, labor and management, and asked for $10 million. When he left the room, the board voted to give him $25 million. We signed an agreement with him, and he recognizes there's a role for unions in the workplace, and there'll be no antiunion activities. We've organized some of the facilities that he's purchased." Even the mighty Carlyle Group, run by celebrated conservative Republicans like James A. Baker, has stuck a toe in the same pond by launching a $750-million "worker-friendly" investment fund, perhaps designed to attract capital from the same labor investors.

In social terms, however, the KPS Special Situations Fund is a far more aggressive pioneer: It takes control of failed or abandoned capital assets and attempts to re-create an American corporation with a very different operating ethos. "We invest in a constructive way," says Mike Psaros, one of the KPS partners. "Instead of going in and slashing and burning and screwing people, we go in and work constructively with the employee groups to figure out what's wrong and fix it. Bottom line: I'm a capitalist. I have investors who demand real returns and these companies have to produce or they deserve to fail and they will. We're seen as labor's guys in Wall Street, maybe a little suspect. On the other hand, we're also seen as hardheaded capitalists. We have an investment theory that is really a different view of life."

The "K" in KPS is Eugene Keilen, a former Lazard Frères partner who pioneered the first major employee-ownership buyout—Weirton Steel in 1980. A decade later, Keilen founded his own advisory firm and designed the worker takeovers of United Airlines and Algoma Steel in Canada, among many other novel transactions. Keilen sits on the board of directors in five KPS-controlled companies. His fund's literature is up-front about its union connections and its goal of "meaningful participation from a company's employees in the restructuring and turnaround process." The firm's early takeovers, Psaros estimates, saved 8,000 to 10,000 jobs "that would have been flushed without those deals." KPS (David Shapiro is the third partner) was launched in 1997 with $210 million and is raising capital for a second fund of $350 million. Most of the initial KPS money came not from unions but from major financial players like GE Capital.

"I went to GE in '97 and said, Look, we have this unique relationship with labor," Mike Psaros recalls. "We have this access to a unique and proprietary flow of investment opportunities. We know how to do these deals. We want you to be our lead investor. GE gave us the use of their name and $10 million." KPS hears about potential deals ahead of others because the "deal flow" comes mainly from labor leaders in industrial unions—paper, steel, autos, machinists, and others—who are trying to save companies and jobs. "We get calls from unions every day, and in ninety-nine percent of the cases there is nothing we can do," Psaros says. "The company is too screwed up, too far gone, makes the wrong product, and so forth. But we also get very interesting opportunities."

KPS is always a control investor, with total command of the board and management, though it sometimes invites in major coinvestors, including the employees. "What we would do as investment bankers, we would go in and take a carcass, a failed enterprise, and try to figure out whether, if you did a bunch of stuff, you could create a viable company," Psaros says. "In some cases, there is a going concern buried under too much debt, an awful management team, a horrible cost structure, usually all of the above. At the KPS fund, we're doing essentially the same work, except now we're doing it as the capitalists. If the deal makes sense, we have the money, we have the bank relationships, the financial resources to do it."

Psaros himself may be thought of as a "working-class capitalist." He was a teenager in Weirton, West Virginia, two decades ago when Gene Keilen's employee-ownership plan saved the steel mill and 10,000 jobs. Psaros remembers going door-to-door with a tin cup collecting quarters to support the workers' takeover effort. "My father worked at the mill and died at an early age," he says. "I watched this guy come in from New York City who quite literally saved our way of life, our town. I said to myself, One day I want to do that—this kid from Weirton who'd never heard of an investment banker." Psaros studied at Georgetown University, majored in finance, and went to Wall Street, where he teamed up with his investment-banker hero.

Blue Ridge Paper Products in western North Carolina is one result: a major U.S. producer of milk and juice cartons and paper cups, with 2,000 employees at six processing plants and the main pulp mill in Canton, North Carolina. Blue Ridge has commanding market share; KPS created this company out of capital assets that Champion Paper was abandoning. During the late nineties, Champion deliberately shrank itself to what investors call the "core competency" so the company would look more attractive to potential buyers. The strategy worked brilliantly for its shareholders. Champion was acquired by International Paper, which paid an enormous premium over the stock price. But the Carolina paper factories were imperiled—viable assets in which Champion had invested more than $600 million.

A Wall Street auction to sell them failed to find any buyers. KPS bought them for $200 million, alerted by an urgent plea from Bob Smith, a vice president of PACE, the Papermakers, Atomic, and Chemical Employees union. "Bob Smith called and said these plants have a right to exist and he was right," Psaros says.

The KPS fund, with GE Capital as coinvestor, put up $35 million in equity capital and borrowed $200 million to acquire 55 percent—control—while the employees, union and non-union, own the other 45 percent through an employee-ownership trust. To finance their stake, the employees agreed to take a painful 15 percent reduction in overall compensation. Workers have four elected directors sitting on the eleven-member board. They are embarked on the promising but very difficult process of changing industrial culture. "It's going to take a lot of time," Psaros says, "but we are transforming what I would call a Stalinist, reactionary, stifling, autocratic, oppressive culture that has existed in those plants for more than seventy years. We are creating a participative, communicative, twenty-first-century culture where the company relies on people's brains more than it does on their backs."

Bob Smith, the union vice president, spoke in the same terms. "For many, many years, American management of labor has been totally authoritarian," Smith says. "You come in and go to work and you check your brain at the door and just do what you're told. Our people were accustomed to that and accepted the adversary culture. Do what you're told and don't worry about whether it's right or wrong, the inspector will catch it, the supervisor will make any final judgments about what has to be corrected. The culture needs to be, Hey, I'm part owner, I've got part of the responsibility for making this operation survive. The quality of the product is no longer the company as such. The company is now partly me."

Cultural transformation advanced fairly quickly in the smaller conversion plants, where paperboard is fashioned into printed cartons and cups, but has proved far more difficult at the main pulp mill. "Many of our people," Smith says, " have grown habituated to, I'll do my eight hours and I don't want to worry about anything else. Then you've got managers on the other side who don't accept change very readily. They talk a good story, but they don't really want to share authority."

This familiar reality in American industrial life, however, does give way to a more productive enterprise—and greater personal satisfaction—as people on both sides of the divide learn to change themselves. Blue Ridge Paper became a more effective and profitable company rather quickly. During its first two and a half years, more than $100 million of expanded cash flow was reinvested back into modernizing the company, buying new machinery, and acquiring another packaging company that expands Blue Ridge's market share. It now makes every Minute Maid carton and has picked up the Florida Natural account. "It's not dumb luck," Psaros says. "It's not just buying cheap and waiting for the market to turn around. Our business is making a series of affirmative decisions—there could be thousands—to turn the company around."

That goal requires the Wall Street insiders to maintain an unrelenting intimacy with the company they own. "In a company like this, the board of directors is almost a ceremonial formality," Psaros says. "We do have regular quarterly meetings, but we're on the phone with our management teams every single day. We're on the phone with the unions, our employees, all the time. We know the leaders of all the union locals in all our plants and, if they have an issue, they give us a ring. It's a huge difference from your plain-vanilla public company that has thousands, if not millions, of stockholders. What it does is, it makes people accountable. It makes me accountable, makes management accountable, makes our employees accountable."

Accountability extends beyond the company to the surrounding community. Paper mills are traditionally notorious polluters, and the Canton mill sits on the Pigeon River, a mountain stream that is a favorite of canoers and hikers. Blue Ridge Products has reduced acidity and removed coloration in the water at an accelerated pace, Bob

Smith says. Champion was not indifferent to the environmental problems, he explained, but its corporatewide approach was slower because it inevitably focused more broadly and was more distant from the local concerns. "What we did is go to the Pigeon River Association and the Sierra Club and say, Look, we live here too," Smith says. "We understand hunting and fishing, the canoeing. We're going to do everything we can to keep it clean and clean it up more, but we need you to help us, not fight us, to be able to get things done. They have assisted us in many situations to get things done, then other situations they've come around and said, Hey, you need to do more. We've gotten color in the water down to where in many cases the sample below the mill is better than above the mill. We've got fish swimming right where effluent comes out, and fish above the mill where they never were before."

The KPS objective, nonetheless, is delivering a splendid return on capital for its investors. Business investments are full of risks; no promises made. But, if things go well, KPS might be expected to "exit" its ownership in four or five years and sell its 55 percent stake to the stock market or other investors, including the employees. "When a firm like ours invests $35 million, our target objective is to compound the capital at an internal rate of return of 25 to 35 percent a year," Psaros explains. Translated into dollars, the $35 million initial investment yields, say, $125 million at sale. The secret is leverage and control. Because KPS borrowed most of the capital for the purchase, it captures all of the appreciated value of the asset, just as any homeowner would when selling a house.

Blue Ridge's 2,000 worker-owners, who accepted a 15 percent giveback for their 45 percent stake of ownership, could decide to cash in too, collecting an equivalent reward of around $100 million. Or the employees might exercise the covenant that gives them first option to buy out KPS's stake and they would own 100 percent of the company. The downside risk is that there will be no buyers—either the paper market will still be lousy at that point or the company isn't performing well or the bids from other investors are too cheap to accept. For better or worse, this risk is at least borne equitably by everyone invested in the firm. Like others, Bob Smith worries about the downside, but he is optimistic. "If we manage the process, when the market goes up, I can see our people making 30 percent plus, maybe as much as 50 percent or more, if things go right," he says. "Even if the market's still shallow, I still see us making a minimum of 20 or 30 percent. So long as people will keep drinking milk and juice, Blue Ridge has the potential to be one of the best assets in the world." The employees, Smith hopes, will decide not to exit, but to buy the whole company.

The essential meaning of Blue Ridge, however, is not about how to save a paper mill or how one can get wealthier by taking risks. The larger meaning is about finance capital's power to advance society's values. Blue Ridge Paper Products is a relatively simple example in which targeted investing has been employed to support "a different view of life," as Mike Psaros put it. In this regard, the techniques of direct-equity investing represent largely unexplored territory since, outside of labor's ranks, very few social reformers have tried to use capital in a tightly directed manner to gain social leverage within capitalism. The techniques are neutral in themselves. Their purposes depend upon who takes charge, on what they expect in the way of returns—financial and nonfinancial—and what they demand as covenants.

One can imagine many variations on the social theme, as people and groups learn how to mobilize and focus their capital for unconventional objectives. Rescuing industrial assets and manufacturing jobs, important as it is, represents only a small corner of investment activity, and the task of reaching into successful corporations with social covenants demanded by the investors is obviously far more difficult. So is the challenge of financing innovative start-up firms that are willing to accept more ambitious social commitments in exchange for patient capital. Given the extraordinary variety of hybridized financial instruments that Wall Street devises, the potential for elaborating specialized interventions is largely unknown. Conceivably, for instance, environmentalists could organize targeted capital investments in major corporations to provide financing for the technological changes in production systems needed to protect nature—the ecological reforms business and finance have been reluctant to make. The returns on targeted eco-capital would be based upon the improved efficiencies these technologies bring to the company. Society's return would be a less destructive industrial system.

So long as the risks are pursued with tough-minded self-discipline, there is nothing in the operating rules of capitalism to prevent any of these departures from the status quo, whether they involve community-loyal investment funds or pressuring pension-fund trustees to alter their investment priorities or punishing the disloyal Wall Street firms or taking control of corporations by making direct-equity investments. Indeed, these are routine practices within the system, employed every day on behalf of narrower objectives and self-interested values. The financial power of society awaits the rise of tough-minded social inventors, investing risk takers with the courage to take control of their own money.

# 5

## Consuming the Future

THE "American consumer" has become such a hallowed institution, it is easy to forget that the great feast of mass consumption is a rather recent phenomenon in human history. It was invented by the twentieth century and made broadly available only during the last fifty years. The plentitude of goods, the exhausting variety of choices, may be regarded as American capitalism's highest achievement because it does resemble a material fulfillment of the nation's egalitarian values. Everyone gets to shop. Even the very poor attempt in forlorn ways to experience the bountiful prosperity visible to them on television. Of course, one's choices are starkly delimited by the inequality of means among the consumers, but everyone is at least free to participate in the endless desires (and the burden of stressful longings). As consumers, we are said to be king. Our mood swings are tracked closely by economists; business people claim we rule over their decisions; while social critics describe acquisitiveness as the national addiction. People from afar, living in other societies, tend to be aghast at our excesses, yet are also enticed.

Someday hence, a century from now or perhaps much sooner,

people will look back at us and ask: What were they thinking? Did Americans not recognize that their unbounded accumulation of things was doomed by its own reckless wastefulness? Didn't they realize that the products and processes of mass consumption were, in a literal sense, gradually killing nature? Americans are beginning, unevenly but generally, to absorb an awareness of the ecological limits and to accept that things must change. The ethos of environmentalism is genuine and growing still stronger, but it is also very difficult to fulfill. Transforming this dimension of American capitalism—disarming the relentless propensity to colonize and destroy the natural world—is surely the highest priority among social objectives, since failure to act promises severe and perhaps irremediable consequences for the future, the unborn generations, and Earth itself. This great goal is also, inescapably, the most radical because, ultimately, it will require a fundamental reordering of the modern industrial economy and how it functions. It also means altering some deeply held habits embedded in American life.

The darkening shadow cast across the mass consumption economy has many threatening expressions: the toxic substances found in living room sofas or personal computers; the relentless mountain of wasted materials that is returned to the earth as useless, often poisonous deposits; the reckless consumption of hydrocarbon fuels with well-known destructive side effects; the consumption of ecosystems for industrial uses or dream houses in the country. No one can say how soon the accumulating damage to nature may reach critical mass—a century from now, a generation or two?—but the scientists most familiar with the facts tend to express the greatest urgency. I will not try to reargue all of the contentious scientific issues, such as global warming, but offer one example to speak for the broader reality. It is the accelerating loss of biodiversity—the "sixth extinction"—for which we the people are evidently responsible.

The *National Geographic,* not usually a voice of doom, reported in its millennial issue that some 50 percent of the world's flora and fauna could be on a path to extinction within a hundred years. And everything is affected: fish, birds, insects, plants and mammals. By [Professor Stuart] Pimm's count, 11 percent of birds, or 1,100 species out of the world's nearly 10,000, are on the edge of extinction; it's doubtful that the majority of these 1,100 will live beyond the end of the next century. . . . A team of respected botanists recently reported that one in eight plants is at risk of becoming extinct.

Such a rate of extinction [the *Geographic* explained] has occurred only five times since complex life emerged and each time it was caused by a catastrophic natural disaster [the last great episode occurred 65 million years ago with the meteor crash that eliminated the dinosaurs]. . . . Today the earth is again in extinction's grip—but the cause has changed. The sixth extinction is not happening because of some external force. It is happening because of us, *Homo sapiens,* an 'exterminator species,' as one scientist has characterized humankind.

This cataclysm does not necessarily predict an end-of-the-world scenario, or the end of human existence, but Professor Pimm raised the issue of moral responsibility: "I think we must ask ourselves if this is really what we want to do to God's creation. To drive it to extinction? Because extinction really is irreversible."[1]

Beyond the science, beyond the economics, the ecological crisis is, above all, a test of character—the American character. We begin with America's conflicted attitudes toward nature and economic progress, because the decisive question may be whether this society can alter long-held sensibilities, and fast enough to avert disastrous outcomes. The new challenge—taking responsibility for the fate of the Earth— is a threshold unlike any other the country has faced previously. We must change capitalism, but also change ourselves.

It is essential to understand that the collision with nature began in American life long before the advent of the automobile and other

155

conveniences, began in fact when the first English settlers arrived on the *Mayflower* and set out to develop the region named New England. Their success provided the formative imprint for who we would become as a people. Their triumph is our inheritance. They encountered a "New Eden" of natural abundance and swiftly made "more" from it: trees, land, wildlife converted to productive uses, commercial trade, and the growing surpluses of stored wealth now known as "capital."

Two profoundly different economic systems thus met in irreconcilable conflict. The indigenous peoples who already inhabited New England lived comfortably enough by following the natural cycles of the seasons, hunting or foraging, planting a few basic crops, fashioning their simple tools and dwellings. Indian clans and tribes accumulated very little in possessions, either as artifacts or surplus food, because their sustenance depended on easy mobility. People converged when and where the salmon were spawning or the wild fruit was ripe; they dispersed across wider territory to hunt game in autumn; they moved homes or villages to new locations when fields were exhausted and cleared new fields, letting nature slowly restore the old ones.

The first settlers often remarked on the idyllic simplicity of how these native people lived, but also on their supposed poverty and laziness, especially the Indian men who seemed to work only when they really needed to. Native Americans, the Puritans decided, failed to make use of all that God had provided them, and this view became the standard justification for pushing them aside (a moral argument repeatedly invoked across the next three centuries of continental expansion). America's original ecological conflict and its consequences are recounted with remarkable depth and dispassion in *Changes in the Land* by historian William Cronon. The author avoids the usual lamentations but does observe: "If English visitors thought it a paradox that Indians seemed to live like paupers in a landscape of great natural wealth, then the problem lay with English eyesight rather than any real Indian poverty."[2]

In 1600, the Indian population in all New England was only between 70,000 and 100,000 people, Cronon estimated, and 80 percent of those lived in the southernmost states where agriculture augmented hunting and fishing. Their nature-based economy was viable, in other words, only if population densities remained quite low. Today, the six New England states support around 14 million inhabitants (far more if one includes New York), which gives a fair measure of how productive the region has become since. The comparison also explains why the Indians' natural economy was essentially doomed once English settlers began arriving in greater numbers. The newcomers were armed with advanced tools and methods (including guns), and they had a very different understanding of nature. The English set out to subdue it.

The new Americans found magnificent stands of giant white pines, four to six feet in diameter, 120 to 200 feet tall or even taller, and these ancient trees were felled to provide ship masts of unprecedented height for the Royal Navy and commercial ships (a technological breakthrough, so to speak, that amplified English naval power and spawned the first great shipyards along the New England coastline). Beavers became pelts in the fur trade and were made into hats, their ponds drained to become the immensely fertile, easy-to-cultivate fields known as "beaver meadows." As the wildlife receded rapidly, grazing livestock replaced game in the food supply and, as domesticated animals increased in number, they soon required fenced pastures, then complicated laws of trespass as well as property damage lawsuits against the owners of wayward hogs and cattle. These new rules were recorded in writing—deeds, contracts, ordinances—and remain encoded in American law.

The conquering spirit of the settlers had theological foundations. Many Indian cultures, then and now, tell an origin story that typically recounts how the people first emerged from the bowels of the earth—born from the body of their mother—and Indian people thus inherited complex kinship relationships with other living species as well as with the spirits of rocks, soil, water, and sky. The Judaic-Christian origin story, recorded in the Book of Genesis, describes a very different premise for human existence. Mankind was created by God in his own image and awarded "dominion over the fish of the sea, and over the fowl of the air and over the cattle, and over the earth and every creeping thing that creepeth on the earth." After expulsion from the Garden of Eden, man was commanded to "be fruitful and multiply and replenish the earth and subdue it." Amid thistles and thorns, he would have to wrest his livelihood from the earth by "the sweat of thy brow," then face death. "Dust thou art, and unto dust shalt thou return." The biblical version sounds grim by comparison, but is also empowering.[3]

Dominion over nature was (and still is) enforced through the concepts of English property law that the first settlers introduced. Wildlife belonged in principle to the king and, by extension, the colonial governments he established. Ownership of land typically was distributed through royal grants to settlers (and swiftly generated the country's first real estate speculators). Natural resources including game accompanied title to the land, though an owner might dispose of trees or minerals separately, selling them to a developer. Property often was "purchased" from the native people (and also expropriated by force), but even the land sales became a bitter source of misunderstanding and bloody conflict, since the Indians did not share the English definition of property.

To Native Americans, ownership was a much more limited idea, conditioned by practical needs and uses. When they "sold" a tract of land to English settlers, they did not assume they were forfeiting all future access to its streams and wildlife or that the transfer was necessarily permanent. Native people "owned" what they had made with their own hands—tools, canoes, dwellings—but, as Cronon explained, "there was little sense of either accumulation or of exclusive use. Goods were owned because they were useful and, if they ceased to be so or were needed by someone else, they could easily be given away." Land "belonged" to the village that occupied it or the people who had cleared a field for crops, but others might continue to use it too, depending on the seasonal abundance and common understandings of reciprocal privileges. "Property rights, in other words, shifted with ecological use," Cronon wrote.

Their system, formally known as "usufruct," premises ownership on one's current use, but without necessarily conveying exclusive or permanent claims. I once heard a latter-day environmentalist summarize the usufruct concept as "take what you need, leave the rest for others." That maxim turns capitalism on its head, of course, since the accumulation of surpluses is central to its forward-looking cycles of investing that promise advancement. The Indians' open-ended sense of ownership sounds impossibly altruistic to modern sensibilities, but they did not regard their doctrine as pious idealism. It was the practical means of insuring abundance for the future. If nobody hoarded surpluses or abused the natural sources of sustenance, there would be enough for all, more or less in perpetuity.

Their lean consumption, including an acceptance of occasional scarcity, is a powerful rebuke to modern excesses, and makes a telling contrast with the ecological dilemma facing industrial-based prosperity. Our system generates overflowing abundance (including the mounds of waste and unsold surpluses), but the plenty is achieved by steadily degrading, even destroying natural systems that are the source of life itself. Essentially, modern capitalism borrows from the future what it cannot repay. Nature is vast but it is not infinite. Thus, as a matter of logic, the present industrial system cannot continue to function in this way without eventually threatening a catastrophic exhaustion of life-supporting Mother Earth. Mass-consumption capitalism, in other words, must come to terms with the larger meaning of "take what you need, leave the rest for others" or else eventually fail as an economic system. Americans, as we shall see, are developing some plausible and promising means for achieving such a reconciliation with nature and without reverting to subsistence living. But will we?

There is not a lot in our national past to predict a peaceful resolution, at least not without some harrowing crisis to force the issue.

In colonial New England, the ecological conflict was finally resolved only by brutal wars of subjugation, as savage as any fought later in the West. The newcomers won; their economics swept away the native version. This same story was subsequently played out repeatedly across the American continent, reelaborating the same principles and practices of production and commerce, usually accompanied by the same conflicts and tragedies (including the obscene economics of owning human beings as chattel property). Yet, despite the dark facts and irreconcilable conflicts in our past, the national history also tells a saga of triumph, of people overcoming vast obstacles to make a better life for themselves, revealing heroic qualities in themselves that also became elements of the American character.

Above all, they were brave, often reckless risk takers. Hardworking, stubbornly optimistic, practical, and innovative, the pioneers set out to alter the future in their own self-interest, yet they were altruistic in their pursuit of common purposes. These qualities and others are revealed in the thousands of local and regional histories, usually written by amateur historians to preserve the pioneer experience, books that are still passed along in families to later generations. One example is *A History of Dickinson County, Iowa,* published in 1902, that recounts how the tall-grass prairie of northwestern Iowa was transformed into some of the most productive farmland in the world.

The author, R. A. Smith, a pioneer himself, began with the "Spirit Lake Massacre" in the winter of 1857, when a remnant band of embittered Lakota Sioux swept through the county's first scattered settlement, murdered forty-two white people, mutilated corpses, and burned cabins. A rescue party from Fort Dodge came out through deep snow to bury the dead and guard against further attacks. Some stayed on, Smith among them, to take up the challenge of developing a prosperous civilization from empty vastness.[4]

The astonishing fact is how swiftly and ingeniously they succeeded. At the outset, the settlers were mostly young men who lived in dank, sod-covered shanties and defended their first corn crops against clouds of ravaging blackbirds. Living on the Iowa frontier was dangerous—another terrible massacre occurred a few years later in nearby Minnesota—and it would be some years before families dared to build their homes out on the open prairie.

Meanwhile, they organized to drain some three thousand acres of prairie swamp and slough (the habitat protected now as wetlands). They took up homestead claims and surveyed town lots, built a fort, a post office, and a small hotel. Two kilns were constructed to make bricks for the new courthouse and first commercial buildings. A sawmill produced lumber for the first fishing boats that plied the chain of small and beautiful glacial lakes (the Sioux had regarded Spirit Lake as sacred waters). Two-masted sailboats appeared soon after, followed by trim little steamboats. Trestle bridges were built to span the narrows connecting the lakes. A clever drawbridge that lowered to let boats through didn't work, so it was replaced by a swing bridge.

Within two or three years of the massacre, Dickinson County had its first doctor, its first regular church services, a mail route, a community-built log schoolhouse, and three literary societies (Shakespeare lived on the frontier too). The county was also engulfed by legal controversies over faulty land titles and broken contracts. Who really owned the newly reclaimed prairie acreage? Who must pay for the new bridges? Lawyers came out from Sioux City to argue the claims. Townships were organized, supervisors elected. The state distributed free seed corn to plant first-plowed prairie.

A decade later, the town of Spirit Lake existed in a handsome commercial block of brick storefronts and the increasingly substantial houses built around the lake. The town had its first bank, shoe store, dry goods store, drugstore, newspaper, a billiard room, and a Masons hall (even a roller rink a few years later). A "pioneer insurance worker" also sold farm machinery. Progress was derailed by the scourge of grasshoppers that swarmed across Iowa in the 1870s, but took off again when the Burlington railroad finally reached Spirit Lake (its construction subsidized by the towns whose voters approved a special railroad tax levy). Three other rail lines appeared in Dickinson County, competing to haul its bountiful grain harvests to urban markets.

The Burlington railroad also built a fabulous resort hotel, the Orleans, at Spirit Lake. It was the largest of many around the lakes, with two hundred rooms, a grand veranda, and nine steeples flying banners, and equipped with American Express and Western Union offices, even a telephone. In one generation, it seems, Dickinson County had progressed from primeval grasslands to a popular vacation spot for newly affluent Americans (and remains so today). The pace of change seems as dizzying as anything in modern life. On July 4, 1895, the county dedicated a tall granite obelisk as memorial to the murdered settlers.

R. A. Smith described all this with understated midwestern pride, careful to avoid boosterish exaggerations and mindful of what was lost. A chapter entitled "Disappearance of the Game" recounted—and meticulously dated—each of the county's final encounters with buffalo, elk, and deer, plus the elimination of foxes, coyotes, prairie wolves, and bobcats. The last herd of elk was sighted in 1871, fourteen years after the massacre, as it moved south along the Sioux River. Scattered by gunfire, the elk fled downriver until "relays of hunters slew to the very last one this fleeing remnant of noble game." Smith likewise reported that "the last Indian killed in Iowa" was a horse thief shot in Dickinson County in 1861. "Of course, there have been many instances of dishonesty and bad faith in dealing with the Indians," he acknowledged, "but that doesn't change the main proposition that in the nature of things it was never intended that this vast continent should be shut off from civilization in order that a few tribes of blood-thirsty savages should be undisturbed." The Puritan rationale held in Iowa too.

Smith wrote reverentially of the early years of struggle. "Men don't know what they can do until they are tested," he said. But he was surprisingly ambivalent about the new life that had been accomplished. "It is better, far better, to have railroads, telegraphs, and telephones, street cars and electric lights, prosperous communities," he wrote. Also, "People are substituting ease, comfort, and luxury for the battle and struggle of the early days. But many will remember with a peculiar regret the really happy lives they lived in the midst of the danger, exposure, and toil of the pioneer days." Furthermore, he observed, "those who suffered most in the toils, labors, and privations of the early days were not the ones to reap the reward of their early sacrifices. The ideal pioneer is not a money maker. . . . The liberal and almost careless openhearted and openhanded hospitality which is ever his most prominent characteristic precludes the possibility of accumulating wealth." The author's mixed feelings toward "progress" sound very American, indeed modern.

So who are we? I have dwelt upon these facts from the past in order to get to that question. Are we the openhearted, inventive, hardworking pioneers remembered by Smith? Or simply an acquisitive people whose desires for greater comfort in life, even luxury, have often been fulfilled by brute force or by appropriating something of value from others, especially from the future? Surely, as history indicates, we are imbued with qualities of both. The question of character is whether we can change.

The American narrative continued onward for many subsequent chapters with repeated conflict and accomplishments even more fantastic. The Great American Desert beyond the hundredth meridian was settled and made to bloom. Rivers were diverted and pumped over mountains to water new cities thriving along the western coastline, where people would eventually manufacture airplanes, movies, computers. Millions came and prospered, building the new life and reiterating those twin American qualities—daring innovation and heedless destructiveness. We are ennobled by the story. Except for recent arrivals, we also are implicated in the consequences.

Progress has taken a perverse turn in Iowa. The harvests are far more bountiful today, thanks to the ingenious machines and applied chemistry of capital-intensive agriculture, but the crops are actually *too* bountiful to be profitable for most farmers. The U.S. system produces more foodstuffs than people can consume or farmers anywhere can sell, so the government keeps them afloat each year with $20 billion or more in federal subsidies. Alongside the surpluses of corn and soybeans, Iowa farmers used to raise hogs but are being driven out of that market by the notorious new "hog factories": huge windowless barns where thousands of animals are raised in dense (and cruel) confinement, fed by clockwork mechanisms, their waste flushed into acres of nearby manure lagoons (one such factory with 5,000 hogs is located at Spirit Lake). The control of food production also has been concentrated. A handful of giant corporations dominate grain and livestock markets and "contract" with the once independent farmers to produce according to the company's "more efficient" terms, take it or leave it. Farmers liken the new arrangement to sharecropping on their own land. Ag economists compare it to the centralized command-and-control imposed by collectivized agriculture in the Soviet Union.

Meanwhile, the Iowa prairie has become an unnatural swamp of migrating chemicals and other pollutants. Iowa experienced 152 fish kills in lakes and rivers during the last six years (5.7 million dead fish, a loss not counted on balance sheets since the fish were not "owned" by the producers of the pollution). Fertilizers run off fields; the huge manure lagoons leak or break down. Iowa's cities now regard farmers as a threat to their health, since water supplies are frequently endangered. Some pollutants migrate in the food itself—antibiotics in chickens, growth hormones in beef, chemical residues on vegetables—and are ingested by unwitting consumers. Biologists worry about the rapid buildup of pathogens and chemicals in the food chain; nobody really knows what the long-term effects will be. Meanwhile, the great legacy bestowed by the ancient grasslands—

Iowa's deep, black topsoil—is migrating steadily into the Mississippi River system. After a century of industrialized farming, Iowa's topsoil is half gone.[5]

What changed in Iowa changed all of the country—the industrialization of production. That great breakthrough in capitalism became the wellspring of modern mass consumption. Other industrialized sectors, much like agriculture, delivered profound and irresistible improvements in life for people of all classes, but also a greater destructiveness toward nature, in new and more elusive forms. The refrigerator, the automobile, jet aircraft, electronic communications: Mass-produced goods eliminated many of the numbing routines of daily work (especially for women), shrank the physical distances, and expanded the reach of our minds, what people see and experience. New conveniences became new necessities. Former luxuries became everyday grace notes. I do not suggest we should learn to do without them or that we would have to do so in order to save the Earth.

The industrial transformation also effectively decoupled consumption from production. In most respects, it is now quite rare for people to consume what they produce. Instead, they buy things made by workers elsewhere in complex production systems—goods that are cheaper and usually better than the homemade. People no longer bake their daily bread (except maybe as a hobby) or slaughter the chicken for Sunday dinner. If they like, they don't even cook the dinner. This particular division of labor generated an immense liberation of time—more time to do something else—but it also mystified the production processes for many Americans too distant to know much about how things are made or where (and contemporary economic pressures also have reclaimed some of the free time from people's lives). Industrialization, less obviously, reduced personal autonomy—the capacity of citizens to be self-directed, responsible actors in their own lives. They went to work for large employers. They lost some measure of control and self-reliance. As I suggested earlier with my grandfather McClure's resistance, people saw their personal skills systematized and converted into portable commodities (an experience familiar to displaced machinists or middle managers in recent years).

More to the point, the major "producers" in the emerging industrialized society were not people at all, but the large and private business organizations called corporations. Corporations grew in girth with the technological breakthroughs of the late nineteenth century and became national in scope as the new railroads connected markets from east to west (just as globalization rides on the new information technologies shrinking the world). The peculiar dominance of these legally privileged business organizations is a central fact of modern American life, peculiar because the corporation's operating structure is, by design, undemocratic, and its internal decisions purposely insulated from public scrutiny and social accountability.

Citizens who try to take responsibility for the ecological destruction encounter a discouraging paradox. While they are exalted as consumers, told that their preferences are the ruling influence in commerce, they don't have a lot of power in the matter. The decision making that will determine the fate of the Earth mostly lies beyond their reach, sheltered within the private corporations. The American consumer may choose to "shop green," and some do, but in the mass market a conscientious individual's choices seem as impotent as selling one's stock after the price has collapsed. Thus, consumers are slyly scapegoated by the business lore, depicted as the all-powerful "marketplace" whose desires cannot be denied, blamed for wrongful decisions they did not make. Corporations themselves also manufacture the desires, yet they resist inquiries into the true content of what they are selling.

So who are we? Despite their weak position, people do still mobilize collectively to defend nature, and sometimes they prevail. I think they are also the new pioneers, among the people who still believe they can change the outcome with pluck and hard work.

Here is my notion of patriotic obligation: Americans will not become fully realized as a people—as a society that fulfills its potential—until we learn, in the spirit of Walt Whitman, to embrace our contradictions, all of them. We embrace the striving, creative accomplishments, but also accept that the grave transgressions and irreconcilable conflicts are inextricably part of ourselves. Instead of pretending to be uniquely virtuous and innocent, as the cheap patriots claim, we learn to see ourselves whole. Because the errors and contradictions are not past, but remain embedded in American life, if not in every citizen, and certainly in the economic and social systems we have inherited. We may make amends for the past, but we cannot undo it. Our main responsibility is to the future. With self-knowledge, we can change the story.

On this new frontier, American ingenuity and risk taking collaborate to take on the destructiveness and disarm it. Our capacity for improvising new realities out of mere hope and hard work becomes the engine for working out new economic relationships with nature (as well as dismantling other debilitating confinements of modern capitalism). The American idea of "progress" takes on deeper dimensions, new meanings beyond the familiar accumulation of "more." Doubters will say that the country is already too settled in long-held habits, that the pioneering spirit died out long ago, drowned in the overflowing abundance. But that is not the country I see, and it is also not our history.

The distinctive quality of American life—what sets us apart from so many other cultures—is our free-wheeling capacity for self-invention. In personal lives and in families, Americans have the space and opportunity (also the nerviness) to change the script now and then, to go off in unpredicted directions, changing our inherited identities and sometimes even our names. The inventive spirit is most visible in American cultural life, the quality in American rock 'n' roll and movies that has charmed the world. In economic affairs and politics the pursuit of transcendental change is far more difficult and usually torturously slow. The story of social progress is not a smooth line, upward and onward. Still, America is far too young, as a nation, to to be yet fully formed. People are still experimenting, exploring.

The best evidence for social optimism is the rise of the environmental ethic itself. This profound shift in American values first emerged a century ago and has steadily gathered force despite the undertow of history and economics pulling in an opposite direction. People do wish to take responsibility for nature, at least to prevent the wanton despoilation. A broad popular consensus has long existed for stronger environmental laws, reflected in a Gallup poll in March 2002 that found 70 percent in support of the environmental movement, and only 5 percent unsympathetic. Even more astonishing, 19 percent described themselves as "active participants" in the movement—nearly one fifth of the population. A narrow majority (54 percent) said protecting the environment has first priority, even if it risks reducing economic gain.

The environmental ethic, however, also has evolved and broadened its objectives. The first stage began in the latter half of the nineteenth century when people began to recognize (as R. A. Smith described) that the original American wilderness was fast disappearing—wild animals and wild places obliterated by economic progress. The political response was the conservation movement, to preserve remnants of wilderness in protected sanctuaries before it was too late. The second stage—contemporary environmentalism—confronted industrial pollution and continues to push for stronger regulatory laws. With few exceptions, however, environmental laws are directed at the threats to human health, not to nature at large, and only then if the pollution qualifies under difficult tests of scientific proof and cost-benefit analysis, in which human life is reduced to bizarre calculations of its supposed economic value, then weighed against the presumed costs of saving life. Despite the popular consensus, the political system generally sets low standards and permits weak enforcement.

The third stage—the ecological perspective—refocuses the problem beyond human beings alone to include the Earth's natural systems and the future of other living things. The "whole Earth" is victimized, in fact imperiled, by modern economic life, ecologists explain, so it would be historically irresponsible—actually immoral—not to confront the larger scope of the destruction. This new understanding raises the stakes enormously. Its logic suggests the ultimate goal must be a zero-damage, zero-waste system, eliminating the many forms of irreversible destruction to the natural world by refashioning production and consumption to mimic nature itself. In effect, industry would reclaim and reuse its materials much the way nature recycles all waste into new food and its ecosystems cleanse and restore air and water. Industry would have to discontinue many toxic components now in standard use and realign its processes in harmony with regenerative ecosystems instead of steadily degrading them.

The imperative, one might say, is to develop an industrial-age ethos that parallels the Native Americans' commitment to sustaining the Earth, eliminating modern excess and wastefulness in the spirit of "take what you need, leave the rest for others." Society would do so as a matter of practical self-interest, but also as its shared obligation to the future. In addition to ingenuity and daring, this great goal obviously requires patience—lots of it—since it necessarily envisions a long era of discovery and innovation, false starts and corrections, toward a distant purpose. Yet the urgency is tangible. We do not have three hundred years to work it out.

To make the prospects for ecological change more visible, I will examine the problem along three broad fronts, each enormously difficult but not impossible, as some people are already demonstrating. The first challenge is the revaluation of costs and prices; that is, identifying the true costs of products and production when ecological and social damage are taken into the accounting. This is not an exercise in bookkeeping, but involves practical efforts to challenge the false valuations of standard economics and enterprise, then to push the system to incorporate true cost pricing in consumption and production much as social investors demand the consideration of broader values in stock prices. The second great task is the redesign and reengineering of industry itself. Inventing the techniques to eliminate wastes and poisons from products and processes, to develop the closed-loop recycling that mimics nature, is likewise a formidable goal, but some early accomplishments suggest grounds for surprising optimism.

The third challenge, perhaps the most difficult, is confronting the exaggerated social power of the modern corporation. Behind their scientific and economic objections, corporate organizations have the greatest capacity to resolve the ecological problem, as well as the other concerns surrounding work, wealth, and democracy in which corporations are centrally implicated. The corporation sits astride these public questions with its narrow sense of purpose and disdain for social accountability and responds with blunt resistance or ephemeral commitments at best. So I will inquire in this chapter and the next into how this privileged form of business organization might be altered to better serve society. The ecological crisis will not be ultimately resolved, I suggest, until Americans also reinvent the corporation.

IN SOME WAYS, the environmental struggle resembles a low-grade civil war spread across the American countryside, in which thousands of scattered local skirmishes are fought over questions of economic value. The conflicts are sometimes neighbor against neighbor, often the community against outsiders, and with rare exceptions nonviolent. People will expend enormous personal energy to save a river or a forest, even swampy wetlands. Faced with intrusive threats to landscape they love, people may suddenly turn into hyperconscientious citizens who study the regulatory rules and take on various goliaths. In most instances, they would probably not describe their efforts as economics—revaluing the true cost of things—but in a larger sense that is what they are trying to accomplish. Consumers, joined sometimes by substantial civic organizations, collectively are attempting, case by case, to force-feed ecological values into the everyday pricing practices of business. When business ignores or resists them, as it typically does, the skirmishers develop creative ways to bang the message home.

The Rainforest Action Network, an international coalition of grassroots groups, set out in 1985 to save the old-growth forests of the world, including the endangered remnants of North America's rain forest along the northwest coastline. Two years later, the network targeted its first boycott at Burger King, which folded after eighteen months of consumer pressure and a 12 percent sales decline. Burger King canceled a $35-million beef contract in Central America that "was turning ancient rain forests into cattle pastures into cheap, greasy hamburgers," as Randy Hayes, the network founder, puts it. With growing sophistication, Rainforest Action eventually devised a two-tiered strategy that has recruited major customers of wood and paper products to the cause: Kinko's, Home Depot, Lowe's, IBM, and some four hundred other companies. These middlemen consumers are then turned on the logging industry. After Home Depot was identified as the world's largest retailer of old-growth wood products, its big-box stores in the United States and Canada experienced hundreds of demonstrations as well as 45,000 customer calls and letters. Who needs this? The company reevaluated what its customers want. When Home Depot announced its new "no old-growth sales" policy, it sent an unsettling tremor through the timber industry.[6]

After winning over a major Canadian logging company to its principles, Rainforest Action next targeted a U.S. giant, Boise (formerly Boise Cascade), which has been an aggressive opponent of government controls on the industry. Boise predictably brushed aside the protests, until it saw some of its own customers, including Kinko's and the University of Notre Dame, begin to cancel purchasing contracts. In early 2002, Boise announced it would phase out its harvest of U.S. old-growth trees, claiming besides this was an inconsequential share of its business. However, an industry spokesman from the American Forest and Paper Association revealed a subtext of corporate resentment. "It's blackmail, any way you slice it," he told *The New York Times*. "As more and more retailers fall victim to this extortion campaign, it could definitely have an impact on the industry." Blackmail? Extortion? These are the consumers who were said to be king.[7]

Rainforest Action, in any case, did not declare victory, but continued the fight against Boise because the company had defined its "old growth" policy in very narrow terms, refusing to halt its international marketing of rain forest timber from other countries or to accept oversight of its forestry practices by an independent accrediting group, the Forest Stewardship Council. So Rainforest Action began launching more demonstrations and recruiting more companies to pressure Boise with contract cancellations. Forest fighting is like that: no easy victories, but a rather shrewd strategy for playing hardball. Consumers are generally in a very weak position, but they are not powerless. With solidarity and long-term commitment, personal values can be translated into real market leverage.

"Most of forest fighting from the 1960s and into the 1990s was trying to get the logging companies to be nice," Randy Hayes explains. "And that's a brick wall; their short-term profit comes from liquidating the old-growth forest. Our middleman strategy of going to the Home Depots and using big customers like Kinko's represents, I think, the biggest victories for the forests ever wrought, except for when forests are protected as national parks." Hayes's idea of ultimate victory—the worldwide halt of old-growth logging in all forest types and a restructuring of the entire global wood products industry— remains a long way off, but the vision has gained plausible focus.

Environmentalist organizations, of course, do still apply enormous pressure on governments to enact stronger regulatory laws across many issues. But the most interesting action is among those who have more or less given up on formal politics, at least for now, and are taking the fight directly into the economic realm, where they go head-to-head with the leading sources of the destruction. The ecological perspective is still too much for the American political system to swallow, particularly given relentless industry resistance. The right wing, allied with and aided by corporations, belittles the protection of ecosystems, wetlands, and forests as a matter of aesthetic taste and not relevant to human well-being. Industry scientists throw up doubts about every new advance. The existing regulatory laws are riddled with exemptions and malleable language, so the standards are vulnerable to endless litigation and political reversals. Altogether, the political arena is most inhospitable to the "whole Earth" perspective.

Yet, outside politics, some ecology agitators are conceivably creating an architecture for protogovernance—rules of behavior, enforcement techniques, and, above all, new public values gaining influence, without benefit of law. Enforcement relies mainly on self-interested, mutual obligations. The Forest Stewardship Council, for instance, was launched by major environmental groups to promote more responsible behavior and accredit companies that prove responsible, but the companies join voluntarily. They accept the FSC standards and inspections because they need its seal of approval, not to satisfy the government, but to satisfy their customers (and sometimes to fulfill the owners' personal values). Unlike a narrow purpose regulatory agency, the stewardship council started with the open-ended premise that ecological protection cannot be separated from social equity or economic consequences. So the "social members"—workers and communities dependent on forestry production—are formally included in the process of establishing performance standards. This "holistic approach," as FSC calls it, should be less vulnerable to capture by the industrial interests, since it includes competing constituencies. It might provide a prototype for a more reliable regulatory agency, if government ever decides to act more purposefully.

Another way of looking at these environmental struggles is to understand that, at their best, they are stitching together new communities of interests within the economic system. People and enterprises, producers and consumers decide to collaborate despite obvious differences because they need each other. Many such alliances are transient and disappear before they reach the stage of sophisticated, long-term strategy. But even those are valuable as an incubator for democratic consciousness. People learn to define objectives for themselves instead of reacting to the government's or to the cramped imaginations of the political parties. Occasionally, people even discover they can prevail, when they act collectively and stick with it.

Developing a convergence of disparate viewpoints is naturally difficult work, since it means bridging distances of culture, place, and political attitudes, including inherited suspicions. For the last few years, I have followed the progress of an upstart group called the Organization for Competitive Markets that was founded by an informal network of farmers and ranchers from the South and Midwest. The concentrated power of the food companies is literally extinguishing the free market for farmers, using their dominant size to extract price advantages or hiring farmers by contract to raise livestock in the confined factories. That arrangement reduces the independent farmer to economic subordination on his own land, roughly the same position of unorganized workers laboring in the industrial system one hundred years ago. The share of contract hog factories rose from 2 percent in 1980 to 10 percent in 1990 and to more than 60 percent a decade later, devastating the income base of farmers who did not submit, David Morris of the Institute for Local Self-Reliance reported. The OCM members are determined to make a last stand against industrialized agriculture before it swallows them too, but they recognize they will get nowhere by themselves. "We're in a death struggle out here, and we're getting our butts kicked," says Fred Stokes, the Mississippi cattle grower and Reagan Republican who is OCM's chairman.[8]

So the farmers have gathered allies from the city, consumers and groups long active in food and environmental issues, the restoration of rural communities, even in animal rights. Joined by antitrust scholars and ag economists, these advocates collaborated on putting together an OCM vision statement for "a whole-food system." It aligns social and economic concerns into one broad agenda, including everything from hog factories to equitable farm incomes, from wholesome food to busting up the corporate oligopolies in agribusiness. Environmental change needs the survival of independent farmers who can break out of the industrialized system, but independent farmers cannot survive without competitive markets and direct marketing to consumers. OCM founders see themselves as a catalyst bringing together kindred spirits who will take on the big boys.

Safe food is fundamental to life, but so is a decent regard for animals. The advocates remind us of an ancient wisdom: How we treat animals will likely be reflected in how we treat each other. Christopher Bedford, a Sierra Club organizer on farm issues who also works for the U.S. Humane Society, thinks the issue of animals ironically humanizes the discussion. "People care about the environment, but it's usually in an abstract way, and they don't really know much about farming because they are so distanced from it," Bedford explains. "But people care deeply about how animals are treated. It's very personal; they have pets themselves. When you explain what this system is doing to animals, people become very upset, and that opens the door to all the other issues: food as an interconnected ecosystem, nature, water, people, animals."

McDonald's ignored protests from People for the Ethical Treatment of Animals when PETA first asked the company to stop the inhumane practices of its beef and poultry suppliers, including needless cruelties in the slaughtering process. Then McDonald's heard from families who bring their children there to eat. PETA is serving now as a trusted consultant to McDonald's efforts for systematic reform.

OCM's outreach was inspired partly by Oklahoma State Senator Paul Muegge, a grain and livestock farmer from Tonkawa and chairman of the Senate agriculture committee, who experienced an odd, new politics unfolding in his home state. "Me and a friend [in the legislature] figured out awhile back [that] we can't beat these treehuggers—they're everywhere," Muegge says. "So we started talking to them, and within a year we got some things worked out. We had alliances with family farmers and environmentalists on the hog-waste issue, and that coalition simply swept over the state." Now, Senator Muegge says, "I'm known as a wacko tree-hugger myself." Building an alternative farm economy alongside the industrialized one is an audacious goal, but the market demand exists for it. Witness the rapid growth of organic-food consumption, the rising fears people feel about the food they eat, the hundreds of localized, often successful rebellions against hog factory pollution. OCM has not yet achieved any real power, but the farmers have a promising strategy. I intend to stay tuned.

On a more prestigious plane, The Nature Conservancy is working on essentially the same idea—the connection between ecology and people's economic circumstances—albeit in less confrontational ways. In environmental circles, the conservancy is the establishment, wealthy and respectable, with exceptional expertise in ecological science. The nonprofit foundation owns and protects some 12 million acres across the nation—vast tracts of forest, streams, rangeland, and mountains that encompass hundreds of precious wild places. TNC usually buys them; some are donated. Its endowment and land holdings total $2.9 billion, financed by millions of contributors, but mainly by wealthy Americans and leading corporations in oil, autos, agribusiness, banking, and other sectors. Protecting pristine nature seems like wholesome, safe philanthropy. During the last decade, however, the organization concluded that not even the Nature Conservancy has enough money to save all the places that need to be saved.

To defend endangered ecosystems, the foundation decided it must engage the local economic conditions and social reality of the people who live and work there: failing farmers with inadequate incomes; small holders in forested mountains; poor people in deteriorating rural communities. Income inequality, it turns out, is an ecological issue. "Personally, I think poverty and sprawl are the biggest threats to biodiversity on the planet, especially in the United States," says Stephen N. Parker, director of economic programs at TNC's Virginia Coastal Reserve. "They go hand-in-hand. When you have rural poverty, people are too poor to insist on zoning and too poor to resist the developers, so they give in to short-term necessity or short-term greed. We aren't going to eliminate greed, but we have to help people shift to long-term values if we want these places to exist one hundred years from now."

To that end, the conservancy has launched a most ambitious venture in economic development at the community level: trying to create jobs and incomes in order to protect nature. TNC has become a working partner with scores of localities (eventually hundreds, it hopes) in systematic searches for alternative lines of business and new value-added farm products, stronger income streams, and the restrained forms of development that can sustain the people on their land while husbanding the natural landscapes. The challenge is immense and requires a belated reversal in the conservancy's past behavior, when it typically entered a community as the large and aloof landowner, indifferent to the local citizens and often despised by them in return. W. William Weeks, a leading advocate for the change and founding director of TNC's Center for Compatible Economics, was persuaded by his twenty years working the standard way—preserving nature by buying it.

"I have done a lot of pure conservation; I did a hundred and fifty land deals in Indiana," Bill Weeks says. "But I know—I *know*—that we're not going to protect biodiversity unless we do this new approach and do it as widely as we can. Ultimately, conservation requires the consent of the people who are being affected. In order to achieve the level of consent we need, we have to pay attention to what those people need. They want things in life beyond pristine nature, and nature can support those things—if it's done carefully. By defending their quality of life we bring more people into the group that believes in conservation and believes that it can be achieved."

The conservancy, as it got know people and communities better, discovered new strength for the cause. "What we have going for us is the people's feeling about remaining on the land," Weeks says. "People really do value the places where they live and work, and the way they make a living on the land is part of what they love about the place. They know what's happening to their way of life and would resist if they could. But if nothing changes, there won't be any family farmers fifty years from now. Everyone will be working for a corporation."

On the eastern shore of Virginia, the long neck of land that runs southward to the mouth of Chesapeake Bay, The Nature Conservancy's 50,000-acre Virginia Coast Reserve is like a secret jewel—the last great stretch of seaward wilderness from New England to Florida. An unspoiled ecosystem runs along the shoreline for roughly seventy miles, largely unknown to the urban populations that flock to developed beach resorts to the north and south. It is a true coastal lagoon system, not a river estuary, and extends from the seaside farms to a chain of fourteen barrier islands over the horizon, in between a great vastness of shallow-water salt marshes and tidal flats. Terns, skimmers, curlews, rail, and Canadian geese are year round. Black ducks and harrier hawks winter over. The songbird migration comes through in spring and fall.

From sunlight and salt grasses the marshes manufacture nourishment. They function like a giant protein factory, producing a nutrient-rich soup that replenishes the food chain, moving from plankton to clams, oysters, fiddler crabs, then to fish, birds, and other wild animals. The marsh also cleans the water—the cleanest ocean water from Boston to Houston, I was told—since there are no cities or factories nearby. The place is beautiful to behold, but also strange to experience, with an unsettling feeling that one is trespassing on innocent terrain, a primeval landscape still existing on its own terms, so close to the navy shipyard at Norfolk, not far from the national capital in Washington. "These islands and marshes look as they did when the English settlers came," says John M. Hall, director of the coast reserve.[9]

For centuries, the ecosystem was protected largely by its remoteness, but that has vanished. Progress is bearing down from north and south. Developers envision a suburban extension from Norfolk and Newport News or genteel parks of country homes for the affluent, accompanied by the usual traffic of cars, boats, people, and pollutants. In that event, TNC would still own the salt marshes and islands, but doubts whether its watery acreage could survive as a functioning ecosystem. Nature is competing, one can say, with real estate prices and the faltering incomes of eastern shore farmers.

The search for alternatives began in 1991 with formation of the Northampton Economic Forum, the place where farmers, watermen, wealthy landowners, impoverished African-Americans, and the conservancy began their continuing conversations about the future. They came up with some plausible remedies. The Hayman, a locally grown white sweet potato, would become a high value-added crop that can plausibly yield as much as $1,000 an acre, if the Hayman brand gets proper marketing. Likewise, shellfish production would expand when the watermen at Willis Wharf adopted aquaculture techniques for clam farming that depend upon clean water for high quality. Bayview, a three-century-old settlement of African-Americans, would generate new work and incomes by reviving the vegetable production and marketing their ancestors had practiced one hundred years before. Bayview's dilapidated dwellings would be replaced by smartly designed reconstruction of both housing and community.

The conservancy, meanwhile, began building the first model houses for low-density vacation development—15 to 25 splendid homes to be sited deftly around a seaside farm where a developer might build 300 to 500. This design enables farmers to keep farming, but also to extract some wealth and income from the rising market

179

value of their land. TNC is buying up some shore farms, then return-
ing the land to private agricultural owners with deeded conservation
restrictions that define how far the limited development can proceed
to be compatible with the ecosystem. "We look at these farms as small
entrepreneurs in a niche market," John Hall says. "Then people ask,
'What the hell is The Nature Conservancy doing developing land?' It
does sound like man-bites-dog."

It would be nice to report that these innovations and others have
succeeded fully and the wondrous salt marshes are saved. Alas, the
ecological-economic dilemma is more deeply rooted and stubborn.
Many important changes are accomplished visibly, but TNC, despite
its deep pockets and expertise, also is groping to discover new relationships that do not have much precedent in American economic
life. In fact, it is trying to protect an ecosystem that includes people.
Like any successful grassroots activist, the conservancy makes mistakes, learns from the failures, and starts again, with a deeper understanding of how difficult it is to make changes in the land. "We're in
the early, early stages of a long, long road," Hall says. Meanwhile, however, the new perspective is already in play in local politics. Two members from the Northampton Economic Forum got elected to the
county board of supervisors. Developers, for the first time, are facing
organized local opponents who have a different plan for Northampton County.

A principal barrier to achieving ecological balance, reflected in
TNC's eastern shore experience and its many other local partnerships, is the stark, often cruel choice the economic system poses
between present and future. People who own productive natural
assets, farmland or forest, can typically earn much higher returns from
selling it for immediate exploitation than if they pursue the patient,
long-term approach with smaller annual yields. Yet the short-term
strategy essentially destroys the nature of their asset, changing their
surroundings into a place they neither wanted nor value: wall-to-wall
subdivisions or a stripped mountainside that is no longer a function-

ing forest. No straightforward way exists for people to reconcile this choice and, for many, there really isn't any choice, since they need the money now. The marketplace is oblivious to the dilemma and, for the most part, so are orthodox economists.

Bill Weeks, an inventive and optimistic social thinker, has envisioned a solution that he calls the "forest bank." TNC would serve as a banker, the trustworthy intermediary that holds and manages the tracts of forestland "deposited" by many small holders, then pays these owners a guaranteed rate of return on the appraised value of their assets, much as a commercial bank pays interest to people on their savings deposits. TNC would not be giving away the money but earning revenue from the forest with the ecologically sound harvesting of trees. The "forest bank" pays an annual return of only 4 to 4.5 percent compared to the 12 to 16 percent an owner could earn by selling to a rip-and-run logging company. But, as Weeks explained, the conservancy promises to deliver something in addition: "forest forever, managed in a sustainable way, not just for sustainable yields but to keep the ecosystem intact and protect the structure of the forest." Is this an acceptable exchange? The conservancy will find out in two experiments it has launched in the Clinch River watershed in southwestern Virginia and the Blue River in southern Indiana.

"Nonindustrial owners frequently harvest when they need the money, and they are usually dissatisfied afterwards," Weeks explains. "They don't like what happened to their forest and often they don't get the full value. All the timber has been taken off and, in economic terms, there's no forest left when they're done. We are giving the owners a way to get cash out of their forest, because these people are not wealthy and they need the money. But the forest is also important to their lives—something they love—and it will still be there for them. They can walk and hunt and gather mushrooms there. Given who we are, they can pretty well trust the promise that their land will stay forest forever. We won't clear-cut. We will build roads and harvest, but in ways that maintain the forest and its biodiversity. Our basic objective is to grow a high-quality forest there. We're going to be very careful about maintaining the value."

The Clinch River runs through Appalachian forest that, except perhaps for a few pockets of old-growth hardwoods, is not of the "nature preserve" quality TNC normally buys. TNC's primary concern is the river's water quality and preserving an enclave of rare aquatic species: freshwater fish and mussels whose habitat extended eons ago throughout the eastern Mississippi River basin. The Clinch is their last refuge. The river has around forty imperiled species, according to forest manager Bill Kittrell, more than any other river in America. As the jobs and income from coal recede, the economic pressure to take down the forest will intensify. The conservancy, in effect, is proposing a more rewarding choice—income *and* living forest. "Why is it necessary to go for a greater return when you can have a working forest that produces a return that isn't based on destroying it?" Weeks asks.

"If we have the numbers right, this could become a self-funding mechanism for conservation," he adds. "At worst, we will have to subsidize a little." That is, if TNC can achieve a large enough scale of operation, around 40,000 acres, its prudent style of timbering should produce a steady flow of revenue that covers both its management costs and the annual returns paid to landowners. The novelty of the "forest bank," however, is forcing a slower pace and smaller scale, at least for now. TNC's lawyers were nervous about calling it a "bank" and running afoul of banking laws. Many of the small owners are enthusiastic about the concept, but were intimidated by legal complexities in the SEC-approved financial prospectus. So the operating details have been simplified and the venture given a less forbidding name, "Conservation Forestry Program." New ideas do sometimes collide with habits of thought and the confinements of old laws.

The "forest bank" idea, whether it succeeds or flounders, is important for its spirit of invention. The essential problem Weeks identified is the gulf between present-day consumption values and people's desire—and need—to conserve natural assets for the long term. So he invented the missing piece: a quasi-financial institution that bridges the gap between time and returns. It does so by coalescing the interests of local people with the interests of an influential sponsor, the conservancy. I think of this as creative deal-making with social purpose. Like any business deal, it won't work unless all parties get real value in return. To be authentic, the transaction also requires democratic consent instead of top-down command by a powerful patron. To be truly effective, it helps if everyone involved brings an ownership stake to the table, something of value they invest in the common purpose, something to withhold if the terms do not seem equitable.

With these ingredients, the bridge becomes an empowering relationship for both sides—a basis for a meaningful social covenant among them—since each expects to gain what one could not achieve alone. Weeks's solution, I note, also creates an economic relationship in the spirit of the New England Indians' original idea of property: ownership rights based on use. In this instance, people will use their forest as needed and leave the rest for the future.

This mode of thinking—inventing an institutional bridge for new economic relationships—could find many fruitful applications across the social landscape, I suggest. Think of it as a new tool for reconciling the contradictions between economic routines and social imperatives, whether the subject is saving ecosystems or rebuilding urban neighborhoods or democratizing the ownership of work and enterprise. It requires imagination and collective action, not to mention hard strategic thinking. The objective is to invent a new form of mediating institution, whether it is called a covenant or compact, a public authority or private foundation, that acts like a trusted fiduciary but also as an active investor, the honest broker who negotiates terms of economic understandings among many parties and holds them responsible. The essence is managing the self-interested cooperation, not control or philanthropic largesse.

A city government (or a private corporation, for that matter) might conclude that, in order to rebuild blighted neighborhoods that will retain their value, it needs to work out a covenant with the people who live there. Those citizens would qualify for an ownership stake in the new houses or enterprises and have an active voice in the development plans, but also assume performance obligations to insure the city gets what it needs from the deal. As leverage, the city might retain the underlying title to the land, while citizens become owners of the structure they themselves develop: homes, businesses, community assets. Such deals, with complex overlapping stakes and obligations, are actually common in finance and business.

To make them work in the social reality, people will have to invent some new institutions. They may create freestanding financial institutions, for instance, whose first loyalty is to the social objectives, that have the professional competence to devise hybrid credit arrangements and to oversee the ongoing economic relationships. Eventually, this new structure of financial activity would need a secondary market like Fannie Mae that buys its secured loans and independent rating agencies to assess both its creditworthiness and social performance. With adventurous thinking, such things are possible. There are many missing pieces.

One way or another, these various examples of ecological reform are about determining the true costs of doing business, the true value of investment returns. The marketplace, given its narrow-minded perspective, has no way to do this by itself, but some people are demonstrating, with hard work and smart strategy, that they can force change in the market valuations, often by applying businesslike leverage on commercial interests. Difficult as this is, it may be the easy part of the problem. Most of the meaningful decision making that will determine the fate of nature lies far beyond the reach of consumers, even when they collectively mobilize to threaten brand names. The more fundamental and crucial decisions are about the production processes. These do not occur in the open marketplace, but within the management realm of corporations, where the public is not allowed.

FOR A COMPELLING image of how future capitalism might look, consider the seashell with its whorled interior or the slender vortex of a tornado or the delight of a small child watching the bathtub water disappear down the drain in a swift, silent whirlpool. An Australian biologist, Jayden Harman, studied the shapes and functions of these vortices in nature and with computer modeling began to design fans, pumps, and turbines that mimic their dynamics—their abilities to move fluids or gases from point A to point B with the least possible effort. Harman's devices have demonstrated astonishing reductions in energy consumption, less wasted motion and much less noise. His start-up company, Pax Scientific, plans to license the designs to industry with potential applications in virtually every sector, from water pumps and air conditioners to ships at sea.

"The fans look like screws instead of standard blades, but you've seen the shapes before in nature," explains Paul Hawken, the ecological businessman who founded Smith & Hawken and is coauthor of *Natural Capitalism*. "The potential for energy savings is huge. The world could save at least 15 percent because something like two-thirds of energy is used to move or cool fluids and gases. And this is just one idea. There are so many things like that out there, it's really exciting. That's where the big change is."

Industrial capitalism, notwithstanding the great accomplishments of human invention, has never approached the functional efficiency of nature—not even close. To the contrary, the wastefulness is prodigious and often deliberate, especially in American capitalism. Waste is designed into many products to create an allure of luxurious excess. Witness the tanklike sports utility vehicle that intimidates the other human-scale cars or a restaurant's overflowing servings of food intended to gratify rather than nourish (the uneaten heapings wind up in the Dumpster). Less visible to consumers but more fundamental to the ecological problem are the systems of production where things get made. These processes are also massively inefficient and neglectful of long-term costs, despite management's supposed obsession with efficiency.

Only 6 percent of the materials that flow through the U.S. production system actually wind up in products, as Hawken and coauthors Amory Lovins and L. Hunter Lovins noted in *Natural Capitalism*. The daily physical inputs consumed by the metabolism of industry amount to twenty times the body weight of every American citizen. The automobile, ostensibly modernized with its computer controls and other electronic charms, actually loses 80 percent of the energy it consumes, mainly through engine heat loss and exhaust. The other 20 percent moves the car.[10]

One is accustomed to hearing such grim facts from ecological activists, but Hawken and the Lovinses are trying to get people to see the good news. This problem is solvable. Americans can do this. Harmony with nature can be achieved (and without stringent material sacrifices) through old-fashioned ingenuity and try-again inventiveness. The ecological crisis will be resolved, peaceably and profitably, through the systematic redesign of products and the reengineering of the production systems—guided by lodestar principles from nature itself.

That is a very tall order, of course, but as *Natural Capitalism* reported, the process is already underway on various fronts with some surprising successes. What may be more startling to conventional wisdom is that the reformation of industry typically produces impressive gains for a company's bottom line—enhanced profit rather than the economic drag predicted by the doomsayers in business. This happy outcome is logical when you think about it, since refashioning industry to protect nature inevitably means tangible savings, reducing the inputs and useless excess through increased efficiency. Eliminating the wasted motion and wasted materials. Building "green" factories and office buildings that both conserve energy and improve human productivity. Reclaiming and reusing the worn-out stuff instead of dumping it in a landfill or the ocean. Redesigning everyday goods like shoes, sofas, and TV sets to eliminate thousands of poisonous substances that are standard ingredients. Restructuring the chemical compounds in industrial processes so they are either derived from natural plant materials or so that the toxics can be remanufactured into usable inputs. In addition to technological progress, the practical relationships between buyer and seller can be altered so that consumer and producer are essentially linked in an ongoing responsibility for what happens to nature.

This vision describes the "next industrial revolution," as Hawken and the Lovinses called it, and they are quite bullish about the prospects for improving everyone's quality of life. "Listen to the din of daily existence—the city and freeway traffic, the airplanes, the garbage trucks outside urban windows," they wrote. "The waste and the noise are signs of inefficiency, and they represent money being thrown away. They will disappear as surely as did manure from the nineteenth-century streets of London and New York. Inevitably, industry will redesign everything it makes and does, in order to participate in the coming productivity revolution."

The evidence for their optimism mainly comes from industry itself, often revealed by humble advances that have vast implications. Anheuser-Busch saved 21 million pounds of metal a year by trimming an eighth of inch off the diameter of its beer cans—without reducing the volume of beer. Pratt & Whitney used to scrap 90 percent of its ingots in making jet engine blades, until it asked the supplier to cast the ingots in bladelike shapes. A 13-pound steel tricycle with 126 parts became a 3-pound plastic version with 26 parts. The glass industry expects to cut its energy consumption in half in coming years simply by reforming its furnaces. New compounds that can substitute for chlorine in paper bleaching will eliminate dioxins while also reducing a paper mill's energy consumption dramatically. A hairdresser in Alabama discovered that human hair soaks up oil from water effectively. NASA tested the proposition and found that 1.4 million pounds of hair in mesh pillows could have soaked up the *Exxon Valdez* oil spill in a week.

Major industrial firms are taking more interest in sustainable technologies, inspired partly by the new political realities facing brand-sensitive corporations. After two generations of environmentalism, the consuming public no longer forgives wanton destruction. And a new generation of corporate managers has come to power who grew up with the same values. When William Clay Ford, Jr., the great-grandson of Henry, became the young, new chairman and CEO of the Ford Motor Company in the late 1990s, he announced a companywide turnaround agenda and made a spirited commitment to sustaining nature. Global warming is "real," he declared. His company will be judged by many standards, Ford's first sustainability report observed, but "none will be greater than our response to the issue of climate change."[11]

DuPont, like many other major names, shifted its policy during the last decade from downplaying or dismissing ecological consequences to a vigorous embrace of environmental responsibility, promising, in the lingo of ecologists, to reduce DuPont's "footprint" on the Earth. Good to its word, DuPont reduced its greenhouse gas emissions during the 1990s by 63 percent, far ahead of the timetable envisioned in the Kyoto agreement on climate change (though the reduction was slight for carbon dioxide emissions, the most threatening element in global warming). DuPont also dramatically cut its total release of toxics into air, land and water from 890 million pounds a year to 550 million pounds and sharply reduced the amount of hazardous waste disposed of by the notorious practice of deep-well disposal, from 187 million pounds to 38 million pounds. That's still a long way from zero, but it demonstrates what industrial engineers and scientists can accomplish when the company wants to get it done.

A lot of this was achieved simply by tightening the plumbing, but the reductions also involved technological breakthroughs. DuPont's molecular research has "down-gauged" polyester film, making it thinner, stronger, and more valuable. Thus, the company literally sells less material for a higher price. Another DuPont process can regenerate film indefinitely from throwaway cameras, making new from used and selling it again. Better living through chemistry, as the slogan said. The three authors of *Natural Capitalism* long-standing and trusted advocates for ecology, assured skeptics: "All three of us have witnessed this excitement and enhanced total factor productivity in many of the businesses we have counseled. It is real, it is replicable."

Another apostle of optimism is William McDonough, a University of Virginia architect who knows the results are real because he has helped create some for major corporations. McDonough designed an ecology sciences building at Oberlin College that generates more energy than it consumes. A new furniture-making factory he designed for the Herman Miller Company in Zeeland, Michigan, looks like a sustainable temple of light and fresh air, with grass and solar panels on the roof and a surrounding landscape that nourishes birds, bees and other creatures. With McDonough's assistance, Ford Motor Company is rehabilitating the severely polluted grounds of its famous River Rouge factory complex in Detroit, starting with an ambitious $2 billion plan that, as CEO Bill Ford told *The Wall Street Journal,* will "transform a 20th-century industrial icon into a model of 21st-century sustainable manufacturing."

McDonough teamed up with Michael Braungart, an iconoclastic German chemist who started out as chemistry director for Greenpeace and was a founder of the German Green party. Their design-consulting firm brings a radically different perspective to business's usual criteria of cost and performance. First, they instruct clients to forget the concept of waste and instead think like nature: "Waste equals food." The world in which we live, they explain, has two operating metabolisms—the biological and the industrial—so every substance produced, consumed, and discarded must be able to serve as "food" for one system or the other. Spent materials become either "biological nutrients" fully digestible in the earth or "technical nutrients" that will be fed back into the industrial system.

"To eliminate the concept of waste means to design things— products, packaging, and systems—from the very beginning on the understanding that waste does not exist," they wrote in *Cradle to Cradle*. "Products can be composed either of materials that biodegrade and become food for biological cycles, or of technical materials that stay in closed-loop technical cycles, in which they continually circulate as valuable nutrients for industry." The future is nourished by the past, just as nature does. Constructing this new industrial food chain alongside nature's—and devising ways to replace and dismantle the destructive system that now exists—is the epic vista before us. "In addition to ecological intelligence and equity, this should also be fun," McDonough said. "It's a celebration, you know. It's not a bemoaning of our limits. It's a celebration of our abundance."[12]

Playfulness is the soul of imagination—the capacity to think anew in freewheeling directions. Braungart and McDonough are gently nudging the environmental movement to get beyond dour warnings and nudging industrialists to let go of hostile obstruction so both can join in the game of reinvention. The playful quality shows up in their own work. They are now consulting Nike on how to make a running-shoe sole that will be biodegradable. They assume this is possible because they have already helped create an upholstery fabric that turns into garden mulch. Their book is not from a tree, they like to point out. Its pages were made entirely, not of paper, but of toxic-free plant materials that the earthworms will reprocess into topsoil.

Their participation in developing furniture fabric as a "biological nutrient" illustrates how complex and immensely difficult it is to refashion the internals of industrial life. DesignTex, a division of Steelcase, the major furniture maker, set out to devise an inexpensive fabric that could be compostable—biodegradable and free of the toxic chemicals and dyes typically used in the textile industry. Sixty chemical companies declined to participate in the project, but Ciba-Geigy, the Swiss firm, agreed to help. The design team went through almost 8,000 standard chemicals and rejected all but thirty-eight that were harm-free and had other qualities positive for nature. In the course of designing the pollutant-free textile, the manufacturing process at the mill was also perforce reengineered—cleansed of poisonous substances and polluted water. The DesignTex fabric, instead of winding up in a hazardous-waste landfill permeated with carcinogens, heavy metals, and endocrine disrupters, is actually safe enough to eat (though not especially tasteful). "When it's worn out and you're through with it, throw it on your garden," McDonough said. "Throwing something away can be fun, let's admit it."

Beyond technology, another significant step toward realizing the closed-loop industrial food chain has emanated from business itself and involves new commercial relationships. In numerous sectors over the last two decades, the leasing of products and industrial inputs has become the widespread and growing practice, instead of outright sale and purchase. Autos, commercial aircraft, office equipment, retail stores, industrial commodities like solvents and other chemicals, all these and other goods are now "rented" to the firms and people who will use them; then the products are returned to the owners, often the manufacturer, when the lease contract expires. The ownership does not change. What is being sold is the right to use the property for its service qualities.

One-third of the new cars in the United States are now leased, not purchased, often for large corporate fleets or individuals who want high-end models like Volvo and Lexus. Dow Chemical leases organic solvents to industrial users and then recovers the material for rehabilitation and resale. Interface, a Georgia carpet manufacturer, pioneered the leasing of office floor coverings, carpeting that is repaired as needed and eventually reclaimed by the company. Carrier, instead of selling air-conditioning equipment to building owners, sells "coolth services"—a contract to provide the use of installed equipment and guarantee comfortable temperatures. For many business reasons, including tax considerations, both parties gain from the transaction of not buying and not selling. Otherwise the practice would not have become so popular. In time, the ecological cause should gain enormously too.[13]

In essence, a leasing contract makes both parties responsible for the product, its proper use and care and its eventual disposal. The lessee agrees to keep it in good repair; the owner makes contractual promises on how it will perform. Either or both could be liable if the product malfunctions or does collateral injury to others, including pollution of air, land, or water. When someone leases a car, the obligations to maintain it are spelled out in the contract and, if the driver doesn't fulfill them, he can be penalized when he turns in the car. The dealer, meanwhile, knows he will get the car back eventually for another rental or sale, so he has a strong stake in preserving its long-term value. For the same reasons, both parties share an ongoing interest in reducing any waste and inefficiencies—mutual costs embedded in the deal. Industrial leasing of chemicals or equipment often includes an explicit agreement to share the savings with the users when operating costs are reduced or waste is avoided.

This business practice, in other words, encourages an ethic of shared responsibility between consumer and producer. It also creates a broader basis for holding people and firms accountable for their actions—including what they do with the product after its value has been exhausted. Whether it is cars or chemicals or routine pollution, the end point in the production-consumption cycle is typically the open dump called nature. A television set, according to Braungart, contains 4,360 different chemicals, many of them toxic, yet when people are through watching the TV, those chemicals typically are disposed of by burying them in the ground. This casual despoilation is pure waste, one of the ways both manufacturers and consumers evade the true costs of commerce. Closing the industrial loop means a system for establishing ultimate responsibility, one that no longer allows random disregard for future consequences.

Take back what you have made and make it into something new. The "technical nutrient" cycles envisioned by ecologists require a disassembly-recovery industry—the missing half of industrial capitalism—that collects the old stuff or spent substances and converts them into new parts or usable materials for new products and processes. "Cradle to cradle," as McDonough and Braungart put it. The prospects of this development is one reason why solving the ecological challenge is bound to create millions of new jobs, even new industrial sectors, rather than destroying them. The U.S. remanufacturing industry already includes more than 70,000 firms and half a million workers, according to Hawken and the Lovinses As McDonough and Braungart preach, the initial design stage is crucial, because virtually every product and process must be reconceived to account for how products and materials will be used again afterwards, to insure designs that allow easy disassembly and conversion to new "nutrients." Could a TV set be refashioned with that end purpose in mind? A car or a computer? Yes, of course. But it takes industrial imagination to do so, as smartly and profitably as possible.

Society obviously has an enormous stake in fostering these cycles of renewal, but Americans should not imagine that they are the vanguard. While some states and localities have adopted recovery and recycling laws, Europe has advanced far more aggressively in enacting "take back" laws that require a manufacturer to reclaim a product at the end of its life; that is, to take full responsibility for the consequences. Twenty-eight countries have such laws for packaging and sixteen for auto batteries (including the United States). Twelve nations are contemplating "take back" laws for electronics. Starting in 2006, the European Union will require European automakers (including the U.S. companies that manufacture there) to take back the cars they made. The EU requirement naturally has prompted design innovation and accelerated the industry's search for sound solutions. After autos, computers and electronics are expected to be next.

Can anyone imagine the U.S. Congress enacting such a law? When? Twenty or thirty years from now? It is possible the Earth cannot wait that long for remedy. The logic of industrial reformation enunciated by the ecological authorities I have cited (and scores of others around the world) is technically plausible, and concrete results are already confirming the vision. Yet optimism falters alongside the awkward political reality in the United States, the largest and most profligate consumer. The U.S. political system is at best in paralysis on the ecological questions, unable to move forward and, in some respects, actively retreating. The system of democratic decision making is neutralized, even captured by the political dominance of business and finance, in which major industrial interests reject the diagnosis of ecological crisis or block the most modest reforms, even if they acknowledge the threat is real. Some companies, certainly, push ahead with their own reforms, regardless, though they too could be impeded by the price advantage that competitors gain by taking the low road.

Given the dysfunctional condition of America's representative democracy, these great public questions are largely in private hands. The rate of progress will be decided within the private business organizations, though everyone faces the implications of inaction. Indeed, decisions about how much progress is tolerable to business interests are often in the hands of the worst actors with the most abusive records, since they exert their political influence most aggressively to veto reform. Yet, in business circles, the good guys do not criticize the bad guys, not in public and never by name. The optimists may have a sound vision, but the pace of actually dealing with this crisis waits upon private players and private interests, including corporate rates of profit.

Global warming illustrates this deformity of the public sphere. On this historic matter, retrograde industrialists have successfully put their short-term financial interests ahead of society's long-term priorities. The issue of climate change involves many contentious complexities, to be sure, but the basics are straightforward. Of the many greenhouse gases, carbon dioxide is by far the most damaging contributor to global warming. In the United States, the leading source of carbon emissions is the electric utility industry, which produces about 40 percent of them, followed by the auto industry in second place. Even as the world's governments were devising a global timetable for steady reductions, the Kyoto protocol of 1997, the American electric-power industry increased its carbon emissions by 20 percent from 1995 to 2000—and cut capital spending on environmental improvements by half (despite industry promises that deregulated energy markets would accelerate environmental gains).[14]

The utility sector's resistance to reform comes mainly from some 360 old and outmoded coal and oil-burning power plants that were exempted from the original standards set by the Clean Air Act of 1970, with the proviso that these unregulated power plants could not expand until they were modernized and adhered to the air-pollution regulations. Instead, the companies proceeded to expand their output enormously so that the "grandfathered" plants now generate more than half of the country's electricity and by far the major share of the sector's air pollution. Neither Congress nor the White House, under both Republicans and Democrats, has yet found the will (and the congressional votes) to make these rogues comply with clean air standards enacted more than thirty years ago, much less yield to proposed new regulatory controls that will curb carbon dioxide.

In the auto sector, the sincerity of Bill Ford's commitment to sustainability was not in question, but his tenure as chief executive proved to be another example of the industry's intractability. Unlike other CEOs, Ford had the power to deliver on his promises, because the Ford family owns 40 percent of the stock and undiluted control. In his first important crucible, however, Ford joined other U.S. auto producers in a fierce and demagogic lobbying campaign that defeated legislation to raise the fuel-efficiency standards for American-made cars and trucks. A higher fuel standard would reduce gasoline consumption per mile and thus reduce carbon emissions. It also would prod the companies to improve emissions technology and move faster on marketing alternatives like electric-powered cars or the new hybrid gas-electric vehicles. Auto lobbyists repeatedly blocked this reform for two decades. Meanwhile, the industry, led by Ford, popularized the gas-guzzling SUVs and light trucks so that the overall efficiency of new vehicles actually has declined by 8 percent. A decade of progress was lost in the 1990s. It appears another decade will be lost in the new century.

Why did Bill Ford retreat from his declared values? Colleagues doubtless warned him that the company would pay a political price if it broke ranks with the industry position. "The problem," a former Ford executive told me, "is carrying out these environmental strategies without getting your fellow industrialists and managers at other companies upset. Throughout the year in Washington, fuel efficiency is just one issue. The penalty is, if you break ranks with them on that, you're standing alone on a lot of other issues." Another industry executive blamed the "power of the marketplace"—cheap U.S. gasoline prices and the allure of large, inefficient vehicles to many consumers. But hiding behind consumer taste is disingenuous, since it was the companies, not consumers, who invented the over-sized SUV and promoted its macho excesses. In any case, the barrier to change is not technological. In Europe, the same American companies produce excellent cars, less gargantuan and gaudy but designed for much greater fuel efficiency and other appealing qualities (Europeans routinely travel at much higher speeds on European highways). The U.S. companies do not market these more efficient models in the United States, perhaps fearful that a lot of Americans would buy them.

In fact, the most likely explanation for Ford's retreat and the auto industry's resistance to efficiency is that ecological reform goes against their basic business strategy. Selling the oversized, heavier, more inefficient vehicles is far more profitable. The U.S. companies earn a much greater return per unit on the behemoths than smaller models, and for four decades they have clung to the strategy of bigness, despite the inroads of foreign producers, because it is the main source of their profitability.

The American industry's long-term performance, in other words, reflects a deep reluctance to innovate in fundamental ways. Yes, Detroit is very shrewd about adding electronics and other conveniences, but remains unwilling to rethink the basic automobile design in any way that would threaten the profit centers of size and wastefulness. This posture has left the U.S. car-makers always a step behind their foreign competitors *and* behind the changing consumer preferences, as the Japanese and European companies consistently introduced appealing new alternatives—cars of smaller sizes and with better manufacturing quality, safety, and greater fuel efficiency.

If one looks back over four decades, the American strategy does not look especially smart. Since the 1960s, the U.S. companies have lost roughly half of their U.S. market share, as they were repeatedly compelled to play catch-up with innovations introduced by foreign competition. The United Auto Workers, once one of the most progressive unions, faithfully aligned itself with the companies' backward-looking strategy, and the union has lost jobs and members more drastically than the employers lost market share. More U.S. losses seem likely ahead, because Japanese auto companies are determined to lead the next market transition—a future when the new cars do not burn gasoline.

Corporate governance, in other words, is a central variable in the ecological crisis. The problems can be solved technologically, but will the companies decide it is in their interest to do so? It seems strange to contemplate, but the fate of the Earth a generation or two from now may hinge less on the technological unknowns than it does on mundane questions of how these large, private organizations are operated: the quality of their business strategies; the character of top executives; their responsiveness to new ideas; the ways in which management resolves the competing claims and preferences. The stakes for the rest of us are enormous.

The authors of *Natural Capitalism* argue, for example, that protecting the Earth's climate can be achieved without the higher energy prices and energy taxes that environmentalists often advocate *if* industry embraces the full array of energy-saving reforms already known to engineering and science. Some sectors like coal, the authors concede, would lose out in the transition, but the government can and should carry people like coal miners through their dislocations into new jobs and other opportunities. If a genuine political debate ever occurs on global warming, it would focus on the pros and cons of these two alternatives: a public-driven agenda of industrial reforms in design and production versus the higher energy taxes and prices intended to drive consumers away from the inefficient products. Both approaches would require government engagement and public money up front, but the tax-and-price strategy guarantees gross inequities for the society, pricing many consumers out of an ability to buy many goods while exempting the affluent from such sacrifice. In a sense, the political choice has already been made, driven by the heavy influence from corporate America. The choice is to resist substantial change as long as possible.

When I asked several optimists about the pattern of corporate resistance, Bill McDonough was undaunted: "Basically, I look at it, and Bill Ford does too, as, we've got to be in business to change our business. That's the reality." When new ideas take form in practical use, he assumes the marketplace will adopt them. "My whole thing is, if we can build something, and it exists, then nobody can say it's not possible," McDonough says. "If I can make a building that makes more energy than it needs to operate, then nobody can say we can't do that."

Paul Hawken, in contrast, despaired about the weak pace of

progress, having observed corporate America's general indifference to the well-understood tools and techniques for reversing the damage. CEOs neglect the opportunities, he explains, partly because Wall Street finance takes no interest in them. "The people who control the flow of funds in this country have a very narrow understanding of where you obtain financial returns," Hawken says. "They have no familiarity with any of the subjects we describe in the book, no training in these matters. They receive no pressure from institutional investors or even the government to consider these choices. They have no accountability for the results of not considering them."

Hawken has begun to worry that when he and others celebrate the brand-name companies that are taking half steps, however laudable, it simply diverts attention from the deeper structural changes that are needed. "What we really need from the corporation is the capacity and the culture in which to tell the truth," Hawken says. "Within these companies, you've got a new generation of younger people, and they know darn well what the story is. I mean, they're not stupid. When you get them together in a room and nothing's on the record, people will be quite candid. We did that a few weeks ago in Detroit—people from auto companies and in high positions—and they're quite concerned. The real problem is, we don't have a culture where people can tell the truth."


THE FUTURE, FORTUNATELY, does not belong exclusively to the large and powerful. It also will be shaped by thousands of small and independent enterprises pursuing the new ideas and nature-friendly products that major corporations ignore or dismiss as impractical, unprofitable. These smaller companies are the innovative leaders in many areas of ecological reform, taking entrepreneurial risks because they believe in the objective and can see future profitability. Since they are new, the pioneer firms have no stake in the past, no need to defend their markets against changing values. Change is essentially what they are selling (one is tempted to call them "pro-life" companies, but the phase has been appropriated for other political uses).

"There are 70,000 to 80,000 companies in the U.S. now whose purpose is—let's use the hackneyed word—sustainability," Paul Hawken says. "Whether it's in agriculture, in chemistry, green buildings, materials, transportation, or water, they are doing the real innovation. Most are small, some large. The bigger ones are innovating on things like fuel cells and hydrogen, and they've gotten money from Ford, Daimler, and United Technologies. Everyone admits that hydrogen is the future after hydrocarbons, it's no longer pie in the sky, only a question of when. But that wasn't the case when the innovators started out. Those early engineers, with the shop in the garage, were struggling too, just like the others are now."

This adventurous business spirit can be glimpsed in many sectors, including agriculture. Small firms with technological prowess and some producer cooperatives owned by farmers are making an audacious market bet on ecology, betting that hydrocarbons will give way to carbohydrates, that petroleum will be significantly displaced by natural materials (mainly farm-grown plants) as a source of fuel and many industrial substances. It does seem fanciful to think the West Central Cooperative based in Ralston, Iowa, population 119, is taking on ExxonMobil for a share of the market in hydraulic fluids, lubricants for chainsaws and heavy machinery, diesel fuel, cleaning fluids, and other petroleum-based products. But West Central Co-op's 3,500 farmer-owners in Iowa grow tons of soybeans and, in addition to operating grain elevators across the state, the co-op makes and sells patented versions of these products—derived from soybean oil, biodegradable and nontoxic. SoyTRUK is tractor-trailer wheel grease. SoyPOWER strips asphalt stains and graffiti from railroad crossings. The Burlington Northern Santa Fe Railroad tested the cleaner and found it to be the most effective.

Terresolve Technologies of Eastlake, Ohio, sells more than thirty varieties of vegetable-based engine oils and lubricants and has established a thriving niche market at golf courses, public parks, and marine-construction firms whose lawn mowers, outboard motors, and heavy equipment used to dispense pollution with the petroleum-based oils. GEMTEK, Agro Management Group, Renewable Lubricants, and many other firms are making everything from wax to home cleaners to water-based paint resins from crop oils: soybean, linseed, canola, rapeseed, and others. They often work in partnership with farmer co-ops. Biocorp of Redondo Beach, California, is trying to succeed where big names like Monsanto and Mobil have withdrawn, marketing compostable plastic trash bags made from cornstarch and cottonseed cellulose. The company has a contract with the U.S. Navy for biodegradable cups and cutlery that can be discarded at sea safely.[15]

Like any other market, the sticking point is price. Some plant-based products are price competitive, others cost more but are competitive because they are more effective and thus do the job with less volume. More to the point, many nature-based products become bargains when the true costs of collateral damage are calculated in the price comparison. Ice-Ban, a deicer made from residues of beer, cheese production, and ethanol, costs a lot more than rock salt but does not corrode highway equipment, concrete roads, and buildings or kill surrounding vegetation. Cities with severe winters have found they save as much as 30 to 45 percent by buying green.

"Tilling instead of drilling," explains David Morris, a forward-looking thinker at the Institute for Local Self-Reliance in Minneapolis. Twenty years ago, he coined the term "carbohydrate economy" and issues a quarterly report of the same name chronicling these pioneering ventures. Morris's long-held conviction is that achieving ecological balance will depend upon restoring incomes and stability in rural communities, and these mutually reinforcing goals succeed only if they originate from the ground up. "We should devolve authority and capacity to the localities as our primary motivation, and the laws should be established to assure that, with the understanding that some things need to be done at higher levels and many need to be done at lower levels," Morris says. "The question is: How do you fashion this from the bottom up?"

More than 150 farmer-owned manufacturing ventures, with more than $3 billion in capital investments, are now operating around the country, engaging in the value-added processes that turn raw crops into higher-priced marketable foods and ecological products, Morris reports. Not all of these enterprises are governed by "green" values—first, they're trying to make money—but all of them are working to create a viable economic alternative to corporatized agriculture. Commodity producers (whether the commodity is coal, coffee, or soybeans) historically have suffered from unstable prices and falling incomes—unless they also control the advanced processing and marketing activities where value is added to their produce along with higher profit margins.

The 21st Century Alliance, based in Manhattan, Kansas, has linked producer cooperatives from eight states that are producing particleboard from straw, tortilla flour, processed pinto beans, and other value-added products. Other farmer co-ops have asked 21st Century about creating an "alliance of alliances" that could cooperatively undertake the tasks of raising capital and sharing skills and risks across many small firms without compromising local control (as John Logue in Chapter 3 proposed for employee-owned companies). That vision echoes the nineteenth-century Populists who believed an authentic democracy required an economic structure organized by and for the many, not the few. In the end, the Populists failed to achieve their concept of a democratized economic system but—who knows—maybe the country is now ready for the idea.

Only major corporations, of course, have the scope and scale to generate dramatic changes quickly, but smaller upstarts play the vital role of leveraging the big boys, as their new products become competitive and popular. In small scattered ways, the coming market shift is already visible. Johnson & Johnson has adopted a worldwide company policy to use only hydraulic elevator fluid made from canola. NAPA, the auto-parts retail chain, is selling automatic transmission fluid made from plants. Germany has fostered Europe's largest market for biolubricants by banning petroleum-based oils for chainsaws and boats on inland waterways. Switzerland, Austria, and other nations are adopting similar prohibitions. In the United States, the infant market for biodegradable trash bags is steadily strengthened as more and more state and local landfills refuse to accept the old kind.

The big boys, however, are also often predators and, if the small innovators are to survive, they need protection, even from friendly embrace. Paul Hawken remarks that, when Ford Motor Company announced with good intentions that it would enter the electric-bicycle business, it resulted in two small electric-bike firms being starved for credit. To bankers, they looked like a bad risk now that they were competing with an industrial giant. Ironically, when small firms do succeed and prosper in the United States, they often disappear. Either they are swallowed up by acquisition or get into financial trouble because they cannot raise the capital needed to sustain growth. These business failures are described as management mistakes, but the consistent pattern suggests that American capitalism is stacked against smaller firms and biased in favor of the very large. If society intends to break out of the political stalemate on ecological issues, it will have to find ways to defend and nurture those pioneers.

Fundamental questions also need to be asked of the major corporations and their exaggerated influence in American life. It is not just the ecological crisis held hostage by their political preferences, but many other important matters across public life. It is not just the market power that makes them awesome, but the power of their social control. A relatively small number of large and private business organizations, a few hundred at most, form the commanding heights of economic life and also intimately shape the social condition, the ways we live, the prices we will pay for prosperity, the boundary lines drawn around society's noneconomic aspirations. How did a society so deeply imbued with the democratic ideal wind up organized and dominated by business organizations that operate on opposite premises? Does the country get what it needs (and deserves) from these privileged organizations? These questions are asked from the conviction that the corporation, as central actor and intelligence in American capitalism, must be redesigned and reformulated too in order to disarm the deeper collisions with society and democracy—and that this is possible to do.

# 6

# Command and Control

THE modern American corporation was fashioned in law and common practice a century ago, when it was essentially relieved of its public obligations and empowered to expand in scope and scale, more or less eternally. The corporation became, without much question, the most effective form for organizing business activity. Indeed, corporations also organize the terms of everyday life, more surely than politics or religion. Yet the corporate institution, while only a century old in its present form, is profoundly dysfunctional in many ways, especially for society's purposes, but also for capitalism's. Some of the systemic disorders were revealed in the contagion of financial scandals that followed the collapse of the wildly inflated stock market. But the dysfunctional nature of the corporation is deeper than executive fraud or phony profits.

The corporation's legally privileged structure and unbounded scale generate a different kind of corruption—the irresponsibility of concentrated, self-aggrandizing power. The commanding heights of corporate control belong to management insiders, a few intimate financiers, and the large-bloc share owners who together are able to impose a narrow-gauged understanding of economic purpose on their own organizations and on the larger society. Given this closely held power, a successful company may remain oblivious to social injuries or the country's neglected priorities, but may also be blind to the corporation's essential purpose: creating real wealth for the future, the material gains that sustain a civilized society. The ecological crisis is governed by corporate indifference; so are most of the other social discontents described in this book. This is what the Reverend Emil Brunner (cited in Chapter 2) meant when he wrote many years ago that capitalism "is irresponsibility developed into a system."

The corporate institution is ripe for reinvention. Since it is the central actor in economic life, Americans are not likely to achieve human-scale aspirations for themselves and society—or to approach an authentic democracy—until the corporation is reformulated in fundamental ways. Obviously, deeper reforms of this nature eventually would require government action, since the structural elements that make the corporation so effective and powerful are embedded in law. But I am not thinking of new regulatory regimes, more of the do-and-don't commandments imposed externally by government. Regulations express and enforce broad public values but, as the financial scandals demonstrated anew, their force and meaning often are undone by the erosions of time, purposeful evasion, and political manipulation.

The behavior of corporations can be altered fundamentally only if organic changes are made within the corporation itself, new power relationships built into the functional design, new understandings encoded in the operating culture. Enforcement might then rely, for the most part, upon internalized forces of accountability—webs of mutual obligations and expectations established among the people and interests who are the company's main contributors (managers, owners, employees, creditors, suppliers, customers, and communities). Once these new relationships are firmly in place, the various constituent members of the firm would perform critical oversight and accountability in the course of their everyday participation. They, in turn, would share the responsibility for seeing that the corporation keeps its obligations to society at large. This ideal is not as utopian as it perhaps sounds. There are such companies operating in America that adhere in varying degree to these broad principles and succeed in business on capitalism's own terms. The problem is, they are a scarce minority.

What exactly is the public purpose of the corporation that entitles it to favored legal status? What should society be able to expect from the corporation? What do we need from it? These are the pivotal questions that ought to be reopened for discussion. The political system is not yet ready (to put it mildly) to undertake anything as fundamental as reorganizing the corporation. But then neither probably is our society. Large, contentious questions of how the business organization should be shaped and governed, constrained and reoriented on behalf of broader social obligations must be answered first, worked out through lots of public inquiry and argument. Convincing solutions likely will be found in real-world experimentation more than in abstract theory, the best answers discovered by people in innovative enterprises rather than government or academia. In scattered ways, such experiments already are underway as numerous citizens—including inventive business managers—set out to create new firms or to change existing ones, devising different operating designs with social imperatives in mind.

A neglected paradox of mature capitalism is that enterprises are more likely to function effectively for the long run—still energetic and profitable, but less destructive and often more creative—when they accept a less domineering role in American life. This counter-reality is not exactly secret, but the knowledge is ignored widely for obvious reasons: It messes up conventional assumptions about the existing power relationships and threatens the steep, top-down pyramid of command-and-control by which most corporations are run.

The companies that break with convention respect people and social norms. They practice inclusiveness because it brings more perspectives and the intimate knowledge of the firm known only to the employees into their decision making. They regard human fulfillment as part of the mission because it encourages a productive and innovative workforce, which is good for business. Many of these companies successfully resisted the frenzied pressures that engulfed business organizations in recent decades. Many others succumbed. American capitalism is spacious enough to tolerate the rare exceptions—so long as they pay their bills and remain profitable. The problem is, the system empowers and often demands the opposite behavior, a short-sighted indifference to people and society's claims.

In this chapter we go back to the origins a hundred years ago and examine some of the legal premises upon which the modern corporation was founded, because they are a principal source of the dysfunctions, as vividly demonstrated in the recent drama of bubble and boom and breakdown. To alter the social obligations of corporations those legal foundations must be modified significantly and conditioned by greater responsibility and accountability. Contrary to conventional dogma, however, the corporate institution would not be injured by such reforms, but should become more effective, both for society's objectives and for productive capitalism. To understand why this is so one also has to appreciate the corporation's inherent strengths, the reasons why it has prevailed as the preferred format for business organization. Those core qualities are not the problem. In fact, they are virtues that can serve society's larger purposes and should be preserved as the corporate institution is overhauled for greater responsibility and accountability.

AFTER THE STOCK MARKET meltdown some business experts attributed the greedy excesses of corporate executives to the "cult of the CEO." Enron, the flagship of scandal, distributed $681 million in rewards to top managers at the very time the company was collapsing into bankruptcy. Dennis Kozlowski, the empire-building CEO of Tyco International, harvested hundreds of millions in salary and stock options, yet (according to his criminal indictment) felt a need to evade more than $1 million in sales taxes on his expensive art purchases. At dozens and dozens of admired corporations, the executives secretively cashed out their own holdings while pushing the retirement savings of their employees into the company's about-to-collapse stock. Greed, disloyalty, and reckless disregard for the law—those were hallmarks of the utopian cult that demanded faith in the strong-willed leader. Many millions fell under the spell.

The rapacious personality type is described by Buddhism as the "hungry ghost," Paul Hawken points out. "In Buddhist iconography, the hungry ghost is depicted as a person with a huge stomach and pencil-thin neck who cannot get enough, whether it's drugs, fame, food, money. He can never get enough. There are a lot of these people running corporations." William Lerach, a prominent plaintiffs' lawyer who has sued hundreds of corporations for defrauding shareholders, observes: "The CEO ultimately gets brought down by the very personality characteristics that made him successful in the first place. How did these guys get to the point where they control a big public company? It's not because they take no for an answer. Their whole life has been fighting and overcoming people who say no, you can't do it, don't do it, it's illegal. These guys say, 'To hell with you, we're doing it, we're getting it done, nobody can stop me.'"[1]

It does seem bizarre, given our democratic values, that such characters were given so much unchecked economic power (stranger still that so many intelligent people believed in the efficacy of inflated egotism). But the hyperpersonalization of corporate power was not a product of social delusion or even of the failures of auditors and directors. It was a consequence of the contradictory corporate structure originally devised a hundred years ago, when professional managers assumed corporate control from the founding titans. Simultaneously, the swelling ranks of public shareholders were fictitiously described as "owners" of the company, fictitious because they had (and have) no genuine control or influence over the "property" they supposedly "own." This original contradiction provided the pretext for the contemporary debacle of scandal and breakdown. The impotent status of shareholders, it was explained in business circles, was at last being corrected through a stern new financial doctrine—"shareholder value"—that kept corporate managements closely aligned with the interests of the absentee owners.

Shareholders, it was said, have at last gained real influence over the companies because "shareholder value" compelled the CEOs to pursue the stockholders' singular objective of earning greater returns (preferably every quarter). The corporation's competing concerns and priorities were thus subordinated or discarded, even including the long-term viability of the company itself, since conceivably the shareholders could gain more from its sale or breakup. Top executives were punished (fired or pushed aside by corporate takeovers) if they failed to take tough measures to enhance the stock price (squeezing the workforce, dumping less profitable divisions, cutting R & D budgets). But executives were richly rewarded when they produced ever greater "shareholder value," since their own pay and incentives like stock options were pegged to the stock price too. In a sense, the doctrine reduced the complex life of a corporate organization to a single number—the daily share price—and its performance was judged abstractly by stock market analysts at a great distance from the actual enterprise.

The supposed alignment of CEOs with shareholders turned out to be a cruel hoax, of course, on unwitting investors. The shareholder logic simply encouraged executives to inflate the returns and thus push the stock price ever higher, ostensibly rewarding shareholders but actually exposing the company to ever greater risk, including the risk of financial implosion. CEOs did not personally share in this risk, however, because the artificial gains in stock prices could still be harvested by those who knew when to get out—insiders like themselves. Meanwhile, the doctrine justified the vast destruction done within the companies and ultimately to the defrauded shareholders too. The newly enacted reforms may temper the levels of greed and fraud but will do nothing to correct the basic deformity in the control of corporations. Doubtless, it is better to have honest auditors and independent directors than not. But more vigilant watchdogs will not correct the problem if they too are committed to the belief that the returns for absentee owners always come first.

The most astonishing fact about the "new economy" breakdown and its subsequent scandals is that none of these outrages was actually new. All of the disorders and fraudulent illusions, the collapsing empires and harsh collateral consequences, have been recurring events during the last century, repeated many times with varying intensity since the modern corporation was formulated. This historical pattern confirms the problem is structural, not personal, made possible by the corporation's flawed and unaccountable power structure. The corporation's negative tendencies—the impulse to dominate, acquisitive overreaching and social neglect—may be suppressed for a time by a hostile social climate or by reinvigorated regulatory enforcement. But these traits surface again and produce the same flagrant damage when the tides of capitalism are swelling or when anxious, ambitious executives decide to ignore the restraints and bull ahead. If one aggressive company breaks through the barriers, others swiftly follow.

Indeed, the corporate institution acquired a rare expertise. It has learned how to eviscerate or evade most of the countervailing forces erected during the twentieth century to domesticate its behavior (e.g., laws that include legal rights for organized workers, antitrust standards, social and economic regulations). In basic character, the corporation resembles a shrewd and muscular wild animal that sooner or later figures out how to break out of its cage. Instead of building new cages, we should investigate the DNA of these creatures.

The decisive alterations that shaped and empowered the modern corporation occurred during several decades starting in the 1880s, and were accomplished through legislation and judicial decisions.

These pivotal changes were driven by the ascendancy of the great national industrial corporations—oil, steel, railroads, electrical generation, and others—new giants that were powerfully present in the critical decisions made by state legislatures, Congress, and the Supreme Court. Popular opposition was either outgunned politically or ignorant of what was occurring.

These long ago alterations in law are important because they form the template for how things work today. The premises are deeply embedded in the economic structure and act like unseen boundary markers between society's aspirations and corporate capitalism's prerogatives. The public's role in formulating expectations for corporations was steadily reduced and walled off from effective assertion, while corporations gained expansive new powers for themselves. The shareholders were cut out of any significant influence, while corporate insiders became more empowered to decide things in isolation, more independent of social influences. And the insiders became personally insulated from the consequences of their actions.

To appreciate the scope of these changes it helps to understand that the corporation originated in early American history as a government-authorized exception to the everyday routines of commerce. Following the English model, the first American corporations existed only if specially chartered by government (instead of the king). They were given explicit privileges and public obligations because these private organizations were able to undertake large projects, like building canals or railroads, that promised great public benefit (George Washington was among the early incorporators; he was chartered to build the C & O Canal westward from the nation's capital). A well-financed collaborative could organize and sustain large tasks and complex business activities beyond the capacity and scattered resources of small independent businesses. Popular resistance to the corporation was fierce throughout the nineteenth century because merchants, mechanics and farmers well understood the power implications of giving competitive advantages to these large, growing business organizations. Nevertheless, by the end of the century the corporation was the preferred form, proliferating because it was so effective and achieving national scope with the rise of the transcontinental railroads.[2]

State-issued charters are still required to incorporate (the reason these private organizations are called "public" corporations), but the obligations to fulfill specified public objectives have disappeared. In the 1890s, states were eager for development and began competing to attract new companies by steadily weakening the requirements in corporate charters—a "race to the bottom" that ended in Delaware which set the least demanding rules for incorporation. This virtually erased any meaningful public demands on corporate purpose. Open chartering was, in a real sense, democratizing because incorporation was thereby liberated from political influence and the usual favoritism toward powerful elites. Anyone can incorporate a new business for any purpose they imagine, no questions asked. But the relaxed terms also enabled corporations to claim open-ended powers for themselves. They became unchecked and undefined institutions unless people somehow mobilized enough political muscle to stop them.

Society, in other words, was put permanently on defense, playing catch-up with new and unanticipated corporate developments, always responding after the fact. The weakness of the public's position is especially relevant to the ecological crisis. Because citizens are unable to define reliable limits on the corporation's purposes and performance in advance, people must passively experience the environmental consequences of exotic new industrial substances or production techniques until the harm becomes visible around them. Then citizens must gather elaborate scientific proof and persuade politicians to take their complaint seriously, while the corporation typically scoffs, denies anything is amiss, and mobilizes its own political resources to block any corrective action. Eventually, if the evidence becomes overwhelming, the company may agree to stop dispensing the dangerous materials into air, land, and water (though some determined companies, like

General Electric, may fight clean-up obligations for a generation or longer).

Biotechnology is only the latest example of these mass-market experiments with nature and human well-being. Genetically altered seed, foodstuffs, and animals may be harmless to the future. The companies say so and persuade government regulators to assent, but the truth is, no one actually knows. And history suggests that corporate assurances of harmlessness are quite unreliable, from lead additives in gasoline to DDT, from carcinogenic food dyes to PCBs. We will find out the truth about biotechnology some years hence when, if there are destructive consequences, the damage already will be widely present in our lives, routinized in commerce and nature.

To ecologists, this approach is dangerously irresponsible, as well as grossly wasteful, since cleaning up environmental mistakes is always far more expensive than preventing them. Public health and environmental leaders advocate a disciplinary concept known as "the precautionary principle" that would require a heavy burden of proof *before* such experiments are commercialized. If that obligation were written into every corporate charter or state laws governing corporate behavior, it would no doubt slow down the process of introducing new products and production practices that seem to promise cost savings or higher quality. But it would assign the unmeasured risks to the proper party—the people who expect to profit—rather than the unwitting public. Managers and investors would be on notice that they are responsible.

The formation of corporate power also was advanced decisively by the Supreme Court during the late nineteenth and early twentieth centuries (the same conservative court that upheld the South's legally sanctioned racial segregation in its notorious *Plessy v. Ferguson* decision). In 1886, the Supreme Court held, with no public argument and little explanation, that the corporation shall henceforth be treated as a "person" for purposes of law, and be entitled to the same constitutional protections previously accorded only to the citizens who are human beings. In particular, corporations could invoke the Fourteenth Amendment's right to "due process," which was adopted after the Civil War to protect the newly emancipated slaves. Personhood was legal fiction, obviously, but it became a most powerful tool for corporate lawyers fending off the demands of citizens and governments.

Over the next fifty years, the Supreme Court made numerous decisions involving Fourteenth Amendment rights, and half of these were devoted to protecting corporations, with less than 1 percent to the rights of African-Americans. The corporate power relationship with citizens was thus shifted to a startling level of inequality, since the corporate organization already has inherent advantages over individuals. Unlike real people, a corporation may exist in many places at once. Or it can reconfigure its body parts and re-create itself in an entirely new form. Unlike real people, a corporation can live forever.[3]

The ascendant corporations, eager to expand in scope and scale, also moved to seize power (and property rights) from their putative owners—the shareholders. Shareholders were a major obstacle to reorganizing the American industrial base, the grand project of acquiring scores of competing firms and amassing them in giant holding companies (conglomerates, we would call them now). Common law at that time still treated each shareholder like a true partner in the firm, and thus unanimous approval was required from the shareholders before a corporation could acquire another company or sell its own assets entirely or make other major structural changes. Led by New York in 1890, states began enacting a remedy for ambitious empire builders: Henceforth, a company could execute its mergers and acquisitions with only majority approval from the shareholders. This change effectively alienated shareholders from their property and secured control of the firm for the insiders, including the largest stakeholders.

This alteration also ignited the first great wave of consolidations and takeovers that led to the gargantuan scale of the largest corporate organizations. That was the objective. The early industrial titans—Carnegie, Mellon, Rockefeller, Du Pont—understood the competitive advantage of utterly dominating a sector. One very large producer could ride out the downturns, while the smaller companies ate the losses. Two or three of these giants together astride a market sector could conspire to set prices and drive competitors into ruin or bleed the customers who had nowhere else to turn. These monopolistic alliances were known then as "trusts" and blanketed everything from trolley cars and cigarettes to oil and steel.

During the recent boom and breakdown we witnessed yet another explosive wave of mergers and buyouts, topping out at $1.4 trillion in acquisition deals during 2000. It was the fifth or sixth such frenzy during the last century (depending on how one counts them). These episodes of consolidation typically are followed by periods of break up and dissolution in which the swollen companies sell off or close down elements of production they have just acquired (the conglomerates may themselves be attacked by financial raiders questioning the rationality of their size and scope). It is as though America has decided that proper corporate structure and scale can best be determined by periodic tournaments of gladiatorial combat.

This time around, the failed conglomerations included dozens of red-hot technology firms, led by WorldCom, that expanded revenue and profit almost entirely by acquisitions, with no real strategy for how to manage all the disparate parts profitably. They flamed out when stock prices collapsed, and many have disappeared. Perhaps the most spectacular failure was the merger of AOL Time Warner, supposedly undertaken on the basis of "synergies" but actually envisioned as a forbidding media empire that would stand astride everything from television and publishing to the Internet. It did not work so well for shareholders, who lost $170 billion in market value, or for the new megacompany itself that was compelled to take an initial write-down of $50 billion, with more to come. Meanwhile, authorities investigated AOL for allegedly cooking its revenue numbers.

More significantly, the modern era of consolidations has created a new galaxy of oligopolies dominating a dozen or more sectors in which a few companies own most of the marketplace and can intimidate or crush minor competition (all of these new formations passed legal muster with the federal government). Three companies own two-thirds of cable television. Five companies control 71 percent of wireless phones. Three mammoth companies, along with two smaller ones, own defense manufacturing. Eight "Baby Bell" telephone companies turned into four. Airlines, semiconductor memory chips, pharmaceuticals, college textbooks, food production, and food retailing—the concentration in these and other sectors seems an ironic outcome for an era that celebrated deregulation and set out to reinvigorate "free market" competition. But this too is an old story. Interludes of intense competition always are followed by the high-stakes rush to reconcentrate market power among a few. Corporations, like human beings, seek stability in their lives and use their predatory size to secure it.[4]

The antitrust laws that originated during the "robber baron" era to contain the overbearing size of industrial giants have been largely neutered. They were never altogether effective, but the social meaning of the legal doctrine has been whittled away steadily (most audaciously during the Reagan era) so that the deep-rooted American skepticism toward bigness and its impact on democratic society has been virtually lost in the law. A restoration and reformulation of the theory and doctrine is urgently needed and might start by changing its name, from the archaic "antitrust" to something fresh and optimistic, like "social trust" policy.

David Morris, the advocate for small, local, innovative enterprises, sees "the deck always stacked against them." The first step, Morris suggests, is to restore the legal presumption that bigger and bigger is always suspect, inherently not better for a free society, and not even for advancing capitalism: "If we just recognized [that] the central principle antitrust embodies is that the burden of proof has to be on those who want to get bigger, there are very few, if any, of these deals that we would approve."

In the early 1900s, as the broad ranks of shareholders were separated from corporate control, the insiders were rewarded with greater rights to be irresponsible through introduction of the "limited liability" corporation. The new doctrine was adopted state by state over stiff resistance in state legislatures. It meant that if the company went bankrupt investors would lose the value of their shares, but no more. Thus, their personal wealth was insulated from any further liabilities stemming from the company they had owned. That may sound logical and necessary to modern sensibilities—a way to encourage entrepreneurial explorers—but it has had the effect of authorizing recklessness. The reform was undertaken, not in behalf of the small shareholders, but for the major investors and other insiders. They could walk away from their failures and start again elsewhere while bankruptcy courts picked over the corporate carcasses they had left behind.

"Limited liability basically shifts the risk of enterprise from the owners to the creditors, including construction companies, suppliers, lenders, and laborers," William G. Roy wrote in his social history of the large industrial corporation. The full costs of failure (whether from stupidity or fraud) are thus "socialized," as Roy put it. That is, the costs are spread across many other parties in society—including wrecked communities—while the architects of the disaster are excused.

Doubtless, this doctrine does encourage a more adventurous capitalism, but it also assigns the losses to people and interests who typically have already been victimized by the failure. We can observe the injustices of "limited liability" in the laborious legal cleanups following the debacles of Enron, WorldCom, Global Crossing, and many other bankruptees. The insiders held onto their mansions and personal fortunes. The losers—creditors, suppliers, shareholders, employees—fought over the scraps, with their claims stacked in descending order of priority—bankers first, employees last. In bankruptcy court, employees always come in last. Indeed, they may have no standing at all unless they can prove fraud or they have an enforceable union contract.

The concept of "limited liability" has also slyly damaged American culture by diluting the ideal of personal responsibility for one's actions. My own family history includes the cautionary tale of a learned great-uncle, Cicero McClure, a farmer in western Pennsylvania who died well before I was born. Uncle Cicero was a director and investor in a small community bank that failed during the great banking panic of 1907. For long years afterward he worked nights as a watchman at an electric power substation in order to repay depositors who had lost their money. They were friends and neighbors. He felt the obligation, whether or not the law required it. I do not recommend such extreme sacrifice for failed investors—it would be unthinkable today—but his story does suggest how much our system of personal values has been degraded by the conventions of modern capitalism.

These various legal premises established long ago all undergird the command-and-control authority of the corporate insiders, especially over the workforce. I use "command and control" ironically because it is the ideological catchphrase always invoked against state-centered socialism or, for that matter, against federal regulatory laws. In the U.S. legal structure, however, it is not the state alone but the corporation where command-and-control is located. This includes intimate powers to tell workers what to do and what not to say (as discussed in Chapter 3). While obviously convenient for managers at the top, their concentrated power distributes many unseen costs throughout the society.

Inherent to this command structure, the corporation functions as a principal source of American inequality, concentrating both power and wealth at the top. It does this by aggregating the surplus value produced from what employees contribute to the firm through their labor and knowledge, then redistributes that value upward and outward to others. Naturally, the insiders do not grant employees a voice in this distribution if they can avoid it. The steep pyramid in incomes—CEOs making more than 500 times what their company's workaday employees earn—would be inconceivable if control of how the surplus returns are distributed was not so closely held. The production of inequality is not inherent to the corporate institution itself, but it cannot be altered unless corporations are reorganized internally.

"The accumulation of wealth and power through large organizations is the modern device for generating inequality," sociologist Charles Perrow explained in *Organizing America,* his study of corporate capitalism. "The bigger the organization, the bigger the surplus is likely to be. . . . It is likely that the larger the organization, the greater the multiple of earnings of top officials over the lowest rank, further centralizing wealth. If an organization buys up other firms, the profits from those employees go to the top. In addition, the larger the firm, the more market power it will have, further increasing profits, and the more political power it is likely to have because of its control of resources (jobs, capital, plants, and equipment, etc.) that are vital to governments."

This fundamental relationship between inequality and the corporation is so thoroughly obscured by business lore and economic mythology that even very sophisticated citizens may not grasp the connection. At a town meeting with management, some five hundred Dow Jones employees, including reporters for *The Wall Street Journal,* complained bitterly about the company's harsh cutbacks in 2002, when scores of senior journalists were fired while senior management and shareholders "didn't suffer any pain," as one employee put it. Dow Jones Chairman Peter Kann was taken aback by the openness of their anger. "It's not an egalitarian place," Kann explained. "No corporation is." Why not? Kann seemed visibly flustered by the question. "That's one of the dangers you face living in a capitalist society," he replied. The employees thought in hard times the sacrifices should be shared by all. Their boss was simply explaining the fundamentals of corporate organization.[5]

When this power alignment first unfolded in history, people did rebel—furiously. From the outset of the modern corporation, working people organized collectively in unions to fight for better wages, control of the workplace, and safe, secure working conditions. Social reformers, likewise, campaigned for standards of decency, respect for human life. Politicians from both parties repeatedly legislated new public rules and requirements to constrain corporate behavior. Mostly forgotten now, these social struggles against corporate power represented the largest mobilization of citizens across fifty years of history, from the Populists in the 1890s to New Deal reformers during the Great Depression.

Early on, however, as the reform efforts were gaining political momentum, the Supreme Court threw a huge log across their path. The property rights of business, the court declared, protected companies from government economic and social regulation. In 1905, the court's *Lochner* decision invoked this logic to invalidate a pioneering labor law enacted by New York state to require a ten-hour workday and safer working conditions in bakeries. The statute was unconstitutional, the justices explained, because it intruded—without the "due process" of law guaranteed by the fourteenth amendment—on business's right to produce profit from its private property. Property over people. The concept generated great outrage, but the court stood its ground. For the next three decades it used the *Lochner* doctrine to block virtually any new social and economic reforms. More than two hundred state and federal laws were invalidated: minimum-wage standards, health and safety codes, workers' right to organize, and many others.

The judicial stranglehold on public action was not broken until deep into the New Deal, when a liberal majority finally was established on the Supreme Court in 1937. The court promptly upheld the new National Labor Relations Act and declared that government has broad powers to protect society's general health and welfare by regulating business activity. That moment opened the modern era of government and its expansive use of regulatory powers, including for environmental protection. Many great accomplishments endure, and corporate behavior and accountability were improved significantly. Yet many reforms also have been effectively gutted, as regulators were captured by counterattacking corporations or regulatory standards fell victim to political reinterpretation, their meaning held hostage to the next election.

In other words, the legal foundations for asserting society's values remain insecure and threatened. The right wing of the Republican party (discreetly encouraged by corporate interests) is determined, in fact, to restore the *Lochner* doctrine as "the law of the land." Conservative litigators and policy groups are promoting a novel constitutional interpretation that, in their own words, would "invalidate the twentieth century." Regulatory actions, they argue, amount to a "taking" of private property by government (just as when government takes private land for a road or public park). Therefore, the affected business interests are entitled to be compensated for any loss, even for marginal intrusions on their profit making.

Under this logic, to put it baldly, government would have to pay the polluters to stop polluting, a doctrine sure to guarantee far fewer environmental laws. That, of course, is the idea. This would throw a tight noose around government's ability to enact economic and social regulations and thus further weaken the public's ability to defend itself. That prospect sounds too bizarre (and reactionary) to be taken seriously, but five justices of the conservative Supreme Court have formally endorsed the constitutional logic of the "takings" theory, though they have not yet found the nerve to apply its full meaning. Possibly they recognize that crippling the public's right to regulate corporations could ignite social rebellion and a governing crisis.[6]

Modern government, meanwhile, continues to elaborate new legal privileges for corporate "personhood," and in some exotic ways that were revealed in the wake of the Enron scandal. A corporation, the public discovered, may turn itself into a citizen of Bermuda for purposes of avoiding U.S. taxes without losing any of the benefits and protections of being American. A corporation may split off elements of itself into "special purpose entities," and these off-balance-sheet partnerships permit a kind of dematerialized accounting. Bank loans become "revenue" on the company's books. Its debts mysteriously turn into "assets." The illegitimacy of these legal deceptions is made obvious when one asks: What if families tried to arrange their financial affairs or tax returns in this manner? They likely would be prosecuted. Congress could clear away all of these corporate tricks by imposing one simple requirement: Companies must report the same set of numbers (revenue, profit, and loss) to the tax collector as they report to their shareholders. It is hard to imagine Congress undertaking such a revolutionary step.

In all these ways the corporation became a uniquely powerful institution and proceeded to use these advantages to become still more powerful. Richard Grossman, codirector of the Program on Corporations, Law and Democracy, a citizens group campaigning for deep reforms, offered a provocative metaphor to summarize the story: "People create what looks to be a nifty machine, a robot, called the corporation. Over time the robots get together and overpower the people. They redesign themselves and reconstruct law and culture so that people fail to remember they created the robots in the first place, that the robots are machines and not alive. For a century, the robots propagandize and indoctrinate each generation of people so they grow up believing that robots are people too."[7]

THE BASIC QUESTION of reform is: Can the corporation be refashioned into a more responsive, less powerful institution without destroying the qualities that make it effective as a business organization? Obviously, altering any of the historic legal premises—moving the boundary markers in society's favor—will be most difficult, but perhaps not as hopeless as generally assumed. Governments do still possess the capacity to redefine the chartering terms for incorporation or to modify other legal protections. The difficulty is finding a state legislature with the will to do so. But some states have acted in limited ways when they saw sufficient cause. A handful of midwestern and western farm states prohibit corporations from owning farmland in agricultural production in order to block the concentration of farm ownership or to discourage notorious practices like the hog factories. During the takeover frenzy of the 1980s a larger number of states enacted antitakeover provisions that enabled boards of directors to stymie the corporate raiders, thus protecting local companies and jobs from the destructive grasp of the conglomerates.

A reform idea with superficial appeal is the wholesale rechartering of corporations by the federal government, proposed by Ralph Nader a generation ago and first championed by some progressive reformers early in the last century. That sounds like a swift, straightforward solution, but aside from the political implausibility, it skips over some hard questions without answering them: To what end will the corporation be redefined? And who will control the new terms? A mammoth federal regulatory agency, the courts, popular plebiscites? Blanket rechartering, in other words, could encounter the same vulnerabilities that undermine the regulatory system. Without first establishing the functional principles in bedrock—what society wants and needs from corporations—the vision is easy prey to the same political manipulations. It seems the wrong place to start.

A more practical approach would begin, less grandiosely, by thinking about the real-world distinctions that already exist in the corporate realm and exploring how these distinctions might be used as leverage points for altering the underlying legal premises. In other words, there are concrete differences in corporate behavior—good, bad, and terrible—that could become the basis for modifying corporate legal privileges, not in search of utopian perfection, but in order to reward what is better and penalize what's worse. The required analysis would be a little like Innovest's comparative tracking of company returns in the context of environmental behavior (described in Chapter 4). But the objective is quite different (and more difficult) because the yield in question is not return to investors but society's satisfaction with the company's performance across many areas of concern.

Measuring a corporation's social responsiveness or the internal accountability of its operating structure and culture cannot be easily reduced to scores and percentages or even legal definitions. But these qualities and others can be gauged concretely by systematic research and reporting. That would start by asking the various contributors or communities how the company behaves. Studying a corporation's actual performance, past and present, alongside its proclaimed values may reveal telling comparisons about which designs for corporate governance consistently produce the better results. Making distinctions, getting beyond generalized bromides, is a way to gain leverage for changing the status quo.

All shareholders are not equal, for instance, despite the conventional lore that pretends otherwise. It is the large-scale investors who become the intimate insiders with management and who control the large decisions that often injure, rather than serve, the broader ranks of distant shareholders (not to mention society). The company treats these big guys differently, since they are often the controlling owners, and so should the law. The "limited liability" protections, for instance, could be modestly scaled back for the inside stakeholders, proportionate to the size of their holdings in the firm and their proximity to power. This would raise the level of risk for those who stand to gain the most from their insider status.

Congress actually took a small step in this direction with the accounting reform legislation enacted in 2002, with a provision that makes it marginally easier to win personal restitution from corporate executives for fraudulent conduct. The same approach could be broadened to cover egregious management failures that do not reveal criminal intent but are profoundly destructive for other parties. The AOL Time Warner merger, for example, is a stunning case of horrendous error by the insiders, betting two large and strong corporations on dubious premises and severely damaging both enterprises, their employees, and shareholders. Yet there is no recourse by which to hold the architects accountable, unless a crime can be proven. Business and finance, meanwhile, campaign to shrink their liabilities still further. Under the banner of "tort reform," they lobby relentlessly for legal ceilings on the damage lawsuits filed against them by injured citizens (and Congress sometimes goes along).

Reducing "limited liability" protection for the designated insiders—increasing their exposure to personal loss—would instill a measure of personal responsibility at the commanding heights. Let those who control things share in the downside costs of their adventures. This new measure of discipline (if one can imagine its adoption) also would provide the leverage for encouraging structural reforms by corporations themselves. Companies, for instance, might be permitted to retain the full scope of their "limited liability" protection *if* they restructure internally to disperse power and ownership so that other contributors become authentic insiders themselves, starting with the employees. Management thus would have to accept greater internal accountability, including legal obligations for disclosure and deliberations with other contributing elements, including the supporting communities, in exchange for retaining their own "limited liability" protection. If they chose not to reform, insiders would face greater financial risk for the consequences of their actions.

Like shareholders, corporations are not all alike either. They exist variously in size, shape, and internal configurations, indeed, in hybrid formats too numerous and complex to describe. The law already recognizes most of these differences in excruciating detail, especially in the tax code, since the obscure distinctions and exceptions typically are enacted at the behest of business interests (much like the corporate legal privileges adopted originally). The usual justification for these myriad exceptions is that whatever makes a corporation more effective (profitable) is bound to improve the overall economy and, therefore, benefit everyone. But is this actually true?

What is largely missing from the political deliberations is the social presence that would ask different questions about what's valuable and what's harmful. A thorough reconsideration of the loopholes and exceptions in the corporate tax code, for instance, would ask whether any of these esoteric arrangements, like the so-called "special purpose entities," actually produce real value for the economy or exist mainly to legalize tax evasion and other antisocial maneuvers. The missing political question is: Why are the corporate "persons" treated so much more generously than living, breathing citizens, especially when the corporate privileges often are used to damage the interests of the human "persons"?

The social inquiry, more broadly, would examine the vast differences in corporate governance, structure, and scale, and seek to discover which corporate arrangements really do provide the greatest benefits, not to the bottom line alone, but for society's noneconomic imperatives. Once such distinctions are established and made clear to the public, government might then begin to exercise preferences and to shrink the operating boundaries for corporate types that consistently injure or neglect or destabilize the society that chartered their existence.

Since the political system obviously lacks the courage, this inquiry will have to be taken up initially by nonofficial "public auditors"—respected authorities, scholars, community leaders, perhaps supported by private philanthropy—who can be trusted to do honest examinations. This "public audit" would require a supple and difficult search—one that depends on field-tested results—but also could open up productive conversations with numerous corporations about how they perform, how they are held accountable. Some of us have strong convictions that a more democratic corporate design works best for society and are confident that a thorough inquiry will confirm this. Everyday Americans might like our logic, but they will want to see living proof.

In any case, these modest suggestions for initiating corporate reform, though intentionally gradualist, are probably not yet ready for prime-time politics. They would be batted away swiftly by business and finance interests with their usual warning to politicians: Don't mess with the golden goose. The corporation, they would caution, functions as the main vessel of our economic prosperity, and anyone who tampers with it will be punished severely by campaign contributors and also by the voters if things go awry. That admonition usually shuts down any serious political discussion. They have a point. It is too easy for critics to assume the modern corporation exists only because of some long ago power grab.

The corporate institution also has prevailed because of its substantive strengths—inherent organizational qualities that deliver real value for society and for the economy. Our discussion thus far has focused on the dysfunctional elements, how corporations acquired their expansive powers and misuse them. But we cannot grasp fully what is dysfunctional in the modern corporation until we also learn to appreciate its virtues.

THE CORPORATION is not the marketplace. That is its essential quality and most important strength. In fact, the corporate organization provides shelter from the storms of the marketplace, the daily buying and selling, the continuous shifting of prices and loyalties. The corporation may be thought of as a kind of protected cloister for sustained economic development, the place people gather to collaborate in complex, long-running processes of innovation and production. These collaborations could not be sustained without some shielding cover from the volatile uncertainties of market exchange.

This distinction is crucial, yet poorly understood. Popular economic discussions skip over it usually, treating markets and corporate organizations as though they are elements of the same thing. Neo-classical economists do not have much to say about the nature of corporations, since the corporate relationship is an awkward exception to their belief that, as Milton Friedman put it, "voluntary exchange" in the unfettered marketplace is the heart of capitalism. Likewise, radical critics who propose to abolish the corporation seem unaware that this would consign everyone, every transaction and every relationship, to the atomizing churnings of the amoral "free market."

Corporations do, of course, engage the marketplace and market competition, buying resources as inputs, selling products, and raising financial capital. But the corporation's organizational nature is the opposite of the market's, a long-running collaboration, not a daily auction. The differences are elaborated lucidly by economist Mary A. O'Sullivan in *Contests for Corporate Control*. The market, she explained, functions in transactions of buying and selling that are highly individualistic, temporary relationships and often even anonymous (a seller need only know the price, not the identity, of the buyer). Market transactions are reversed easily (buy something one day, sell it the next). And the market's power is dispersed so widely among the participants that none can claim to control it (unless they have acquired the lopsided dominance of an illegitimate monopoly).[8]

The corporation, by contrast, is a collective effort, a fixed relationship among people, resources, and interests. It makes irreversible decisions. And essentially it is in charge of itself. The company integrates people and resources in complex, ongoing processes and coordinates the contributions from many diverse players (that is, manages them). Unlike the market, the corporation has to make commitments of capital that cannot be easily undone: building new factories; hiring and deploying workers; allocating resources to fixed objectives with a recognition that the results may not be known for months or years. The corporation, though always tossed about by market forces, makes its own decisions. Insiders determine the core strategy—where to deploy capital, the people, and the machines, and for what purpose. Then the managers adjust strategy and performance, more or less continuously, in response to the real-world results.

This stripped-down description sounds grossly simplified because it leaves out the webs of external forces that surround the corporate organization and constantly bear down on its internal decisions: the changing tides of customer taste and demand; the confidence levels of creditors and investors; the great unknowns of technological change or the threat of a competitor firm that develops a shrewder strategy and better methods for accomplishing the same purpose. Still, this organizational sketch should make the central point clear: The collaborative nature of the corporation accomplishes what markets never could do alone. It brings people together for long-term objectives and keeps them together and engaged in the complexity until the goals are fulfilled (or perhaps till the company goes bust).

Clearly, a coordinated assembly of people and resources is a more cost-efficient way to undertake complex tasks than going into the marketplace every day to buy the right machines and technical knowledge or to hire skilled workers to keep production lines going (though companies do hire "temps" and consultants). Because the company controls its own resources internally, it may ignore the daily market deviations. The company knows (at least believes) its resources are organized uniquely to produce new, added value at the end of the process. That is, the creation of new wealth, the corporation's permanent goal.

More from less. Mineral ore goes in the door and comes out as steel or aluminum. Others take up the metals and make large-body commercial aircraft. And so on. None of this can be accomplished by buyers and sellers participating in daily price auctions. It requires an organization with an idea of the future and the permanence to see it through. The corporate form has prevailed, I suspect, not so much because of its cost-efficiencies, but because it so faithfully mirrors the forward-looking narrative at the core of capitalism. The corporation is the instrumental expression of that brilliant dynamic (described in Chapter 4) in which a capital investor envisions the future, sets out to make the vision come true, collects his returns, and tries again. And, yes, corporations must be profitable in order to participate in this virtuous cycle.

These fundamental attributes are what might be called the nonnegotiable qualities of the corporation; if any are missing or severely compromised, the goose is definitely endangered. O'Sullivan's book describes three core conditions the corporation must have to function: secure commitments of finance capital; effective integration of its many organizational elements; finally, insider control. All of these are necessary to sustain production, and to envision the future accurately. With insider control and solid information the "strategists" at the top level of the firm are able to make the best-informed decisions about allocating capital, based on what they have learned from the company's own participants about its processes and products. Without these three qualities the company loses control of its own destiny to financial markets and eventually loses the creativity that keeps it alive.

If O'Sullivan's terms define the essential latitudes for corporate organization, then a broad vista is open for reform—an enormous space for significantly altering corporate structure and behavior without disturbing the core virtues. "Insider control," for example, does not lead inexorably to the rigid, top-down managerial structures that are commonplace. If "insiders" were redefined to include all the other participants in the firm, sharing ownership and voice in the decision making, then organizational integration arguably would be enhanced by the democratic ethos. Certainly, a corporation needs well-informed managers who are empowered to manage. It does not require demented egotists at the top of a very steep pyramid.

Furthermore, these core elements of corporate organization actually are undermined by many of the contemporary practices embraced by corporate management. The overbearing pressures from outsiders—stock market analysts and financial advisers—may overwhelm a company's ability to make its own, self-informed decisions about deploying capital for the future. The disciplinary doctrine of "shareholder value" deliberately induces financial insecurity on the company—the very opposite of the secure financial commitments a company needs to think beyond its immediate horizon. The recurring managerial initiatives to "downsize" and "rationalize" may deliver short-term financial gain, but they also can hollow out the company's dynamic integration of its many working parts. These forces are more than distractions; they may contribute to failure.

Whether a company succeeds or fails essentially is determined by what goes on inside the organization, not by outside kibitzing or tampering, no matter how useful that might be. The essence of the successful corporation, as O'Sullivan explains in a telling phrase, is its function as a "learning collectivity." Only through continuous, collective learning among participants and managers is the company able to innovate, to discover new insights about itself and its objectives. And only innovation gives it the ability to survive and flourish; that is, to produce genuinely new value that can compete with others trying to do the same. Innovation, in these terms, simply consists of discovering new methods or products that deliver greater quality or cost savings or advanced capacities over whatever existed before.

Thus, the company's innovation gives it an edge in the market competition, protects it from falling behind. To achieve this, obviously, a company must want to learn. It must give employees and other collaborators reasons to share in the curiosity about how things might be done differently, better. The successful company sustains an atmosphere that brings forth from within the "collectivity" what people learn and discover among themselves from their work.

This idealized description seems a long way from how critics depict the corporation and, for that matter, will seem fabulously mistaken to many of the people who work inside corporations. Many business organizations do not function as a "learning collectivity," except in a few specialized positions, and privately would dismiss the concept. Some very large corporations are essentially exempt from learning and innovating because they have achieved overwhelming market dominance and their size, in a sense, protects them from new ideas. Other companies are routinely (and usefully) exploiting old discoveries, plowing the same furrows year after year, with no incentive to change much. These exceptions remain secure and profitable, but only so long as no one enters their market and disrupts it with new and better thinking.

This quality—the capacity for innovation—ought to be the first, most important social test of corporate governance. Regardless of how the firm is organized, does its organizational control system inspire innovation or suppress it? Do the "strategists" commit capital to innovative priorities because they are steadily informed by the "learners" scattered throughout the company? Or do they focus capital on empty financial plays that may generate returns but do nothing for the company's future well-being? This is a far different yardstick than the usual questions applied to corporate governance—how many directors are "independent" or whether the auditors are rotated every few years— but it speaks more directly to the core reality of the corporate institution and to what society wants and needs from it.

For society's purposes, innovation is probably the most critical standard (even more so than for investors) because organic institutional change can hardly occur without it. The innovative corporation has the capacity to confront larger social discontents and injuries within itself—income inequity or ecological damage that perhaps flow from its own behavior—and search for viable solutions. The "learning collectivity" has an inquiring spirit, a habit of exploring different paths uncertain of the outcome but unhobbled by the existing routines. It takes a self-confident CEO to undertake such forays into the "new" not knowing what the costs or payoff might be. It takes a self-confident workforce to cooperate with such experiments and make them succeed. When a company does manage to correct social problems it becomes the model for other firms—and the standard by which others can be rebuked or penalized.

The most dramatic example of social necessity is the ecological crisis. Industrial transformation—re-creating products and processes to reduce and eventually eliminate the destructive consequences for nature—cannot proceed without the willing expertise of innovative companies. The country needs corporations capable of doing this. Above all, it needs a system of corporate governance that leads (and pushes) companies to embrace the goal as its mission. For social purposes, the substance of innovative performance matters more than organizational form. Nor does it matter whether a company pursues the challenge of invention to gain economic advantage or to fulfill its felt social obligations. Effective corporate governance recognizes that motives of self-interest and social obligation are compatible and mutually reinforcing.

Likewise, on a scale similar to the ecological challenge, the United States is not going to overcome globalization's relentless downward pressures on U.S. wages and jobs unless it fosters a sustained era of domestic industrial innovation. As management expert Peter Drucker and others have warned, American production will remain competitive worldwide only by moving to higher levels of quality and skills, creating superior, distinctive products and preparing the workforce to perform with greater sophistication and innovation. Otherwise, as Ron Blackwell of the AFL-CIO explains, technology allows the high-end products to be converted swiftly into mass-produced commodities that are readily manufactured elsewhere by low-wage workers. Without innovation, the high-wage jobs continue to migrate to foreign production. The widening gulf of wage inequality becomes a permanent chasm in American society. Innovation is not the whole answer, of course, but a necessary component of confronting both ecological destruction and income inequality.

Skeptics will point out that "innovation" has become such a well-worn cliché in management circles that the label is cheerfully applied to anything, including the antisocial practices I have described: the nasty new ways to squeeze the workforce; appealing new products that conceal destructive consequences; notorious innovations like the automated hog factories. This is true enough, but these "improvements" are transparently false innovations and easily distinguishable. Typically, the supposed "savings" are achieved by ignoring the true costs of the new product or process. Or by failing to examine the future consequences. Or by deliberately pushing those costs and risks off on other parties. Identifying what constitutes genuine new value as opposed to the artful redistribution of liabilities is a critical distinction, but the task of determining which is which becomes easier when all of the contributors to a firm are involved.

In sum, if O'Sullivan's "learning collectivity" becomes the standard by which corporations are judged, then the system for corporate governance has to be refocused on a different set of values, with more intrusive questions, but also more human-scale content. The governance test would be about operating qualities within a corporation far more than external legalities or financial reports. Such a shift would not eliminate the need for prudential checks and balances—auditors and directors who are supposed to provide independent oversight; trustworthy reporting to shareholders—though, as we have seen, those agents are not terribly effective at preventing financial fraud and other large abuses. A new regime of oversight would measure performance in concrete ways—tracking a company's learning-and-innovating capacity—and require an internal structure that plausibly promotes these same qualities. As previous examples illustrated and real-world experience demonstrates, there are various organizational patterns that can lead to the same outcome—a corporation structured to generate authentic innovation. The proof will be in the results, not the form.

Essential design elements would involve mechanisms that foster the fluid integration of "learners" with "strategists"; channels up and down for mutual accountability and inquiry within the firm; and formal commitments to the corporation's shared goals (statements of intent that are perhaps less than an enforceable contract but more concrete than public relations press releases). This platform implies the need for shared ownership among the many contributors as an anchoring fact that gives concrete meaning to the new power relationships and assures standing for those who are not in charge. A company might theoretically accomplish all this without shared ownership—some companies do—but participatory work systems based on good faith alone are always vulnerable to change with the next CEO.

More important, ownership provides an accepted legal foundation in property rights for redefining the meaning of "insiders" inclusively. The people who own and control the firm would become an expanded group of those who are genuinely engaged in the life of the company, not a mere handful of key decision makers. The broad ranks of shareholders would not lose anything in this new arrangement, but the fiction of their "ownership" would be discarded. Passive shareholders would thus have the same influence they have now—not much. That would change only if they choose to make direct, secure commitments of capital to the company, investments that are more permanent than the easy exit available to them in the stock market. One can imagine a new variety of mutual funds that aggregate many small investors to manage such investments, adhering to articulated values and specified objectives. Collectively, the small shareholders would then exercise the same sort of focused investment power that now belongs only to wealthy large-bloc holders. In other words, shareholders who take actual responsibility for the firm can share in governing it. Others will remain distant bystanders.

Men are not angels, as James Madison warned us, and especially not angelic when they are attempting to govern themselves. Nothing about corporate governance by workers or, for that matter, by communities guarantees that they will be wiser or more responsible to social obligations, less selfish or less foolishly shortsighted. A democratized internal structure ought to encourage greater trust and mutual accountability, fusing the judgments of many perspectives, but in human institutions there are no final remedies for folly and error. On the other hand, it is hard to imagine that worker-owners would do worse than some of the recently celebrated titans who, with assistance from sheeplike directors and malleable auditors, enriched themselves by destroying the companies.

What the new "insiders" would bring to the table is their own everyday knowledge of the company, the personal investment of their lives, and their own diverse, independent social conditionings. Employees see things the managers do not see. Most are invested for the long term. This might sometimes incline many employees toward more conservative strategies than the CEO—change can be threatening—but their skepticism might be well-founded (or sometimes wrong). But, surely, the value choices of the broader group provide a more reliable bedrock for a company's direction than the whims of distant stock market analysts.

A corporation can adopt a democratized ownership and operating culture, but a company is not a political democracy and cannot function like one. A democracy (as we have witnessed frequently in modern politics) may decide not to decide and instead do nothing. A company does not have that luxury. It cannot survive without making decisions, continuously and concretely, including decisions unpleasant for some contributors. One expects the managers, for instance, to eliminate unnecessary jobs in the interest of all the owners. A different ownership base might, however, accept obligations to the people who lost the jobs. Shared ownership means sharing the risks as well as the rewards. An innovative company might adopt universal wage adjustments or paid furloughs for the hard times, so that everyone takes a hit when the market turns sour and costs need to be reduced. These and other mechanical solutions exist for reducing the stress and inequity that occurs within companies, including the segmented exploitation of temp workers. Closely held power has no incentive to try any of these since it directly benefits from the inequalities.

But these reforms will not eliminate the need for hard choices. In short, the executive needs the authority to act—to have the last word—and he can't rely on majority opinion to protect him. One can imagine many systems of checks and balances—the "manage-ment team" approach and formal consultations with other "teams" within the company—that establish the executive's power to act without re-creating the "cult of the CEO." The broadened ranks of insiders, for instance, might exercise a "vote of confidence" every two or three years, a regular opportunity to reconsider strategy and vent complaints about the management. A negative vote wouldn't neces-sarily remove the CEO from office, but it would send a strong signal to the board of directors that something is seriously amiss.

A company perpetually at war with its own employees is most unlikely to foster innovation or even recognize learning as an impor-tant asset. In the modern era, workers are often reduced to the status of severable commodities—just another "market input"—while the "efficient" corporation keeps its distance from long-term commit-ments or two-way relationships. Temp workers are the extreme exam-ple, but the same distancing has occurred far up the line, including the middle managers and technical workers who are most vital to the learning-innovating processes. Where did managers get the idea that an insecure and adversarial culture would encourage risk taking and creative thinking? It probably emanated from the financialization of corporate managements, when engineers and old-school managers were displaced by the "numbers guys" from finance. The ascendancy of neoclassical economics also lent support, since it depicts individu-als as bundles of self-interest who can be satisfactorily understood through a single motivation—their desire for gain.

Charles Perrow, the sociologist, has ridiculed the economist's brit-tle understanding of human nature by comparing it to *The Invasion of the Body Snatchers* "where human forms are retained but all that we value about human behavior—its spontaneity, unpredictability, self-lessness, plurality of values, reciprocal influence, and resentment of domination—has disappeared."

Perrow's larger point is that the corporation is a social organization itself. Whatever else it may be, it exists inescapably as a social organization, since it brings people together in relationships with each other and with the company. What Perrow, O'Sullivan, and other critical voices are suggesting is that the well-being of the corporation as a business enterprise cannot be separated from its qualities as a social organization. If one dimension is dysfunctional, then the other cannot be unaffected. That seems so elementary, it should hardly need to be said. Yet the ethos of the modern corporation promotes the contrary view—that the organization exists above and apart from the people who come and go within it.[9]

But what if the "numbers guys" are wrong? What if deterioration in the social organization foretells the decline of the business enterprise? This would occur, not as a matter of human sentiment, but because the firm gradually loses this sustaining process of learning and innovating, a capacity that depends upon those unmeasurable human qualities cited by Perrow, like "spontaneity, unpredictability, selflessness." The linkage between business and social realities would be more widely appreciated if economists were equipped to examine economic life in more supple human terms. The evidence is abundant; corporations striving to revive their innovative spirit begin by promoting an inclusive, collective identity with their contributors.

The "learning collectivity" is further threatened by the question of scale. As companies succeed and grow larger, the distance naturally lengthens between the top managers who make the strategic decisions and others who know the working realities within the firm. When a company begins to acquire other companies, the connection is strained further. When a corporation becomes a conglomerate composed of many unrelated businesses, the collective learning process becomes so tenuous it often disappears. Then key decisions on how to deploy capital are more likely driven by external financial considerations, like the profit potential of acquiring still more companies or dumping others, than by what the company knows about itself. "It all depends on the relationship of the strategists with the learners," O'Sullivan wrote. "If those at the apex of the conglomerate are willing to leave strategic control in the hands of those who are integrated with the learning processes that generate competitive success in the various businesses, an integration of strategy and learning may be preserved. Unless the integration is institutionalized, however, it will be vulnerable to strategists who seek to make a reality out of the illusion of a unitary control structure for the corporate enterprise as a whole."

The "illusion of a unitary control structure" is precisely what did in so many empire builders during the boom of the nineties. Their acquisitions had an abstract logic that made sense to executives at the top (and to their investment bankers), but inside the company people could see that the rapid, undigested growth was a formula for confusion and loss of purpose—literally destroying the accumulated knowledge within the collaborative. Size by itself does not necessitate such an outcome. Some very large companies—Johnson & Johnson, Merck, Hewlett-Packard, and others—appear to have retained the internal fluidity of learning and decision making as they expanded because central command allows a significant measure of self-direction within operating divisions or because the inherited culture supports innovative thinking.

Thermo Electron, a successful high-tech innovator in Boston, addresses the same problem by continually spinning off "new" companies—dozens of them—to produce and manage the newly discovered applications ready for commercialization. The new firms—Thermo Gas Tech, Thermo Moisture Systems, Thermo Polysonics, and so on— remain partially owned by the mother company, partly by managers and staff, and perhaps also by stock market investors, depending on each situation. Thus, the original company has had children and even grandchildren, as economist David Ellerman puts it.

The overbearing size of the largest corporations, nevertheless, still forms a barrier to creativity in the American economy because it has the effect of squelching innovation by others, intentionally or inadvertently. Smaller entrepreneurial firms, struggling to get a foothold for their new ideas, often are crumpled by the mere presence of a major player with deep pockets. Netflix, a promising Internet start-up that developed a way for people to rent DVD movies online, saw its share price collapse by the news that Blockbuster Video was investigating the same approach. As Bob Tedeschi wrote in *The New York Times,* "the potential Netflix story line began to sound familiar: a popular Internet debutante meets traditional company in dark alley, emerges with no friends and a balance sheet in serious need of medical attention."[10]

Above a certain size, getting bigger and bigger does not deliver new economies of scale; it simply walls off the threat of innovative competition. Companies use their size to guard their turf against intruders and, because they have greater financial resources and technological and marketing skills, they can literally smother the new guys who come along with a better idea. If that fails, they can buy them. When the upstart competitor is eliminated, the big boys decide for themselves whether this new idea is useful and profitable or should be consigned to permanent storage. That does not describe the market competition Adam Smith had in mind as the "invisible hand." It resembles instead the schoolyard bully who gets his way in the playground games because other kids know it is futile to challenge him.

The government, by retreating from antitrust enforcement and narrowing its application, has effectively decided that bullies are okay, even good for the economy. ExxonMobil, the mammoth oil merger blessed by the authorities, has made itself into the leading advocate for *not* doing anything about global warming. Citigroup and J.P. Morgan Chase—the much celebrated banking conglomerates created in the 1990s—were swiftly in the crosshairs of government investigations for funny-money lending to Enron.

Would any of this hopeful talk about innovation alter the behavior of Ford and General Motors? Or convert those reactionary electric utility executives to the cause of environmental reform? Probably not. Those companies are large and politically well protected. They are like old mules who know how to plow the same furrow effectively, but are too settled and stubborn in their ways to learn (much less invent) new ways to improve their social behavior. The auto companies likely will stick to their familiar routine (bigness and waste over efficiency) until the Japanese or European car companies eat their lunch—that is, take away more U.S. market share by offering new and fundamentally different cars. Then the Americans will follow, as they had to in the past. The electric utility industry probably won't reform until government makes it do so or their market is seriously disrupted by innovation—the emerging new era of solar power and other renewable sources. Both examples illustrate the social necessity of finding ways to protect the new kids on the block—the small, creative firms—against the predatory power of long established corporations.

For the long term, imagine that antitrust law is transformed into a broader, more effective legal doctrine called "social trust." This new approach would start by reestablishing the original presumption that very large business organizations are inherently suspect—not good for us—because their concentrated power undermines democratic society as well as the learning-and-innovating capacities of the economy. A "social trust" policy would not set out to break up the oversized companies that already exist, but would draw a hard line against allowing new ones. The burden of proof would be on those corporations above a certain size that intend to merge or acquire others to grow much larger. Can society trust them to be creative rather than destructive? For evidence, people would examine the company's past performance and, more important, demand plausible justifications for why bigger will advance creativity instead of damaging it. Smaller firms would have standing to examine these claims and show why the greater concentration will stifle innovation and generate other social-economic costs.

The basic idea is to create a new measuring gauge for corporate behavior and structure, one that vaguely resembles the environmental impact statements required to examine the ecological consequences of major projects. A "social trust" impact statement would ask rigorous questions and produce a yardstick for measuring corporate promises against subsequent performance. Initially, the "social trust" process might not require the full force of law enforcement, but it could provide a platform for negotiating new terms with the largest corporations and encouraging self-reforms in their operating cultures. In some sectors, where the concentration is so far advanced that breaking up the oligopoly is required, government might compel companies to accept concrete social obligations (including broadened ownership) in the process of disassembly. This leverage could become a backdoor route to amending corporate charters, case by case, in search of basic principles that may eventually be applied generally. None of this seems especially radical, but don't hold your breath waiting for congressional action on "social trust" policy.

The ultimate objective is to internalize values of responsibility within corporate organizations accompanied by political mechanisms that will protect the values from eroding in the future, because impermanence is another threatening reality for the learning collectivity. A depressing irony of American corporate history is that many of the companies now regarded as antisocial rogues were once the opposite—dynamic, innovative corporations that enthusiastically fulfilled social obligations and even pioneered social reforms ahead of government. Human institutions do change with time, of course, driven by new economic circumstances and different leaders. But one of the most troubling failures of the existing corporate-governance system is that a "white hat" company can morph into a "black hat" without disturbing its bylaws or legal obligations.

General Electric, once again, is an outstanding example. During the 1920s and through the Depression years, GE was one of the most progressive corporations. It introduced workers' councils in company plants, pioneered profit sharing, pensions, mortgage assistance, and other labor relations reforms. That era was known as "corporate liberalism" and doubtless reflected the country's political sensibilities at the time. The then accepted theory of corporate governance held that top executives and directors should represent all of the diverse interests of the many different stakeholders in the firm, from shareholders to employees, adjudicating their conflicts and ensuring that every contributor was treated equitably. GE and many other leading companies practiced this and preached it. Owen Young, the GE co-executive (cited in Chapter 3), prophesied that one day the workers would own the company and "use their capital as a tool," rather than the other way around.[11]

This did not happen. After World War II, GE remained progressive on some matters (racial equality, for one) but steadily hardened to the right (and launched Ronald Reagan's career as a conservative tribune). By the 1980s, GE had embraced the tough-minded command-and-control values promoted by Jack Welch. Notwithstanding the company's nostalgic TV commercials, General Electric is no longer known as an innovator. Basically, it is a diversified holding company that acquires companies already dominant in their sectors, then dumps them if they lose their commanding position. This strategy certainly has been good for "shareholder value," though not for the Hudson River and other places despoiled by GE operations. The "new" General Electric raises irresponsibility to a proud creed.

The mutability of corporate values is a crucial part of our problem. Many forces—intensifying global competition or perhaps the mental fatigue of an aging organization—may explain why a company discards or loses its original values and culture. Whatever the causes, the impermanence demonstrates that a corporation needs a stronger anchor to its social commitments than the good intentions of the chief executive. The stakeholder theory recently has come back in fashion (at least among some reformers and politicians), but amounts to no more than a wishful restatement of corporate liberalism. The sentiments are noble but will remain empty and perishable if they are not firmly anchored in the actual power relationships within the corporation. Broadened ownership and various internal mechanisms I have mentioned may be essential supporting conditions, if not a guarantee.

The hard part is the culture within a company—the living relationships of a social organization. Culture is a far more elusive condition because it cannot be imposed from outside nor dictated from above. It cannot be written down nor faked. If a company proclaims its commitment to equity and innovation, people inside will know from their everyday experience whether or not the values are real. Given shared seriousness, however, such a cultural reality is not a utopian vision. I turn to one existing example, a company that has sustained these values for many decades and succeeded brilliantly in business. It doesn't describe perfection or provide all of the answers. But it does fulfill what architect Bill McDonough said about his "green" buildings. If it exists, they can't say it's impossible.


HERMAN MILLER INC., a leading manufacturer of office furniture and furnishings with a sales peak of $2.2 billion, can be thought of as a brilliant anomaly. It operates on the old-fashioned human-scale values inherited from a family business and yet the company is best known as the source of world-class innovation. For four generations it has repeatedly developed industry-changing products that regularly win "best design" awards. In a business sector notorious for pollution, Herman Miller became a pioneer in assuming responsibility for systematically reducing the ecological consequences of its production. The environmental initiative originated not with management, but among conscientious employees. All of Herman Miller's 7,500 employees are shareholders who are further encouraged to think and act like owners by a bonus system based on the company's performance in creating new economic value. Yet their collective stake is far too small, only about 15 percent, to guarantee control and, in that sense, the company is "owned" by public shareholders at large. Yet the management does not take instruction from the kibitzing of stock market analysts.

"Analysts—have you ever seen an analyst who didn't want you to do more than you did?" CEO Michael Volkema remarks. "But you've got to decide whether the analysts are going to run the company or are the leaders going to run the company. Surely, if I wanted to maximize the profits of this corporation, I could stop investing in the future. But I don't know whether that would be a good thing long term for all the different constituents, whether it's customers or employees or shareholders."

As CEO, Volkema has the last call on major decisions of strategy and capital deployment, but he works within an elaborate weave of managerial teams and layered consultations. He also works without an executive contract. "Herman Miller has never given their top leaders contracts," he explains. "We are 'at will' employees. It's a little different from most corporations." Actually, it's a lot different. During the 1990s, while Volkema's company was reelaborating its concept of "corporate community," America's major corporations were discarding such talk as outmoded sentimentality. He naturally hesitates to criticize, since those companies are among his best customers.

"You can always bump into those individuals who think capitalism is about math and money," Volkema acknowledges. "Anyone who reads about the origins of capitalism knows it is much more than that. The corporation was commissioned to fill some sort of social purpose; it's not just about making money. There are people who misunderstand the system and get perverted results."

Like most remarkable institutions, Herman Miller is too idiosyncratic to be a model others could replicate easily, but its story lends insight into the dynamics of corporate culture and how values can be sustained over a very long time. Herman Miller has endured through eighty years of business without losing its character. It has struggled, prospered, altered its basic business strategy, expanded enormously, reorganized internally, changed executives—all without sacrificing the core values implanted by its founders. Respect for the individual at every level. A faithful obligation to community and larger purposes. A smart, energetic commitment to discovering something new and beneficial, then producing it profitably for people.

Above all, the Herman Miller story demonstrates how the social organization within a company can reinforce—and guide—its business enterprise. The company, like any other, has experienced setbacks and disruptions, including recessionary shoals that collapsed sales and forced layoffs. Yet it has managed to navigate the rough times without losing its singular reputation, confirmed every year by numerous awards from industry and government. It is repeatedly rated by academics and media as one of the "most admired" and "best managed" and "most ethical" companies. *Fortune* magazine put it on its original list of the "100 Best Companies to Work for in America."

Herman Miller first made its reputation a half century ago when it introduced the Eames chair designs—symbols of modernity and functional design at its best. A contemporary successor is the company's Aeron chair and both have achieved museum status. In the 1930s, Herman Miller was an obscure maker of home furniture based in Zeeland, Michigan, struggling to keep up with the annual decorative elaborations dictated by changing tastes in the home-fashion market. Its founder, D. J. DePree, decided to break free of all that and instead focus on honest, problem-solving designs that filled living needs and would last. He recruited some of the era's great designers as cosmopolitan partners: Charles and Ray Eames, Gilbert Rohde, George Nelson, and Isamu Noguchi. They generated a stream of distinctive, beautiful objects on the leading edge.

Innovation became a fixed tradition. In the late 1960s, based on a design concept of "planned nonobsolescence" developed by Herman Miller's research corporation, the company introduced a radical new approach to the business office: the movable architecture of the open-plan office system. Herman Miller gets the credit (or blame, if you prefer) for revolutionizing the white-collar workplace in the modern corporation. In the 1990s, it won design awards for ergonomic innovations in both chairs and office systems.

D. J. DePree was the formative spirit of Herman Miller Inc. (named after his father-in-law) and DePree's voice and views still echo through company lore as the institution's received wisdom. A seminal teaching involves his experience back in 1927, when the company was still very small, with the sudden death of a skilled mill-wright. When DePree visited the man's family, saw some of his poetry and handicrafts, and heard personal recollections, he was shaken to realize that he had not really known this man, not at all. "God was dealing with me about this whole thing, the attitude toward working people," as DePree recounted many times afterward. "I began to realize that we were either all ordinary or all extraordinary. And by the time I reached the front porch of our house, I had concluded that we are all extraordinary. My whole attitude had changed."

Out of this encounter DePree announced a vision: that a business should be "rightly judged by its humanity" and that everyone involved in the workplace has the right to identity, equity, and opportunity. As the story suggests, DePree was an observant Christian, a Baptist who taught Sunday school into his elderly years and was once president of the Gideon Society that places the free Bibles in hotel rooms. His social context—Zeeland and other small towns in western Michigan—was settled by the Dutch Reformed pioneers, similarly devout and conservative on the political spectrum of Protestantism. Their Calvinist faith includes a strong belief in providence, the conviction that one exists on Earth within God's protection and grand design, that therefore one has purposes to fulfill, and on that basis, one will ultimately be judged. This world view, the opposite of irresponsibility, clashes directly with the organizing assumptions of the modern industrial system.[12]

Michael Volkema explains: "At a time when Henry Ford was saying, just give me your hands [for assembly-line work], and that set the stage for the industry view of workers as a kind of production tool, DePree was awakening to the perspective of human beings as complex, unique individuals. As a consequence, he felt he was going to be dealt with himself by how he dealt with other people. Dealing with the whole person—mind, body, spirit—that became the basis for virtually everything people now see in us as unique."

A sociologist or theologian might recognize the relevance more readily than a business school economist. Herman Miller did not become a "Christian company" and, indeed, DePree surrounded himself with worldly characters of many religions, including at least one comanager who was an up-front atheist. The providential viewpoint, nevertheless, provided a kind of managerial road map for running the business. Are we creating something genuinely new in the world and useful? Is everyone given a chance to fulfill their particular talents and purpose? What does a business decision mean for the distant future? Life is a gift; use it wisely and well.

Innovation, equity, tolerance—these values seem in jarring contrast with contemporary stereotypes of religious conservatives (mainly inspired by the political exertions of the Christian right). They are understood as people hostile to modernity and change, suspicious of anyone who does not share their articles of faith. To the contrary, Volkema insists, faith can be a wellspring of innovation. "I always wonder how people who have a world view that we're just a bunch of molecules—the randomness of it all—could ever believe that they can create anything new," he says. "If you take a more providential view of the world and just look around at the wonders of the creator, you can believe in the creative capacity and the ability to design things that didn't exist before. It is true that people who lie and cheat and steal won't be very successful in our company. But, regardless of their worldview, people who believe in the dignity of other human beings will do very well."

The operating culture of every organization, however, is sooner or later tested by big change and, for business corporations, change often means trial by success—the corrosive effects of rapid growth. The decisive moment for Herman Miller occurred in 1970 when, having launched its revolutionary new approach to office design, the company had prospects for a dramatic expansion, from a workforce of five hundred or so to many thousands. But the opportunity would require enormous amounts of outside capital to finance the new factories and worldwide marketing. "Going public"—issuing stock shares for the first time—is usually the point when the founding values are dissipated, even destroyed. By 1977, Herman Miller had 2,500 employees dispersed at many new locations, and its original profit-sharing plan, innovative when it was adopted, had been eclipsed by change. Hugh DePree, who had succeeded his father as CEO and shared the same values, undertook the most difficult task of systematizing these convictions within a much larger business organization.

His method was to launch and formalize a structure for employee participation. An intense exercise in self-scrutiny followed, involving virtually all segments of the company and led by an ad hoc committee of fifty-four people elected by their coworkers. They produced a formal understanding that the employees are collectively the insiders at Herman Miller, and therefore they act as the controlling owners responsible for the firm. A new management plan worked out internal structure and numerous mechanisms for participation at every level: work teams; caucuses and councils; monthly business reports; "state of the union" tours by executives. The plan also established various performance gauges, monitoring workplace results as well as the company's financial performance. Herman Miller now targets EVA for "economic value added," a deeper measure of long-term wealth creation than profits or stock prices. These indicators are the handles through which workers can exercise responsibility and hold each other accountable to the whole enterprise, including executives.

"Each person must have the opportunity to own the business through personal value added," Hugh DePree explained. "These ownerships must be risk ownerships, shared within the business itself and based on the owners' commitment of their lives and resources."

In that spirit, a few years later, employees organized their own companywide Environmental Quality Action Team that began identifying the ways in which the company could eliminate wasteful consumption and toxic pollution, as well as push new-product design toward the ecological imperative of disassembling worn-out products and reusing the materials. The company has incorporated these elements and others in its design protocol for all newly launched products and, meanwhile, works at steadily improving the ecological ratings of existing products. Veneer finishes on furniture were shifted to a water base, and air emissions of volatile organic compounds were reduced by 90 percent. The Aeron chair is now 60 percent recyclable; the Caper chair is 100 percent. The statistical gains are impressive (and win more awards for Herman Miller), but perhaps more impressive is the company's product-by-product reporting system that makes clear how much more remains to be achieved. "No business is truly sustainable today," Volkema says. "We all have to be on an aggressive journey."

Herman Miller managers still worry about size and the dangers of becoming too big to retain the internal strengths of community. "For us, what we try to think about is how we define community," Volkema says. The "challenge for the larger organization is, there's really no way to define a tight-knit, agile community when you start to get to 10 or 30,000 employees. Somehow you have to define subset communities that have a clear line of sight on how they can add value to the larger effort. Our plant sites are 500 or 1,000 or 1,200 people—I think that's the outer limit of where you can define community." Recall that Joe Cabral, CEO of the much smaller Chatsworth Products (cited in Chapter 3), thought a work team of

150 was the outer limit for sustaining a sense of "family" among coworkers. Either way, scale may threaten productive values if employees lose their identity in the firm.

But, if Herman Miller employees are the controlling insiders and effectively the owners, what about all those absentee shareholders who hold 85 percent of the company's stock? In theory, they might be organized by a corporate raider to overturn this arrangement, but that seems most unlikely, since Herman Miller has been such a good long-term investment. If one invested $1,000 in its shares back in 1970, the holdings would have been worth $108,000 by 2001 (compared to $18,000 from investing in the S & P index). Furthermore, the distinctive qualities of the company are themselves alluring to patient capital, attracting socially responsible investors and investment funds as well as major fiduciary institutions that are not inclined to argue over short-term results. "I would be worried when the short-term market mentality begins to drive a company's business strategy," Volkema says. "I think that's a danger, especially for an innovator who has to have a special patience to be able to invent the things that don't exist today."

Innovation justifies—even requires—human-scale patience in the business strategy. "One of the things we've learned is that not every-body's innovative," he says. "So you have to understand everyone's unique talents and enable them to do what they do best. Somebody has the spectrum to envision something new, then the rest of us can see the logic of it. Innovation is not going to be done by committee. And that gifted person with the new ideas is not the same person who's going to commercialize it and bring it to market." Volkema's managerial description of these human interactions reminds me of sociologist Perrow's list of the intangible human attributes: "spontaneity, unpredictability, selflessness, plurality of values, reciprocal influence, and resentment of domination."

If you ask how Herman Miller has retained its character, the answer may be simply that it created the space for those human virtues to flourish, including "resentment of domination." By doing so, despite its changing circumstances, the company appears to have constructed a web of mutually reinforcing qualities within the organization, qualities that protect the core values from the usual intrusive pressures. If that sounds too touchy-feely for sound business management, recall that Herman Miller outperformed the S & P by 500 percent over thirty years. Shareholders are attracted by these corporate values (and perhaps silenced by the returns). The board of directors does not seek to hire swashbuckling CEOs. "That is not going to happen here because the culture wouldn't allow it," Volkema observes. The company attends to the individual but operates on the idea of community. "I think anything that has sustainable greatness," he says, "always at its heart has an ambition for the larger number rather than for a single person." These values, in turn, reproduce themselves in the people who want to work for this company and the people it wants to hire.

"We have been blessed by those workers and by the culture that attracts people who are conscientious," says Mark Schurman, director for corporate communications. "D.J. would say it is providence."


CAPITALISM, as we have observed, is evolving continuously from its own inventive energies and, presently, the corporate institution is exploring the potential of a new, dematerialized form, sometimes described as the "virtual corporation." A large corporation, thanks to the reach and precise control provided by modern communications technology, no longer needs to amass vast capital assets of its own— the centralized production centers of massive factories and work-forces. Instead, it may organize far-flung networks of allied firms to do the heavy lifting. The center thus becomes the brain and central nervous system, the systems integrator who coordinates complex activities from afar and asserts the strategy and design standards for others to follow. This power to coordinate and control is based primarily on the corporation's knowledge, not its real estate, its capital value anchored in brand names and patents.

Microsoft, never an especially large employer, got out of manufacturing altogether but still effectively asserts its market power (illegally in some cases, it turned out) through the creative control of its technology. Globalized production, whether it is Nike's sports shoes or Boeing's large-body commercial aircraft, has created webs of relationships by outsourcing production to myriad suppliers, many of whom compete with one another for the next contract. The franchise systems built around brand names and famous logos are simpler expressions of the same idea. Quality depends upon uniformity and strict adherence to performance standards. The center has the power to discipline or exclude anyone who falls short or declines to accept the network's terms.

In this new world, it is access to the network, not capital ownership itself, that becomes the crucial determinant of who flourishes or fails, social critic Jeremy Rifkin explained in *The Age of Access*. Wal-Mart, given its overbearing size, arranges exclusive supply contracts with a few selected producers and purchases from them on a massive scale (everything from prepackaged meat to home appliances). The exclusivity gives it the power to underprice smaller competitors and drive out the diversity of local retailers; it also effectively shuts out the marketplace itself. Suppliers are left in a highly dependent position, essentially producing for one all-powerful customer. "New forms of institutional power are developing that are more formidable and potentially more dangerous than anything society experienced during the long reign of the market era," Rifkin warned.[13]

The power implications are already visible in some sectors like agriculture, where farmers raise livestock (chickens, hogs, and beef) under contract to a handful of major corporations in agribusiness. The farmers are relieved of price volatility, to be sure, but they become trapped by many other risks (they own any hogs or chickens that happen to die). Once engaged by contract agriculture, farmers will have little or no bargaining power to resist the dictated terms, and usually nowhere else to turn if the company stiffs them. Take it or leave it—farmers are becoming sharecroppers on their own land. Many urban franchisees similarly are confined to powerless positions. As this new, lopsided arrangement spreads across various sectors, the power alignment begins to resemble the same anti-competitive market dominance that companies once achieved through monopolistic concentrations of ownership, only this system does not violate the existing antitrust laws.

Clearly, if these nonmarket networking relationships become the future format of the corporate institution, legal reforms are urgently needed, laws both to guarantee the bargaining rights of less powerful players and to protect independent enterprises from a predatory network determined to colonize an entire sector without owning it. Neither the courts nor politicians are yet ready to confront the implications, but pressures are slowly beginning to focus political attention. Groups of independent farmers, as well as scattered dealers, franchisees, and community retailers, are agitating for legislative reforms to protect honest market competition—just as small-business interests led the lobbying for the original antitrust laws a century ago. Knowing the history of how corporations amassed their power, one recognizes difficult political struggles ahead.

And yet there is also an optimistic subtext. The new technologies that make corporate networks plausible and effective are also tools well suited to the revival and redevelopment of smaller, independent, and diversified companies. Upstart firms can overcome many of their natural handicaps by fashioning similar alliances with like-minded independents but based on more equitable, cooperative relationships. Networks can share knowledge and professional expertise that is usually beyond the means of smaller firms. Indeed, they can share preferential markets as committed customers for each other's output. They are governed by mutual self-interest, not by a single, all-powerful center.

The industrial park of employee-owned companies envisioned by those Ohio workers and managers (cited in Chapter 3) does not have to be located on a single piece of real estate. A collaborative network among like-minded companies might be extended across very long distances, just as major corporations disperse their production around the world, but without sacrificing the self-direction of the individual firms. "An alliance of alliances," as the farmer cooperatives called it, that shares credit access or spreads market risk among many. This development might require a new type of service firm, mobile specialists who work for many companies at once, as partnerships cooperatively owned by all of them. Galaxies of smaller companies may also need the services of a trustworthy integrator—a manager who helps coordinate the market interests of the network but does not control it.

The political and economic barriers to any of these ideas are formidable, obviously, since the redistribution of power is seldom achieved without intense opposition from the status quo. But the road to genuine reform need not begin with challenging the most savvy, well-entrenched business organizations. The first stage, more plausibly, involves small-scale invention, either creating new firms based on new social understandings or negotiating new relationships with existing companies that deliver mutual benefits both to the enterprise and for its surrounding social context. Much of the activity I have described in this book essentially represents large and small steps toward this goal—reinventing and restitching the relationships within capitalism. The deep, long-term political objective of such innovation is to create a significant counterreality—viable capitalism functioning under new terms—that is large enough to become a visible alternative for people and institutions to embrace, as consumers, workers, and investors—and as citizens. That bottom-up redevelopment, slow and tentative as it may seem, is the necessary predicate for changing big-picture political forces, and for changing the rules for the biggest corporations.

Truly adventurous pioneers might experiment with the audacious challenge of designing a new corporate charter for their own enterprise; that is, literally redefining the purpose and obligations of their business organization up front, both as a formal commitment to broader social intentions and as fair notice to investors, partners, and employees that this corporation is different from the herd. Given the density of existing corporate law and securities regulation, this process may require legislative authorization, the willingness of state governments to permit a "social charter" corporation as an experimental exception to business as usual. Bill Weeks of The Nature Conservancy was trying to solve this legal problem when he sought SEC certification for the investors in the novel "forest bank" idea (cited in Chapter 5). The approach did not succeed entirely in that instance, but the concept could aid inventiveness, a concrete way of establishing the distinctive operating values that will make a new enterprise responsible and accountable.

New chartering terms also could help small firms overcome one of the principal barriers to survival: the lack of secure commitments of finance capital. Innovative entrepreneurs, pursuing social objectives in their enterprise, might negotiate terms for the corporation's charter with contributing communities or major creditors, including pension funds, who want to advance the same goals. In effect, they would work out covenants with investors to assure patient capital for the firm's development in return for explicit commitments to social obligations and responsible behavior. Abundant capital exists, as we have seen, but what's missing are reliable connections between the two—legal understandings that enable investors to evaluate the risks of good intentions on a more concrete basis than wishful thinking.

There are no established blueprints for how to accomplish these new arrangements—no proven methods that guarantee success—but there are lots of thriving examples scattered around the country (a few of them described in this book). People will study what exists, borrow ideas, and modify them to match their own circumstances and ambitions. Progress will unfold in the great American tradition of loose-jointed pragmatism—copy what works, discard what fails, and try again until you get it right.

The founding principles of the new social corporation are, likewise, not fixed elements or universally required commitments, though the broad outlines are suggested by the various examples in this book. I identify six essential social purposes that, contrary to conventional dogma of American capitalism, are not inherently incompatible with successful enterprise and, in fact, should reinforce a profitable, innovative corporation. These qualities have largely been excluded from the standard corporation by design or popular default to the existing power alignments. Think of these as six key steps toward establishing self-enforcement within a responsible business organization.

The corporation must produce real new wealth, profit in the narrow meaning but also genuine value added to the material basis for sustaining a civilized society.

The active objective of the corporation is to achieve harmony with nature, instead of borrowing assets from the future, with the understanding that disturbing nature is inescapable, but destroying it is neither required nor free.

The system of internal governance reflects a democratic understanding that one way or another all of the company's insiders "own" it and together accept the risks and responsibilities for its behavior, and that the governance mechanisms ensure participatory decision making and the equitable adjudication of inevitable differences.

The corporation, in addition to its standard obligations to investors or creditors, undertakes concrete covenants with the communities that also support it in different ways (perhaps even granting forfeitable performance bonds that will serve as formal instruments of mutual obligation and trust).

The company's mission includes promoting unbounded horizons for every individual within it, whatever their personal potential and ambitions might be.

The corporation commits to defending the bedrock institutions of the society, from the viability of family life to the integrity of representative democracy.

No one should entertain utopian visions of perfection on any of these points. Human institutions are always subject to folly and error and failure since human beings are prone to the same. What we are trying to envision is a framework of relationships that empowers business organizations to resist the low road and gives its participants the ability to hold the functional reality of the organization to its long-term purposes. Given the legal history of corporations, it probably helps to put these points in writing, codify them in ways that people recognize as genuine. But, of course, actualization requires a shared culture within the organization—mutual understandings that no one can actually see but everyone recognizes as real.

In that regard, I suggest a seventh essential quality more elusive that any of the others: a culture that encourages altruism. The idea of altruism—selfless acts on behalf of the whole—has become exceedingly unfashionable in our time. Indeed, it seems to have withered in the shadow of "economic man" whose self-interested motivations are the entire premise of how modern capitalism is organized. Only a fool, it is assumed, would act on behalf of the larger group without a direct promise of payback for himself. Yet we do regularly witness the glaring exceptions: the brave firefighters who accept grave personal risks (even near certain death) as part of the job; the soldiers willing to die for their country. On a less dramatic scale, altruistic sacrifice is a visible value in many immigrant groups, where family members and even nonrelatives contribute time and energy collaboratively to some larger struggle and distant goals of the community. Think of the Korean families who labor long hours in a small, struggling grocery store or who pool meager personal savings to enable someone else in the community to buy a retail enterprise and gain a small foothold toward future prosperity. In any healthy family, the same altruistic spirit motivates nurture of the children, an unshakable commitment to do whatever is required for their future, no questions asked about the reward for personal sacrifice. Whether one assigns this form of altruism to genetic inheritance or learned behavior, the results are usually dismal when this quality is missing from a family.

Altruism originates in such feelings of kinship and reciprocal trust—overriding obligations one feels toward advancing or defending the group without any immediate prospect of return. People do it because it feels right. Their reward is often an exalted sense of satisfaction. Richard Petti, a mathematician who has worked as a management consultant to major corporations, has witnessed within corporate cultures a reality that discourages and even punishes altruistic behavior. Telling the truth, for the greater good of the overall company, will not likely be welcomed by bosses or coworkers and, Petti observes, may get you fired. Yet the practical functioning of any healthy community—or any business organization—requires that some level of personal commitment to the greater good must be present above and beyond the question of equitable financial incentives. Perhaps it is the satisfaction of participating in something larger than self or the knowledge that one is contributing to the distant future beyond one's own mortality.

It is an enduring mystery of human nature (especially mysterious to economic orthodoxy) and not easy to describe what exactly is needed to promote such behavior. A company that reciprocates personal trust and shared values with its contributing members seems far more likely to produce mutual commitments to the whole enterprise, but only if the reciprocity is authentic. In any case, Petti has observed, a culture or a corporation that one way or another does encourage altruistic behavior will very likely endure over competitors who do not. Likewise, a society that suppresses this human attribute on behalf of mean-edged combat is likely to feel impoverished, regardless of the material accumulation.

Constructing the alternative reality of new corporations represents a crucial starting point that can eventually alter the behavior of corporations at large by raising public expectations and eventually producing new legal standards and structures. But meanwhile, reformers are not without some influence over the shape and behavior of established business organizations. As I have described, people can amass collective influence on companies as vigilant customers. As injured shareholders, they also can sue for fraudulent accounting and other corporate offenses. Plaintiffs' lawsuits are now establishing that, alongside multimillion-dollar damage awards, shareholder litigation also can win corporate governance reforms from defendant corporations. The new rules and obligations won in this are so far modest, but it is another potential lever, one taken seriously by managements because so much money is at stake. Greater leverage, now only in its infancy, is available through the coordinated power of direct investing by labor unions, their pension funds, or other major sources of capital. In exchange for their infusions of capital, these purposeful investors could gain controlling stakes in companies and negotiate investor covenants that alter the operating values or ownership structure on behalf of social purposes.

The most promising front is perhaps the slow but broad awakening of the fiduciary institutions to their own responsibilities for corporate governance, and the recognition that antisocial behavior by corporations does damage to the overall economy and therefore to the broad investment portfolios of major pension funds and others. Pension trustees are, in fact, injuring their own beneficiaries when they encourage reckless irresponsibility among the companies they own, though the fund managers have not yet developed an effective way of policing this behavior, or of rewarding or punishing companies on the basis of their social consequences. James P. Hawley and Andrew T. Williams, the business economists who elaborated the theory of "universal owners" (cited in Chapter 4), have proposed that pension fund managers begin to exercise much closer, systematic scrutiny of how companies "externalize" costs by pushing them off on others—and to use the data as a new scorecard for investment decisions. "Because of potential adverse consequences, fiduciary duty compels institutional owners to have in place a process for tracking and analyzing these developments, that is, some form of risk analysis," Hawley and Williams wrote. If major pension funds begin such universal monitoring of corporate behavior, then major corporations will have no choice but to do the same—or else lose their access to trillions of dollars in capital.[14]

In other words, reformers face an enormous mountain, but they are not impotent. As they proceed with various localized initiatives and experimental organizations of business, they will quickly recognize that there are many kindred spirits around the country working on various aspects of the same great challenge. When citizens learn to focus their potential influence—coordinating the leverage available from consumer to investor, from worker to citizen—the idea of reform will begin to seem more threatening to the established order. Resistance is likely to be political, the established corporations employing their political resources and vast machinery of public relations to block or discourage (or co-opt) the energies of change.

All of these issues will sooner or later wind up as a political fight, perhaps much sooner than the pioneers would like, since they are so outgunned by business and financial interests. Government and the political system, however, are inextricably woven into the fabric of American capitalism. In the final analysis, it is impossible to reinvent one domain without also reforming the other. For that struggle, as many reformers well understand, their government is on the other side.

# 7

# Public Works

FROM the earliest days of the republic, government has been a central actor in developing American capitalism, and doubtless it always will be. Government's role is obvious to anyone who reads a little of the national history, yet the conservative orthodoxy has managed to obscure the relationship by asserting confidently that private enterprise will flourish if only government would get out of the way. Actually, capitalism would be bereft and feeble if government were not always standing close by with a helping hand.

Government provides public capital (that is, taxpayers' money) to finance innovative ventures regarded as too risky and unpromising by private investors. At every level, government builds the infrastructure to foster economic development and subsidizes private enterprises in numerous ways. More fundamentally, government defines and protects the rights of private property and routinely enforces the business contracts between private parties. The libertarian vision of a lost Eden in which enterprise prospered free of political interference is utter mythology. Business people appear to understand this better than the ideological theorists.

What business conservatives really mean when they plead for smaller government is a less active role for government as defender of society's broad claims—the many laws and regulations that restrain the behavior of business and finance on behalf of society's general health and welfare. In those terms, government has indeed grown weaker—though not smaller—during the triumph of laissez-faire ideology in the last generation. Yet, even in an era of deregulation, government did not draw back from attending to business and financial interests; it became more responsive and more generous. Corporations, likewise, did not reduce or dismantle their political operations. The sophisticated lobbying intensified. Far more business money was devoted to electing friendly politicians, with excellent results for the donors. As the overall consequence, government is now less vigilant on society's behalf than it was—after all, that was the candid purpose of deregulation and the campaign contributions. Yet, if anything, government is now more intrusive in the economy, especially when it decides to reward or rescue individual firms or entire industrial sectors from their free-market mistakes.

The plain fact is that reinventing capitalism is impossible to achieve without reformation of government as well, since the two realms are intricately interdependent. The kinds of organic change described in this book—fashioning new, more responsible relationships within capitalism—cannot be done by government edict (even in the unlikely event government wanted to act). But neither can these changes fully succeed unless government's own deformed relationships with capitalism are corrected. Because my subject is capitalism, I do not intend to recount all that has gone wrong with the political system, though obviously its failings are relevant. Representative democracy has reached an advanced state of decay (see the analysis I elaborated in *Who Will Tell the People,* published in 1992) in which roughly half of the electorate declines to participate as voters, even in presidential elections. The continuing deterioration is directly related to the growing political dominance of business and finance interests, though not entirely explained by it. Restoring popular faith in democratic governance and the people's capacity to influence important governing decisions is a great and complicated challenge, one that will not be achieved by changing the parties in power or by the gradual breakdown of the conservative economic orthodoxy (which appears to be underway).

In fact, rectifying the operating principles of government may be harder to achieve than introducing viable alternatives within private capitalism (an ironic point, since citizens in a democracy are supposed to have more direct influence over political matters than on private enterprise). Politics, however, is highly centralized by comparison. The rules and institutional structures are formalized and legally more confining, without much space left for freelance inventors to experiment with eccentric ideas. The political marketplace, more significantly, is now structured like a two-company monopoly in which the two major parties jointly hold exclusive title to the electoral process and share the same strong interest in blocking out any smaller competitors. Like any corporation with a comfortable monopoly, the collaborating political parties are self-absorbed and risk averse when it involves reforming the electoral system. Why disturb established market positions by tinkering with provocative, untested ideas? Local and state politics, though blanketed by the same arrangement, are much more porous and, therefore, more promising as the first place to change things.

The two parties do, of course, have important differences and compete intensely for control of the government, but they also collaborate with each other to limit the exposure of all incumbents to genuinely competitive elections (typically, fewer than 10 percent of congressional seats are truly contested). Polling numbers on party alignment vary from season to season, but the population is now divided into roughly three equal parts—Republican, Democrat, and independent—and only the nonaffiliated, disorganized independents have demonstrated long-term growth. The Republican party, because it is more ideologically cohesive and thus can exercise much tighter internal discipline, is usually able to accomplish larger goals in power, knowing some Democrats will always join in supporting its agenda of cutting business taxes or boosting defense budgets. Democrats try to paper over their deep internal divisions by sticking to a few familiar issues and avoiding novel ideas that might upset one voter bloc or another. Party politics, in other words, is unpromising terrain for innovation.

The two-party control over access to elective office is not exactly an accident or an act of nature. It was instituted deliberately through laws and judicial decisions early in the last century that stacked the terms of entry against any outsiders and gave privileged legal status to only Republicans and Democrats, presumably to encourage political stability, but also to suppress rising immigrant populations and other nonestablishment influences. In contrast, throughout the nineteenth century new minor parties were formed regularly, regionally and nationally, to promote different agendas and grievances and to challenge the dominant party coalitions. These new party formations seldom gained power (the Republican party is the large exception), but some of them gained enough traction to push the political debate in new directions or to see their new ideas and causes co-opted by Democrats or Republicans. That era of flexibility had its chaotic moments, but the new parties also regularly renewed the democratic discourse, a healthy ventilation by bottom-up political thinking that is now effectively suppressed by the major party monopoly and their financial backers, assisted by major media and other establishment institutions.

For these reasons, the most needed measures of political reform may be the electoral changes that would weaken the monopolistic hold on politics and public discourse, creating more space for alternative voices in election contests and liberating the great diversity of political opinions from the suffocating limitations imposed by the two parties. The simplest version of such changes would replace the winner-take-all rules of elections with ballots that allow voters to make first and second choices, voting first perhaps for a minor-party candidate, but also casting a second-choice vote that would be counted only if no candidate has won a majority. Thus, voters have a greater variety of choices and can express themselves directly for fervent causes. The reform might even persuade more Americans to vote.

This change—a device known as "instant runoff voting"—is unlikely to threaten the dominant status of the two major parties since both would get a lot of the second-choice votes. But it might compel them to listen more earnestly to alternative viewpoints and to incorporate a broader range of issues and interests in their agendas. In order to win, they might have to become responsive—and convincing—to a broader range of the electorate or else face the risk of eventually losing their dominant position. Genuine competition is how democracy was supposed to work, a self-correcting instrument designed to connect the popular will with governing power, not to sustain party institutions and insiders in perpetuity.

Both major parties, for obvious reasons, are hostile to such reforms. After all, the system works for them. Why reform it? Nevertheless, a few localities (most notably the city of San Francisco) are starting to adopt variations on this small-d democratic experiment, hoping to accommodate public pressures for a more open and diverse electoral system (for a full account of the possibilities, read Steven Hill's *Fixing Elections: The Failure of America's Winner-Take-All Politics*). I am pursuing a different, more fundamental accusation about government and politics, one in which both Republicans and Democrats are implicated.

The modern American state—encompassing governance at the local, state, and national levels—has lost the capacity to distinguish between public works and private gain. And this failure has profound consequences for the society that are far more destructive than the obvious symptoms of corruption involving money and politics. Over many years, the two parallel purposes—public benefit and private returns—have become steadily fused by the crude logic holding that whatever helps the advance of enterprise may be regarded as beneficial for the general public too. The meaning of public value is thus so adulterated, government is effectively relieved of strong guiding principles. It acts promiscuously on behalf of seemingly random demands and threats.

The public decisions on how to dispense money or preferences thus have become confused or, less charitably, deranged. And government begins to resemble a house of indulgences, dispensing favors and forgivenesses, rationalized by arcane economic calculations but driven more often, as everyone understands, by raw political favoritism. Among other consequences, the government itself thereby promotes inequality, since the distribution of public awards closely follows the misalignments of wealth and influence already existing in society.

These practices are enormously wasteful—hundreds of billions in public resources converted to private gain—but wasted money is the least of the consequences. Nor is this another futile lament against the tyranny of special interests. In a democracy, one man's idea of "special interest" is always another man's righteous cause. The contests among them arise naturally, inescapably, in politics and, in the absence of an all-wise despot, there always will be the sloppy, frustrating, often wasteful imperfections of democratic decision making. We accept the persistence of excess and error in the contract for self-government, so long as the governed retain the power to correct the errors.

The confusion of governing purpose has far more damaging consequences, however. Government loses its ability to envision the broader, long-term story of society's permanent interests. Its potential power to alter the shared future of the country is forfeited to immediate commercial needs, farsightedness vetoed by the here and now. In its debased condition, the government is persuaded to transfer the ownership of public assets into private hands—a scandalous corruption of property rights, but definitely helpful to capitalist enterprise. And it is now the routine reality that the government in Washington works at cross purposes with itself, aiding with one hand the very behavior that it allegedly opposes with the other.

In these terms, the federal government has become strangely weak, notwithstanding its size and awesome powers. Pulled this way and that, yet incapable of taking big leaps forward, government seems confused about its original purpose or, if you prefer, corrupted by its allegiance to capitalism's needs. This incapacity, I suspect, has contributed greatly to the weakened public faith in government. People harbor contradictory complaints and may not grasp the intricacies, but they do know the benefits are not aimed their way.

In essence, the governing system has become a reactionary influence in the generic meaning—backward looking. It works hardest to support the old over the new, to sustain the status quo created in the past, to defend "what is" against "what might be." In theory, government at every level is not opposed to innovation and small, innovative enterprises or to many larger changes sought by social reformers. As a practical matter, however, government usually takes its stand with the very large and well-established business organizations. Generally, it wants what they want. On major matters, it is most reluctant to do anything they oppose. The political objective we explore in this chapter is nothing less than relearning the meaning of "public works." I am anxious to revive a principled understanding of how government and capitalism are meant to interact in order to restore strong governing principles that not only include society's interests but that serve society first.


In 1825, when the Erie Canal was completed across New York State, connecting the Hudson River valley with Lake Erie in the west, it was a seminal moment for American politics. The state government of New York built the canal and borrowed the money to do so. The waterway covered 425 miles from Albany to Buffalo, included 83 locks and 18 aqueducts along the way, and created the first westward route for waterborne commerce through the Appalachian mountain range. In an age before railroads, cars, or airplanes, it was a transforming event in the nation's economic development.

New York City, able to ship goods to the interior frontier, surged with commercial traffic and surpassed Philadelphia as America's largest seaport. Buffalo and Cleveland would boom, first as trading centers and later as industrial cities. Ohio followed New York's precedent and built a canal system southward from Lake Erie to the Ohio River at Cincinnati, celebrated as "Queen City of the West." East Coast manufacturing was thus linked by barge to the Mississippi River system, and midwestern agriculture shipped its produce eastward on the return trip. People flooded into the new territory too, following the trade routes and populating America's middle prairie. This is how America expanded in its early stages, and the major developments were done by government taking the role of public financier and builder or as the powerful partner of private capital.

What sounds natural and inevitable today was enormously controversial at the time. DeWitt Clinton, mayor of New York City, took up the cause of promoting the Erie Canal, and he was elected governor on the issue. Then and now, any measure that unites city and upstate interests is smart New York politics, but the larger question was whether government could properly undertake anything as stupendous and risky as "Clinton's folly." After all, it would cost $7 million, far beyond the means of New York taxpayers (bond financing would be repaid by tolls on the barge traffic). Thomas Jefferson had dismissed the idea as "little short of madness." Congress embraced the project and agreed to finance it, but President James Monroe vetoed the measure on the grounds that it was unconstitutional. Governor Clinton's risk taking, nonetheless, paid off dramatically for the country.

The Erie Canal represents the prototype for public works that prevailed for generations after. Government commits resources of money and land—including its unique capacity to borrow huge sums of capital—for projects that promise general public benefit as well as private gain. Some individuals do get fabulously rich from the results, but the personal accumulations seem incidental alongside the larger significance for the nation: The future is substantially altered for all; indeed, an utterly different future is made attainable by the government's purposeful intervention.

The subject of public works is disparaged in modern circles as the retrograde pork-barrel politics of "pouring concrete." But it is a good starting place for understanding how modern governance has become deranged in purpose. Most politicians remain devoted to public works spending—building something real like roads and bridges, dams and airports—because, unlike most government spending, it creates visible, lasting accomplishments voters can see and use. Who knows, the sponsor may even get his name on the bridge.

The great era of railroad building following the Civil War grossly expanded the terms of public works as federal and state governments, even local taxpayers, picked up much of the tab for the construction and provided gargantuan subsidies in cash and free land. In all, the seven railroad companies that built the transcontinental lines were awarded huge tracts of real estate equivalent to 9.5 percent of the acreage in the continental United States; 38 percent of those corporations' value came from the government. Political corruption was among the "social costs"—though not as injurious as the forced separation of Indian tribes from their land and property rights. The national railroad companies easily manipulated small, weak governments, including the one in Washington, with crude directness—often straightforward bribery—that makes modern political money seem discreet and restrained by comparison. Still, despite the looting and waste, the railroads did get built. Their existence effectively reshaped the nation.[1]

Moreover, the railroad building was accompanied by a public works project of grandly egalitarian intent: the Homestead Act of 1862 that literally redistributed national wealth in the form of undeveloped land to propertyless Americans, including the rush of new immigrants. Each family of settlers owned their 160 acres *if* they developed it: built a house, dug a well, plowed at least ten acres, and lived there for five years. The issuance of free land for western settlers took thirty years of political agitation and the rise of Abraham Lincoln's new Republican party to win approval as national policy (free land to settlers was among the reasons Republicans remained the majority party for more than half a century). Many families struggled and failed; many also fell prey to land speculators and indebtedness, or they were lured by the railroads to occupy false-front "towns" in impossible desert circumstances. The law was poorly designed in some ways, corrupted in others.

Nevertheless, Lincoln's Homestead Act was probably the nation's greatest single stroke of economic development channeled directly through people, instead of through business organizations. In the end, despite the failures, some 80 million acres of government land became the private property of families, earned through "sweat equity," as we now call it. Homesteading was the small-d democratic model of public works, but with the same thrust of creative potential as canal building. Rivals in social importance are the New Deal's mortgage-credit subsidies that opened home ownership to the broad middle-class, or the GI bill passed after World War II that made higher education possible for millions of veterans from humble origins, profoundly enhancing equality of opportunity while the workforce rose to higher levels of skill.

In present times, some advocates suggest a parallel between employee ownership and homesteading. Instead of land, equity shares in corporations are the income-producing capital asset more relevant to our economic circumstances. Government, it is argued, should provide access to low-cost capital to finance the broadened distribution of equity ownership, capital that workers could borrow to purchase their company's stock shares, then repay from their enterprise's returns, more or less as homesteaders "earned" their property by farming and ranching on the land. The social benefits would profoundly deepen the stability and responsibility of people and families just as home ownership did.

In the twentieth century, as industrialization eclipsed agriculture, government's engagement in economic development shifted toward technological content. Many of its foremost interventions were justified by the necessities of war or the portents of war, with no need to argue over how the public might benefit. The most extraordinary chapter was World War II, when Washington spending force-fed an economy still struggling to overcome the Depression. More to my point, the federal government pumped capital into key technological innovations in emerging industries—literally hiring the companies and building the factories to develop new sectors that would make over the U.S. economy. In a span of five years, the nation's gross national output increased by more than 75 percent (per capita income grew during wartime by more than 40 percent, but since consumer goods were unavailable the rising incomes were channeled into savings and investment). The basic industries that powered America's postwar prosperity were built on government capital: electronics, petrochemical synthetics, aircraft frames and engines, shipbuilding, steel, and nuclear power, among others.

Much of that innovative focus continued in peacetime but, thanks to the Cold War, the direction of economic development remained largely a project of the Defense Department (even the Interstate highway system was justified, with a wink, as necessary for national security). The military-industrial complex, one might say, succeeded the great railroads as the major industrial user of public capital and the enduring nexus of all-purpose political influence. Boeing's first large-body commercial aircraft, the 707, was a knockoff of the transport plane it had developed for the military. NASA's space program relied on the same companies that developed technology and hardware for the Pentagon (and NASA's many design innovations were harvested most thoroughly by the European consortium that developed the Airbus to compete with Boeing).

The Internet is one of the many technological accomplishments nurtured into being by government. Washington devoted many years to financing basic research on the concept and finding solutions to design problems, long before private capital saw the commercial possibilities, much less the revolutionary implications for communications and social relations. These formats for public works continue to operate in many, many variations. Some do indeed amount to wasteful pork. Others simply fail to overcome the obstacles in what seemed worthwhile risks. Still others, particularly in the fields of science and health, deliver great value and incalculable public benefits.

Yet, over time, a new logic of private gain gradually was insinuated into the meaning of "public works," a governing rationale that allows and, in some instances, commands government to take responsibility for the well-being of the private enterprises themselves, to aid and defend them in prosperous circumstances, or to rescue them from bad times, or simply to enhance their profitability in the name of serving the general public interest. This shift in governing purpose—often papered over with artful economic arguments, sometimes frankly acknowledged—essentially accepts the private gains as a worthy end in themselves, regardless of how vague and remote the public benefits may be. This dilution of public purpose originated with the activist government of New Deal liberalism in the crisis of the Great Depression, when Washington intervened with direct aid and regulated the private sector on many fronts. After decades of resisting on principle, most conservatives eventually got on board and engaged in their own version of helping-hand government, unembarrassed by the ideological contradictions with their espousal of smaller, less intrusive government. The two major parties have somewhat different preferences about which enterprises and sectors are most deserving, but there is no longer much disagreement on the main point. Both embrace the same corrupted principle.

Government at every level, from City Hall to the capital, exists now to make the economy go, to assist almost any sort of private enterprise that might be expected to create jobs and incomes, profit and growth, and therefore can claim to benefit the citizenry at large. "Good times" are the open-ended public purpose, and who can be against that? The usual method is to award special benefits directly to enterprise—companies and banks, entire sectors of commerce and industry, even individual firms that ask for help in a politically persuasive way. The awards take many forms: money; legal concessions; tax forgiveness; even the private property government confiscates from other citizens to advance commercial or industrial projects in the name of the general welfare. These favors naturally go disproportionately to the largest, most politically adept business organizations.

Silicon Valley, home base of the semiconductor industry, portrays itself as entrepreneurial and independent of old-style industrial politics, but it sought and received $800 million from Washington to research new elaborations in semiconductor design. The federal money went only to the fourteen largest chip makers, names like Intel and National Semiconductor, who were given preferred status over two hundred smaller competitors. The ostensible purpose was to help the U.S. industry catch up with Japanese companies that had gained the majority share of the world market, and American companies did catch up, but not from any research breakthroughs. They recovered because they were protected by a "voluntary" import-limiting agreement that conservative Ronald Reagan secured from Japan (one of many import barriers erected by the Reagan Republicans at the behest of various sectors).

The auto industry cashed in on the Clean Car Initiative, a similar research consortium formed by the Clinton administration to encourage the Big Three auto companies to develop a "new generation of vehicles." Ford, GM, and Chrysler took the money, more than $2 billion, but thus far have succeeded in not producing any "clean cars." More efficient, smaller, pollution-free automobiles would, as previously explained, upset their profit strategies, so they fiddled around with the research funds while selling still larger, less efficient vehicles. Despite Detroit's sly resistance, the public subsidy may have obliquely advanced the cause of environmental innovation, because Japan took the U.S. effort seriously as a competitive threat and responded aggressively. At Detroit's insistence, Toyota and other Japanese companies that manufacture cars in the United States were excluded from the consortium, and they feared it would lead to a genuine breakthrough—just as earlier alliances of American know-how and government capital had produced so many great industrial advances. The Japanese accelerated their own clean car efforts, determined to steal the lead, and they have.

The competitive pressures of globalization are now a familiar rationale for subsidy. The Export-Import Bank provides more than $50 billion in loan guarantees on trade deals, government insurance against risk that is devoted overwhelmingly to a handful of the largest corporations: Boeing, General Electric, Lucent, Caterpillar, and others. The premise of the Ex-Im subsidies—increased U.S. exports will increase U.S. jobs—is contradicted by an inconvenient reality. Virtually all of the leading corporate beneficiaries of Ex-Im aid have been reducing their U.S. workforces for many years, most of them drastically. In fact, the agency often underwrites deals in which new manufacturing capacity is created in China or Mexico to compete with U.S. production. "Reverse Robin Hood," reporter Leslie Wayne called it in *The New York Times.* "[T]he bank has become a tool for an elite group of politically well-connected corporations to get sweetheart deals and cheap financing courtesy of American taxpayers."[2]

The libertarian Cato Institute compiled a list of 125 programs of direct subsidies for business, totaling $85 billion, that it labeled "corporate welfare." Notwithstanding "free trade" rhetoric, government still does protect many industries, not for national security or economic necessity, but simply because they are politically well-connected. Sugar is one of the most notorious examples. American consumers pay $2 or $3 billion extra each year because import quotas block cheaper sugar from abroad (typically produced by impoverished nations in the Caribbean and Latin America). The domestic price supports provided to American sugar growers cost another $1.4 billion, and nearly half of that money goes to the largest 1 percent of the farms (much like the federal subsidies for other agricultural crops). Sugar plantations are, meanwhile, notorious polluters from their chemical runoffs that threaten the Florida Everglades, among other places.[3]

Similar subsidy systems or defensive legal arrangements are in place for a long list of other sectors, from timber to nuclear power, in which producers are excused from the full costs of their operations or from various legal obligations they find burdensome. The federal government has paid to build some 340,000 miles of logging roads in the publicly owned national forests so timber companies can harvest the trees. Then the government authorizes money-losing timber commodity sales that cost the taxpayers another half billion a year. Or government may compensate enterprises for the discomfort of having to comply with the law, especially environmental law. The damaging effects of the hog factories eluded federal attention for many years but, when EPA finally adopted very mild (some would say toothless) rules to protect clean water, Congress followed up by promising to pay up to $450,000 per farm to comply with the regulations. If the past is any guide, taxpayers will someday be called upon to provide much greater sums to clean up the ruined landscapes left behind by corporatized farm factories, as they have paid for other sectors of agriculture, mining, and manufacturing.

The logic of promoting private gain as "public works" has become thoroughly localized too, as states compete for industrial investments by giving away huge sums of public money. Marriott International succeeded in extorting $44 million in subsidies from the state of Maryland in exchange for *not* moving its corporate headquarters to Virginia. Marriott's proposed move, it turned out, was a ruse designed to shake money out of Maryland's taxpayers, but state and local politicians did not have the nerve to call the bluff. In Ohio, Daimler-

Chrysler won a package of $280 million in "incentives" not to leave Toledo and instead build a highly subsidized Jeep factory. General Electric asked for a two-thirds reduction in property taxes on its Appliance Park plant in Louisville, Kentucky, which dates back to World War II. IBM sought $1 billion in reduced tax assessments from San Jose, California.

In Alabama, the state government distributed nearly $1 billion during the 1990s in various subsidies to attract foreign automakers— first Mercedes-Benz, then Hyundai, Toyota, and Honda. Alabama pride swelled at the presence of famous corporate logos, but the state remains at the bottom in educational attainment and forty-third in per capita income. Alabama's government awoke from its splurge of corporate favors to discover a fiscal crisis of underfinanced schools and other neglected priorities. The governor reversed course and began trying to recover some of the lost millions in revenue. Some six hundred out-of-state corporations, he found, were gaming the state tax code to pay zero taxes on some $800 million in profits, while they played one state legislature against another in the pursuit of more tax breaks. This form of economic development—whether one calls it corporate bribery or corporate extortion—directly undermines the broad public purposes once regarded as state government's first obligations.[4]

At the federal level, tax avoidance is perhaps the largest "public works" project. Unlike the states, the federal government has no constitutional requirement to balance its budget, so political decisions to add business tax exceptions and preferences do not visibly subtract from other priorities. Nevertheless, Robert S. McIntyre, director of Citizens for Tax Justice and a formidable watchdog of proliferating tax loopholes, estimated that $195 billion was dispersed through the tax code in fiscal 2000 to benefit business investors or subsidize business products. "One can easily calculate that personal and corporate tax rates are about 20 percent higher than they'd need to be if these tax preferences for business and investment did not exist," McIntyre testified. Alternately, if these special favors were withdrawn, government would have ample funding to solve the enduring weaknesses in the health care system or to shore up Social Security. Because tax forgivenesses appear nowhere in the line-by-line budget and do not require annual appropriations, a representative can stand for fiscal soundness while still funneling the money to favored business interests. "Politicians can have their cake and eat it too," McIntyre explained. "In recent years, this has made tax subsidies the tool of choice for many politicians."[5]

One of the most outrageous examples is the arcane provision that allows U.S. companies to move their corporate headquarters offshore, typically to Bermuda or a Caribbean island, for the sole economic purpose of avoiding the U.S. corporate income tax (in the wake of Enron-style accounting scandals, an embarrassed Congress rushed to reconsider that one). Much larger tax concessions are just as specious in purpose and results. Accelerated depreciation allows businesses to write-off machinery and buildings much faster than the assets actually wear out—a wasteful tax incentive on its face, purported to stimulate new investment spending. Trouble is, countless economic studies have failed to find any correlation between accelerating this tax break and increased investment (often the two are trending in opposite directions). The tax credit for corporate "research and experimentation" has a similar history: no evidence whatever that it actually induces companies to spend more on research, but abundant examples of how corporate accountants flagrantly stretch the meaning of "research" to cover ordinary operating expenses.

At a minimum, McIntyre proposed, tax subsidies should be subjected to the same formal, annual evaluations applied to the government's direct spending programs. Is the tax subsidy designed to serve an important public purpose? Is it actually helping to achieve those goals? Are the benefits fairly distributed or targeted to those who do not really need or deserve government aid? Are the tax breaks carefully administered? "Few, if any, business tax subsidies could pass these tests," McIntyre said.

The biggest beneficiaries, as he has documented over many years, are America's biggest corporations. In the early 1980s, after the Reagan administration's tax-cutting binge, half of the 250 largest, most profitable companies paid no federal income tax at all over three years, despite $250 billion in aggregate profit. GE was again a leader in the field, earning $6.5 billion in profit and collecting a $283 million tax refund from the government. Many of the scandalous loopholes were reduced or closed by the 1986 tax reform legislation, but the government gained no revenue because the political trade-off required a steep reduction in the top *personal* income tax rates paid by the wealthy, including corporate executives. Through the 1990s, corporate loopholes steadily crept back into the tax code, so that by 2000 McIntyre found that forty-one corporations were again paying less than zero—and earning tax rebates of $3.2 billion on $25.8 billion in profits.[6]

The political foundations for reducing business taxation are bipartisan. Democrats came to the practice naturally, elaborating new purposes for the specialized relief introduced during the New Deal. Republicans joined the game during the 1970s, weary of always being the naysaying minority party and anxious to win elections with their own version of "feel good" politics. The "supply side" economic doctrine allowed good conservatives to abandon fiscal rectitude in favor of aggressive tax cutting for business and individuals in upper-income tax brackets. As a practical matter, bipartisan majorities are easily formed for helping business avoid taxes. After the terrorist attack of September 11, 2001, Congress swiftly enacted a $15 billion bailout for major airlines—while declining to provide emergency aid for millions of laid-off workers—and added $43 billion in enlarged tax favors for enterprises generally.

The federal government has been deranged by corporate power in another, more fundamental function: its duty to define and protect property rights. In our time, it is the public's property, not private property, that government fails to protect. The contemporary logic of market fundamentalism espoused by conservatives has (with passive assent from many liberals) gradually engineered an enormous transfer of the public's common assets to private ownership. What assets? Land, water, sky. The electronic spectrum of broadcasting airwaves, originally established in law as owned by the people and managed by government in their behalf. The inherited knowledge of science and learning, now increasingly captured by private patents, copyrights, and other expanding forms of "intellectual property" protections. Even the public's space is shrinking, quite literally, in more prosaic ways. The land devoted to public uses—parks, schools, civic buildings, and others—has decreased by one fifth since the 1950s, according to the American Planning Association.[7]

The privatization of public assets has accelerated in this era of new technologies so rapidly and broadly that critics suggest corporations have captured not only politics, but the law. In the simplest terms, people have lost valuable common assets and will now often pay for what used to be free—actually, for what they used to own—mainly because these were given away by federal regulators and legislators. Congress "lent" $70 billion in broadcasting spectrum to the major television networks as an inducement to encourage their conversion to high-resolution digital television (the networks have failed to convert, but they are hanging onto this scarce public resource, which becomes far more valuable as wireless telephones and other uses need it to expand). Water has become a precious commodity, as population increases and so many natural sources have been contaminated or exhausted, so public water systems and resources are acquired by private business as a major new profit center (bottled water also became a hot new product because industrial pollution spoiled rivers and aquifers and underfinanced public systems failed to maintain safe, unpolluted water supplies).[8]

The colonization of public knowledge by private patent is a more complex process, but the same interests are steadily claiming ownership of technologies and methods that not so long ago were regarded as common assets available to all, from seeds to surgical techniques and even life forms. Perhaps the most egregious example is the pharmaceutical industry that essentially rides free on the taxpayer-funded basic research done at the National Institutes of Health and other public laboratories—then gouges consumers with inflated prices for patent-protected prescription drugs. The government provides roughly half of the billions spent on drug research and takes the big risks by developing the basic compounds and breakthrough discoveries. Then the companies take those results, develop and test them as new medicines, and collect windfall profits on products the unwitting citizenry helped pay for (occasional efforts in Congress to correct this injustice are regularly stymied by the drug-industry lobbyists).

A generation ago, when the federal government was more resolute, it used its power as owner and buyer to compel wider and even free distributions of the new knowledge derived from its R&D investments. Military procurement, funding for university research in electronics and other fields, and antitrust policy were all managed to induce companies to share—or else face legal inquiries into their monopolies. As the semiconductor industry developed, government exerted strong influence by buying production for defense from small, fledgling firms as well as from the major names. AT&T settled an antitrust suit by agreeing to diffuse its production knowledge to other firms, and the company was enjoined from seeking royalties.[9]

"Who owns the sky?" Peter Barnes, founder of Working Assets, a socially responsible telephone company, asked that question as the title for his book describing how citizens could share in the returns if the public's common assets became market commodities. The trading of "pollution rights," as Barnes explained, creates a cost-price system for compelling companies to reduce air pollution and rewards those who achieve the greater reductions because they can sell their surplus "pollution rights" to other companies that have not met the standard. Barnes's provocative proposal suggested that every citizen should be the initial owners of these government-issued certificates and could collect income from their appreciating value—instead of the companies who trade them. Who does own the sky, anyway? I think it belongs to eternity, not to corporations and not to present-existing citizens.

But Barnes's proposal echoes the thinking of Thomas Paine, the original radical of the American revolution, who envisioned the common inheritance as one important way to promote a society of equality. Paine suggested the natural capital of land, water, and resources—plus the technologies handed down from previous generations—should be held in trust as a common inheritance and managed for the people by government, instead of for the relatively few private owners. The common owners of inherited knowledge and physical resources could lease these assets to private users for modest royalties, provided the assets are not abused. Like Barnes's idea, Paine envisioned a stream of common income regularly distributed equally to all citizens. Tom Paine's ideas proved to be too radical for his contemporaries, the founders, and they are way too radical for today's governors.[10]

Even in a well-functioning representative democracy one expects messy excesses and random contradictions. Some level of disorder and even looting is probably inevitable, given the interests and factions continuously contesting for public favors. But when excesses become the norm, when favoritism flows consistently to the most powerful interests, one knows the democracy is sick and malfunctioning. The consequence for American governance means that public institutions are regularly acting at cross purposes with themselves, blindly undercutting their own stated values and obligations, contradicting the society's agreed-upon goals. These conflicted purposes can be seen in three distinct dimensions.

First, the political rationale for business subsidy—more jobs and faster growth—has empty, enervating results for society because the government's own macroeconomic management of the economy cancels any theoretical benefits. Tax forgivenesses and directed subsidy may very well enhance the performance and profit of specific firms, but they cannot enlarge overall employment and output in the economy, not when the Federal Reserve's monetary policy or the executive branch's fiscal policy are pushing in the opposite direction. During most of the last twenty years, the Federal Reserve Board has enforced its own ceiling on economic growth rates and deliberately kept unemployment at artificially high levels for the purpose of containing price inflation. Whether or not this was wise policy, it trumped everything else. Thus, when certain companies or sectors are rewarded with stimulative favors, the result at best is to give them an artificial edge over competing firms and sectors that received no help. The net sum for society is not more jobs or faster growth, only additional advantages for a favored few.

Second, a governing system habituated to such indulgences sows greater inequality among its citizens—the opposite of democratic intentions. This accusation is inescapably true for state governments financing one private corporation's new factory and not others, but true as well for Congress dispensing tax forgivenesses to certain large organizations but not smaller ones. The insidious result is that public wealth flows to the benefit of certain income classes—generally to the shareholders and insiders of the favored firms—while any collateral benefits for communities or workers are derivative "trickle down" at best. Government's "redistribution" of income is routinely deplored when the recipients are weak and struggling people but widely applauded as "sound economics" when the beneficiaries are already affluent and successful.

The corrosive effect of such contradictions is that a political system in the habit of tolerating "reverse Robin Hood" as standard practice is led to accept deeper compromises with principle. A stark example is how easily the political community has acquiesced in recent decades to the doctrine known informally as "too big to fail." Selected enterprises are rescued from failure because the governors decide the economic system will somehow be endangered without them, so government bails out and restores major banks and broker-ages, airlines, insurance companies, or other troubled ventures.

The regular rules and standards of economic life are suspended temporarily for the largest financial organizations—some of which have been rescued more than once during the last twenty years of tur-moil. In effect, their losses are "socialized" and the broad ranks of tax-payers pay for their mistakes. A generation ago, such interventions were rare and always provoked highly charged debate; as they become routine in financial disruptions, the list of supplicants grows longer. Popular cynicism is confirmed, but neither liberals nor conservatives have a convincing explanation for how public interest would suffer if the "big boys" simply were allowed to fail, the subsidy spent on re-placing them.

Finally, the profligate use of business subsidies regularly collides with the public purposes embodied in many of the government's own laws and regulations. Ecological protection is the most dramatic example among many. The tax code rewards waste in numerous ways, while government preaches efficiency in production as the shared economic policy. Tax code provisions and direct subsidies, for instance, give favorable incentives to the exploitation of virgin timber, newly mined minerals, and manufactured materials, while effectively penalizing companies that employ recovery and reuse of the spent, discarded materials. While government enforces labor standards and decent working conditions, it simultaneously rewards the companies that are flagrant violators. Government subsidizes businesses in the name of job creation, but fails to notice that the recipients of public money are reducing their workforces.

Government, in other words, is implicated in many of the social and economic injuries that its policies ostensibly are attempting to curb. Such contradictions in the governing system are like a contest that pits pious civic sentiments against government's everyday list of clientele. Sentiment generally loses, the clients win. The political con-fusion is wasteful and wrong—blatantly unfair—but that is not the gravest injury. When government proceeds in so many contradictory directions, society itself becomes confused about priorities. When every long-term goal of the public must be vetted by the standard of what private enterprise wants or needs, then citizens find it extremely difficult to act on the future or even see the future clearly. Efforts to engineer a gradually reformed capitalism obviously are made much more difficult when the public sector's exertions are often pulling in the opposite direction.

Reordering the economic system must, therefore, also involve untangling government's bad habits, then restoring a set of governing principles for public works that is more discriminating between public and private gain, more farsighted in focusing on what society wants and needs for its distant future. The politics of accomplishing this will be very tough, since it means taking on the most powerful interests and the deeply ingrained behavior of the political system. Still, the guerrilla action is already underway in the countryside.

THE PORK BARREL of modern politics is wonderfully ambidextrous and corrupt. It looks bluntly old-fashioned in the ways it pours lots of concrete and orders up mountains of questionable hardware for national defense and other public purposes. Yet it also operates with etherealized sophistication in its use of arcane legal concessions or tax breaks to deliver boodle to private interests. The action is sustained by a very old operating principle of democratic politics—logrolling—the cooperative code of "you help me get my boodle, I will help you get yours, or at least we will not stand in each other's way." The harvesting of public money is now dominated by the modern equivalent of political machines, those skillful, relentless organizations called corporations.

The enduring and natural weakness in representative democracy, easily exploited by special interests of every kind, involves the uneven intensities of political desires and exertions. The general public's broad interest is seldom aroused or forcefully focused on subsidiary matters like pork barrel, but the intended beneficiaries are always intensely mobilized to secure their subsidies. This is as true for farmers and insurance agents as it is for major banks and multinational corporations. Who really understood, for example, how the tax code was being steadily gutted by thousands of obscure definitional changes and peculiar "incentives" benefiting business interests? The lawyers and corporate accountants knew, of course, since they often drafted the legislation; so did selected lawmakers who promoted these obscure amendments on behalf of clients and patrons. But, as a practical matter, neither the news media nor conscientious legislators nor the public at large can possibly keep up with this kind of fine-print politics, beyond occasionally demanding "reform" or an end to "corporate welfare."

The interplay of interest-group logrolling is not going to be expunged from American democracy. As a practical reality, only general rules of governing principles can possibly draw a line against this sort of political behavior. Yet disciplinary rules are themselves extremely difficult to establish, because nearly every sector of society and the economy may fear it has something to lose if real discipline is achieved. It is hard to find an honest cop anywhere on the block and, in this contest, there are no disinterested judges.

This prosaic reality played out again during the 1990s, when an impressive bunch of political advocates came together from left and right to organize a frontal assault on "corporate welfare." They called themselves the "odd bedfellows coalition" and ranged from Ralph Nader, labor, and environmental organizations on the liberal side to some very conservative antigovernment groups like the Cato Institute. The left-right coalition brought together activists experienced in the Washington labyrinth, astute critics of the system's excesses with good connections in both parties. They failed to accomplish much of anything. When the coalition drew up its target list of corporate subsidies, participants agreed that everyone must have the right to veto their own "sacred cows"—the programs their own political base feels are important or too controversial to challenge. The lengthy list of eligible targets swiftly dwindled to a few trivial items. The coalition sputtered out of existence. Washington is too compacted with interwoven interests, too habituated to cooperative back-scratching, to serve as a good starting place for reform.

Meanwhile, however, promising progress is underway among state and local governments, where reformers are tackling essentially the same problem. Diverse coalitions of homegrown interests are challenging the corporate largesse handed out by their states, cities, or counties, and these grassroots agitators are winning real reforms. A viable political movement gradually is forming around the question of fraudulent public works. Once it has developed sufficient strength and cohesion, the movement intends to take the issue to Washington and confront the federal pork barrel too. Indeed, if we are lucky, these reformers may be creating a schematic for establishing new governing principles that can restore the original intent of public works—a government that serves society first and helps people develop a different, brighter future.

Across the fifty states, corporations have turned "economic development" into what can only be called a racket. They siphon off some $50 billion every year from state and local treasuries in the name of creating new jobs and enterprise. Like most rackets, this one operates largely in secrecy, privately negotiating deals with political leaders on tax abatements and other forms of aid, with little public disclosure or accountability. The corporations have developed great acumen at pitting the states against one another and employ deep squads of consultants to lend a scientific aura to their search for public handouts. They dangle the prospect of a new industrial plant before several localities and ratchet up the bidding war among anxious public officials. They game the state tax codes in a similar fashion so that a substantial chunk of corporate income escapes state taxation anywhere. They make exciting promises that are frequently not kept, whether they are promising to build a new factory or threatening to close an existing one. Both methods succeed in diverting public resources to private gain.[11]

The process is basically a shakedown in which the mark is government itself. Most governors well understand what's going on but figure they have little choice but to play since, if they refuse to pay the bribes, other governors will. Poorer states engage for obvious reasons, but the leading industrial states also have been drawn into the competition, for fear of losing established employers to a higher bidder. When the New York Stock Exchange shakes down New York City for $400 million with a threat to become the Jersey City Stock Exchange, one knows the greed is out of control. Peter Fisher, professor of urban and regional planning at the University of Iowa, found that the effective state corporate income tax rate fell by 40 percent from the 1980s to the 1990s, eroded by proliferating giveaways that companies win in these irregular deals. In twelve of the most industrialized states, from New York to Ohio to Texas, Fisher discovered that manufacturing companies in many sectors can win a negative tax rate simply by building a new factory. That is, the state government owes them money, much as the federal government pays billions in tax refunds to very profitable corporations.[12]

People began to fight back in earnest during the deindustrialization of the 1980s, angered by deceit and broken promises and the heavy losses of industrial jobs. Organized labor led the fight because companies were moving unionized production both overseas and to low-wage states offering major tax avoidance. A telling wake-up moment occurred in 1992 when General Motors closed down its Willow Run assembly plant in Ypsilanti, Michigan, after harvesting $1.3 billion in local tax abatements with its promise to keep the 4,500-worker factory operating there. When Ypsilanti sued and lost, workers discovered there was no promise—only a GM press release, not a legally enforceable written agreement. The Michigan jobs moved to Texas, where GM harvested new tax breaks.

Ironically, the public officials in Arlington, Texas, wisely demanded a so-called "clawback" agreement before signing off on their tax give-away. If GM runs away again, it has to give back the money. That commonsense demand has become a model for other localities and, since then, seventeen states and scores of local governments have enacted similar clawback provisions covering industrial subsidies. After United Airlines got nearly $300 million from Indiana to locate maintenance facilities in Indianapolis, it fell short on its promised investment and the airline paid a $32 million penalty. Connecticut enacted a novel rule for its tax subsidies to Pratt & Whitney, long a major employer in the state. If the company's Connecticut employment declines, it loses its tax credit proportionately and loses it totally if its Connecticut jobs decrease by more than 6 percent. Meanwhile, nine states, including Ohio and Minnesota, have adopted full disclosure on all tax deals. And some sixty-five jurisdictions have requirements on the quality of the jobs. "We have moved from confrontation and litigation to agreements in black and white," says Greg LeRoy, a leader in the union-allied Good Jobs First organization.

In recent years, LeRoy explained, the developing network of activists reached a critical take-off point. Its members began asking broader questions about the nature of these subsidies and what they actually produce for communities and taxpayers. The complaints are no longer limited to dishonest dealings or purloined tax revenue, but are drawing distinctions about so-called development subsidies that do more harm than good. Greg LeRoy recites some of the new questions that are being asked:

"Should subsidies keep going to companies that pay poverty wages and thereby stick the taxpayers with hidden costs like Medicaid and food stamps? Should subsidies keep going to companies that fail to provide health care or deny workers the right to organize a voice at work? Should subsidies keep taking money from our schools, while the school boards have no say? Should subsidies keep going to polluters who fail to comply with emissions standards? Should subsidies keep paying companies to flee inner cities and older suburbs and fuel suburban sprawl? Should subsidies keep paving wetlands and plowing up cornfields for Wal-Mart and Home Depot? Should subsidies keep going to factory farms?"[13]

This broader conversation about the social consequences has greatly expanded the ranks of groups joining the fight and enlarged their political goals. The corporate pork barrel, federal as well as local, routinely subsidizes destructive, antisocial behavior by private enterprise while government then spends the taxpayers' money to ameliorate the consequences for society. This contradiction is illogical and wasteful, but it also garbles the meaning of public purpose. Is the government on society's side in these matters or pushing in the opposite direction? At the local level, more and more citizens have figured out that public works in the modern sense may act as an engine of social destruction, not progress.

One reason numerous states and localities are enacting new disciplinary standards and controls for corporate subsidy is that politicians and officials are now being confronted by broader ranks of critics. Teachers and school administrators are in the fight; so are environmental groups like the Sierra Club and Friends of the Earth. Antisprawl activists and local development groups see the contradiction—the tax subsidies and infrastructure aid subvert their efforts to achieve "smart growth" in metropolitan areas. Transit planners and civic groups want to prohibit corporate subsidies for any project not located in the transportation grid of existing highways and rail. The "living wage" campaign, which has won legislation in scores of cities and counties, wants to compel any tax-subsidized company to observe a floor of livable wages and benefits for its workers. The National Family Farm Coalition wants to ban government subsidy for hog factories and other corporate encroachments. A network of twenty-three groups in the State Tax and Fiscal Analysis Initiative is exposing the malign impact of corporate subsidy on budgets and competing public priorities. The many public interest watchdog groups associated with Ralph Nader organize active opposition; so do mainstream good government organizations. Scholars from many academic disciplines are developing the evidence.

These allied interests, I should add, are a long way from prevailing, but their wingspan is broadening and their acceleration is impressive. Like any new political formation, this one wins where it can, usually by educating and mobilizing local citizens, then pressuring the local government handing out the corporate subsidy and the corporation with its hand out. Some efforts engage public officials and companies in bargaining for "community benefits agreements" that may cover everything from the quality of the jobs and wages to environmental performance to financial commitments for affordable housing, child care centers, worker training, and other public goals.

In Los Angeles, the Figueroa Corridor Coalition for Economic Justice, a broad phalanx of labor and community organizations, negotiated a milestone agreement with the developers (including right-wing billionaire Rupert Murdoch) of the new Staples Center, a huge hotel-and-entertainment complex expected to collect $75 million in city subsidies. Under the new terms, the project will include $1 million for neighborhood parks, inner-city hiring and job training, living wage standards, affordable housing units for 20 percent of the development, union organizing rights, and many other distinctive features. Citizens *can* acquire power if they organize and bargain smartly.

It also helps if the government officials sympathize with the objectives. Beverly Stein, board chair of Multnomah County, Oregon, which covers the suburbs east of Portland, held out for an elaborate and expensive list of social concessions from two semiconductor manufacturers, LSI Logic and Fujitsu, seeking $100 million in long-term county tax abatements. As a state senator, Stein had voted against the high-tech subsidy program—too costly and unnecessary, she thought. So when she was elected county chair, Stein was willing to drive a hard bargain and would not have been especially distressed if the companies rejected her terms. Fujitsu did and dropped out. But LSI Logic, a specialty chip maker from Milpitas, California, wanted the Oregon plant location for the quality of life, and the company agreed to go far beyond the standard agreement. The company now spends as much as 25 percent of its annual tax savings on community impact improvements. It recruits and trains local low-wage workers for the manufacturing jobs and is committed to high levels of work-force retention and internal promotion. To prepare the unskilled workers, it helps fund the Mt. Hood Microelectronics Training Center. It also subsidizes new housing units for low-income families and child care services for workers, especially entry-level parents. LSI Logic has signed on to an environmental goal of "no impact"—a distant objective, to be sure—and is reporting significant progress in reducing and recycling its toxic wastes, performing far beyond the regulatory standards.

Oregon is not a typical situation, of course, since it possesses the natural assets that high-end companies want and seek. But its standard-setting approach, called Benchmarks, gives expression to what the communities want from economic development. And self-confident public officials like Beverly Stein manage to shake a lot more out of the corporations than even they expect. "We made it so hard to win, Fujitsu withdrew," Stein recalls. "With LSI Logic, the subsidy is expensive, but we sure did get what we wanted. Because they're hiring the same people we were trying to help, and getting those people trained for middle-income jobs and career ladders." When I ask her about employee ownership, Stein replies: "That's one thing I missed. I wish I had thought about having them give us some equity or stock for the people who work there. I don't know if I could have gotten it, but I would have tried."

City by city, state by state, people gradually are setting the bar higher for corporate subsidy and attempting to break up what is essentially a zero-sum game among the states—stealing each other's jobs by offering larger and larger bribes of public money. Ultimately, as reformers understand, they cannot break up this racket until they take the fight to Washington. Congress has the power to shut down these practices by using the federal tax code to tax away the corporate windfalls or, alternately, setting rules that force the contest in more positive directions. "There's not yet a sufficient organized base to produce a coherent federal debate," LeRoy acknowledges, "and I don't see how we get the federal debate going without a lot more state agitation. And it's hard. You've got to stick to your guns. You've got to stand on principle."

On the other hand, once they can develop sufficient political strength and cohesion to make this a national issue, then the debate will be focused on the federal pork barrel too. Says LeRoy: "If, four years from now, we have twenty states with disclosure laws instead of nine, and twenty-five states with clawback provisions instead of seventeen, and fifty states with job-quality standards instead of thirty-seven, I think a federal debate will be inevitable. The jobs debate has been corrupted by the corporations and not enough people understand that yet. But, once they do, it leads them to sweeping thoughts about changing the system, and then there's no turning back. Then we can take on the federal tax loopholes, the federal subsidies for low-end employers, the subsidies for sprawl, and all the other things people oppose."

The federal pork barrel, while more complex and vastly larger in scale, operates with the same perverse disregard for the consequences. It hands out hundreds of billions without any serious scrutiny of whether people at large actually benefit—or are injured—by these uses of public money. When the debate does someday confront Washington, it will be obvious that the grassroots reformers already have created some important boundary markers and enforcement mechanisms—rules and conditions that will be useful in reforming the meaning of "public works" at the federal level. We are not there yet. Still, in the meantime, we can start to envision the general principles that ought to govern the corporate pork barrel, principles that force the national government away from corrupted uses and toward rules of investment that are truly public in purpose. Here is a rough first draft to consider.

First principle: Do no harm. The present system is utterly contradictory in the ways that the federal government subsidizes the very
antisocial behavior it ostensibly is trying to curb, financing many of
the deleterious practices of capitalism described throughout this
book, from increasing inequality to ecological destruction. At a minimum, one would think, taxpayers should not have to pay for the confinements and injuries they encounter in economic life. For starters, a
registry of repeat offenders—companies that persistently fail to comply with the law, whether it is the tax code or environmental standards—might be declared ineligible for public aid of any kind. A new
analytical system will also be needed to sort out the fraudulent and
destructive subsidies from those with genuine public value.

Industry and industry-friendly economists have devised elaborate
systems of cost-benefit analysis to determine whether the benefit of
new regulations exceeds the costs to enterprises and the economy,
measured in dollars. Despite its many fallacious assumptions, cost-
benefit accounting is now standard in the federal government and
regularly used by industry to block many valuable measures that
would benefit public health and welfare. Perhaps it is time to turn the
tables and analyze the costs and benefits of the several hundred billion
dollars in public subsidy for business and finance. Reformers will have
to develop a more supple and sophisticated analytical system, one that
examines the rewards versus the injuries not in dollars alone, but in
terms of society's own long-term aspirations. This task cannot be left
to economists alone, since their orthodox model does not even recognize nonmonetary considerations, those values that cannot be
bought or sold.

Second principle: If the government does not get what it paid for,
then the corporate beneficiaries must return the money. That sounds
straightforward, and some state governments are beginning to enforce
this principle, but the federal subsidy system is so sloppy and unaccountable that it presently has no basis for even knowing whether it
has been swindled (and it seldom asks). Washington resembles the case

of Ypsilanti writ large—ripped off by nonenforceable corporate press releases. The many billions in federal tax subsidies, as Robert McIntyre and others have documented, are distributed on vaguely stated expectations of economic gain, administered permissively by tax officials, and if any agency should inquire into a company's actual results, the company mobilizes its congressional supporters to warn off the investigators.

In other words, the first step is obvious: Get it in writing. Like any private sector creditor or investor providing capital to an enterprise, Washington should demand a contract. Every company, including those claiming the numerous tax-avoidance provisions, should be compelled to execute a binding agreement that describes what it will deliver in exchange. This would force government to define precisely what the subsidy is supposed to achieve. And many would-be beneficiaries would flee from the prospect of having to commit themselves legally to deliver what they have promised. With full disclosure, the discipline might also foster a public bargaining process that interested third parties could monitor and influence in defense of social priorities.

Third principle: When public resources are deployed to rescue or enhance particular profit-making firms, the public is entitled to a quid pro quo of comparable value. That is, if the taxpayers are required to bail out corporations in trouble or invest in their technological advancement, the government should claim hard assets in exchange—ownership shares and stock options or warrants the government can redeem dollar-for-dollar once the companies are restored to profitability. The Chrysler bailout of 1980 and the recent bailout for the airline industry employed this device, but most federal bailouts—especially in banking and finance—do not. More often, when major banks or dominant corporations face horrendous losses from their own folly and error, they are deemed "too big to fail" by the government and, with a shrug, it will "socialize" the losses by dumping them on the general taxpayers. During the last generation hundreds of billions in bad debts have been shifted from private balance sheets to the public's, with nothing in return. This is unjust, and also encourages the financial recklessness as well as the corporate impulse to grow still larger and thus qualify as "too big to fail."

Once government has established its claim to corporate equity in return for all but the most trivial public assistance, the exchange could be harnessed to advance broader public purposes, including the democratized ownership of capital. Government would not itself be more than a temporary holder of the corporate equity, but it could invent ways to redistribute this public wealth like a latter-day Homestead Act, financing employee ownership trusts or distributing shares to capital accounts held by virtually all U.S. citizens or transferring some assets to local stewardship by community trusts or public authorities acting as community investors and watchful participants in the companies. The Capital Ownership Group, an international policy forum based at Kent State University, has developed "Fair Exchange" legislation to start down this road (though Congress may not be ready for such big ideas). Deborah Olson, a labor lawyer who is COG's executive director, explains that broadened ownership "can bring corporate 'citizens' back under civil society control," while it also reduces wealth inequalities. The equity-exchange concept has potential globally for accountability from multinational corporations. It could also be required by states handing out major subsidies.

Fourth principle: The goal of public works investment must be long-term improvement, directed at life in the next generation, even when dealing with cyclical economic disturbances. That quality is what made the Erie Canal so valuable to American history: It changed the prospects for Americans not yet born while it also expanded the economic landscape of the developing nation. One can look back at other breakthrough public projects and recognize the epic contributions government made to advancing American life in permanent ways. That quality has been greatly diluted by the open-handed modern state, trivialized to the point where the generational perspective is nearly lost in politics. This principle naturally would provoke enormous argument over what exactly does serve the next generation (and it always would be difficult to hold politics to the standard). Still, there is a good human reason why politicians like to build bridges and highways and schools. They feel their exertions are leaving something permanent for the future, something valuable that may still exist after they are gone. Likewise, for instance, financing early childhood development for those Americans born to unpromising circumstances would be understood as longterm investment, altering lives and improving society a generation hence.

These suggested principles do not exhaust the possibilities, but mainly I am trying to illustrate how people and politicians might begin to think differently about the role of government in economic development. When one considers how the grassroots reformers are trying to impose order on out-of-control corporate subsidies, it is easy to imagine how some of their ideas could contribute to a broader reform of government. The tax code, for an obvious example, lacks any serious correlation with the parallel objectives of government, beyond the usual expectations for economic growth and job creation. A serious tax overhaul might create incentives of a different kind: grading corporations on the established behavioral standards and awarding favors only to those who meet the performance tests. You don't get to use the new tax break unless you are contributing measurable positive results in your community (imagine a local referendum on whether the company qualifies as a good citizen).

The regulatory system, likewise, routinely is abused and ignored by many interests because they know they will face very little penalty if they are caught. If regulatory enforcement was integrated with the eligibility rules for tax privileges and direct subsidies, corporate managers might be made to pay a real price—significant dollar losses—for failing to meet the emissions standards or for violating their workers' rights. Conversely, the company that consistently surpasses the legal minimums and develops promising innovations for social progress should be treated generously, rewarded in the bottom line terms that matter to managers and investors.

Given the historically entrenched habits of politics and the adverse power equation, it may even require a constitutional amendment to establish these principles in law and practice. That too would be a very steep uphill struggle. But, as the right has demonstrated, a well-formulated proposal for making fundamental change through amendment to the Constitution can be a powerful vehicle for educating and mobilizing the broader public—and for agitating the minds of elected officials. Big government and little government could be restricted by commonsense commandments. Do no harm to the public with the public's own money. Get what you paid for or take the money back. Collect a quid pro quo for the public's investment. Invest only in the distant future, not in somebody's quarterly returns.

These ideas sound quite fanciful, I recognize, because all are so distant from the politics we know. It would help if one major political party or the other made common cause with those grassroots agitators and decided to take on the difficult reform of corporate subsidy. That is not going to happen—not yet anyway. It cannot happen until there is a much larger and louder army of citizens marching on the politicians, connecting many diverse perspectives and interests behind a coherent agenda, threatening complacent incumbents with nasty surprises at election time. If the Republican party is not going to do this for people, nor the Democrats, then one way or another people have to do it for themselves or it will not be done.


"TELL ME A STORY," the child asks at bedtime. The mother or father obliges, reading a familiar folktale or maybe spinning out a made-up adventure. For a few intimate moments they are suspended together in the narrative's action, deliciously anticipating how the story ends, even if they already know. Storytelling is the ancient comfort at the core of human consciousness. It is the way we imaginatively organize past, present, and unknown future into a manageable reality. Chaotic events and infinite possibilities become a story with a distinct beginning, middle, and end, an ordering that helps mere mortals make sense of life's experiences, including those that have not yet occurred. People tell small stories to themselves all the time, as routinely as thinking through the day ahead. I go to work, shop for groceries, bathe the kids, call Grandma. Sometimes, the story is the hoped-for narrative of one's life. I study hard, then go to college, get a good job, have a loving family. I get the raise and we go to the beach. Everyone, meek and powerful alike, guides their existence with such private narratives.

And society tells itself stories too. These are the shared public narratives that describe the future for people, recall the honored past, and sanctify the national character. Who we are, what we wish to become. To my mind, public storytelling represents the high art of politics and its noblest function, if it is done honestly, convincingly. When you think of great political leaders from the past (Lincoln is my ideal), they were effective in altering the course of history because they were compelling storytellers. With words and images they summoned people to an imagined drama of national life, and their stories often became true, in large part because people came to believe in them. A leader can disarm the future for us by describing its beckoning promise and, in a functioning democracy, this task does not belong to political leaders alone. Anyone, in theory, may contribute to the national narrative (if they can make themselves heard) and democracy, at its best, is about choosing freely among competing visions. I do not bring up this idea of narrative as a lofty metaphor, but as a reasonable representation of the country's actual dilemma.

America needs to develop a new narrative for itself. The old story line is no longer working to the mutual benefit and general satisfaction of the society and, in fact, does great damage to many lives and to our prospects for the future. Yet we seem unable to see our way clearly—to imagine fully an alternative version people may plausibly follow. To invoke again the language in my opening chapter, the country is stuck in the narrative of "more," the pursuit of unbounded material abundance that has been a driving purpose from the beginning. Yet, in our new condition beyond scarcity, the economy of more seems to have turned upon itself, tearing down social fabric and weakening essential institutions like family, piling up the discontents and destruction right alongside the growing plenty. The political system, far from assisting people to reimagine their future, is thoroughly enthralled by the logic of more, intimidated by its stern dictates, and resolute in protecting the existing order from significant change.

In such unpromising circumstances, people may grumble about confinements on their lives or the other visible injuries to society, but it's very difficult for them to see any escape other than to intensify their own pursuit of more. This country, though fabulously wealthy compared to others, now tells itself a strangely masochistic version of the American dream: If you really want to be truly happy, you will need to get really, truly rich. Most people understand this is a mirage; at least, they know it is an impossible fantasy for themselves. So they tend to the necessities of their lives and nurture the attainable pleasures, including accumulation, as best they can. Go shopping, rent a video for the kids, and remember, buy a lottery ticket.

Government, many citizens feel in their bones, is not going to resolve this great dilemma for the country, let alone for them personally. They do not expect government even to try. Politicians, especially at the national level, cannot confront the larger dimensions candidly (presuming some politicians do grasp the matter) because that would put them in conflict with the enduring national story of more—the story that government itself works to advance. If an elected official did boldly describe a competing narrative of vastly different choices, it would likely amount to career-ending self-immolation, another lame politician trying to speak for a popular movement when none yet exists.

The decay of American democracy, I suggest, is substantially related to this enervating disconnect in American public life. Why follow politics? It's not about me, not about anything real. People at every station are conscious of the tension between their lives and the economic imperatives of more; they understand a lot about the destructive social consequences and frequently articulate their frustrations and anger in private conversation. Yet the subject remains taboo in politics, not addressed or even acknowledged by the governing dialogues.

Taking on capitalism sounds too radical—and vaguely un-American, like a plot to overthrow the mighty engine of more. The implicit ambition of this book, nonetheless, has been to describe the alternative narrative—at least, to sketch the outlines of a promising new story for our future—and to make it sound plausible for ordinary citizens, if not to their leaders. The core of my argument is that the resolution of these deep conflicts and discontents must begin with organic changes within American capitalism itself. And that people themselves can do this, despite the inertia of government and the overbearing power of established economic interests. Yes, the national dilemma also involves social pathologies and the frailties of human psychology—the alluring forces of irresponsibility, ignorance, arrogance, greed—but ministering to people's failings is attacking the problem from the wrong end.

It is the economic system of American capitalism that is the heart of the matter, the originating source of the dilemma. As it presently functions, capitalism encourages the human pathologies—embodies irresponsibility as a central requirement in its operating routines—and gives most participants very limited capacity to behave otherwise. People have to accept those terms in pursuit of economic well-being and, in doing so, they are compelled to surrender their ability to exercise any responsibility for the consequences. Empowering people to take ownership of their work and of the investing consequences of their wealth and savings, to take responsibility for their roles as consumers and citizens, should be understood, not as new burdens, but as opportunities to expand the boundaries of one's life. These tasks involve moral obligations, in the fundamental sense, both to others and self and the unborn future. They will engage one in the content of life that lies beyond material gains, where the returns are measured in greater human fulfillment.

The evidence for my optimism is located among the pioneers, those Americans already working in various ways to dismantle or reengineer the status quo. They seem scattered and marginal to be sure, but are making real progress. I believe in their potential because I have seen what they can accomplish and, above all, because I think their ideas and efforts are aligned more accurately with the country's actual circumstances than is the inherited story line of more. Knowledge is power. When more people come to know and understand the options, these ideas can prevail.

What is it that these people want from the economic system? More space for life itself. More power (and thus more responsibility) for ordinary people to determine the content of their lives, work, and community. More equity in the distribution of rewards; more justice. More conscientious nurturance of society's softer assets: the babies and children, the fate of the Earth and other living things, the grace notes of community life, the untapped possibilities for personal self-realization. "More of the opportunities to cultivate our better natures," as Samuel Gompers declared in 1893.

In essence, reform-minded pioneers seek to establish a different understanding of more—the pursuit of a more fulfilling and ennobling existence, an opportunity the economic system effectively denies to most people. Imagine this narrative: Inventive Americans, having conquered scarcity and accomplished great plenty, set out to discover how to live wisely and agreeably and well with the abundance. Secure in material terms, they hope to learn at last what it means to be fully human. That was Keynes's prophesy. That is the country's new story.

Their principal focus, as a result, must be on the actual composition of economic growth rather than on the gross numbers reported as ever-growing Gross Domestic Product. The status quo forces in business and politics (joined by fellow-traveling economists) will argue, as they always do, that such reform might endanger the golden goose itself, threatening to replace prosperity with no-growth stagnation. That familiar claim is the powerful enforcer in politics, and not just among politicians. Who can be against more jobs, more income, more profit and plenty? Reformers see through the mask, however, and recognize that GDP is not neutral science, as advertised, but actually an opaque expression of capitalism's amoral value system, posing as statistical evidence of progress. In the real world, where people live, the GDP numbers help to falsify the story of more. What economics reports as growth is often for society loss and decline.

Professor Herman E. Daly of the University of Maryland is a former World Bank economist who rebelled against the fictitious nature of economic orthodoxy and became a pioneer in exposing the intellectual fallacies. Daly, with true detachment, stepped back and asked of the Gross Domestic Product: more of what? He examined what economics counts as growth and what it ignores. It counts every activity and transaction that can be measured in dollars, but neglects the value of everything else—literally leaves it out. Nature adds nothing to growth until someone cuts down the trees. Or a river becomes the free dump for factory wastes. Children are worthless too, unless one estimates their lives as a stream of future income or calculates the economic demand when they need clothes and shelter. Community well-being and personal security do not show up anywhere in the accounting. Those goods are not counted, economists would say, because how could you? They are unpriced assets, neither bought nor sold. Priceless, Daly would observe, does not mean worthless.

The distortions become more profound. Economics counts any and every economic activity or exchange as a positive contribution to GDP, regardless of the negative impact it may have for people and society. Crime is therefore understood as an important generator of economic growth; the more crime, the more market demand for hiring cops and security guards, for building more prisons. Disease and illness are positive factors for the same reason (and the health industry works hard to discover new ailments to heal). So are car crashes, train wrecks, or other events society understands as major disasters.

Less visible disasters like pollution, work stress, poverty, or family dis-
solution are not deducted from growth. However, the cost of cleaning up the social consequences afterward has a plus value for GDP.

These crude examples greatly oversimplify Daly's analysis (for
enlightenment, read *For the Common Good,* coauthored with theologian John B. Cobb, Jr.). But the point is fairly straightforward: Economics makes no distinction among positive and negative economic
activities on the grounds that objective scientific analysis cannot consider such social values. After all, one man's disaster may be another's
source of income. Yet, by refusing to make any distinctions, economics is effectively making a profoundly influential value choice for the
unwitting society. The choice is an economic system bereft of values.
When society accepts statistical growth as its shared measure of
progress, the society has effectively surrendered its own values to capitalism's.[14]

To make the contradictions visible, Daly and Cobb constructed a
more balanced measure of economic growth—the Index of Sustainable Economic Welfare—that deducts the negative costs of economic
growth, the familiar collateral damage like environmental despolia-
tion and depletion of resources, and crime, poverty, and other forms
of social deterioration. Though these negative consequences can only
be partially quantified, the act of counting them produces a dramatic
reversal in the picture of progress. Instead of the robust growth in per
capita income that the standard data reported in recent decades,
Americans were experiencing a steady erosion in their economic
well-being. The country was getting steadily poorer, not richer, its
wealth declining once the accounting was true to reality. "A long-
term trend that is indeed bleak," the authors reported.

Inspired by Daly and Cobb's insights, many others are now
extending the investigation by creating various social indicators and
other analytical measures to help people see the damaging trade-offs
concealed by the GDP version of growth. These efforts range from
the Genuine Progress Indicator produced by a San Francisco organi-

zation called Redefining Progress and state-sponsored measures like Oregon's Benchmarks to the Calvert-Henderson Quality of Life Indicators, a dense catalog of social-economic trends produced by social critic Hazel Henderson and the Calvert Group of socially responsible investment funds. The federal government, of course, still operates according to the narrow mindset of formal economics. Until a new, more honest GDP is constructed for official use, the political debates about growth and how to achieve it will continue to be confused, based on self-destructive illusions.

Herman Daly's larger warning to society is that the standard pattern of growth is self-defeating. The long-held assumption that more output and more consumption eventually would overcome poverty, inequality, and other symptoms of social decay has demonstrably failed. Yet the growing ecological destruction is, meanwhile, on a collision course with the natural limits of the Earth. Ultimately, growth cannot continue unless something gives—either an industrial transformation to eliminate the destruction or a sharp cutback in material abundance.

The essence of sustainable development, Daly explains, is an economy focused not on gross quantity with its negative consequences but on more enduring quality—more value and efficiency, less waste, in everything the economy produces and consumes. "If technology can easily and greatly increase efficiency, then the transition could be relatively painless," Daly wrote. "If not, it will be more difficult." More from less—that is capitalism's great virtue. If properly pursued, more from less will lead once again, not to stagnation or deprivation, but to a more fulfilling future.

To put this challenge in historical context we need to appreciate that the United States is still a relatively young country, a mere adolescent alongside older nations and ancient cultures. Through most of their history, only two hundred years or so, Americans and their enterprises and government have focused energetically on development: building the canals and railroads; pioneering new territory and new industries; acquiring the education and business capacities to advance economic life in heroic dimensions. That process is not going to end entirely, but the main focus of innovative efforts must shift now. Redevelopment, we might call it. That is, reconstructing, modifying, and improving the quality of what already exists in the established prosperity while correcting old mistakes.

In many ways, redevelopment of an already formed economy is far more difficult than pioneering. We are not plowing unbroken prairie or building new towns and cities. The cities already exist, many in ruinous decay. Some of the prairies have become chemical swamps; some of the towns have lost purpose and populations. Relieved of the stark questions of survival, Americans must now attempt to reconstruct the interior landscape of American life. That is tougher territory. It is already populated with settled institutions, public and private, that are naturally resistant to change and often encrusted with age. Altering the familiar habits and routines, dislodging the established power relationships—those are imposing mountains to cross.

In the life of nations this new stage might be called maturity. Having grown muscular, talented, and much admired for its successes, can America ripen into a well-balanced society, acquiring the social graces and farsightedness of adulthood? Or does it simply keep repeating the adolescent excesses, like a stunted child who is unable (or unwilling) to grow up? Circumstances suggest that, whether they know it or not, Americans are in the midst of choosing between those two story lines. A happy ending is not foreordained.

The transformation Herman Daly envisions requires deep alterations in the economy, but he sees this ultimately as a test of national character and spiritual faith. "Sustainable development will require a change of heart, a renewal of the mind, and a healthy dose of repentance," Daly wrote. "These are religious terms and that is no coincidence because a change in the fundamental principles we live by is a change so deep that it is essentially religious, whether we call it that or not. . . . We are creatures endowed with creativity but also subject to limits, and we have obligations to our Creator to care for Creation, to maintain its capacity to support life and wealth."

GOVERNMENT AT EVERY LEVEL obviously has the power—enormous power—to alter the economic landscape on behalf of this vision. It can help finance the shift to employee-owned enterprise by providing low-cost credit and tax breaks, much as it did to universalize home ownership. It can raise the requirements for achieving ecological balance and stiffen penalties for the destruction. It can redefine the fiduciary obligations of financial institutions so they invest other people's money in the true interests of the owners and beneficiaries. It can refocus public works subsidies on the industrial innovations needed to achieve eventual harmony with the natural world. It can enact new civil rights legislation on behalf of workers and families. It can develop a new social trust legal doctrine that defines the scale and public obligations of corporations.

All these and many other reform measures would be valuable and someday, one imagines, they might be enacted. But, at the risk of disappointing some readers, I am not at this point going to offer a lengthy catalog of legislative goals. Such a list seems premature. It might simply reinforce the false notion that government can make this happen for us.

For conservatives as well as liberals, a reflexive reliance on the federal government as the main vehicle for reforming society is a well-established habit, but is grossly inadequate for the present circumstances. First, the political system's present response to most of these propositions ranges from indifference to hostility, attitudes not altered by changing presidents or party control in Congress. Given the underdeveloped support for fundamental reforms, it might even be dangerous to ask Congress to legislate on these matters. Having observed the national government up close across nearly four decades, I have developed an enduring wariness toward its good intentions. I have seen too many important ideas and worthwhile initiatives deformed and eviscerated by the very legislative process that enacted them.

Compromise is always part of lawmaking, but both political parties are now adept at enacting hollow laws that appear to serve large public purposes but are actually wired with special-interest traps that guarantee continued evasion and meager results. This is especially true of regulatory law, but the risk is present even when public money is committed to innovative experiments. The projects' operating terms and original purposes often are diluted by legislators in order to spread the money around as widely as possible. Advocates typically accept the changes in order to get their bill through Congress, but the debasement often proves to be fatal. When the reform project does not produce the intended results it is declared a failure, and promising ideas are abandoned. Congressional hunger for pork is natural enough, but in the absence of strong governing principles or internal party discipline, worthy objectives are vulnerable to high-minded caricature.

The greater danger of seeking federal action prematurely is that doing so may very well smother promising experiments underway at state and local levels, forcing new ideas to conform to a centralized uniformity before these ideas are developed fully and field-tested in practical circumstances. Federal government interventions have produced historic accomplishments, particularly in establishing rights for excluded and exploited groups, but federal legislation also typically preempts the field for Washington. Once the standards are determined nationally, local grassroots groups lose their leverage on the issue and, once marginalized, they often lose their energy and focus. What the country needs at this point is an era of robust experimentation and self-education—large and small efforts, widely dispersed, to develop and test numerous approaches toward redefining the meanings of more. Change of such fundamental dimension, if it is to succeed, requires people to learn how to do things differently, and that knowledge must be deeply, broadly planted in people's everyday experience. That is impossible to achieve from the top down.

Enacting state and local laws thus offers more promising ground for politics. Washington, meanwhile, could help by clearing away some of the legal obstacles erected for status quo interests and by encouraging the reform spirit without trying to manage it. The federal government, for instance, might help pay for state networks of "field agents" who assist people with the technical questions of reform, something like the agricultural extension agents who teach new methods to farmers. What are the mechanics of engineering a takeover by employee owners? Or designing democratic governance within the firm? Or launching a community-owned investment fund? How does a town or county generate jobs from a strategy based on education and other forms of community self-improvement? For that matter, how do people even start to think about this new story in terms of their own surroundings?

As these questions suggest, the great value of human-scale exploration is that ordinary citizens gain new capabilities in the process—personal strengths they didn't know they had—and, in time, some of them will emerge as the innovators and the leaders with the self-confidence to promote their own homegrown solutions as available models for others. Some Americans, we now know, are already doing this (and some colleges and local governments are helping them).

The country, as a whole, is not there yet. And there is no playbook to follow, no central office with a ten-step plan. We do not yet know enough to claim settled solutions and, meanwhile, millions more must be persuaded to join the search. This kind of politics requires great patience and, above all, patience with one another. The new narrative, appealing and promising though it may sound, must first be told by people, one to another.

ODD AS IT MAY SEEM, citizens need to learn how to think like capitalists. That is, they need to develop their own forward-looking narratives for the society and figure out how to make them come true.

The brilliant, creative core of capitalism, as I discussed earlier, is the story that entrepreneurs and capital investors tell themselves about the future. How they intend to alter it, what they expect to gain in return, where they will raise the capital to accomplish their vision. Many of their stories turn out to be flawed or mistaken, of course, but the capacity to envision a set of future events and then act to fulfill them is a central source of capitalism's strength and its dominance of society. People do the same thing in their private lives, for family and self. But Americans collectively are weak and astonishingly underdeveloped in the art of looking forward together and intelligently developing a plan for what they intend to become, as a community or a nation, as a people.

Society, in effect, leaves the future blank and passively lets capitalism fill in the picture with its own imaginative stories. Business and financial enterprises are expertly equipped to handle the task. After all, it is what they do routinely with the formulas and formats learned at business school for "running the numbers." Strategists and bankers know how to estimate potential risk and return in new ventures. R&D turns technological discoveries into marketable comforts and conveniences. Entrepreneurial insight teases out a new line of products from society's everyday frustrations or yearnings. And their wishful narratives are hard-tested in the marketplace.

The basic shortcoming in business planning, however, is that the strategists are necessarily judged by a narrow gauge of performance—the return on capital. They do not get paid for solving social problems. Given the political passivity, they seldom are penalized for causing social problems. What business enterprise creates, nevertheless, does alter the fabric and structure of American life, for good and for ill. It pulls country and community in unforeseen directions that other citizens had no opportunity to examine or resist.

Society's voice is largely missing because it has no grand story to tell as counterpoise to the well-focused plans of enterprise. In theory, government might fill that void but, for various historical reasons,

American government no longer does much planning beyond subsidiary questions like highway routes or the blowsy campaign promises of office seekers. Some attribute this to the fervent individualism of Americans—the desire to live free of encumbrances, an enduring suspicion of government power. Yet, in earlier stages of American development, the pioneering efforts typically were based on a shared public vision of the future and employed elaborate systems for cooperation between citizens and government. In the crisis of the Great Depression the federal government explicitly engaged in formal systems of planning, and its agencies were a source of some major reforms, programs that addressed economic and social problems as one. Those were extreme times, and the New Deal's planning systems are now largely defunct, discredited by the business propaganda denouncing "socialist" central planning. As a consequence, business and finance do the planning for America now, to the extent that anyone does.

Despite this historical impasse, a rather extraordinary—and hopeful—countertrend has arisen spontaneously around the country in recent years. People are once again starting to tell their stories to one another, ambitious stories about what they think their communities can become, cautionary stories about the mess their town or city is turning into. These efforts are scattered for now, still searching for the right setting in which to be heard, the right format to be convincing. They sometimes are allied with local or state governments, sometimes not. In either case, these forward-looking citizens have no power whatever to change anything. Their potential power lies in persuading other citizens to think differently about the future—at least to think about it—and to develop a renewed belief that people can change things. Possibly, I am making too much of these efforts to reinvent citizenship, but I see them as perhaps a harbinger of "new politics"—from the bottom up and seeking to restore people's voice in their future.

In Oregon, the legislature created a "progress board" whose members (including Beverly Stein of Multnomah County) developed "a strategy for Oregon that addresses the economic, social, cultural, environmental and other needs and aspirations of the people of Oregon." The board came up with some ninety benchmarks and handed out grades: F for urban highway congestion; C+ for per capita income; D for civic engagement; D+ for eighth graders using alcohol, cigarettes, and drugs. No overall category, not even the state's buoyant economy, scored higher than C+. "Most parents would not welcome this report card," the board observed. It assigned "ambitious but realistic" goals, both for the short-term and a decade hence, then described the existing values and visions for change: "Family life is at the top of our list of personal values, while civic affairs [now] are near the bottom." "Oregon's workforce will be the best educated and trained in America . . . equal to any in the world by 2010." "Oregon will support thoughtful growth management strategies." These are yardsticks for public officials, but also for those citizens who decide to think for themselves.

The civic pride of Orlando, Florida, was bruised when a private group, the Healthy Community Initiative, issued its "Legacy 2000" report, a portrait of social-economic trends that reveal the city's "slow decline" as a livable community. Air pollution, poverty, drug use, traffic headaches. The local consumption of fossil fuels is in "condition red." The 25 percent of children living in poverty are on a path to become 40 percent. Orlando's "Good Life Index," the group declared, scores 60 on a scale of 100. County chairman Mel Martinez complained that this was a "disservice" to the community. "I would give us an 80," he protested. "I mean, I know there are challenges out there—I hear you—but we're working on them."

In the small town of Tifton, Georgia, people undertook a similar process of self-examination and grandly declared the community of 17,000 intends to become "the reading capital of the world." Toward that end—developing the civic asset of well-educated people— Tifton created its own fiber-optic system, connecting schools, homes, and businesses to the digital world. The town wired itself and owns the system, instead of waiting on private enterprise.[15]

Sustainable Seattle began in the early 1990s as an amorphous network of private citizens who were worried by the rapid deterioration of their city's splendid qualities due to the relentless expansion (economic growth most communities would envy). These citizens started a running discussion of local conditions, and their reports on social indicators have since become part of the rhythms of Seattle civic life (and inspired many other localities to attempt the same). The group's favorite indicator—the disappearing wild salmon—spoke to Seattle's deep self-identity as a nature-friendly place to live. "The fish are like the canary in a coal mine," author Robert Sullivan explained. The salmon may save us from ourselves, the mayor suggested.

The wild salmon are not saved, and neither is Seattle. The political conflicts are fierce and bruising. Nevertheless, an intense conversation is underway among people who are arguing over economic-social trade-offs that were always present, though never confronted. Citizens are also compelled to deal with other citizens they had not encountered before. Constructing a self-portrait of how we live turns out to be one small step toward democracy.

"Indicators are a very subtle agent of change," Alan AtKisson, one of Sustainable Seattle's founders, explained in *Believing Cassandra,* "because they work in two relatively invisible dimensions: individual consciousness and social process. . . . Inside the process are concealed a host of new concepts, values, initiatives and inspirations." AtKisson described seven "principles of sustainability" and his first one is this: "Think long-term. . . . Start by keeping the world of your great-grandchildren in mind." Around the country, scores of variations on the same theme are constructing self-portraits, some with narrower focus and some more aggressively, but all trying to confront deep structural questions about economic life and how it shapes the future.[16]

In Austin, Texas, one of those booming cities blessed with high-tech industry, the city council created the Austin Equity Commission to investigate the "disappearing middle." Its chairman is Ray Marshall, University of Texas economist and former U.S. secretary of labor. The little appreciated reality of places like Austin—highly educated university towns with a fast-growing technological economy—is that these so-called "creative cities" generate rising income inequality, greater and faster than the country as a whole, as reporter Bill Bishop has explained in the *Austin American-Statesman*. The high-tech economy, as it is presently organized, demands a workforce of poverty and plenty—more lousy low-wage jobs alongside the premium employment for computer engineers and business professionals. That mix threatens the overall quality of Austin's future in numerous ways, as it piles up social deterioration in the midst of greater wealth. Ultimately, this threatens the economic prosperity, too. As the Austin commission reported, the accumulating disparities "could become a major barrier to sustainable economic growth."[17]

Silicon Valley, anchored by San Jose, California, has the greatest income inequality in the country. And the South Bay AFL-CIO Labor Council organized a similar collaboration with local business managements and governments to confront the phenomenon of growing wage inequality. Does the reality of high-tech represent another "canary in the coal mine"? Certainly, it is a vivid example of how local sensibilities may recognize a threatening reality the national government ignores, perhaps because it does not see it. Washington is oblivious and doing whatever it can to promote the present format for high-tech development (and, in return, solicits bountiful campaign money from the industry's leading corporations and investment bankers).

The paradox of high-tech inequality is not merely a local problem, and the implications are not trivial for the nation. Silicon Valley, Austin, and the other high-tech centers are represented as the future of the U.S. economy, the model that scores of other cities are trying to emulate, the advanced technological production federal authorities assume will save us from the competitive forces of globalization. But what if this new form of salvation simply recreates more of the old familiar social losses? A society extremely divided by the walled differences of class and income, the social deterioration that always accompanies inadequate incomes: fractured families, slum housing, crime, stunted lives. Since neither political party seems willing to face these facts at the national level, it may be that these local inquiries, frail as they seem, are our best, only hope for putting the truth on the table before it is too late.

Across the country, people are engaged in many parallel mobilizations that seek to turn the narrative of "more" into a more positive story. In some older cities, various local businesses, historic preservationists, and neighborhood activists have come together to block big-box retailing, the suburban-style mall projects that city governments tend to subsidize heavily in the name of economic development, but that obliterate the character and diversity of the urban landscape (and also bulldoze viable, older stores and neighborhoods). Roberta Brandes Gratz, author of *Cities Back from the Edge,* described these confrontations as motivated by a different sense of what city life should be. The people are insisting on "organic regeneration" rather than massive teardowns and sterile copycat shopping malls. They have triumphed in enough places, she wrote, "to demonstrate how downtown revitalization really works."[18]

In farm country, the state of Oklahoma has established the Oklahoma Food Policy Council, following the example set by Iowa. The councils are developing an alternative story about the food we consume: the value of local food production as more safe and wholesome, less destructive environmentally, and a way out for smaller family farms up against deteriorating incomes and corporatized agriculture. Making space for locally produced foodstuffs also could be a political predicate for shutting down the hog factories and other of agribusiness's abusive practices. Who knows, it might even be a first step toward developing a new antitrust doctrine.

"Slowly but steadily the food culture of Iowa and other states is changing," said Neil Hamilton, chairman of the Iowa council. "The local foods movement is nationwide and it is helping consumers and communities consider where food is grown and how food-buying decisions can support local farmers and businesses. . . . But the local food movement would not have so much energy if the food didn't taste great and if consumers didn't benefit as well as producers." Is food an economic issue or a social issue? It is both, of course, like the other examples. People are trying to see this subject in its entirety—the economy of food and the social consequences for people—and then figure out how the two can be reconciled to mutual benefit.[19]

The homegrown initiatives are easy to dismiss, even ridicule as touchy-feely wishful thinking. They represent "soft politics" since they have no actual power to accomplish their goals. Indeed, some efforts are deliberately distanced from the power of local government because it often looks like a hopeless swamp layered with hostile special interests. Communities, one has to add again, are not angels either, any more than workers. Nothing guarantees that grassroots aspirations will be virtuous and equitable or that those in control will respond to high-minded goals. It all depends. Still, I see these examples as confirming evidence that people will assert themselves, whatever the barriers or handicaps, and that they are resourcefully inventing ways to do so. Their willingness to take on very large public questions, with no obvious means for resolving them, suggests an American character quite different from the hapless lambs manipulated by business marketing or atomized by the abstractions of formal economics.

In essence, the process of using social indicators to construct social narratives tries to apply the principles of ecology to human systems—the man-made systems of economy and community. As Bill Weeks of The Nature Conservancy explains, when scientists study an ecosystem, they begin by doing a "stress analysis" that identifies the points of deterioration the natural system is experiencing. Then they develop a narrative to explain how and why these symptoms of breakdown are occurring. That analysis usually suggests solutions—what has to be altered to restore balance to the ecosystem and, thus, its sustainability. People essentially are trying to adapt the same mode of thought to their surroundings and, compared to ecological science, the initial efforts are only primitive, first steps into complex and unknown territory.

The social narratives are still missing many pieces and lack the sophisticated methodologies that business and finance apply routinely for narrower objectives. Major corporations, as usual, got to the idea first, and well ahead of citizens. Some firms have elaborate systems for constructing alternative scenarios of their future, including potential interactions with society that might disrupt their story. Sometimes the business planners even invite their leading critics to contribute scenarios to the game, since popular resistance is a major business risk for new products like genetically altered plants and animals.

Citizen storytelling so far lacks the rigor of what business does and has not moved far beyond static indicators. The citizens will need to develop further the art of storytelling, capturing the fluid dynamics of multiple interconnected events, constructing a dramatic flow that leads to plausible strategies and convincing resolutions. For a glimpse of what I mean, read Eric Schlosser's *Fast-Food Nation*. He is a brilliant storyteller, not a policy thinker, and his well-rounded account of the rise of the fast-food industry includes every important business element and social consequence, from the founding entrepreneurs who saw the social need for McDonald's (cheap, quick family restaurants) to the modern-day "dark satanic mills" where the animals are slaughtered and the workers maimed and brutalized. Other, less complex examples of social-economic narratives are the short portraits of industrial sectors like *The Sneaker Book* by Tom Vanderbilt, published by the New Press. He explained how brand-name sports gear originated in American yearnings for fitness and wound up in Asian sweatshops where exploited children manufacture the expensive sneakers.

These books implicitly teach one how to think about the economy and society in an altogether new way.[20]

The pioneers need not feel bad about shortcomings in their story-telling. After all, they have only just begun, and what they are attempting is far more ambitious than anything the business strategists undertake. These citizens essentially are trying to integrate the divergent elements of social reality and the working engine of economic life into a coherent story that is more promising for society than the reigning narratives of self-centered capitalism. This is very difficult to achieve (and most innovators would probably not describe it so grandly). In time, however, as forward-looking communities develop more expertise and attract a wider following, I expect they will progress to more inclusive narratives, more ambitious story lines.

What, for instance, is the narrative of children in our society? Not the bromides we tell ourselves, but the actual terms and conditions imposed on kids growing up in America? We know there is something wrong with the present story, since symptoms of distress and breakdown, even violent rage, are all around us and not limited to the children in poverty. Children, it seems obvious, need more nurturance, but they may also need more of their own childhood—the space to discover the innocent, unprogrammed delights of the new; the time to encounter life's gorgeous diversity and learn there is joy in idle curiosity. At present, it seems, children are put on an assembly line, quite early in their lives, and "managed" toward economic goals of production and income. Their performance will be "tested" regularly along the way as the measurable "output" of the education system. If they pursue advanced education, we leave them saddled with mountainous debts. That makes good sense to an economist, but it is a nasty thing to do to young people whose personal narratives are still fresh and forming. The worth of their lives, they are told, will be measured in those same narrow terms.

A broader understanding of education's purpose exists: nurturing children so they will feel at home in the world; equipping them to experience the fullness of their own lives, the joys of doing honest work. That perspective has been marginalized by the business model and will not be restored easily. A new narrative might start from the premise that commodifying children's lives is not good for them and, in the long run, not for society. In the presence of abundance it ought to be possible to reconsider education and refashion it as a cornerstone for a more fulfilling prosperity.

There are many provocative questions waiting to be asked in new ways. What is the narrative of the elderly, for instance, now that we might live to be one hundred? Theodore Roszak in *Longevity Revolution* described the growing "retired" population as America's great new social asset, not the financial burden described by politics and economics. He foresees a profound opportunity to reintegrate senior citizens with society as the "honored elders" and perhaps surrogate grandparents, listening and teaching the rest of us, but above all, as valuable workers, doing real tasks the society needs, including for money incomes. Might Americans recover some of the lost virtues of the extended family without the old confinements? Might Roszak's vision of longevity suggest a workforce that is growing, not shrinking, as the grim right-wing critics of Social Security argue? We can tell a happier story about the economics if we think more positively about the society.

For that matter, we await a more convincing narrative about how to rescue America's decaying democracy. We know the authenticity of the representative system is in steep decline, know also that the periodic reform efforts have only trivial effects. Political reporters like to write about the 50–50 country, so closely divided between the two major parties, but actually this is a 25–25 country in presidential elections and a 20–20 country in the off-year congressional elections (when 90 percent of House contests are predetermined by the bipartisan monopoly's gerrymandering). Instead of dwelling on the failings of those bad citizens who decline to participate in elections (50 to 60 percent of the adult population), a new narrative might focus on reforming the failed institutions of political life (including the concentrated and homogenized media). The inquiry might ask why Republicans and Democrats are entitled to their arranged monopoly on political power when both fail utterly to engage the country as a whole. Or, as this book suggests, we might recognize that the deeper deformities in our democracy do not originate in elections, but in the malformed power relationships that rule over economic life.

As forward-thinking communities develop new stories for themselves, sooner or later they must inevitably turn to the question of power. Yes, people are in a weak position to accomplish many things, especially changing larger economic conditions governed beyond local reach. But people are not as powerless as they perhaps imagine. What this book has described are the interlocking realms within capitalism—work, capital, consumption, corporate organization, and public governance—that are also the principal points for leveraging change. Each of these areas can become the entry points for acquiring power once people learn to act more purposefully as investors, managers, workers, consumers, and citizens.

This requires collaboration among many disparate people and interests, collective action that people will have to organize for themselves, since neither major political parties nor leading economic institutions seem able or willing to assist. Organized people, however, making use of their varied skills and personal assets, have the power to create a new texture for crossruffing power—webs of coordinated pressures that can convince an existing institution to alter its operating values or that collectively build new institutions from scratch. The efforts must be mutually rewarding and reinforcing for the collaborators, working on different fronts on behalf of broadly shared values and goals. That is always difficult to arrange, of course, but potentially an awesome force and quite unexpected by the status quo.

An employee-owned firm aligns itself with community aspirations and, together, they take on a firm that is doing damage to their future. Or they create a local investment fund of their own that rechannels their savings into preferred development. A major pension fund, in response to its constituent beneficiaries, withdraws its assets from antisocial corporations and invests in more responsible enterprises. A consumer-sensitive retailing sector finds itself squeezed by mobilized investors, workers, and customers, all advocating the same shift in values. An elected government, relying for its authority on passive voters, finds itself suddenly turned out of office.

Gentle persuasion is always the preferred approach, but hard-nosed applications of power are necessarily the more reliable agents of change. These uses of power involve the same hardball practices that are daily routines among capitalism's insiders: withdrawing resources and committing the assets elsewhere; squeezing vulnerable firms; rewarding those who are responsive; punishing the recalcitrant in numerous ways; taking control and ownership; demanding contractual terms of accountability; negotiating covenants for investments that spell out mutual obligations and responsibilities. I do not expect corporate managements and elected governments to remain oblivious once they see this new power as real. They will fight back, if they can, using any means available, including tactics that are illegitimate and vicious. Beneath all the complexities of this subject, reinventing capitalism is essentially a struggle to rearrange power in America. No one should look for an easy victory.

Newly created institutions, whether banks or companies or community investor funds, obviously involve great risks, but they may also be the most promising vehicles for fostering demonstrable change, more promising than waiting for the major players to accept new operating values. I won't recapitulate all the possibilities, but they are the missing pieces in modern capitalism: trustworthy financial firms and accountable business corporations; new patterns for ownership and governance; new mediating institutions for capital that adhere reliably to different values because they are accountable to the interests of only one party (the organizing workers, investors, consumers) and not to the mammoth institutions of Wall Street.

Communities also may have to invent some institutional surrogates for government, quasi-public, not-for-profit trusts or foundations that can fill some of the long-term functions that government has mostly abandoned (while the voters work on converting elected politicians to the new perspectives). A community trust, for instance, could serve as the community's stakeholder and honest broker, holding equity shares in locally based corporations with the right to kibitz their behavior and governance, negotiating covenants with businesses on behalf of local aspirations, or perhaps providing the lubricating capital for new enterprise development, including takeovers by employee owners. Above all, the community trust would be required to concentrate on the distant future, above and beyond the seasonal interests and conflicts of electoral politics.

Somebody has to ask the big questions for the future and articulate a new story, someone with enough capital and clout to command respect from established power. Some 550 community foundations, often funded by local philanthropists, exist around the nation and give aid to worthy, needy causes. Perhaps some of these might evolve into a broader role. But the community trust I envision would be closer to an independent public authority, perhaps even chartered with very limited governing powers and very modest public financing, with trustees bound by public accountability but not controlled by the mayor or governor. The trust could hold equity shares and covenant bonds for the community, like "earnest money" from the corporations that receive public subsidy. Ideally, the trustees would be required to focus *only* on long-term projects—the public works that are generational investments designed to improve the social reality over the next twenty or twenty-five years. Think of the world that will exist for your great-grandchildren, as Alan AtKisson suggested, for that is the inheritance you will leave them. When citizens and elected officials have learned again how to think about their legacy in those terms, then perhaps elected governments will reclaim that role and the community trusts can be phased out.

Many of these suggestions are fanciful projections of what is possible, playful but plausible stories about how this country may unfold in the years ahead. I do not claim with certainty that any of these ideas will themselves be realized, but since I am not alone in thinking this way, I expect the future to generate more and better ideas—more sophisticated and sharply focused and tested by practical experience. What I do claim, with considerable confidence, is that Americans in amazing variety will keep poking inventively at the economic system, looking for ways to get a handle on its operating routines and power structure, tinkering with new approaches that can truly change the nature of American capitalism. Modest changes at first, perhaps local and limited, but with grander ambitions in mind.

# 8

# Thinking Forward

U NDOUBTEDLY, the most audacious assertion in this book is that Americans are capable of doing this, that they have the heart and head to see the possibilities for themselves and to see them through. My convictions about the capacities of ordinary people are deeply grounded, beliefs I learned from my mother and father and absorbed from their stories of family forebears. This understanding was powerfully confirmed by my experiences as a reporter over many years, as I encountered ordinary citizens of every station in a multitude of situations. The national history, properly understood, makes the same point about us.

This country, as I have observed in previous books, has its full quota of fools and scoundrels, but on the whole the people are quite remarkable, resourceful, and serious about their lives, often courageous in the worst circumstances. It is sometimes difficult to see this through the fog of the mass market—the media caricatures of who we are and the clever marketing images that conjure desires from popular fantasies. But we are not a nation of addled sheep (at least not most of us).

Okay, that is what I believe. But I am willing to concede that, in this period of history, confidence in the people may be the minority view. Certainly, the governing elites in business and finance as well as government, regardless of political preferences, operate on bleaker assumptions about the human condition. High-minded stewardship, they tell themselves, requires a rather constant manipulation of the soft-headed populace, deftly steering the people toward correct outcomes, even if people are too stupid to understand their own best interests.

What's worse is that many ordinary Americans—maybe most of them—believe this too. At least, many have internalized from experience the notion that they have been assigned lesser roles in the grand scheme and there's nothing to be done about it. Like it or not, the obstacles are simply too formidable to overcome. The frontier is closed; the pioneering is history. This self-doubt and resignation may be the greatest barrier to realizing an alternative future, one in which people at large can participate from their various angles in the decisions that govern their lives.

One of this book's implicit objectives is to encourage a little impudence, especially among younger people. I do not expect my prose to blow away their caution and skepticism. But I do hope they keep their minds open to the possibility that some of what I have observed may be right and that it speaks to their own experiences and thinking. If so, they need to ask some questions, to entertain more doubts about the system, less doubt about themselves. Curiosity and doubt are the first steps toward action, especially when accompanied by well-earned anger at the way things are.

Historian Lawrence Goodwyn of Duke University, a friend and wise counselor who teaches the history of social movements, once explained it for me. "The first thing we have to do is license in people a degree of doubt and curiosity," Goodwyn instructs. "We need untrammeled curiosity. We live in a damaged culture, and people are inhibited more than intimidated. Getting rid of complacency means expanding our curiosity. Then we need to encourage an insurgent temperament. If we can't actually create this in our time, we can at least show the next generation that it's possible to think this way."[1]

All of us have a lot to learn. It would help if some institutions of learning decided to focus more aggressively on this terrain where society collides with capitalism. Americans know many, many things but, ironically, they are largely ignorant of how their capitalism functions. Colleges and universities might introduce "capitalist studies" alongside other specialties and, to be truly bold, they should attempt to reintegrate economics with sociology (the two disciplines were once regarded as inseparably connected). A university course might resurrect famous old arguments from the past that examined the nature of capitalism and its relationship to society—names like Schumpeter, Veblen, Polanyi, Keynes, and Brunner, and other authorities I have invoked. They knew how to think about capitalism and economics free of the intimidating mathematical formulas. In the same spirit, a few brave business schools might begin teaching a deeper social perspective on capital finance and corporate management, a more systemic moral inquiry than the "business ethics" courses.[2]

The general inertia and passivity, in any case, are not the end of the story. "Never doubt that a small group of thoughtful, committed citizens can change the world. Indeed, it's the only thing that ever has." That remark has been attributed to Margaret Mead but, whoever said it, the observation resonates down through our history. In democracy, the deep politics originates in social reality, not in legislative halls. People everywhere have the ability to alter social reality, at least in their own surroundings. When they decide to act on their convictions, sooner or later the politics will follow. A meaningful minority can change the nation. I saw it happen in my lifetime. The civil rights movement—composed of the humblest, weakest citizens in the land—set out to liberate themselves from the racial caste system and, as Martin Luther King, Jr., prophesied, they liberated a lot of white people too. This is a long road, surely, but every small change advances someone's circumstances. Every small advance is a signal to others that change is possible, that maybe they too are licensed to entertain doubts and curiosity.[3]

Let us suppose for the moment that more and more people do proceed along the paths of reform I have described, joining the others who are engaged already, and that their ideas begin to gain traction and wider visibility in the society, even in the higher realms of politics. As that occurs, Americans will discover, as I suggested early on, that indeed they must change themselves too. Part of that process is ennobling—developing a larger sense of self—but part of it also involves discarding some inherited baggage from our culture and history. We are governed in our reflexes by the folklore of small prejudices and visceral suspicions toward certain others, our buried assumptions about who in this society is a good guy and who isn't, about who is capable of leading and who must follow. Those of us who do "brain work," for instance, are encouraged to believe we are special human beings. That is a cultural lie. It has to be challenged.

Notions of rank ordering and class are expressed everyday by the particular clothes we wear or the cars and trucks we choose to drive. If you stand back a few paces from American society and look at who we are, you can see we are a highly delineated assembly of very different people, and everyone knows intuitively how to read the tribal markings and the colorful (sometimes feeble) expressions of our individual identities. We Americans seem to like it like that, always have and probably always will. Our variegated society would seem quite bland if we lost the gaudy distinctions. I am not proposing everyone throw away their designer-logo shirts or suppress the peculiarities we all cherish in ourselves. Individualism, even the shallow kind, is our birthright.

What I do suggest is that the unresolved dilemmas of our modern situation allow us—in fact, require us—to lower our guards a bit and reconsider distant others in a new light. Not as potential buddies or next-door neighbors, but as necessary allies for the tasks ahead. Given the complexities of modern economic organization, people will not get very far unless they recognize that many of the old dividing lines among us are no longer accurate or helpful. And the kinds of collective action required for serious change must be developed through new alliances of interests that jump across the old boundaries of class, race, occupational status, even political labels in surprising new ways.

I have hinted at these possibilities throughout the book with my examples of active pioneers. Some of them are "humanist-populist-capitalists," some are poor people. Some are "radical" ecologists out to transform industrial life, and some of *them* are from the Republican establishment. Some are forward-thinking labor leaders, others are middle managers who used to regard unions as the main problem. Some are wealthy investment bankers, some are failing farmers, accountants, or animal-rights activists. It's a very rich social mix, gorgeously unlikely in the American fashion. These types seldom talk with one another. In this economic system and this culture, it is difficult to do so. Yet some of these folks have recognized that, at a fundamental level, there is a mutuality of interests across the dividing lines. They want to uncover these connections, make them visible, use them to broaden the power of their insurgencies. They are not doing this because they are nice people (though many of them are), but because it looks like the only strategy that might succeed.

The social paradox of our modern plenty can be crudely reduced to this: People do need one another, despite the differences, if they are going to work their way out of this predicament. We don't have to love the strangers, but we do have to deal with them. The society of "more" instead tends to run away and build walls, find a dream house in the countryside, and then keep others out, lest the newcomers obliterate the sanctuary. In the long run, as people are gradually discovering, there's no place to hide in the ever-abundant society. The economy of more has been driven by an ethos of individual self-seeking, especially in recent decades, but that mode of thinking will not deliver an escape from society's conditions. The very, very wealthy may build remote castles and moats, but the rest of us (and our great-grandchildren) are going to be living in the general fabric of society, and we know it is deteriorating amid the accumulating goods. For most of us, the only remedy lies in what has always been the paradox of American life: Collective action is required to achieve individual self-realization. People open the path for each one's individual pursuit of potential only by working together to liberate life's possibilities for all.

In fact, I will go further and say that this era may be the very first time in American history in which it is possible—and necessary to self-interest—for people to deal with one another across the inherited boundaries. A lot of young people, though probably a minority, seem to understand this and are living accordingly. They are not scared of the "others," but interested in them. They are participating in the cultural and class differences as enrichment to their own experience, luxuriating in the variety which, after all, is among the country's greatest assets. Meanwhile, general abundance also is steadily scrambling the economic distinctions that shaped our inherited identities—a fact that makes a "new politics" seem possible.

What exactly does "labor versus capital" mean if the workers are trying to become the owners of the company? Who are the "capitalists," for that matter, when the pension funds hold the savings of the American workforce and, along with other fiduciaries, are effectively the owners of the broad stock market? Who then really benefits if profit is derived from destructive wastefulness? And what is a community's true destiny when rampant growth is despised on one side of town as a malevolent force, while it represents salvation for the other side? These are not sentimental questions, but profoundly knotty political challenges. At a minimum, they require people to consider the other side's self-interest and to search for what might mutually resolve the conflicting aspirations. Otherwise, we will continue along the familiar path of power struggles in which the weaker side always loses and the social deterioration deepens further, and this is what we call "progress."

If my premises are correct and Americans do proceed collectively toward more supple definitions of progress, they may encounter a surprising dividend—the human comfort of mutual dependency. Sociologist Richard Sennett has provocatively proposed that we reconsider the opposing virtues of self-reliance and dependency—the human need to depend upon others. In private life, he observed, dependence ties us together in the warming expectations of human relationships, as children rely on adults or family members and neighbors know they can turn to one another in need. In the public realm, however, we are supposed to be grown-ups—self-sufficient adults free of all that—and social shame is directed at those who fail to accomplish independence. This ethic has advanced ferociously in recent years in both economic and political realms, most obviously in the welfare reform Sennett was discussing, but more generally as companies "liberated" families from reliable pensions or the other social contract guarantees.

Self-sufficiency begins to feel chillier, lonelier. For many families, their anxieties are embarrassing. Sennett suggested that what people may be feeling in their lives is a form of public shame akin to those at the very bottom—"an inner sense of incompleteness, whatever the hard evidence of achievement or gratification." The public shame is misdirected, he argued, because a human neediness for dependence on others is as natural to adults' live as to children's. Instead of hiding or running away, people may discover fuller lives by learning to accept their mutual need for others. Dependence, Sennett observed, also fosters "an enriching sense of mutual trust."[4]

Let us conclude on a mountaintop, speculating about a blue-sky future we cannot yet see but that might lie over the horizon. If Americans do undertake the redevelopment of the country's interior landscape (and they begin to succeed), that may change nearly everything else in the way our society is organized. I can imagine corporations that are, on the whole, smaller and more nimble, more responsive and cooperative, interconnected with other firms and social interests. No longer preoccupied with fending off government intrusions, businesses might even assume certain social obligations that are now exclusive functions of government. Government might be smaller, maybe not. Certainly, it would have to reformulate the ways it asserts its powers and become far more discriminating about who gets rewarded and who gets punished, become less intrusive in some areas, more forceful in others. The principles of economics would look utterly different, since the meanings of profit, loss, and productive output would be revalued to conform better with society's understandings of what is gain and what is loss.

The point is, adjusting to the realities and responsibilities of abundance can open the door to rethinking long-settled functions and institutions, including how government deals with social and economic problems. If companies, for instance, operate their own internal wage-sharing systems that cushion all of the workers in downturns, then government might play a smaller role in providing benefits, though it could take a more forceful position in denying favors to the companies that still operate the old way—penalizing the weakest employees for the firm's bad fortune. When enterprises truly have internalized the ecological goals, the country would still need regulatory systems to punish the rogues, but the enforcement design might be turned upside down, rewarding those who excel with the greatest progress and raising the bar steadily higher for what society regards as standard performance.

One choice example is the divided governing structure by which the federal government now manages the economy, the macroeconomics of fiscal and monetary policy conducted separately and often at cross purposes by Congress, the executive branch, and the independent Federal Reserve. L. Randall Wray, a free-thinking young economist at the University of Missouri–Kansas City, has produced an ingenious reformulation that could integrate these functions in a more rational way. It starts by creating a pool of public works jobs that will be always available to the unemployed at an adequate but below market wage floor—thus the federal government acts permanently as the "employer of last resort." Washington then would use this labor pool as the principal mechanism to apply stimulus or restraint to the overall economy, like an automatic stabilizer. In boom times, workers naturally would move off the government job program and into bet-ter-paying jobs available in the private economy. The government's spending would thus shrink. When the economy is slack or contract-ing, more workers would have to opt for the last resort jobs, and so government would be pumping more money into the economy, countering the down cycle.

This system, Wray asserts, would produce a moderating stability for the economy—the harmony of low inflation and low unemploy-ment—and it could resolve irrational governing arrangements based upon the inherited conflicts between labor and capital, debtors and creditors. His concept is an innovative departure that I find convinc-ing, but we cannot really know without a lot of public inquiry and political debate. In the present framework, we cannot even talk about such an idea, much less pursue it.[5]

Short of an epic crisis, a depression or world war, this country al-ways has had difficulty developing mutual trust and united purpose across its many different people and interests. The principal explana-tion, I suspect, is the enduring chasm of inequality. While the founders said we are all endowed equally by the Creator with certain inalienable rights, we are not all born on the same page. Some of us were born lucky and others not (even within families) and these differences in fortune typically multiply in economic terms throughout our lives, with more good luck or bad breaks along the way. The country's deeper social and economic divisions cannot be healed by pretending otherwise or by dispatching missionaries to "fix" those who had the bad luck to be born without inheritance.

Governing institutions, especially the system of rights that protect private property, reflect a mistrust and uneasiness felt on both sides of the divide. *They* want to take what I have. Or, alternatively, *they* are keeping me from what I need and want. A very wealthy society, where there is plenty to go around, ought to be able to resolve this amiably, but the welfare state in this country certainly did not succeed, and instead has been steadily weakened. The American ideal of equality has always been in tension with the ideal of individual freedom, the public meaning of equality always undercut by the reality of stark differences. This question is utterly out of fashion for now, but I predict forward-looking Americans will return to discussions of inequality and how it might be overcome. As many voices in this book suggest, American society will not be complete, fully mature and self-respecting, until the nation has restored meaning to this compromised national value.

The conquest of scarcity, in fact, opens up new thinking about what equality may mean in the future—and new approaches toward achieving it. If the abundance is general and people have adapted their lives to the new opportunities for self-realization, then the goal of maximization for them is no longer simply a matter of piling up more wealth and material accumulation. The main goal is to maximize their lives—what Keynes meant by "living wisely and agreeably and well"—and maybe what the founders really meant by "life, liberty and the pursuit of happiness." We already can see some Americans making such choices in their lives, trying to reintegrate the work of "living" with their other ambitious, broader vistas.

Under general conditions of secure abundance, the substantive meaning of inequality becomes less tangible too. Increasingly, inequality will be defined by the objective barriers that prevent some people from realizing the human experience before them, the fullness of living on Earth with all of its absorbing relationships and activities now that material wants like food and shelter are no longer the principal reason for struggle. Remember, we are not all born on the same page and we do not expect to all travel the same road (we do not even like the same music or worship the same deities). But everyone, regardless of status or skills or accident of birth, is entitled to their life—the capacity to live out one's own unique story—as thoroughly as one is equipped to do, as adventurously as one hopes for. Jeremy Rifkin addressed this question in *The Age of Access* by warning that in the networked world of multinational corporations and commodified public spaces, many people may simply be shut out—denied access to work or public conveniences or to the common ideas and accumulated public knowledge.

The Canadian economist C. B. MacPherson anticipated the postscarcity age a quarter century ago and argued for a new system of rights that guarantees for people the capacity to live fully. The original argument for democracy, MacPherson noted, was that democracy would maximize "man's human powers, that is, their potential for using and developing their uniquely human capacities." Not as a consumer, he said, but as "a doer, a creator, an enjoyer of his human attributes." MacPherson reiterated those attributes: rational understanding, moral judgment and action, aesthetic creation and contemplation, the emotional activities of friendship and love, religious experience. "Man is not a bundle of appetites seeking satisfaction, but a bundle of conscious energies seeking to be exerted," he insisted. As a socialist, MacPherson was convinced that capitalism and the market system would never adjust to demands for human equality in these terms. The challenge, one might say, is to prove he was mistaken.[6]

A new approach to confronting inequality can be found in capitalism's cornerstone—the protection of property rights—only, someday hence, this society has to assign protective rights to the private property of self—the life each of us by nature does own—as an American birthright to realize one's life as fully as spirit and curiosity may carry us. I cannot begin to provide proper wording for the Constitutional amendment, but this is really a new version of a very old dream (like many other ideas in this book). Think of Franklin D. Roosevelt's "Four Freedoms" speech of 1941, in which he articulated "freedom from want" and "from fear" as achievable goals for a nation soon at war. Or remember Tom Paine's concept for sharing the common wealth of our inherited knowledge. The impulse to make "life, liberty and the pursuit of happiness" into a more tangible guarantee has been around a long time.

The meaning of these new rights, MacPherson argued, begins at a minimum with the right to participate in the productive economy—that is, jobs and incomes for all who seek them. Many of us would add health care, decent housing, advancing education, and other substantive guarantees, because access to these opportunities now represents the bare necessity for realizing one's life in this complicated modern world. Awhile ago, the state of Montana rewrote its Constitution and added the citizen's right to clean air and clean water. Surely, the United States can guarantee as much to its citizens. After all, life is fundamentally dependent on the good health of nature. Opponents will object that this means more lawsuits, but lawsuits are the way in which capitalism enforces its contracts, so why should citizens be denied this way of defending themselves? America is indeed a litigious nation and has been since the beginning, starting especially with legal actions to enforce property rights. The idea of property is sanctified in law and custom, even though the meanings of "property" have become increasingly abstracted and etherealized. Life is surely as real as stock shares or debentures or futures contracts. Certainly, it is more valuable.[7]

Essentially, we are talking about guaranteeing a platform for life that everyone shares from the start, regardless of circumstances, and that is not subject to political cancellations or managed as a patronizing handout. It comes free with citizenship in this very wealthy nation. Some will fritter it away, no doubt, while others will surprise us (and themselves) with the interesting lives they develop. Even with the platform, we would not all wind up at the same place or with the same bank account—how could we?—but the enduring tensions between equality and individualism would be reduced greatly, if not fully resolved, by this powerful new commitment from the society to its future—everyone's future.

The country, to put it mildly, is not ready for this, not yet (I did say this was speculation). Still, the concept may look more plausible and practical in years ahead, as more people come to recognize the enervating conflicts embedded in "more" and where they are leading us. As it presently functions, the economy is certain to generate still greater inequality, still more pointless impoverishment of lives, more social destruction, more empty political combat, more wreckage for future generations to clean up. The logic of reform is powerful, but it may become harder for many Americans to accept in the immediate future if, as I expect, the squeeze on middle-class incomes and mass consumption intensifies (the likelihood described at the book's opening). The national character always is strained and tested in the hard times; some people turn to reactionary fantasies. Many people quite naturally will retreat to defend family and self, and who can blame them? Still, if you read the history, Americans also often find their way to new ground in the hard times, advancing their understanding and embracing once radical ideas because they have been compelled to think more deeply about the way things are and how they might change them. We simply do not know which way people may turn.

What I want to believe about our country is that, though it seems deeply settled in its patterns of wealth and power, we have only just begun the story of who we are, what we might become as a nation. Americans today know a lot of things their forebears couldn't have known. We have routine experiences that would have astonished and frightened them. It is possible that some of the ideas that were tried in the past and failed to prevail are now within our grasp, mainly because Americans are at last ready for them, equipped now with the knowledge and confidence to make them succeed. That sounds wishful, and it is. That is what I choose to believe.

# Acknowledgments

PETER MILIUS, to whom this book is dedicated, was a reporter, editor, and editorial writer at *The Washington Post* for more than three decades and recognized by Washington insiders as a rare and valuable asset in the nation's capital. A man of liberal values, Peter understood politics and government at a very deep level, indeed knew more about the buried complexities and political wrinkles than most of the people who come to Washington to serve in government. And he shared his understanding generously with all. His editorials in the *Post* were crafted like tutorials, designed to keep the debate honest on all sides and, at the same time, argue with authority for the humane and reasonable (he would say sensible) resolution of social and economic issues. Given this role in an era of harsh conservative reforms, he was bound to lose on a lot of questions and did. Yet, as many of us admired, Peter stood his ground—congenially, expertly, tenaciously—knowing that each incremental triumph in public policy would be vital to the circumstances of people somewhere and that his intellect and values could help them win.

There was a heroic quality to Peter's generosity and his patience with the human condition. When he died suddenly in early 2002, Linda Greider, my wife, said simply: "Peter had good karma." This was true—people felt it in him at work and at home. As national editor at the *Post,* Peter took a physical delight in editing the smart, tough reporting, particularly if it shredded pompous evasions from powerful figures. He also found personal joy in teaching (and prodding) younger reporters to dig deeper, lending them the nerve to try and celebrating their success. He and I were kindred spirits. We worked alongside each other at the *Post* and earlier at the *Louisville Times,* our children grew up together, we shared frequent laughs about the antic side of politics and later on swapped grandchildren stories. Peter was patient with me, too. He would listen to my outsized declarations and analysis with a benign attentiveness, then say something wry like: "Well, you may be right, you may be nuts. But good luck to you." I do not know if Peter ever read Wendell Berry, but he might have. The poet's instruction to be joyful despite the facts is from the poem "Manifesto: The Mad Farmer Liberation Front."

In writing this book, I owe a special debt of gratitude to Alice Mayhew, whom I have been so fortunate to have as the editor of all my books published by Simon & Schuster. Usually in the past, Alice has left me alone for three or four or five years to write the book, then she applied her astute, scrupulously professional scrutiny and judgment to the finished manuscript. This time, having read the first five chapters, she and her deputy editor, Roger Labrie, invited me to lunch where they gently, but clearly, suggested: start over. It seems odd now to look back on that exchange with pleasure, since it was withering at the time. But Alice was adroitly rescuing me from confused intentions, in fact liberating me to write a stronger, more ambitious book than the one I had started. Such moments are why she is a great editor. Thank you, dear friend, thank you, thank you, thank you.

I also once again feel lucky and grateful to have Lynn Nesbit as wise friend and agent. For more than twenty-five years, she has expertly supervised my relations with editors and publishers and contributed her own deft sensibilities to my sense of direction. My thanks also to Roger Labrie, who patiently nudged me to stay on course and to the very skillful copyeditors, production, promotion, and marketing people at Simon & Schuster, in particular Victoria Meyer, Aileen Boyle, Gypsy da Silva, Rachel Burd, and John Wahler.

I am likewise indebted and grateful to the brilliant editors of *The Nation* magazine, where I write regularly, for their generous forbearance as I struggled to finish this book. In particular, I thank Katrina vanden Heuvel, the editor, and Karen Rothmyer, managing editor, as well as the publisher, Victor Navasky. Amid the current smugness and resignation, *The Nation* offers a free-thinking tonic for the national spirit—the strongest voice of dissent in American public life—and it's pure fun for me to write for its pages. I recommend it as stimulating reading, especially to young people yearning for a vibrant democracy and social justice.

The ideas and knowledge in this book are mostly borrowed from others, including some of the living thinkers and doers trying to re-shape the future. I cannot possibly name all of them here, but I want to thank the following in no particular order for their help and thinking: Arnie Graf, Jonathon Lange, Bill Weeks, Jim Coleman, John Logue, Deborah Olson, David Ellerman, Chris Mackin, Jeff Gates, Ron Blackwell, Jeremy Rifkin, Paul Hawken, Herman Daly, David Morris, Robert McIntyre, Greg LeRoy, Tom Schlesinger, Jane D'Arista, Bill Bishop, Jim Hawley, Robert Monks, Chris Bedford, Peter Camejo, Gary Dorrien, Fred Stokes, Michael Stumo, and Larry Goodwyn. Apologies to those I've missed.

Finally, I depend upon the warmth and strength of my family—especially the clear thinking and confident values of Linda Furry Greider—and upon our children and their spouses, Cameron Greider and Lalou Dammond, Katharine Greider and David Andrews. Above all else, we all draw our optimism from the four grandchildren—Lucy and Byron Greider-Andrews, Clara and Isabel Greider. We look at them and see that the future is bright.

# Notes

## 1. THIS NEW MOMENT

1. The life expectancy changes are from Robert William Fogel, *The Fourth Great Awakening & The Future of Egalitarianism,* University of Chicago, 2000. Housing and consumption comparisons are from Clair Brown, *American Standards of Living, 1918–1988,* Blackwell, 1994.

2. Among the harrowing events of homesteading was birthing a child without a doctor or any modern conveniences. Rachel Calof wrote: "I must say that personally the most dependable state of affairs during the many years I lived on the prairie was pregnancy, and soon I was again carrying my usual load. I was determined that this pregnancy and birth would be better than the preceding ones . . . but such was not to be. As my pregnancy progressed, the weather turned rainy and gray and I became vaguely fearful and despondent. As my time approached my depression grew. I prepared my delivery table as usual, spread with straw, but this time with a clean cloth on top, while at the same time crying uncontrollably. I felt certain this time I would not come out of it alive." *Rachel Calof's Story: Jewish Homesteader on the Northern Plains,* J. Sanford Rikoon, editor, Indiana University Press, 1995.

3. Clair Brown's landmark study of consumption (cited above) is a richly detailed portrait of American lifestyles across the twentieth century, captured in five snapshots: 1918, 1935, 1950, 1973, and 1988. Her remarks on typical working families' consumption in 1988 are from the *Boston Review,* Summer 1999.

4. Money as a living thing. Suze Orman, *The 9 Steps to Financial Freedom,* Crown, 1997.

5. I am indebted to Cathy Mulder, a student at Franklin and Marshall University, for the complete 1893 quotation from Samuel Gompers. It is found in *The Samuel Gompers Papers,* Volume 3, University of Illinois Press, 1989.

6. John Maynard Keynes's prescient essay, "Economic Possibilities for Our Grandchildren" can be found in *Essays in Persuasion,* Harcourt Brace, 1932.

7. Louis Uchitelle described the deterioration of homeowners' equity position in *The New York Times,* January 19, 2001.

## 2. THE SOUL OF CAPITALISM

1.  Amartya Sen argues that self-interest has a far broader meaning in human relations than the narrow one defined by formal economics. "The motivation pattern that dominates Japanese business has much more content than would be provided by pure profit maximization," he wrote, "a motivation structure that departs, in some significant spheres, from the simple pursuit of self-interest which—we have been told—is the bedrock of capitalism." See *Development as Freedom*, Alfred A. Knopf, 1999.

2.  Reverend Emil Brunner's denunciation of capitalism was from *The Divine Imperative*, published in 1932. He and the other Social Gospel thinkers are revived for reconsideration by Gary Dorrien in *Soul in Society: The Making and Renewal of Social Christianity*, Fortress Press, 1995.

3.  Karl Polanyi's description of "the self-regulating market" as utopian is a good fit with the globalization debates in our own time. *The Great Transformation, The Political and Economic Origins of Our Time*, Beacon Press, 1944. The French historian and cultural essayist Raoul Vaneigem observed rebellions of humanist liberation across centuries in *The Movement of the Free Spirit, General Considerations and Firsthand Testimony Concerning Some Brief Flowerings of Life in the Middle Ages, the Renaissance and, Incidentally, Our Own Time*, Zone Books, 1994.

## 3. WORK RULES

1.  Elaine Bernard, *Dollars and Sense*, September/October 1999.

2.  Unions have frequently invoked work stoppages to protest excessive demands for overtime. *America@Work*, published by the AFL-CIO, February 2000.

3.  Russell L. Ackoff, *The Democratic Corporation: A Radical Prescription for Re-creating Corporate America and Rediscovering Success*, Oxford University Press, 1994. Reform progress was described in steel, apparel, medical electronics, and imaging manufacture by Eileen Appelbaum, Thomas Bailey, Peter Berg, and Arne L. Kalleberg in *Manufacturing Advantage: Why High-Performance Work Systems Pay Off*, Cornell University Press, 2000.

4.  The Silicon Valley data are from "Growing Together Or Drifting Apart? A Status Report on Social and Economic Well-Being in Silicon Valley," Working Partnerships USA and the Economic Policy Institute, 1998. WashTech, an association of software professionals in Washington state affiliated with the Communications Workers of America won $97 million in damages for Microsoft's "permatemp" workers. The "rise of the virtual employer" is from *Blueprint*, the policy newsletter of the Task Force for Reconstructing America's Labor Market Institutions, MIT, July and October 1999. Bureau of Labor Statistics surveys on "non-standard" jobs are analyzed in "No Shortage of 'Nonstandard' Jobs," a report by the Economic Policy Institute 2000.

5.  The AFL-CIO polling study of young workers, "High Hopes, Little Trust," was published in September 1999.

6.  American Management Association survey, *Wall Street Journal*, April 17, 2001. The manager's remark on stress is from an article by Tony Horwitz on workplace surveillance, *Wall Street Journal*, December 1, 1994.

7.  Richard Sennett, *The Corrosion of Character: The Personal Consequences of Work in the New Capitalism*, W. W. Norton, 1998.

8. GE Executive Vice President Frank P. Doyle's acknowledgment is from a conference of the Jerome Levy Institute, April 28, 1995.

9. For those interested in an accessible discussion of the history and distinctions among various forms of self-ownership, see *Perspective on Work,* December 2001, and essays by David Ellerman, Christopher Mackin (a consultant to employee-owned firms), and Jeff Gates. Gates is author of *The Ownership Solution: Toward A Shared Capitalism for the 21st Century,* Perseus Books, 1998, perhaps the best single-volume explication of employee ownership. A descriptive primer on cooperatives can be found in E. G. Nadeau and David J. Thompson, *Cooperation Works! How People Are Using Cooperative Action to Rebuild Communities and Revitalize the Economy,* Lone Oak Press, 1996.

10. Sociologist Charles Perrow of Yale University made these observations on the development of corporate bureaucracy in *Complex Organizations: A Critical Essay,* McGraw-Hill, 1986 edition.

11. Human Rights Watch usually investigates abusive treatment of workers and other citizens in poorer nations, but its report, "Unfair Advantage: Workers' Freedom of Association in the United States under International Human Rights Standards," describes the dramatic reality of how Americans are deprived of their legal rights by employers. Human Rights Watch, August 2000.

12. The Labor Party's paper, "Toward a New Labor Law," argued that by basing the NLRA's regulatory powers on the Constitution's commerce clause rather than the Bill of Rights, the door was opened to the political attacks and retrenchments of subsequent years. Labor Party publication, Washington, D.C.

13. Owen D. Young of General Electric was quoted by Robert A. G. Monks and Nell Minow in *Corporate Governance,* Blackwell, 1995, and by Margaret M. Blair in *Ownership and Control, Rethinking Corporate Governance for the Twenty-first Century,* Brookings Institution, 1995.

14. An authoritative account of the Mondragon cooperatives and how they developed is in William Foote Whyte and Kathleen King Whyte, *Making Mondragon: The Growth and Dynamics of the Worker Cooperative Complex,* Cornell University Press, 1988.

15. A summary of comparative studies on ESOP companies' business performances can be found at the National Center for Employee Ownership's website, www.nceo.org.

16. John Logue and Jacquelyn Yates explore, with scholarly rigor, the everyday difficulties of creating successful worker ownership in *The Real World of Employee Ownership,* Cornell University Press, 2001.

## 4. IMPERIOUS CAPITAL

1. Karl Marx's resonant jeremiad is from *The Revolutions of 1848,* Penguin, in association with the *New Left Review,* London 1973. Joseph A. Schumpeter's great discourse, originally published in 1942, is *Capitalism, Socialism and Democracy,* HarperPerennial, 1976.

2. The wealth statistics are from Edward N. Wolff, "Why Stocks Won't Save the Middle Class," in *Unconventional Wisdom: Alternative Perspectives on the New Economy,"* Jeff Madrick, editor, Century Foundation Press, 2000.

3. The shift from individual to institutional dominance of stock ownership is a worldwide phenomenon occurring in many other advanced economies as well. The statistics are from the U.S. Federal Reserve Board, reported by Robert Clow in the *Financial Times,* October 16, 2001.

4. Robert A. G. Monks and Nell Minow first described the idea of "universal own-ers" and how pension funds' span of ownership "endows them with a breadth of concern that naturally aligns with the public interest." The goal, they explained, "is to find a way to maximize wealth creation over time, in a manner that does not impose inappropriate costs on third parties or on society as a whole. . . . Inappropriate costs can include agency costs imposed on investors as reflected, for example, in excessive CEO pay." Their book was *Watching the Watchers: Corporate Governance for the 21st Century,* Blackwell, 1996. A subsequent book by Monks elaborates practical evidence for the concept: *The New Global Investors: How Shareowners Can Unlock Sustainable Prosperity Worldwide,* Capstone, 2001.

James P. Hawley and Andrew T. Williams focus the implications more explicitly on the realm of institutional investors, especially major pension funds, and describe ways in which the concept may be advanced. Hawley and Williams, *The Rise of Fiduciary Capitalism: How Institutional Investors Can Make Corporate America More Democratic,* University of Pennsylvania Press, 2000.

5. The data on Keynes's investment record is from Robert G. Hagstrom, *The Essential Buffett; Timeless Principles for the New Economy,* John Wiley & Sons, 2001. The text of Keynes's stock market critique is Chapter 12 in *The General Theory of Employment, Interest, and Money,* Harcourt Brace, 1964, the book that, in 1936, elaborated the theory that came to be known as Keynesian economics.

6. The evaporation of bull-market gains for mutual funds was reported by Carol Vin-zant, "Royally, Straight-Out Flushed," *Washington Post,* October 7, 2001.

7. The estimate of financial fraud is from *Working Capital,* Fall 1999, the bulletin of the AFL-CIO's Center on Working Capital. I saw no need to reelaborate the details of financial scandals, since the public has been well exposed to the facts by now. For a succinct analysis of the systemic failings uncovered after the fall of Enron, see my article, "Crime in the Suites," in *The Nation,* February 4, 2002.

8. Details on stock turnover are from Dean Baker and Anchon Fung, "Collateral Dam-age: Do Pension Fund Investments Hurt Workers?" and the introduction by Leo W. Gerard, president of the United Steelworkers of America, in *Working Capital: The Power of Labor's Pen-sions,* Cornell University Press, 2001. The book, edited by Fung, Tessa Hebb, and Joel Rogers, is an excellent explication of the issues and possibilities for union activism in finance capital.

9. For details on the rapid expansion of social investing, see "2001 Report on Socially Responsible Investing Trends in the United States," Social Investment Forum, Washington D.C. (www.socialinvest.org). A companion report, "Increasing Investment in Communities," describes the proliferation of new banks, venture capital funds, and other financial institutions that channel scarce capital to local enterprises and projects with social values and objectives in the forefront of their objectives.

10. Social investing's performance is discussed by Amy Domini, *Socially Responsible Investing: Making a Difference and Making Money,* Dearborn Trade, 2001, and Peter M. Camejo, *The SRI Advantage: Why Socially Responsible Investing Outperforms,* New Society, 2002.

11. The Innovest documentation and company reports are proprietary materials, that is, sold to mutual funds, pension-fund trustees, and other financial managers. The sectoral dif-ferences Innovest identified are from Robert A. G. Monks, *The New Global Investors: How Shareowners Can Unlock Sustainable Prosperity Worldwide,* Capstone, 2001.

12. Alfred Chandler's account of how the market for capital assets has changed American business management provides a somber climax to his saga of twentieth-century capitalism, *Scale and Scope: The Dynamics of Industrial Capitalism,* Harvard/Belknap, 1990.

13. Some of America's very best newspapers, like *The New York Times* and *Washington Post,* remain family-owned, and the Sulzberger and Graham families retain full control while still enjoying access to Wall Street capital by issuing "B shares" to the public that have no voting rights. The insulating device is probably less important, however, than the families' determination to set their own priorities rather than accept the financial market's. For a good account of the modern dilemmas facing the newspaper business, see Michael Janeway, *Republic of Denial: Press, Politics, and Public Life,* Yale University Press, 1999.

14. Details on local capital funds, community banks, and other pioneer institutions can be found in the Social Investment Forum reports cited above.

15. Senator Long's vision for Buffett-style mutual funds was related by Jeff Gates, who served Long as general counsel of the Senate Finance Committee. A more practical alternative exists for investors who can buy shares in Buffett's company, Berkshire Hathaway. Though the share price seems forbiddingly high, Buffett continues to beat the market consistently. The one exception was the recent period during the stock market bubble, when even Buffett could not top its deranged valuations.

16. Details on the direct-equity investing sector and the Carlyle Group are from Katharine Campbell, "Money Raising as an Art Form," the *Financial Times,* November 6, 2001, which reported that U.S. funding rose to $157 billion in 2000, then fell off sharply as financial markets deteriorated. Details on Chase Manhattan and J. P. Morgan are from Tom Schlesinger, director of the Financial Markets Center.

## 5. CONSUMING THE FUTURE

1. A decade ago, the National Academy of Sciences and the Royal Society of London jointly concluded that if these and other trends continue, "science and technology may not be able to prevent either irreversible degradation of the environment or continued poverty for much of the world." *The National Geographic*'s millennium supplement, "Biodiversity: The Fragile Web," was published in February 1999 and is regarded as a classic among environmentalists. The National Academy of Sciences–Royal Society statement was cited by retired U.S. senator Gaylord Nelson, founder of Earth Day, in a thirtieth-anniversary speech, April 22, 2000.

2. The origins of American economic life are illuminated brilliantly by William Cronon, *Changes in the Land: Indians, Colonists, and the Ecology of New England,* Hill & Wang, 1983. Among other virtues, Cronon's book is a model of how to understand economy, politics, and society as a whole fabric, rather than in the narrow slices created by separate academic disciplines. Another rewarding book on the colonial legacy of English property law, tracing the history of one 2,000-acre tract of land in Massachusetts, is by John Hanson Mitchell, *Trespassing: An Inquiry into the Private Ownership of Land,* Addison-Wesley, 1998.

3. My broad summary of theological differences is derived from my own reporting among American Indian tribes.

4. R. A. Smith's book was published in Des Moines by the Kenyon Printing and Manufacturing Company in 1902. The full title is *A History of Dickinson County, Iowa, Together*

*with An Account of The Spirit Lake Massacre, and the Indian Troubles on the Northwestern Frontier.*
It was a book passed along to our family because my wife, Linda Furry Greider, is descended
from the pioneer Smiths of Lake Okoboji in Dickinson County. The author was her great-
uncle, known in family conversation as "Uncle Rod," though he died long before she was
born.

5. Farm pollution in Iowa was described by Elizabeth Becker in *The New York Times,*
February 10, 2002. Evan Eisenberg lamented that the prairie soil "is half gone. What is left is
half dead, the roiling, crawling life burned out of it by herbicides, pesticides, and relentless
monocropping." See Eisenberg's *The Ecology of Eden,* Alfred A. Knopf, 1998.

6. For a fuller account of the ecological perspective of groups like the Rainforest Action
Network, see Randy Hayes, "Restructuring the Global Economy," Johns Hopkins University Symposium "Paragon or Paradox? Capitalism in the Contemporary World," March 14,
2002. The network's website is www.ran.org.

7. Boise's policy change was reported by Greg Winter, *New York Times,* March 27, 2002.

8. The rise of hog factories is described by David Morris in "Hogging the Market," *The
New Rules,* Institute for Local Self-Reliance, Fall 1999. For my account of the Organization
for Competitive Markets and its viewpoints, see "The Last Farm Crisis," *The Nation,* November 20, 2000.

9. I toured the eastern shore marshes in an open launch with Bill Weeks and other conservancy workers on a late afternoon in autumn when the fading sunlight gave a golden tint
to the vast acres of marsh grasses. For ecological detail, I have drawn from Curtis J. Badger, *A
Naturalist's Guide to the Virginia Coast,* Stackpole Books, 1996.

10. Amory Lovins and L. Hunter Lovins are founders and co-CEOs of the Rocky
Mountain Institute, which has long been an incubator of technological reform to meet the
ecological crisis. Their coauthor, Paul Hawken, is also author of *The Ecology of Commerce,*
Harper Business, 1993. Together they wrote *Natural Capitalism: Creating the Next Industrial
Revolution,* Little, Brown, 1999.

11. William Clay Ford, Jr., and his vision for sustainable manufacturing was described by
Jeffrey Ball, *Wall Street Journal,* May 15, 2001.

12. William McDonough and Michael Braungart, *Cradle to Cradle: Remaking the Way We
Make Things,* North Point Press, 2002.

13. The mechanics and implications of leasing products and materials are discussed in
*Natural Capitalism* and by Jeremy Rifkin, *The Age of Access: The New Culture of Hypercapitalism,
Where All of Life Is a Paid-for Experience,* Tarcher Putnam, 2000.

14. The retrogression of the utilities industry on carbon emissions was reported by Jim
Carlton and Rebecca Smith, *Wall Street Journal,* June 14, 2002. For an account of the politics
of resistance on global warming, see my article, "Carbongate," in the *Amicus Journal,* Summer
2001.

15. Examples of eco-businesses in agriculture are drawn from articles by Jessica Nelson,
Michelle Carstensen, Sarah Hannigan, and others in the *Carbohydrate Economy,* from 1999 to
2001, published quarterly by the Institute for Local Self-Reliance, Minneapolis, Minnesota.

## 6. Command and Control

1. The rewards for Enron executives amid the company's failure included $67 million
for Chairman and CEO Kenneth Lay, who resigned in disgrace, Kathryn Kranhold and

Mitchell Pacelle, *Wall Street Journal,* June 17, 2002. Dennis Kozlowski's excesses are described by David Leonhardt, *New York Times,* June 4, 2002. For further discussion of the cult of the CEO, see my article on William Lerach, the country's leading plaintiffs' lawyer in shareholder fraud litigation, "Is This America's Top Corporate Crime Fighter?" *The Nation,* August 5, 2002.

2. For the history of corporate power, I have drawn upon Morton J. Horwitz, *The Transformation of American Law, 1870–1960, The Crisis of Legal Orthodoxy,* Oxford University Press, 1992; Mary A. O'Sullivan, *Contests for Corporate Control: Corporate Governance and Economic Performance in the United States and Germany,* Oxford University Press, 2000; David Kairys, editor, *The Politics of Law: A Progressive Critique,* Basic Books, 1998; Charles Perrow, *Organizing America: Wealth, Power and the Origins of Corporate Capitalism,* Princeton University Press, 1992; and William G. Roy, *Socializing Capital: The Rise of the Large Industrial Corporation in America,* Princeton, 1997.

3. The consequences of the Supreme Court's *Santa Clara* decision of 1886 were reviewed in the 1930s by Justice Hugo Black, who determined that corporations, not emancipated slaves, were the principal beneficiaries; see my book, *Who Will Tell the People: The Betrayal of American Democracy,* Simon & Schuster, 1992.

4. A dramatic account of the new oligopolies astride so many sectors was provided by Yochi J. Dreazen, Greg Ip, and Nicholas Kulish in *The Wall Street Journal,* February 25, 2002.

5. The exchange between Dow Jones employees and Chairman Peter Kann was reported by Paul Tharp in "Kann Gives Angry WSJ-ers A New Lesson in Capitalism," *New York Post,* December 5, 2002.

6. The so-called "takings" doctrine, however, has been borrowed by U.S. multinational corporations and insinuated into U.S. trade agreements as "investor protection." In particular, Chapter 11 of the North American Free Trade Agreement sets up private arbitration tribunals where foreign investors may sue national governments (including the United States) for damages done by regulatory laws. The public is excluded from these secrets forums. The same format is sought by business interests (and already authorized by Congress) for future trade agreements, including the proposed Free Trade Area of the Americas. See my article, "The Right and U.S. Trade Law: Invalidating the 20th Century," *The Nation,* October 15, 2001.

7. Richard Grossman and the Program on Corporations, Law and Democracy (POCLAD) have led a nationwide campaign of education and agitation around the subject of corporate power. Among other ideas, POCLAD argues for the rechartering of all corporations. His remarks on "robots" are from "Can Corporations Be Accountable, Part 2," originally published in *Rachel's Environment & Health Weekly,* August 6, 1998.

8. O'Sullivan's book fuses a business economist's understanding of business organizations with a social perspective on the values in play and it has deeply informed my own thinking. She also provides a valuable guide to the competing academic theories on the corporation. With advanced degrees in business and economics from Harvard, she is an assistant professor of strategy and management at INSEAD in France. Mary A. O'Sullivan, *Contests for Corporate Control: Corporate Governance and Economic Performance in the United States and Germany,* Oxford University Press, 2000.

9. Charles Perrow's observation, cited by O'Sullivan, is from "Economic Theories of Organization," *Theory and Society,* 15: 11–45.

10. Bob Tedeschi's "E-Commerce" column on Netflix, *New York Times,* August 12, 2002.

11. The history of General Electric and other leading corporations once dubbed "welfare capitalists" is recounted by Mary O'Sullivan in *Contests for Corporate Control.*

12. Stories of D. J. DePree's leadership are told in many company documents. I am drawing upon the book written by his son, Hugh DePree, who succeeded him as CEO, *Business As Unusual: The People and Principles at Herman Miller,* published by the company in 1986.

13. Among his many profound and provocative insights, Jeremy Rifkin suggests that Hollywood's culture industry, organized with capital deal-making as the core of its power, represents a model other sectors are now emulating. *The Age of Access: The New Culture of Hypercapitalism, Where All of Life is a Paid-for Experience,* Jeremy P. Tarcher/Putnam, 2000.

14. Professors James P. Hawley and Andrew T. Williams describe strategies for developing a strong new governance role for fiduciary institutions in their proposal "The Center for the Study of Fiduciary Capitalism," Saint Mary's College of California, fidcap.org.

## 7. PUBLIC WORKS

1. The statistics on railroad subsidies are from Charles Perrow, *Organizing America,* who wrote of that era: "We must add ease of corruption to the usual factors of production."

2. The Export-Import Bank's distorted policies are described by Leslie Wayne, "A Guardian of Jobs or a 'Reverse Robin Hood'?" *New York Times,* September 1, 2002.

3. Cato Institute's catalog of "corporate welfare" was described by Stephen Moore and Dean Stansel, "Ending Corporate Welfare as We Know it," Cato Policy Analysis No. 225, May 1995.

4. Marriott's deception of Maryland officials was revealed by Jay Hancock, "Marriott Used Va. As Ruse to Raise Md. bid," *Baltimore Sun,* March 27, 1999. The corporation privately informed Virginia economic development officials that it intended to remain in Maryland, but asked them not to reveal this so that Maryland would not back off its bid. Other details on federal and state subsidies are from: sugar and timber, "Green Scissors 2000: Cutting Wasteful and Environmentally Harmful Spending," Friends of the Earth, Taxpayers for Common Sense, U.S. Public Interest Research Group, and other organizations; hog factories, editorial, "The Curse of Factory Farms," *New York Times,* August 30, 2002; state incentives, Robert Tomsho, "In Toledo, a Tension Between School Funds and Business Breaks," *Wall Street Journal,* July 18, 2001; Rick Brooks, "How Big Incentives Won Alabama a Piece of the Auto Industry," *Wall Street Journal,* April 3, 2002; and Shailagh Murray, "Sweet Home Alabama No More," *Wall Street Journal,* September 30, 2002.

5. Robert McIntyre's remarks are from testimony before the House of Representatives' budget committee, June 30, 1999.

6. The renewed tax-free status of major corporations was reported by Citizens for Tax Justice in "Study Finds Resurgence in Corporate Tax Avoidance," October 19, 2000.

7. The contraction of public space is cited by John DeGraaf, David Wann, and Thomas H. Naylor in *Affluenza: The All-Consuming Epidemic,* Berrett-Koehler, 2001.

8. A compelling survey of the usurpation of common assets by private industry can be found in David Bollier, *Silent Theft: The Private Plunder of Our Common Wealth,* Routledge, 2002.

9. The federal government's complicity in the loss of public assets to private interests is made clear when one recognizes how its stewardship has been degraded in the last two

decades. Details on the more vigilant approach are from Mary A. O'Sullivan in *Contests for Corporate Control.*

10. Peter Barnes's innovative proposal for a sky trust is found in *Who Owns the Sky? Our Common Assets and the Future of Capitalism,* Island Press, 2001. I am indebted to Alfred F. Anderson of the Tom Paine Institute in Eugene, Oregon, for educating me on Paine's conception of how to organize the common inheritance. Anderson uses Newt Gingrich as a foil for illuminating the lost understandings of Paine and others about democratic society in *Challenging Newt Gingrich, Chapter by Chapter,* Tom Paine Institute, 1996.

11. A diverse literature has developed on the consequences of state and local economic development subsidies. Many of the facts here are drawn from the work of the Institute on Taxation and Economic Policy (ITEP) in Washington and, in particular, an excellent primer, "No More Candy Store: States and Cities Making Job Subsidies Accountable," published by Good Jobs First of ITEP and written by Greg LeRoy with Richard Healy, Dan Doherty, and Hany Khalil.

12. State tax erosion is calculated by Peter Fisher, "Tax Incentives and the Disappearing State Corporate Income Tax," *State Tax Notes* magazine, 2002, available from Tax Analysts, Arlington, Virginia.

13. Greg LeRoy's questions are from his keynote address to the "Reclaiming Economic Development" conference that brought together some 150 groups active on the issue, July 11, 2002.

14. *For the Common Good: Redirecting the Economy toward Community, the Environment and a Sustainable Future,* Beacon; Herman Daly and John Cobb's seminal work, was first published in 1989 and revised in 1994. Daly's comments in this section are taken from his later book of essays, *Beyond Growth: The Economics of Sustainable Development,* Beacon, 1996.

15. The Oregon Benchmarks details are from "Achieving the Oregon Shines Vision: The 1999 Benchmark Performance Report," Oregon Progress Board, March 1999. Details on Orlando's Good Life Index are from the *Orlando Sentinel,* July 6, 2000. The progress of Tifton, Georgia, was reported by the newsletter of the Kerr Center for Sustainable Agriculture, Poteau, Oklahoma, Winter 2000.

16. Robert Sullivan's "canary in the coal mine" is from his article, "And Now, The Salmon War," *New York Times,* March 20, 1999. The rise of community groups like Sustainable Seattle is recounted by Alan AtKisson, *Believing Cassandra: An Optimist Looks at a Pessimist's World,* Chelsea Green, 1999.

17. To describe the high-tech paradox of greater inequality, I have been educated by the extraordinary work of reporter Bill Bishop of the *Austin American-Statesman* and his occasional series on "Cities of Ideas," in which he asks big questions about the nature of America's changing economy. Bishop is that rare reporter who sets out to understand the larger realities of his community and his country but goes far deeper than the official version. One can find his work at statesman.com, and I recommend it to citizens trying to understand their economic surroundings and to reporters as a model of how their work is done properly. In particular, I drew upon Bishop and Mark Lisheron in "Austin's service class is losing its way out," *Austin American-Statesman,* November 3, 2002.

18. Roberta Brandes Gratz described the urban political combat in "Preserving the Urban Dynamic," *The Nation,* April 23, 2001. Her book with Norman Mintz is *Cities Back From the Edge: New Life for Downtown,* John Wiley 1998.

19. Neil Hamilton of the Iowa Food Policy Council is quoted in "The New Agriculture," *Field Notes,* Kerr Center for Sustainable Agriculture, Winter 2001.

20. Eric Schlosser's book is *Fast-Food Nation: The Dark Side of the All-American Meal,* HarperCollins, 2001. With wit and brevity, Tom Vanderbilt tells the not unrelated story of how the industry of expensive athletic shoes evolved. *The Sneaker Book: Anatomy of an Industry and an Icon,* New Press, 1998. New Press is publishing a series of similar industry-sector profiles.

## 8. THINKING FORWARD

1. Lawrence Goodwyn, a great teacher and wise friend, is the author of *The Populist Moment: A Short History of the Agrarian Revolt in America,* Oxford, 1978. His brilliant account of barefoot farmers setting out to change their surroundings is one of those forgotten sagas of ennobled citizens and it asks implicitly whether modern Americans, well fed and well educated, have the same capacities.

2. As an undergraduate at Princeton University more than forty years ago, I encountered the department of economics and sociology and took many of the latter courses, none of the former. The economists, who think of themselves as hardheaded scientists, subsequently won a separation from their much disparaged colleagues, the sociologists. I would say that this intellectual conceit—economics is objective, society is not—helps explain how formal economics became separated from reality.

3. I have borrowed the Margaret Mead quotation from Alan AtKisson's *Believing Cassandra.*

4. Richard Sennett's observations are found in a short essay, "On welfare and the psychology of dependence," Daedalus, *Journal of the American Academy of Arts & Sciences,* Summer 2000.

5. I have given a barebones sketch of Randall Wray's reconception of macroeconomics that necessarily leaves out the rich complexities but is designed to tantalize. The full story can be found in L. Randall Wray, *Understanding Modern Money: The Key to Full Employment and Price Stability,* Edward Elgar, 1998.

6. I discovered the work of C. B. MacPherson through Jeremy Rifkin's book *The Age of Access,* and found that MacPherson had articulated years before some of the half-formed ideas I was struggling to express—an experience of discovery that is humbling but also exhilarating. MacPherson was so resolutely in opposition to the market economy and its depredations that he could not see the possibilities for alterations within capitalism. I have drawn here from "The Maximization of Democracy" in *Democratic Theory: Essays in Retrieval,* Oxford, 1973.

7. U.S. Representative Jesse L. Jackson, Jr., son of the civil rights leader, has explored this terrain in an interesting book, written with Frank E. Watkins, *A More Perfect Union: Advancing New American Rights,* Welcome Rain Publishers, 2001.

# Index

ABP pension fund, 119
abundance:
    consumption expectations spurred by,
      14, 15
    economic anxiety in age of, 12–14
    inequality in age of, 334–36
    inherited identities blurred by, 330
    as modern economic condition, 9–18,
      300–301
    social consequences of, 20–21, 31
    unequal distribution of, 16–18, 21,
      25–26
accounting:
    cost-benefit, 295
    fraud, 113, 225, 261
Ackoff, Russell L., 53, 86
Adler, Paul, 86
AFL-CIO, 55–56, 58, 138, 139–40,
    141–42, 234, 315
*Age of Access, The* (Rifkin), 254, 335, 348*n*
AIG, 145
Airbus, 273
aircraft industry, 55, 254, 273
airline industry:
    employee ownership in, 68, 88–89
    government bailout of, 280, 296
    hub system adopted by, 127–28
air pollution, 32, 188, 195, 282–83, 336,
    346*n*
Alabama, corporate subsidies in, 278
ALCOA, 86
Algoma Steel, 143, 146

altruism, 259–60
American Airlines, 128
American Bar Association, 77
American Federation of Labor, 10, 66
American Forest and Paper Association,
    171–72
*American Standards of Living* (Clair
    Brown), 11–12
Anderson, Alfred F., 349*n*
Anheuser-Busch, 187
animal rights, 164, 174, 175
antidiscrimination laws, 78
antitrust laws, 217–18, 241, 242, 255, 282
AOL Time Warner, 216, 226
architecture, energy efficiency in, 189, 198
assembly, freedom of, 49, 69
AT&T, 282
AtKisson, Alan, 314, 323
Austin Equity Commission, 314–15
auto designs, energy inefficiency of, 186,
    195–97, 242
auto industry:
    assembly-worker injuries in, 53–54
    environmental issues and, 188, 189,
      195–97, 199, 200, 275–76, 346*n*
    government subsidies in, 275–76,
      277–78
    manufacturer reclamation in, 193–94
automation, 56–57

Baker, James A., 135, 145
bakeries, automation in, 56–57

banking conglomerates, 241
bankruptcy, 218–19
Barber, Randy, 103
Barnes, Peter, 282–83
Basques, cooperatives operated by, 73, 74,
  90, 91
Bayview, 179
beavers, 157
Bedford, Christopher, 175
*Believing Cassandra* (AtKisson), 314
Bell Atlantic (Verizon), 53
Benchmarks, 293, 306, 313
Berkshire Hathaway, 345*n*
Bernard, Elaine, 52
Berry, Wendell, vii, 339
bicycles, electric, 203
big-box retailing, 316
bin Laden family, 135
Biocorp, 201
biodegradable fabric, 190–91
biodiversity, 154–55, 177
biotechnology, 214
birds, extinctions of, 155
Bishop, Bill, 315, 349*n*
Black, Hugo, 347*n*
Blackstone Group, 145
Blackwell, Ronald, 58, 138, 139, 140,
  141, 142, 234
Blasi, Joseph, 86
Blockbuster Video, 241
Blue Ridge Paper Products, 147–51
Blue River forestland, 181
Boeing, 55, 127, 254, 273, 276
Bofferding, Charles, 55
Boise (Boise Cascade), 171–72
bookstores, chain vs. independent, 129
Borges, Frank, 130
Braungart, Michael, 189–90, 192, 193
broadcast industry, 32, 281
Brown, Clair, 11–12, 14, 17, 18, 19–20,
  85, 341*n*
Brown, Curtis, 70, 86
Brunner, Emil, 35–36, 37, 45, 206, 342*n*
Bryant, Joseph, 53
Buddhism, hungry ghost archetype of,
  209
Buffett, Warren, 133–34, 345*n*

BUILD, 72, 73
building trade unions, 143
Burger King, 171
Burlington Northern Santa Fe Railroad,
  200
Burlington railroad, 162
Bush, George H.W., 135
Bush, George W., 140
business schools, 327

Cabral, Joseph, 80–83, 88, 92–93, 131,
  251–52
California Public Employees' Retirement
  System (CalPERS), 105, 110, 112,
  135, 140–41
Calof, Rachel Bella, 3–4, 341*n*
Calvert Group, 116, 117, 306
Calvert-Henderson Quality of Life Indicators, 306
Calvinism, 248–49
Camejo, Peter M., 119–20
Canada, labor-sponsored investment
  funds in, 143–44
Canadian Pension Plan, 145
C & O Canal, 212
capitalism:
  Christian critiques of, 35–36
  Cold War support of, 26
  deleterious impact of, 24–25, 28, 39,
    44–45, 100–101, 302
  economic efficiency vs. social respon-
    sibility in, 35–47
  environment in, *see* environmental
    issues
  in Europe vs. U.S., 33–34
  fiduciary, 106
  flexibility of, 26–27
  forward-looking aspect of, 26, 40–41,
    230–31, 310–11
  government as counterforce to, 31,
    311–12
  Hawley and Williams's three stages of,
    106
  income inequality in, *see* income
    inequality
  in Japan, 34, 342*n*
  laissez-faire, 36–37, 264

legalized fraud of power relationships
in, 60–64
managerial, 106
personal, 106, 133
regenerative principle of, 40–41
three classic factors of production in,
94
capitalism, reform of:
criteria for economic growth in,
303–8, 332
education and, 327
in financial system, 98, 99–100, 102,
109–10, 115–20, 131–32, 143–52,
321–22
grassroots work in, 48, 309–10,
312–17, 321–22, 325–27
limitations of political sphere in,
29–35, 308–10, 320–21
in local development efforts, 312–17
long-term sustainability as focus of,
306, 307–8, 313–17, 323
personal isolation vs. interdependency
in, 328–32
power rearranged by, 322, 323
self-interest in, 34, 47, 302, 303, 342*n*
*Capitalism, Socialism and Democracy*
(Schumpeter), 101
Capital Ownership Group (COG), 297
carbohydrate economy, 201–2
Carlucci, Frank, 135
Carlyle Group, 135, 145
Carnegie, Andrew, 106, 216
Carrier, 191–92
casual labor, 70
Caterpillar, 276
Cato Institute, 276, 287
Center on Working Capital, 138, 139,
344*n*
CEOs, 208–11
without contracts, 246
cult of, 208–9, 238, 347*n*
interests of shareholders vs., 210–11
wages of employees vs., 63, 125, 220
Champion Paper, 147–48, 150
Chandler, Alfred D., Jr., 123, 345*n*
*Changes in the Land* (Cronon), 156, 345*n*
Chase Manhattan, 135–36

Chatsworth Products Inc. (CPI), 80–83,
131, 251
childbirth, 341*n*
children:
economic valuation of, 304
education of, 30, 272, 319–20
labor of, 31, 36, 318
Christianity:
capitalist critiques rooted in, 35–36
nature in, 158
providential worldview in, 248–50, 253
service as goal of, 35
Chrysler, 275, 277–78, 296
Ciba-Geigy, 191
*Cities Back from the Edge* (Gratz), 316
Citigroup, 113, 241
Citizens for Tax Justice, 278
civil rights movement, 327–28
clawback agreements, 290, 294, 295–96
Clean Air Act (1970), 32, 195
Clean Car Initiative, 275–76
Clinch River watershed, 181, 182
Clinton, Bill, 275
Clinton, DeWitt, 270
Cobb, John B., Jr., 305
Coca-Cola, 104, 134
COG (Capital Ownership Group), 297
Cold War, 26, 273
Coleman, James, 75, 76, 77–79
collective bargaining, 32, 66
college education, 272, 327, 350*n*
college faculty, tenure of, 75–76
Communications Workers of America,
53, 342*n*
communism, 26, 27, 36, 63
community benefits agreements, 292
community development banks, 132
community trusts, 323
Congress, U.S.:
accounting reform legislation of, 225
airline bailouts passed by, 280
compromise legislation in, 309
elections of, 265, 320
employee takeovers facilitated by, 81
Erie Canal funding from, 270
local venture-capital funds supported
by, 144

(Congress, U.S., *cont'd*)
  public assets sold by, 280–81
  *see also* government
Conservation Forestry Program, 182
conservation movement, 168
  *see also* environmental issues
conservative ideology, 265
  property rights in, 222, 280–81
  small government in, 30, 32–33,
    263–64, 274
  tax cuts in, 280
conspicuous consumption, 2
Constitution, U.S.:
  amendment process of, 299
  fourteenth amendment, 215, 221
  labor rights based on, 69, 343*n*
  slavery recognized in, 61
  thirteenth amendment, 61, 69
consumption:
  conspicuous, 2
  environmental impact of, 154–55,
    159, 166, 170–72, 188, 213–14,
    316–17, 345*n*
  modern production removed from,
    165–66
  of necessities vs. luxuries, 11–12
  precautionary principle and, 214
  pressures toward increase of, 10–11,
    15, 17, 153–54, 185
  resistance to, 14–15
  wealth distribution inequalities and,
    17–18, 153
*Contests for Corporate Control* (O'Sullivan),
  229, 347*n*
cooperatives, 65, 69–74, 90
corporate liberalism, 244, 245
corporations, 205–62
  CEOs of, 63, 125, 208–11, 220, 238,
    246, 347*n*
  clawback agreements with, 290, 294,
    295–96
  democratic structure introduced in,
    227–28, 235–38, 250–53, 258
  direct-equity investments in, 135–37,
    143–49, 150–51, 345*n*
  ecological solutions backed by, 170,
    197–99, 202–3, 251, 258

  emergence of, 166, 211–14, 221–22
  employee takeovers of, *see* employee
    ownership
  exaggerated influence of, 203–4
  inequality modeled in, 52, 219–21
  innovative capacity of, 228–30,
    232–36, 239–41, 245, 247–48, 249,
    252
  internal accountability in, 226,
    250–53, 258
  as "learning collectivities," 232–33,
    235, 239–40
  legal personhood of, 214–15, 222–23,
    227, 347*n*
  limited liability of, 218–19, 225, 226
  local influences on, 323
  mergers and acquisitions of, 123–26,
    134–35, 215–18, 224, 226, 239–40
  mutability of values in, 243–45
  network model of, 253–56
  offshore headquarters of, 279
  organizational nature of markets vs.,
    228–30, 241
  pension funds managed by, 104–5,
    140
  public disempowerment caused by
    rise of, 212–14, 221–22
  rationalizing moves of, 81, 127, 232
  reinvention of, 206–8, 223–28, 231,
    235–38, 242–43, 256–62, 347*n*
  responsibility diluted by, 219
  shareholder governance of, 215, 261
  size of, 215–18, 233, 239–41, 251–52,
    275–76
  social commitments of, 99, 170, 234,
    242–45, 246, 248–53, 257–62,
    292–93, 308, 322
  state-issued charters of, 213, 224
  stock price as rating of, 122–23, 210
  subsidies for, *see* government support
    of business
  tax dodges of, 223, 226–27, 278–80,
    286–87, 288, 289–90, 292–93, 298
cost-benefit accounting, 295
covenants, financial, 144
CPI (Chatsworth Products Inc.), 80–83,
  131, 251

*Cradle to Cradle* (McDonough and
    Braungart), 190
craft guilds, 66
creation myths, 157–58
creative cities, 315
credit card debt, 18
crime, economic valuation of, 304–5
Cronon, William, 156–57, 158–59, 345n
culture, homogeneity of, 129
curiosity, 326–27

Daimler-Chrysler, 277–78
Daly, Herman E., 304, 305, 306, 307–8
D'Arista, Jane, 103
debt, personal, 18
Defense Department, U.S., 273
Delaware, incorporation rules in, 213
democracy:
    in corporate organization, 227–28,
        235–38, 250–53, 258
    decline of, 30
    economic, 60, 65
    elections in, 264, 266–67, 320–21
    equality of developmental opportuni-
        ties in, 335
    income polarization in, 21, 84
    popular faith in, 264–65
    workplace authoritarianism as barrier
        to, 52
Democratic party, 266, 280
dependency vs. self-reliance, 331
depreciation, tax incentives on, 279
DePree, D. J., 247, 248, 249, 253
DePree, Hugh, 250, 251
Depression, Great, 9, 36, 45, 81, 110, 273,
    274, 312
deregulation, 33, 37, 217, 264
DesignTex, 190–91
*Development as Freedom* (Sen), 34, 342n
direct-equity investing, 135–37, 143–49,
    150–51, 261, 345n
    deal flow in, 143, 146
    leverage in, 136–37, 150
    liquidity in, 136
disassembly-recovery industry, 193
discrimination lawsuits, 78
Domini, Amy, 117

Domini 400 Social Index, 116, 117
doubt, 326–27
Dow Chemical, 191
Dow Jones:
    global sustainability index of, 117
    labor vs. senior management of,
        220–21
downsizing, 81, 125
Drucker, Peter, 103, 234
Dubinsky, Rick, 89
Du Pont (company), 188–89
Du Pont, E. I. (industrialist), 216
Dutch Reformed Church, 248

Eames, Charles, 247
Eames, Ray, 247
"earnest money," 323
economic democracy, 60, 65
"Economic Possibilities for Our Grand-
    children, The" (Keynes), 15–16
economics:
    integration of sociology with, 327,
        350n
    neoclassical, 229, 238
    supply side, 280
economic value added (EVA), 250–51
EcoValue investment-risk ratings, 118–19
education:
    on capitalism, 327
    college, 272, 327, 350n
    federal grants for, 272
    school vouchers for, 30
    social goals of, 319–20
efficiency, 19
    community values and, 35–48
    as environmental issue, 185–94, 245,
        251
    in nature, 185
    in workplace, 53–55, 85
Eisenberg, Evan, 346n
elderly, 320
elections, 31, 263–67, 323
    congressional, 265, 320
    in democracies, 264, 266–67, 320–21
    presidential, 264, 320
    voter participation in, 264, 320
electric bicycles, 203

electric utility industry:
  air pollution generated in, 32, 195,
    346*n*
  corporate governance of, 242
Ellerman, David, 50, 60–62, 63, 64–65,
  84–85, 240
emissions standards, 32, 188, 195, 346*n*
Employee-Owned Network, 90–91
employee ownership, 59
  in airline industry, 68, 88–89
  community trust financing of, 323
  contractual relationship reversed in,
    64–65
  in cooperatives, 65, 69–74, 90
  creativity fostered in, 82
  in employee-ownership trusts, 146,
    148, 150–51
  in employee stock ownership plans,
    64–65, 81–84, 85, 87, 88
  ethical responsibilities of, 77–78
  government subsidies of, 272–73, 297,
    308
  labor union promotion of, 68, 146
  of major corporations, 88–90, 146
  in partnerships, 65, 75, 76–79, 90
  performance improved by, 85–88
  scarcity of financial resources for,
    92–93
  self-discipline developed in, 71
  social activism of, 321–22
  in steel industry, 68, 88, 146, 147
  support system networks for, 90–92
  trust required in, 74
employees:
  antidiscrimination protection of, 78
  businesses owned by, *see* employee
    ownership
  corporate bankruptcy standing of, 219
  corporate ownership changes and,
    124
  employer loyalty to, 55–56, 237, 238
  as "human resources," 61
  job loss feared by, 12
  in middle management, 53, 67
  pension funds of, 103–5, 107–10, 117,
    119, 125–26, 137–44, 261–62,
    344*n*

  personal satisfaction of, 51–52, 57
  respect for, 248–51
  surveillance systems used on, 56
  time demands on, 12, 18, 53
  in white-collar vs. manual-labor jobs,
    57–58
  *see also* labor; labor unions; workplace
employee stock ownership plans
    (ESOPs), 64–65, 81–84, 85, 87, 88
energy efficiency, 72, 186, 189, 196–97,
  198
engineers, 55
  humane values implemented by,
    79–80
Enron, 104, 112, 113, 139, 208, 218, 223,
  241, 279, 346*n*
environmental issues, 154–204
  agricultural pollution, 31, 164–65,
    174–76, 179–80, 200, 202, 277,
    316, 346*n*
  air pollution, 32, 188, 195, 200,
    282–83, 336, 346*n*
  auto industry and, 188, 189, 195–97,
    199, 200, 275–76, 346*n*
  biotechnology firms and, 214
  consumption limited by, 154–55, 159,
    345*n*
  corporate governance and, 170,
    197–99, 202–3, 213–14, 234, 251,
    258
  energy efficiency and, 72, 186, 189,
    196–97, 198
  environmental stress analyses of,
    317–18
  family farmers and, 174–76, 179–80
  forest protection, 171–72, 173,
    181–82
  government subsidies as disincentives
    on, 277, 285
  government support of, 175–76, 308
  hazardous waste disposal, 188, 192
  income inequality as, 177
  industrial efficiency and, 152, 185–94,
    245, 251
  innovative small firms and, 199–202
  in local socioeconomic realities,
    174–83

oil spills, 187–88
political shifts in, 33, 172–73, 175–76
popular support of, 166, 168–69,
    170–72, 175–76, 188, 245
power plants and, 32, 195
precautionary principle in, 214
in social investing, 117–20
species extinction, 154–55
state constitutions on, 336
sustainable development and,
    200–202, 306, 314, 317
and trading of pollution rights,
    282–83
traditional capitalist avoidance of, 20
in U.S. frontier settlement history,
    156–63, 306–7
water pollution, 149–50, 164–65, 176,
    277, 281, 336
whole Earth perspective of, 168–70
Environmental Protection Agency (EPA),
    32, 277
Erie Canal, 269–71, 297
ESOPs (employee stock ownership
    plans), 64–65, 81–84, 85, 87, 88
*Essential Buffett, The* (Hagstrom), 133–34
European capitalism, 33–34
EVA (economic value added), 250–51
Export-Import Bank, 276
extinction, rate of, 154–55
Exxon, 104
ExxonMobil, 200, 241

fabric, biodegradable, 190–91
"Fair Exchange" legislation 297
family life:
    altruism in, 259–60
    elders included in, 320
    working hours in, 52, 53
farming:
    conservation practiced in, 174–76,
        179–80, 200, 202
    contract, 164, 254–55
    corporate ownership bans in, 224, 291
    environmental damage from, 164–65,
        277, 316, 346*n*
    federal subsidies of, 164, 277, 291
    hardships of, 3–4

hog, 164, 174, 176, 224, 277, 291, 316
    on industrial vs. family scale, 164–65,
        174–76, 202, 291, 316
    livestock, 157, 164, 171, 174–75, 176,
        224, 254, 277, 291, 316
    local foods movement in, 316–17
    mechanization of, 6, 7–8
    plant-based products developed from,
        200, 202
    prairie, 3–4, 161, 164–65, 346*n*
    self-ownership in, 65
    self-reliance in, 5–7
    shellfish, 179
fascism, 45
*Fast-Food Nation* (Schlosser), 318
Federal Communications Commission, 32
Federal Reserve Board, 284
feudalism, 50, 51, 58, 63
Fidelity, 140
fiduciary capitalism, 106
Figueroa Corridor Coalition for Eco-
    nomic Justice, 292
financial system, 94–152
    collateral consequences ignored in,
        97, 107–10, 125, 126–28
    conflicts of interest in, 98, 140
    debt vs. equity in, 95
    fraud in, 113, 130, 225, 261
    government regulation of, 112, 113,
        126, 206
    innovative alternatives to, 98, 99–100,
        102, 109–10, 115–20, 131–32,
        143–52
    power concentration in, 96, 128,
        129–32
    short-term focus of, 98, 108, 114, 124,
        134–35
    social landscape reshaped by, 97–98,
        125, 321–22
    unreliability of forecasting in, 95–96,
        126
    *see also* pension funds; stock market
Fisher, Peter, 289
fish populations, 150, 164
*Fixing Elections* (Hill), 267
Florida, state-employee pension fund of,
    105

Florida Natural, 149
food:
   in fast-food industry, 318
   local production of, 316–17
   safety of, 31, 164, 214, 316
Ford, Henry, 106, 188, 249
Ford, William Clay, Jr., 188, 189, 195,
   196, 198
Ford Motor Company, 188, 189, 195–96,
   203, 242, 275
forests, 171–72, 173, 181–82
Forest Stewardship Council (FSC), 172,
   173
*For the Common Good* (Daly and Cobb),
   305
"Four Freedoms" speech (Roosevelt),
   335
401(k) plans, 105, 140
fourteenth amendment, 215, 221
franchise networks, 254, 255
freedom, workplace incursions on, 49–58
Friedman, Milton, 36–37, 229
Friends of the Earth, 291
frontier development, 156–63, 271–72,
   297, 306–7
FSC (Forest Stewardship Council), 172,
   173
fuel-efficiency standards, 196–97
Fujitsu, 292, 293
fur trade, 157

Gannett newspapers, 128
Gates, Jeff, 345*n*
GDP (Gross Domestic Product), 303–6
GE Capital, 146, 148
General Electric, 57, 69, 104, 108–9,
   213–14, 244, 276, 278, 280
General Motors (GM), 242, 275, 289–90
Genesis, Book of, 158
Genuine Progress Indicator, 305–6
GI bill, 272
Gideon Society, 248
Giles, Tracy, 53–54
Gingrich, Newt, 349*n*
Girard, Leo, 143–44, 145
Global Crossing, 218
globalization, 166, 234, 254, 276, 316

global warming, 188, 194–95, 198, 241
GM (General Motors), 242, 275, 289–90
Goldman Sachs, 140
Gompers, Samuel, 10, 15, 303
Good Jobs First, 290
Good Life Index, 313
Goodwyn, Lawrence, 326–27, 350*n*
government:
   community surrogates for, 323
   as counterforce to capitalism, 31,
      311–12
   as "employer of last resort," 332–33
   innovative reform resisted by, 269, 309
   macroeconomic management of,
      283–84, 332–33
   as protector of public assets, 268,
      280–83
   public faith in, 264–65, 269
   *see also* political system; regulation,
      government
government support of business, 31, 263
   in auto industry, 275–76, 277–78
   clawback agreements in, 290, 294,
      295–96
   cost-benefit analysis of, 295
   dilution of public purpose in, 267–69,
      274–75, 278–80, 285–86, 291
   "earnest money" in, 323
   four guiding principles of, 294–98
   inequality furthered by, 268, 284–85
   in infrastructure improvements,
      269–72, 273, 291
   largest firms favored in, 275–76, 277,
      280, 284–85
   long-term goals emphasized in,
      297–98
   macroeconomic management vs.,
      283–84
   in military-industrial complex, 273
   new disciplinary controls on, 287–99
   in research investments, 273–74, 282
   state location incentives as, 277–78,
      288, 289, 348*n*
   tax exceptions as, 278–80, 287, 288,
      289–90, 292–93, 298
   taxpayer bailouts in, 296–97
   trade policy used in, 275, 276–77

Graf, Arnold, 73–74
Gratz, Roberta Brandes, 316
Great Depression, 9, 36, 45, 81, 110, 273, 274, 312
*Great Transformation, The* (Polanyi), 44–45
greed, 35, 40, 93, 209
Greenspan, Alan, 12
Greider, Harold W., 80
Greider, Linda Furry, 338, 346*n*
Gross Domestic Product (GDP), 303–6
Grossman, Richard, 223, 347*n*
guilds, craft, 66

Hagstrom, Robert G., 133–34
Hall, John M., 179, 180
Hamilton, Neil, 317
Harman, Jayden, 185
Harris Corporation, 81, 82
Hawken, Paul, 185, 186, 187, 193, 198–99, 200, 203, 209, 346*n*
Hawley, James P., 106, 109, 261–62, 344*n*
Hayes, Randy, 171, 172
hazardous waste disposal, 188, 192
health insurance, 70
Healthy Community Initiative, 313
Heartland Industrial Partners, 144–45
Heartland Labor Capital Network, 143–44
Henderson, Hazel, 306
Herman Miller Company, 189, 245–53
Hewlett-Packard, 240
high-tech production, 54, 314–15
Hill, Steven, 267
*History of Dickinson County, A* (Smith), 160–63, 345*n*—46*n*
hog factories, 164, 174, 176, 224, 277, 291, 316
Home Depot, 171, 172, 291
home ownership, 18, 84, 136, 272, 273, 308
Homestead Act (1862), 271–72, 297
homesteaders, 3–4, 84, 341*n*
Honda, 278
Humane Society, U.S., 175
Human Rights Watch, 67, 343*n*
hydrogen technology, 200
Hyundai, 278

IAF (Industrial Areas Foundation), 72
IBM, 171, 278
Ice-Ban, 201
immigrant groups:
  altruistic sacrifice in, 259
  ethnic solidarity in, 74
import barriers, 275, 276–77
income inequality, 16–18, 51
  capitalist tendency toward, 21, 41, 62–63, 80
  corporate structure as model of, 52, 219–21
  in democracies, 21, 84
  as environmental issue, 177
  mass consumption affected by, 17–18, 153
  property-rights solution to, 334–36
  in technological economy, 234, 315–16
independent voters, 265
Index of Sustainable Economic Welfare, 305
Indians, *see* Native Americans
individual expression, 46–47, 334
individualism, 312, 318, 329–30, 336
Industrial Areas Foundation (IAF), 72
industrialization, 165–66, 273
inequality, *see* income inequality
inflation, containment of, 284, 333
information technologies, 96, 166
initial public offerings (IPOs), 122, 126
innovation:
  in corporations, 228–30, 232–36, 239–41, 245, 247–48, 249, 252
  government resistance to, 269, 309
  by small firms, 199–202
Innovest, 118–20, 225, 344*n*
instant runoff voting, 267
insurance, health, 70
Intel, 275
intellectual property, 281
Interface, 191
International Paper, 147
Internet, 82, 129, 241, 274
Interstate highway system, 273
investments:
  direct-equity, 135–37, 143–49, 150–51, 261, 345*n*

(investments, *cont'd*)
diversification of, 114–15, 134
  by individuals vs. fiduciary institu-
    tions, 106, 343*n*
  liquidity of, 114, 115, 136
  in local enterprises, 131–32
  mutual funds, 13, 131, 134, 140
  in socially responsible corporations,
    99, 107–10, 116–20, 252, 322,
    344*n*
  by small investors, 13
Iowa:
  agribusiness in, 164–65
  frontier development in, 160–63
  local foods production in, 316, 317
IPOs (initial public offerings), 122, 126
irresponsibility:
  distant ownership as cause of,
    100–101
  generalization of, 45–47
  as moral obligation, 37, 244, 302

Janeway, Michael, 129
Japan, socially responsible capitalism in,
    34, 342*n*
Jefferson, Thomas, 270
job creation, 130, 193, 283–84, 285
job loss, fear of, 12
Johnson & Johnson, 203, 240
J. P. Morgan, 113, 136
J. P. Morgan Chase, 135–36, 145, 241

Kann, Peter, 220
Keilen, Eugene, 146, 147
Kelso, Louis, 81, 83–84, 85
Keynes, John Maynard, 39, 134, 138–39,
    303, 334
  on liberation from economic struggle,
    15–16
  stock market critiqued by, 110–12,
    113, 114, 115, 122
Kiernan, Matthew J., 119
King, Martin Luther, Jr., 327–28
Kinko's, 171, 172
Kittrell, Bill, 182
Knight-Ridder, 128–29

Knights of Labor, 66
Kohlberg Kravis Robert, 135
Kozlowski, Dennis, 208–9
KPS Special Situations Fund, 145–48,
    150
Kruse, Douglas, 86
Kyoto protocol (1997), 188, 195

labor:
  aging of, 320
  business subsidies challenged by, 289,
    290, 292
  casual, 70
  child, 31, 36, 318
  as commodity, 45, 60–64, 249
  direct investing by, 143, 261
  in foreign sweatshops, 318
  investment strategies in support of,
    140–51
  management opposition to, 46, 148
  manual, 57–58
  nonstandard, 54
  personal rights surrendered by, 49
  technological displacement of, 85
  temporary, 53, 54, 69–74, 238, 342*n*
  wages of, 14, 17–18, 63, 72, 84, 85,
    125, 220, 234, 291, 315–17, 332
  *see also* employee ownership; employ-
    ees; workplace
labor laws:
  constitutional rights as basis of, 69,
    343*n*
  corporate property rights vs., 221–22
  deterioration of, 32, 67
Labor party, 69, 343*n*
labor unions:
  decline of, 66–67, 68, 90
  employee ownership engineered by,
    68
  in negotiations with employee own-
    ership, 88–90
  pension funds managed by, 105,
    137–38, 139–40, 141–42, 143, 144,
    261
  of professionals, 55
laissez-faire capitalism, 36–37, 264
Lakota Sioux, 160, 161

land:
    ownership of, 158, 159, 271–72
    public, 281
Landmark Partners, 130
Lange, Jonathon, 73, 74
law firms, partnerships in, 75, 76–79, 90
Lay, Kenneth, 346*n*
leasing contracts, 191–92
leisure class, 2, 11
Lerach, William, 209, 347*n*
LeRoy, Greg, 290, 294
leverage, in direct-equity investing,
    136–37, 150
limited liability, of corporations, 218–19,
    225, 226
Lincoln, Abraham, 272, 300
liquidity:
    in direct-equity investing, 136
    in stock market, 114, 115
livestock farming, 157, 164, 171, 174–75,
    176, 224, 254, 277, 291, 316
living wage campaign, 72, 291
local foods movement, 316–17
*Lochner* doctrine, 221, 222
logrolling, 286, 287
Logue, John, 90–92, 130–32, 202
Long, Huey, 81
Long, Russell, 81, 134, 345*n*
*Longevity Revolution* (Roszak), 320
Lovins, Amory, 186, 187, 193, 346*n*
Lovins, L. Hunter, 186, 187, 193, 346*n*
Lowe's, 171
LSI Logic, 292–93
Lucent, 276

McClure, Cicero, 219
McClure, Franklin S., 5–8, 66, 165
McDonald's, 175, 318
McDonough, William, 189–90, 191, 193,
    198, 245
McIntyre, Robert S., 278–80, 296
Mackin, Christopher, 83, 85–86, 89
MacPherson, C. B., 335, 336, 350*n*
Madison, James, 236
Major, John, 135
management style:
    democratic, 235–38, 250–53

in employee layoffs, 12
in ESOPs, 88
participatory, 86–87
teamwork approach in, 53
managerial capitalism, 106
market competition, 41, 228–29, 230,
    241, 255
Marriott International, 277, 348*n*
Marshall, Alfred, 61
Marshall, Ray, 315
Martinez, Mel, 313
Marx, Karl, 21, 63–64, 94, 100, 101
Mead, Margaret, 327
media conglomerates, 32, 129, 216, 217,
    321
Mellon, Andrew, 216
Mercedes-Benz, 278
Merck, 104, 240
Microsoft, 54, 254, 342*n*
middle management, 53, 67
military-industrial complex, 273, 282
Milius, Peter L., 338–39
Minow, Nell, 109, 344*n*
Minute Maid, 149
Mondragon cooperatives, 73, 90
    ethnic solidarity in, 74, 91
Monks, Robert A. G., 109, 113, 344*n*
monopoly power:
    regulation of, 31, 216, 217, 255, 282
    of two-party politics, 265–66, 267,
        320–21
Monroe, James, 270
Montana, environmental rights in, 336
moral responsibility, seven areas of, 42–43
Morgan Stanley, 119, 141
Morris, David, 174, 201–2, 217–18
Mt. Hood Microelectronics Training
    Center, 293
*Movement of the Free Spirit, The*
    (Vaneigem), 16
Muegge, Paul, 175–76
Murdoch, Rupert, 292
mutual funds, 13, 131, 134, 140

Nader, Ralph, 224, 287, 291
NAPA, 203
Narcotics Anonymous, 70

NASA, 187–88, 273
National Family Farm Coalition, 291
*National Geographic,* 154–55, 345*n*
National Institutes of Health, 282
National Labor Relations Act (NLRA),
    (1937), 67, 221–22, 343*n*
National Semiconductor, 275
Native Americans, 156–59, 161, 162, 169
    in New England, 156–57, 160
    property rights and, 158–59, 271
    usufruct and, 159
*Natural Capitalism* (Hawken, Lovins, and
    Lovins), 185, 186–87, 189, 198
nature:
    engineering based on, 185
    in Genesis, 158
    in Native American cultures, 157–59
    short-term profits vs. conservation of,
    180–83
    *see also* environmental issues
Nature Conservancy (TNC), 176–83,
    257, 317
Navy, U.S., 201
Nelson, George, 247
neoclassical economics, 229, 238
Netflix, 241
New Deal, 84, 112, 221, 272, 274, 280,
    312
New England, Puritan settlers vs. Native
    Americans in, 156–57, 160
newspapers, family vs. corporate owner-
    ship of, 128–29, 345*n*
New York:
    Erie Canal in, 269–71
    state-employee pension fund of, 105,
    140–41
New York Stock Exchange, 289
Niebuhr, Reinhold, 36
Nike, 190, 254
NLRA (National Labor Relations Act)
    (1937), 67, 221–22, 343*n*
Noguchi, Isamu, 247
nonstandard jobs, 54
North American Free Trade Agreement,
    347*n*
Northampton Economic Forum, 179, 180
Notre Dame, University of, 171

Oberlin College, 189
OCM (Organization for Competitive
    Markets), 174–76
"odd bedfellows coalition," 287–88
office furniture industry, 245, 247–48,
    250, 251
Ohio Employee Ownership Center,
    90–92
oil spills, 187–88
Oklahoma Food Policy Council, 316
Olson, Deborah, 297
Oregon, benchmark system on growth
    management in, 293, 306, 312–13
Organization for Competitive Markets
    (OCM), 174–76
*Organizing America* (Perrow), 220
Orlando, Fla., Good Life Index of, 313
Orman, Suze, 13
O'Sullivan, Mary A., 229, 231, 232, 235,
    239, 240, 347*n*
Ownership Associates, 83, 85

Paine, Thomas, 283, 335–36, 349*n*
paper industry, 147–51, 187
Papermakers, Atomic, and Chemical
    Employees union (PACE), 148–49
Parker, Stephen N., 177
participatory management, 86–87
partisan politics, 265–66, 267
partnerships, 65, 75, 76–79, 90
patents, 281–82
Pax Scientific, 185
Payton, John, 77
pension funds:
    corporate management of, 104–5, 140
    direct investing by, 143
    of labor unions, 105, 137–38, 139–40,
    141–42, 143, 144, 261
    long-term social interests of, 107–10,
    138–42, 261–62, 322, 344*n*
    of public employees, 105, 119, 138
    shareholdings of, 103–4, 117, 119,
    125–26, 139
    U.S. totals in, 103
People for the Ethical Treatment of Ani-
    mals (PETA), 175
permatemps, 54, 342*n*

Perrow, Charles, 66, 87, 220, 238–39, 252
personal capitalism, 106, 133
Petro China, 140
Petti, Richard, 260
pharmaceutical patents, 282
Philip Morris, 104
Pigeon River, paper mill on, 149–50
Pimm, Stuart, 155
plant-based products, 200–201, 202, 203
plant extinctions, 155
*Plessy v. Ferguson,* 214
POCLAD (Program on Corporations,
    Law and Democracy), 223, 347*n*
Polanyi, Karl, 44–45, 342*n*
political system:
    capitalist reforms of, 29–35, 298–99,
        308–9
    contemporary indifference to, 23, 264,
        301–2, 320
    corporate lobbying in, 264
    elections in, 263–67, 320–21, 323
    environmental issues belittled in,
        172–73, 194–95
    grassroots vs. federal levels of, 308–10
    logrolling in, 286, 287
    media concentration and, 321
    money in, 31
    partisanship in, 265–66, 267
    workplace authoritarianism and, 52
    *see also* government
pollution, *see* environmental issues
*Populist Moment, The* (Goodwyn), 350*n*
Populists, 202, 221
poverty:
    children in, 16
    as permanent subcategory in eco-
        nomic system, 21
    social definition of, 17
    unchecked development and, 177
powerlessness, 14, 39, 46–47
    in workplace vs. political sphere, 52
power plants, 32, 195
prairie farming, 3–4, 161, 164–65, 346*n*
Pratt & Whitney, 187, 290
precautionary principle, 214
private schools, voucher funding of, 30
professional workers, unionization of, 55

professors, tenure granted to, 75–76
Program on Corporations, Law and
    Democracy, (POCLAD), 223,
    347*n*
*Property & Contract in Economics* (Eller-
    man), 60*n*
property rights, 63–64, 157, 221, 222,
    236, 263, 333–34, 335–36
    intellectual, 281
    in Native American cultures, 158–59,
        271
    public assets and, 32, 268, 280–83,
        348*n*—49*n*
Psaros, Mike, 145–46, 147, 148, 149, 150,
    151
public assets:
    broadcast airwaves as, 32, 281
    private acquisition of, 268, 280–83,
        348*n*—49*n*
public relations, 39–40

Quality of Work Life (QWL) movement,
    53
Qusenberry, Suzie, 54

*Rachel Calof's Story* (Calof), 3–4, 341*n*
racial discrimination, 78, 214
railroad construction, 162, 166, 213, 271,
    273
Rainforest Action Network, 171–72
Ransom, Avis, 71–72
rap music, 11
Reagan, Ronald, 109, 144, 174, 217, 244,
    275, 280
Redefining Progress, 305–6
reform, incremental process of, 28, 29
regulation, government, 309, 332, 347*n*
    badly deformed state of, 30, 32, 33,
        218, 222, 263–64, 298
    deregulation and, 33, 37, 217, 264
    of financial system, 112, 113, 126, 206
    of monopoly power, 31, 216, 217–18,
        255, 282
Republican party, 265–66, 272, 280, 329
*Republic of Denial* (Janeway), 129
research and development (R&D), 108
    tax credits for, 279

retirees, 320
Rifkin, Jeremy, 103, 254, 335, 348*n*
*Rise of Fiduciary Capitalism, The* (Hawley
    and Williams), 106, 109
Rockefeller, John D., 106, 216
Rocky Mountain Institute, 346*n*
Rohde, Gilbert, 247
Roosevelt, Franklin D., 335
Roszak, Theodore, 320
Roy, William G., 218

salmon, 314
Samuelson, Paul, 61
savings:
    in pension funds, 103
    U.S. aggregate levels of, 18, 102–3
scarcity, 18–19, 20, 334
    *see also* abundance
Schlosser, Eric, 318
school vouchers, 30
Schumpeter, Joseph A., 100–101
Schurman, Mark, 253
*Scope and Scale* (Chandler), 123
Scudder Investments, 13
Seattle, Wash., growth management in,
    314
SEC, 140, 257
self-interest:
    altruism vs., 259–60
    in reform of capitalism, 34, 47, 302,
        303, 342*n*
self-ownership:
    current levels of, 65
    historical departure from, 65–66
    *see also* employee ownership
self-reliance vs. dependency, 331
semiconductor industry, 275, 282,
    292–93
Sen, Amartya, 17, 34, 342*n*
senior citizens, 320
Sennett, Richard, 56–57, 331
Shapiro, David, 146
shareholder fraud litigation, 261, 347*n*
shareholder value, 124–25, 126, 127, 210,
    232
shellfish industry, 179
shopping malls, 316

Sierra Club, 150, 175, 291
Silicon Valley, 54, 82, 275, 315
Sioux, 160, 161
slavery, 29, 61, 62, 66
Smith, Adam, 241
Smith, Bob, 148–50, 151
Smith, R. A., 160, 162–63, 168,
    345*n*–46*n*
*Sneaker Book, The* (Vanderbilt), 318
social contract, 97, 125
Social Gospel movement, 36, 44
socialism:
    European capitalism influenced by,
        33–34
    New Deal criticized as, 312
    religion allied with, 36
socially responsible investing, 34, 99,
        107–10, 116–20, 252, 322, 342*n*,
        344*n*
Social Security, 140, 320
social trust legal doctrine, 242–43, 308
sociology, integration of economics with,
    327, 350*n*
Solidarity (employment agency), 69–74,
    87
Solidarity Fund, 143–44
South Africa, antiapartheid boycotts of,
    77
Southwest Airlines, 128
soy products, industrial application of,
    200
special interests, 268
special purpose entities, 223, 227
speech, freedom of, 49, 67, 69
Spirit Lake, Iowa, development of,
    160–62, 164
sports gear, 318
sport utility vehicles (SUVs), 185, 196
Staples Center, 292
states, business incentives offered by,
    277–78, 288, 289
State Street Global Advisers, 140
State Tax and Fiscal Analysis Initiative,
    291
Steelcase, 190–91
steel industry, employee ownership in, 68,
    88, 146, 147

Stein, Beverly, 292, 293, 313
Stockman, David, 144–45
stock market:
  corporate performance measured in, 122–23
  fundamental fallacies of, 97, 110–15
  individual investors vs. fiduciary institutions in, 106, 343*n*
  liquidity in, 114, 115
  middle-class investors in, 102
  mutual funds in, 13, 131, 134, 140
  pension funds in, 103–4, 117, 119, 125–26
  small investors in, 13, 19
  as source of capital, 120–21, 122
  start-up companies in, 121–22
Stokes, Fred, 174
storytelling, 299–300, 318–19
sugar, U.S. import quotas on, 276–77
Sullivan, Robert, 314
supply contracts, 254
supply side economics, 280
Supreme Court, U.S., 214–15, 221–22, 347*n*
sustainable development:
  environmental issues and, 200–202, 306, 314, 317–18
  as focus of capitalistic reform, 306, 307–8, 313–17, 323
  income disparity and, 314–16
  local initiatives in, 312–13, 314–17
Sustainable Seattle, 314
SUVs (sport utility vehicles), 185, 196
sweat equity, 88–89, 272
sweatshops, 33, 318

Taft–Hartley pension funds, 141
"take back" laws, 193
"takings" legal doctrine, 222, 347*n*
tax policy:
  corporate tax avoidance and, 223, 226–27, 278–80, 286–87, 288, 289–90, 292–93, 298
  depreciation in, 279
  employee takeovers facilitated by, 81, 83
  on venture-capital funds, 144

Teachers Insurance and Annuity Association—College Retirement Equities Fund (TIAA-CREF), 105
teaching assistants (TAs), 75
Tedeschi, Bob, 241
television, 15, 281
temporary workers, 53, 54, 238, 342*n*
  employment agency cooperative owned by, 69–74
tenure, academic, 75–76
Terresolve Technologies, 200–201
Thermo Electron, 240
thirteenth amendment, 61, 69
TIAA-CREF (Teachers Insurance and Annuity Association—College Retirement Equities Fund), 105
Tifton, Ga., civic fiber-optic system in, 313–14
timber industry, 157, 171–72, 181–82, 277
TNC (The Nature Conservancy), 176–83, 257, 317
tobacco industry, 77, 107, 115, 116
tort reform, 226
Toyota, 53–54, 276, 278
transportation infrastructure, 269–71, 273, 291
Trillium, 116
trusts, 216
  laws against, 217–18, 241, 242, 255, 282
21st Century Alliance, 202
Tyco International, 208–9

unemployment levels, 284, 333
unions, *see* labor unions
United Airlines (UAL), 68, 88–89, 146, 290
United Auto Workers, 197
United for a Fair Economy, 125
United Steelworkers of America, 68, 88, 143
"universal owner," 109, 344*n*
upholstery fabric, biodegradable, 190–91
urban development, 291, 292, 313–16
utilities industry, 32, 195, 242, 346*n*

Vanderbilt, Tom, 318
Vaneigem, Raoul, 16
Vanguard, 140
Veblen, Thorstein, 2, 79–80, 83
Verizon (Bell Atlantic), 53
Virginia Coastal Reserve, 177, 178–79
Volkema, Michael, 246, 249–50, 251, 252, 253
voter participation, 264, 320

wages:
    of CEOs vs. workers, 63, 125, 220
    decline in, 14, 17–18
    high-tech polarization of, 315–17
    living wage campaign and, 72, 291
    protection of, 332
    technology as depressive effect on, 85, 234
wage slavery, 66, 84
Wal-Mart, 254, 291
Washington, George, 212
*Watching the Watchers* (Monks and Minow), 109, 344*n*
water supplies, 149–50, 164–65, 176, 277, 281, 336
Wayne, Leslie, 276
wealth:
    of individuals vs. fiduciary institutions, 106–7
    *see also* income inequality
Weeks, W. William, 177–78, 181–83, 257, 317, 346*n*

Weirton Steel, 146, 147
Welch, Jack, 244
welfare state, 32, 85, 334
West Central Cooperative, 200
wetlands, 161, 178–79
Whalen, Christopher, 126
Whitman, Walt, 167
*Who Will Tell the People* (Greider), 264
wilderness preservation, 168, 176, 178–79
Williams, Andrew T., 106, 109, 261–62, 344*n*
Williams, Lynn R., 68, 88
Wilmer, Cutler & Pickering, 75, 77
Wolff, Edward N., 102
women in workforce, 18
Working Assets, 282
workplace:
    cultural stereotypes in, 58
    employee ownership in, *see* employee ownership
    erosion of personal control in, 49–58
    hierarchical power distribution of, 50–51, 52, 58, 60, 64, 68, 84–85, 148
    powerlessness in politics vs., 52
    *see also* employees; labor
World Bank, 60, 304
WorldCom, 216, 218
World War II, 10, 272, 273
Wray, L. Randall, 332–33

Young, Owen D., 69, 244

# About the Author

WILLIAM GREIDER is the bestselling author of five previous books on seemingly impenetrable institutions that govern our lives, including *One World, Ready or Not* (on the global economy), *Who Will Tell the People,* and *Secrets of the Temple* (on the Federal Reserve). A reporter for forty years, he was formerly a national correspondent and editor at *The Washington Post* and a columnist for *Rolling Stone.* He is now the national affairs correspondent for *The Nation.* He lives in Washington, D.C., and invites reader comments at williamgreider.com.